Fantasy in the Grotto

Sinica Leidensia

Edited by

Barend J. ter Haar
Nicolas Standaert

In co-operation with

P.K. Bol, D.R. Knechtges, E.S. Rawski,
W.L. Idema, H.T. Zurndorfer

VOLUME 169

The titles published in this series are listed at *brill.com/sinl*

Fantasy in the Grotto

Otherworldly Adventures in Classical Chinese Literature

By

Timothy Wai Keung Chan

BRILL

LEIDEN | BOSTON

Cover illustration: Liu Chen and Ruan Zhao kept by two maidens in the grotto. Section 9 of *Liu Chen and Ruan Zhao Entering the Tiantai Mountains* 元趙蒼雲劉晨阮肇入天台山圖卷. By Zhao Cangyun (active late 13th–early 14th century). Yuan dynasty (1271–1368). Handscroll; ink on paper. 8 7/8 in. × 18 ft. 5 in. (22.5 cm × 564 cm). Section 9. The Metropolitan Museum of Art of New York City. Accessed 25 July 2024. https://www.metmuseum.org/art/collection/search/39545

The Library of Congress Cataloging-in-Publication Data is available online at https://catalog.loc.gov

Typeface for the Latin, Greek, and Cyrillic scripts: "Brill". See and download: brill.com/brill-typeface.

ISSN 0169-9563
ISBN 978-90-04-72037-4 (hardback)
ISBN 978-90-04-72092-3 (e-book)
DOI 10.1163/9789004720923

Copyright 2025 by Koninklijke Brill BV, Plantijnstraat 2, 2321 JC Leiden, The Netherlands.
Koninklijke Brill BV incorporates the imprints Brill, Brill Nijhoff, Brill Schöningh, Brill Fink, Brill mentis, Brill Wageningen Academic, Vandenhoeck & Ruprecht, Böhlau and V&R unipress.
All rights reserved. No part of this publication may be reproduced, translated, stored in a retrieval system, or transmitted in any form or by any means, electronic, mechanical, photocopying, recording or otherwise, without prior written permission from the publisher. Requests for re-use and/or translations must be addressed to Koninklijke Brill BV via brill.com or copyright.com.
For more information: info@brill.com.

This book is printed on acid-free paper and produced in a sustainable manner.

This book is dedicated to
Paul W. Kroll, Stephen H. West, and David R. Knechtges

Contents

List of Figures and Tables XI
Preface and Acknowledgments: "A Tale of Two Worlds" XII
Abbreviations of Frequently Cited Sources XV

Introduction: Fantasy in the Grotto 1
1 Key Concepts and Terminology 6
2 Research Questions and Chapter Synopses 11

1 Life-Prolonging Food and Its Magic in Early Chinese Narrative 15
1 Introduction 15
2 Eating and Journeying in Early China 19
3 Eating and Spatiotemporal Dimensions in Early Texts 24
4 Eating as a Means to Transcend Time 27
5 The Blessed Land; Plums and Peaches 36
6 Sesame: Transcending Time and Space 42
7 Time-Travel Fantasy in the Literary World 47
8 Other Magical Food Items 49
9 Conclusion 51

2 In and Out of the Transcendents' Grotto: from Zhang Zhuo to Yuan Zhen and Bai Juyi 53
1 Introduction 53
2 From Grotto to Chamber: Zhang Zhuo's *You xianku* 55
3 Romance in Reminiscence: Yuan Zhen's "Story of Yingying" 61
4 Liu Chen and Ruan Zhao in Yuan Zhen's Love Poetry 69
5 Poetic Nostalgia of the Grotto: Bai Juyi's Remonstrance 76
6 A New Discourse on Enlightenment 83
7 Conclusion 90
   Appendix 91

3 Roaming, Roleplay, and Rhetoric in Liu Yuxi's Peach Spring Adventures 95
1 Introduction 95
2 The Homesick Fisherman 98
3 The Interlocutory and Introspective Peach Blossom Spring 104
4 Encountering the Daoist Lad Transcendent 110
5 The Frustrated Fisherman 115

    6   Gentleman Liu's Travel in Time and Space   119
    7   Conclusion   125
         Appendix   125

4 **The Transcendent by the River Sending Off Gentleman Ruan: Grotto Romance in Tang–Song Lyrics**   134
    1   Introduction   134
    2   Part 1   137
        2.1   *In Search of the Transcendent in Tang Songs*   137
        2.2   *The "Celestial Transcendent"*   138
        2.3   *"Farewell My Transcendent" in the Secular Realm*   144
        2.4   *The Transcendent by the River*   148
        2.5   *The Transcendent Seeking Transcendence in the Grotto*   151
    3   Part 2   157
        3.1   *Ruan Zhao Returning Home: an Amorous Poet Unveiled*   157
        3.2   *Liu and Ruan's Transcendence and Return to the Mortal Realm*   158
        3.3   *How to "Remember the Transcendent's Beauty"*   162
        3.4   *The Grotto Transcendent in the Northern Song*   165
        3.5   *Writing as Reminiscence of the Peach Spring*   173
    4   Conclusions   176

5 **The Confucian Scholar in Love with the Transcendent in Yuan–Ming Contexts**   180
    1   Introduction   180
    2   Mortality or Immortality: the Values of the Literati   182
    3   Liu and Ruan's Accidental Straying to Mount Tiantai   185
    4   Beautifying Traumas and Obliteration of Value   191
    5   Within and without the Grotto: Enlightenment and Benightedness   196
    6   Breeze, Flower, Snow, Moon, and Liu and Ruan in Yuan Drama   199
    7   Conclusion   203
         Appendix: Text Inscribed on Zhao Cangyun, "Liu Chen and Ruan Zhao Entering the Tiantai Mountains"   205

Epilogue: the Divine Ladies in Love: Romantic Detention in the Liu-Ruan Tradition and *The Odyssey*   206
    1   Introduction   206
    2   Recurring Romance and the Realm of Remembrance   207
    3   Expedient Means and the Intended Morals   211

4   Otherworld and This-World   212
5   Human Needs and Values   216
6   Real and Unreal   221

Works Cited   223
Index   249

Figures and Tables

Figures

1   The two girls inviting Liu and Ruan to their home   193
2   Banquet in the grotto   193
3   Re-visiting the grotto   194

Tables

1   Eating and time dilation in works dated from the 1st to 5th centuries   33
2   Characters, settings, and plot features in the three stories   67
3   Sections in Yuan's and Bai's poems   85
4   Protagonist *xian* in "The Transcendent by the River" songs anthologized in *Poems Gathered from Among Flowers*   152

Preface and Acknowledgments: "A Tale of Two Worlds"

This book journeyed over many years before it finally moored. The earliest research work related to this project was inspired by my relocation from the southern hemisphere back to the north on Christmas Day 2005. This move echoed the frequent moves I had taken before: from Hong Kong to Guangzhou, Beijing, Boulder (CO), Columbus (OH), San Diego (CA), Boston (MA), Sydney (NSW, Australia), and back to Hong Kong. When Rip Van Winkle returned home, twenty years had passed, and his home had changed beyond recognition. When Odysseus regained his kingdom in Ithaca, it had also been twenty years since he left. In the disguise of the swineherd, only Argo—a puppy when his master left—recognized Odysseus. (His maid only recognized the scar on his foot.) Liu Chen and Ruan Zhao returned from a magical journey to find their home a strange land. Upon my return home, I found Hong Kong a drastically altered place, and all these classic homecoming stories carried deep personal significance. After a period of reflection and research, I wrote a paper entitled "A Tale of Two Worlds."[1]

While "A Tale of Two Worlds" contrasts magical realms hidden within medieval China with the political reality of the time, my academic career has spanned more than two worlds. Not long after my return to Hong Kong, my students Tyler C. Pike and Scheherazade Rogers visited me from Sydney, bringing along some *qi* 氣 (vital breath) and new inspiration for the project. This topic developed further through conversations with Barbara Hendrischke during her visit in April 2007. Rip Van Winkle and Odysseus were both with us in our chats, along with the *Taiping jing* 太平經, as Barbara presented me with an autographed copy of her newly released translation.[2] Two months later, Derek Herforth invited me to share my research ideas in the Chinese Seminars Series at the University of Sydney, where I had previously taught for five years. Liu Chen and Ruan Zhao were the protagonists in this talk, which was attended mainly by my colleagues-cum-friends, including: Lily Hsiao Hung Lee, Mabel Lee, Helen Dunstan, Wang Yiyan, and Shirley Chan. I am particularly grateful to Derek for his stimulating remarks on that occasion. "A Tale of Two Worlds" was published the following year and, after a long period of contemplation

---

1 Chan, "A Tale of Two Worlds."
2 Hendrischke, *The Scripture on Great Peace*.

PREFACE AND ACKNOWLEDGMENTS　　　　　　　　　　　　　　　　　　XIII

and effort, became a lemma for the present book. I was fortunate to have been invited to present this material in various stages of its maturity by Paul R. Goldin (University of Pennsylvania, 2013), Wang Ping (Princeton University, 2013), Stephen H. West (Arizona State University, 2016), Liu Xianglan 劉湘蘭 (Sun Yat-sen University, 2017), and Tsuchiya Masaaki 土屋昌明 (Senshu University, 2017, 2023).

The decade-long research work for this book was supported by several research grants. The most important of these was a 2014 six-month sabbatical leave from Hong Kong Baptist University (HKBU), which allowed me to spend three months at the University of Washington under the guidance of David R. Knechtges. The program allowed me to make efficient use of the excellent collections at Suzzallo and Allen Libraries and the Tateuchi East Asia Library. During my visit, Shen Zhijia and Wang Ping offered much support. My research was also funded by several schemes: a two-year grant by the Research Grant Council, Hong Kong SAR Government, under the General Research Fund (2013–15); and Hong Kong Baptist University's Faculty Research Grants (2013, 2016, 2017). The HKBU's Staff Development Grants enabled me to present my work at conferences (2013, 2014, 2016). For access to numerous primary and secondary sources, HKBU Library played a pivotal role. I also made extensive use of the East Asian Library of Stanford University, the East Asian Library of the University of California, Berkeley, the University of Tokyo Library, University of Kyoto Library, and Tōyō Bunko 東洋文庫. During these research trips, I received the help and support of colleagues and friends, namely, Robert Ashmore, Ronald Egan, Tanaka Issei 田仲一成, Tokura Hidemi 戶倉英美, Akihiro Michisaka 道坂昭廣, and Yutaka Yokote 橫手裕. I am especially grateful to Hasebe Tsuyoshi 長谷部剛, who, during my 2017 research trip, drove me to the historic site of the Urashima Tarō 浦島太郎 legend in the Tango 丹後 Peninsula (north of Osaka) and provided me with abundant relevant source materials. Special thanks also go to Sato Koichi 佐藤浩一 for his assistance for my visit to Tōyō Bunko and for his continuous help in checking my Romanized spellings of author names and book, article, and journal titles of Japanese sources.

My approach to literary scholarship was formed by my supervisors Professor Ge Xiaoyin 葛曉音 (Peking University) and Professor Paul W. Kroll (University of Colorado). Stephen H. West has been a lifelong friend and patron, who, when I was at the mouth of the grotto, brought me into the realm of Western Sinology. David R. Knechtges has also guided me for more than two decades. Ralph J. Hexter exposed me to the world of Western classics and helmed my studies of Western literary history and comparative literature. Two old friends,

Robert Ashmore and Nicholas Morrow Williams, have always offered great help and inspiration.

Some of the basic ideas and content of chapters 4 and 5, and the Epilogue were previously published in three Chinese articles, although they have been greatly expanded and revised. They are:

1. "Dongxian ge song Ruanlang gui: Ou ci guiqing qiantan" 洞仙歌送阮郎歸——歐詞閨情淺探 (Songs of the Grotto Goddess Sending Master Ruan Home: Feminine Lovesickness in Ouyang Xiu's *Ci*-poetry). In Zhang Hongsheng, ed. *Song Yuan wenxue yu zongjiao* 宋元文學與宗教. Shanghai: Shanghai guji chubanshe, 2015, pp. 329–51.
2. "Rusheng yuxian: Liu Chen Ruan Zhao chuanshuo zai Yuan Ming yujing zhong de shidai yiyi" 儒生遇仙——劉晨阮肇傳說在元明語境中的時代意義 ("The Confucian Students Met the Fairies: the Saga of Liu Chen and Ruan Zhao in the Contexts of Yuan-Ming Dynasties"). *Journal of Chinese Studies* 中國文化研究所學報 67 (2018): 41–62.
3. "Shennü youxin: Aodexiusi yu Liu Chen Ruan Zhao yanyu gushi yiyun de bijiao yanjiu" 神女有心——奧德修斯與劉晨阮肇艷遇故事意蘊的比較研究 ("The Nymph in Love: A Comparative Study of Odysseus's and Liu Chen and Ruan Zhao's Romance"). *Guoxue xinsheng* 國學新聲 5 (Taiyuan: San Jin chubanshe, 2014), 239–306.

Two former students from the University of Sydney, Scheherazade Rogers and Tyler C. Pike (mentioned above), deserve prominent acknowledgment. Scheherazade edited my conference abstracts and papers that became the main content of this book. Tyler did thorough editorial work on the manuscript. His editing work encompassed not only the grammar, style, and format of the writing, but also gave me useful feedback and prompted me to rewrite several sections.

During the review process, I received invaluable feedback and criticism from the anonymous readers arranged as part of the publication process. They pointed out numerous mistakes and flaws and prompted me to reconsider various issues and re-write/revise different parts in the manuscript they found problematic. I am wholeheartedly indebted to these reviewers' efforts to help me improve the quality of the arguments, translations, and structure of the writing.

Finally, and most importantly, my heartfelt gratitude goes to my family. My parents cannot read or write but they made the utmost effort to offer financial and spiritual support for my education. My wife Zhang Hong and our son Andrew have been vitalizing me with inexhaustible *qi*, manifested as love, inspiration, and encouragement.

Abbreviations of Frequently Cited Sources

BJYJJ   *Bai Juyi ji jianjiao* 白居易集箋校. Ed. & comm. Zhu Jincheng 朱金城. Shanghai: Shanghai guji chubanshe, 1988.

BJYSJ   *Bai Juyi shiji jiaozhu* 白居易詩集校注. Ed. & comm. Xie Siwei 謝思煒. Beijing: Zhonghua shuju, 2006.

CCBZ   *Chuci buzhu* 楚辭補注. Comm. Wang Yi 王逸 (fl. 89–158); sub-comm. Hong Xingzu 洪興祖 (1090–1155). Beijing: Zhonghua shuju, 1983.

CSJC   *Congshu jicheng* 叢書集成.

DHGC   *Dunhuang geci zongbian* 敦煌歌辭總編. Ed. Ren Bantang 任半塘. Shanghai: Shanghai guji chubanshe, 1987.

HCLS   *Han Changli shi xinian jishi* 韓昌黎詩繫年集釋. Ed. & comm. Qian Zhonglian 錢仲聯. Shanghai: Shanghai guji chubanshe, 1984.

HHS   *Hou Han shu* 後漢書. By Fan Ye 范曄 (398–445). Beijing: Zhonghua shuju, 1987.

HJAS   *Harvard Journal of Asiatic Studies*.

HJJJ   *Huajian ji jiao* 花間集校. Comp. Zhao Chongzuo 趙崇祚 (early 10th c.); ed. Li Yimang 李一氓. Hong Kong: Shangwu yinshuguan, 1978.

JAOS   *Journal of the American Oriental Society*.

LKXQJ   *Li Kaixian quanji* 李開先全集. Ed. Bu Jian 卜鍵. Shanghai: Shanghai guji chubanshe, 2014.

LYXJ   *Liu Yuxi ji jianzheng* 劉禹錫集箋證. Comm. Qu Tuiyuan 瞿蛻園. Shanghai: Shanghai guji chubanshe, 1989.

QSC   *Quan Songci* 全宋詞. Comp. Tang Guizhang 唐圭璋. Beijing: Zhonghua shuju, 1988.

QSGSD   *Quan shanggu sandai Qin Han Sanguo Liuchao wen* 全上古三代秦漢三國六朝文. Comp. Yan Kejun 嚴可均 (1762–1843). Beijing: Zhonghua shuju, 1987.

QTS   *Quan Tangshi* 全唐詩. Comp. Peng Dingqiu 彭定球 (fl. early 18th c.), et al. Beijing: Zhonghua shuju, 1960.

QTWDC   *Quan Tang Wudai ci* 全唐五代詞. Comp. Zeng Zhaomin 曾昭岷, et al. Beijing: Zhonghua shuju, 1999.

SBBY   *Sibu beiyao* 四部備要.

SBCK   *Sibu congkan* 四部叢刊.

SKQS   *Wenyuange Siku quanshu* 文淵閣四庫全書. Rpt. Taipei: Taiwan shangwu yinshuguan, 1983–85.

SSJ   *Shisanjing zhushu* 十三經注疏. Comp. Ruan Yuan 阮元 (1764–1849). Rpt. Beijing: Zhonghua shuju, 1983.

TPGJ	*Taiping Guanji* 太平廣記. Comp. Li Fang 李昉 (925–996), et al. Beijing: Zhonghua shuju, 1986.
TPYL	*Taiping yulan* 太平御覽. Comp. Li Fang, et al. Beijing: Zhonghua shuju, 1985.
WX	*Wenxuan* 文選. Comp. Xiao Tong 蕭統 (501–531); ed. Hu Kejia 胡克家 (1756–1816). Rpt. Beijing: Zhonghua shuju, 1979.
XQHWJ	*Xian Qin Han Wei Jin Nanbeichao shi* 先秦漢魏晉南北朝詩. Comp. Lu Qinli 逯欽立. Beijing: Zhonghua shuju, 1983.
XXSK	*Xuxiu Siku quanshu* 續修四庫全書. Shanghai: Shanghai guji chubanshe, 1995.
YWLJ	*Yiwen leiju* 藝文類聚. Comp. Ouyang Xun 歐陽詢 (557–641), et al. Shanghai: Shanghai guji chubanshe, 1982.
YXKJZ	*You xianku jiaozhu* 遊仙窟校注. Eds. & Comms. Li Shiren 李時人 and Zhan Xuzuo 詹緒左. Beijing: Zhonghua shuju, 2010.
YZJJZ	*Yuan Zhen ji jiaozhu* 元稹集校注. Comp. & Comm. Zhou Xianglu 周相錄. Shanghai: Shanghai guji chubanshe, 2011.

Introduction: Fantasy in the Grotto

In early fifth-century China, a tale was created that would become a cornerstone in the history of Chinese romantic literature. First anthologized in a collection of *zhiguai* 志怪 ("recording the uncanny") narratives called the *Youming lu* 幽明錄 (*Record of the Hidden and Manifested*), attributed to Liu Yiqing 劉義慶 (403–444), this tale concerns a journey to another realm undertaken by two men named Liu Chen 劉晨 and Ruan Zhao 阮肇. In this realm they were saved by two beautiful ladies who offered them delicacies and sexual pleasure, but, upon returning home, seven human generations had passed. This 500-character folk tale (see Chapter 1) is not considered a literary masterpiece, and it is not particularly romantic, but it served literary masters throughout history as a core reference in the depiction of romantic encounters. The complexity of these Liu-Ruan references increased over time as writers took greater liberties with the source material. Together with the tale of Liu and Ruan, the later texts form a tradition we call the literature of "grotto fantasy" or "grotto romance." This tradition featured prominently in Chinese literary history but has yet to be examined systematically. Situating these texts according to how they adapt the grotto fantasy tradition is crucial to understanding their aesthetic achievements.

We make three new observations about grotto fantasy in its different incarnations. First, the original Liu-Ruan tale accrues new narrative elements over time. These are not just evolutions of interpretation or creativity in poetic reference. Rather, the Liu-Ruan tale itself appears to evolve as it is adopted by new generations of artists. The second observation involves the story's female protagonists, originally depicted as a group of benign vamps. They eventually came to be recast in a triple role of female entertainer, Daoist priestess, and spiritual transcendent, and this triple association proved remarkably consistent in most subsequent grotto fantasy work. Third, the Daoist-influenced feature of "time dilation" and its associated dangers became a flexible literary instrument and a defining feature of grotto fantasy literature.

These three observations underline how unstable the original text of the Liu-Ruan tale was. In its instability, it stands out relative to other early narratives. It was not an instability born of scribal variance or the vagaries of oral transmission, but rather of an enduring perception that the text lent itself to accretive flexibility, enabling the expression of multifarious themes and emotional range.

Among early medieval narratives that became equally popular, no other text engendered a tradition with comparable range and cohesion. We might, for example, compare the Liu-Ruan tale with the stories of Gourd Elder 壺公,[1] E Lühua 萼綠華, the divine ladies of Mount Wu 巫山, and other popular tales discussed throughout this book. While all of these became sources for colorful allusion and reference, we fail to find a tradition of works stemming from any of them that contribute to an evolution of the original tale and its contemporary relevance. The only exception is, perhaps, Tao Qian's 陶潛 (aka, Tao Yuanming 淵明, 365–427) "Record of the Peach Blossom Spring" ("Taohuayuan ji" 桃花源記).

As we shall see in Chapter 1, Liu Chen and Ruan Zhao's fantastical journey was predicated on the mystical properties of the fruit of the peach tree. Tao Qian's is the other peach-related tale that looms large in the history of Chinese literature.[2] We look at this text in more detail in Chapter 3; for now, suffice it to say the tales differ in important ways, particularly in the inclusion in the Liu-Ruan tale of sexual pleasures. Nevertheless, they were often grouped together because they both read as journeys to an otherworld. One such typical collective grouping is found in the Daoist encyclopedia, *Xianyuan bianzhu* 仙苑編珠 by Wang Songnian 王松年 (10th c.). The compilation rubric of "juxtaposition of examples" (*lianzhu* 連珠; lit., "linked pearls") in this book includes the two peach spring tales in the same entry. The entry reads:

> Huang Zhen, Wuling, Liu and Ruan, and the Peach Spring; the tradition says: Huang Daozhen the fisherman, a native of Wuling, rowed his fishing boat and suddenly entered a peach spring grotto where he met some transcendent beings. Liu Chen and Ruan Zhao were natives of the Shan district. They gathered medicinal herbs on the hills of Tianmu, got lost, and entered a peach spring grotto where they met some transcendent beings. They stayed there for one half year before returning home and saw their descendants seven generations removed.
>
> 黃真武陵劉阮桃源：傳云：漁人黃道真，武陵人，棹漁舟，忽入桃源洞遇仙。劉晨阮肇，剡縣人也，採藥於天姥岑，迷入桃源洞，遇諸仙，經半年卻歸，已見七代孫子。[3]

---

1 Rolf A. Stein's translation. See Stein, *The World in Miniature*, 67, 70, 72, 294.
2 Stephen R. Bokenkamp points out that the peach spring depicted in the *Scripture of Five Talismans* (*Taishang Lingbao Wufu xu*, HY 388) "is the direct source of inspiration for T'ao Ch'ien's 陶潛 (365–427) well-known 'Record of the Peach Flower Font' 桃花源記." See Bokenkamp, "The Peach Flower Font and the Grotto Passage," 65.
3 *Xianyuan bianzhu* (HY 596), 1.18a. The fisherman in Tao Qian's tale as Huang Daozhen is first recorded in a fifth-century work, *Wuling ji* 武陵記, quoted in TPYL 49.4a. The relevant fragments (mainly from *Taiping yulan*) collected in *Han Tang dili shuchao*, 358–60, are attributed

INTRODUCTION: FANTASY IN THE GROTTO

Juxtaposing the Liu-Ruan tale and Tao Qian's "Record" as foundational texts about encounters with "transcendent beings" or "transcendents" (*xian* 仙)[4] was a taxonomy that persisted throughout the centuries. But the encounter with *xian* in Tao Qian's narrative was not a romantic one. The love theme unique to the Liu-Ruan tale became a marked feature of works in the grotto romance tradition in the Tang, and this theme continued to grow and bloom in Song-dynasty lyrics and beyond.

This study is by no means intended as a survey of works related to the Liu-Ruan tale.[5] We are, instead, focused on careful reading of major works that most creatively embody core themes of grotto fantasy. These are works that, in most cases, have not been read as grotto fantasy before.

As such, the present book adopts thematic analysis, in that we concentrate on the development and literary force of grotto fantasy themes over large swathes of time and across a variety of literary and other forms. As opposed to studies that focus on individual writers or significant brackets of time in the literary tradition, thematic studies demonstrate artistic imperatives and opportunities offered by certain archetypal, recurrent subjects. Through identifying the archetypal elements of journeying in Eastern-Han texts that predate the grotto fantasy tradition, we establish the early distinction between "this-world" and an "otherworld" in which time passes differently. We explore the motif of magical eating as a means of surviving transitions to and from "time dilated"

---

to Huang Min 黃閔 of the Southern Qi dynasty. An entry "Taohua yuan" is found in *Soushen houji*, 1.4. Wang Shaoying notes that the text was descended from the *Wuling ji* and *Xianyuan bianzhu*. Chen Yinke argues that the note on Huang Daozhen was given by Tao Qian himself; but Wang Shaoying disagrees and regards it as a retrospective fabrication. See *Soushen houji*, 1.5, n. 2. Richard VanNess Simmons points out that this note is found in a Yuan-dynasty edition of Tao's collected works, *Jianzhu Tao Yuanming ji* 箋註陶淵明集, but the note is not in a Southern Song edition. See Simmons, *The Sōushén hòujì*, 36, n. 19; Tang Han 湯漢 (ca. 1265), comm., *Tao Jingjie xiansheng shi zhu* 陶靖節先生詩註, 4.19a.

4 We present a detailed analysis of the term below. Here, suffice it to note that Tao's account of the Peach Blossom Spring does not include any overt mention of "transcendents," a term that accrued to the tradition later. The only related term, *shen* 神, may be found in Tao Qian's poem, rather than the prose introduction preceding it, in the couplet, "Their wondrous traces were hidden for five hundred years, / Then one day the divine realm was thrown open" 奇蹤隱五百，一朝敞神界. See *Tao Yuanming ji*, 6.167. Tao's account of the Peach Blossom Spring gave direct rise to the *Yuefu* (Music Bureau) poem titled "Ballad of the Peach Spring" ("Taoyuan xing" 桃源行). Wang Wei 王維 (701–761) was an early poet to represent the realm as "spring of the transcendents" (*xianyuan* 仙源). Liu Yuxi 劉禹錫 (772–842) calls the residents of the realm "仙子" (*xianzi*; transcendents). See *Yuefu shiji*, 19.1269–70; *Wang Wei ji jiaozhu*, 1.16–17; *QTS*, 125.1257–58.

5 A recent comprehensive study of variations of the Liu-Ruan tale is Xu Wei, "Liu Ruan gushi de wenben cengci," 59–76.

worlds. The book considers narrative themes and their cultural underpinnings, and how these change over time. We focus on Daoist worldviews, alchemical thought, fantasy and romance, and political turbulence, and their impact on the genealogy of the grotto romance on its road to maturity and sophistication. In addition to a detailed analysis of the device of time dilation, we also deal with other themes, motifs, and images specific to the grotto fantasy tradition, such as love, eating and drinking, the grotto, the peach blossom, departure, and nostalgia. We explore how these elements, along with other historical-cultural trends and ethos, combine to form an archetype.

The importance of defining the Liu-Ruan archetype is that we can then analyze why and how this archetype is adapted, warped, and combined with surprising new elements. In a given poem, a nod to the Liu-Ruan tale may look just like any other allusion, but when read alongside other poems and other works over time, it becomes clear that the Liu-Ruan tale was an inherently different kind of source in the eyes of Chinese literati. It maintained an enduring attraction to later writers because of its continuously expanding possibilities in the expression of romantic sentiment. One such possibility was to conflate the Liu-Ruan tale with aspects of Tao Qian's "Record." Cross pollination between references to these two iconic sources became a convention of grotto fantasy, and essential to our appreciation of the aesthetic value of these works.

The accrual of new elements illustrates a reciprocal cycle: the Liu-Ruan tale as a central reference in the repertoire of amorous literature, and the transformation of the tale in new hands. As is often the case in premodern Chinese literature, this cycle reflects a preoccupation with memory itself. More specifically, this is, as Stephen Owen demonstrates in his thematic study of memory in Chinese literature, an attention to the veil between the present and the remembered, rather than a focus on the remembered per se:

> The force of literature lives in that gap, that veiling, which simultaneously promises and denies access. ... The artwork is framed, closed to the world around it: it may replace the real world, but it does not merge with it.[6]

Often, what is remembered in verse is a combination of a private personal past with curated recollections from the literary tradition. In this combination, the poet transforms private memories into familiar historical or literary tropes. Owen describes this process as "how the vivid and private memories of one's own past have become fused with vivid images from the poetic past, how the

---

6 Owen, *Remembrances*, 2.

particular becomes a stylized type." We shall observe this same process at work in grotto fantasy, but the conventions of the tradition complicate the presentation of memory. Time dilation, in particular, becomes a prominent complication that opens up a range of literary possibilities.

As a contrast between realms in which time passes differently, literary time dilation also enabled grotto fantasy writers to explore related contrasts, such as transience and eternity, or worldly and transcendent. In the Liu-Ruan tale, the allure of the worldly draws Liu Chen and Ruan Zhao back to the mortal world, although their return is catastrophic. This catastrophe may have been intended as a quasi-religious lesson. The mechanism of the struggle involves a loss of power resulting from a long absence from home and family.

Their powerlessness due to displacement (being in the wrong place at the wrong time) in turn becomes an ideal device to create narrative tension. We find this tension in the irreversible consequences of ladies left alone and bereft after sending off their lovers, men left anguished upon confronting the impossibility of returning to the grotto, and literati bemoaning an overthrown dynasty. To the maidens, the duration of the grotto romance is an eternity; therefore, they seek to detain their lovers to keep the romance eternal. The extremely slow speed of time in the grotto (relative to mortal time) thus lends itself to the artistic depiction of anxiety over the *different* way time passes in certain circumstances rather than the passage of time in general.

Interculturally, an appropriate comparison with the mundane/transcendent tension in the Liu-Ruan archetype is Odysseus's fear of the loss of his kingdom during his long absence from home, and his indulgence in romance with the three ladies, Kalypso, Cerce, and Nausikaa, in their respective otherworldly settings.[7] From the perspective of these divine ladies, however, their desire to detain Odysseus is predestined to be frustrated because the romance cannot result in legitimate marriage (see Epilogue).

The Liu-Ruan tale might not have been popular in the heyday of *zhiguai* narrative, but it found a new vogue when *zhiguai* ebbed some two centuries later. Subsequently, literary interest in the tale burgeoned in the Tang and maintained its popularity throughout pre-modern history. This belated appreciation of the tale bordered on literary zealotry. The tale was not only adapted broadly by writers of narrative but also by masters of *shi* poetry, lyrics of popular tunes in the Tang, *ci*-poetry of the Tang and Song, Yuan–Ming drama, and early Ming visual art. These works drew nourishment from their common

---

7 Nausikaa is described as: "like the immortal goddesses for stature and beauty." See Richmond Lattimore, *The Odyssey of Homer*, Book VI, line 16 (p. 102). Scheria was such a peaceful kingdom, Odysseus could have stayed and forgotten about his own kingdom, Ithaca.

source while changing it to suit their purposes. In turn, they elevated the profile of the Liu-Ruan tale in China's literary history (and beyond).[8]

1   Key Concepts and Terminology

A full appreciation of the Liu-Ruan tale and its later adaptations relies upon the concept of a "grotto heaven," which is a kind of paradise enclosed within the human world.[9] The setting for the two men's saga is tinted with Daoist lore. Both "grotto-heaven" (*dongtian* 洞天) and "blissful land" (*fudi* 福地) are terms that stem from esoteric terminology in early Daoism.[10] According to Lee Fong-mao, the notion of thirty-six grotto-heavens was formed no later than the end of the Eastern Jin (420) and derived from some concepts in the "weft texts" 緯書 (apocryphal writing) of Han times.[11] These locales, Lee adds, refer to "a notion of transcendent realms adjacent to the mortal world but different in substance." The adjacent realms are distinguished, according to Lee: "whether or not one can see the transcendent beings and obtain the esoteric documents." Visits to this grotto-heaven are often portrayed as accidental, prompting Lee to label them "accidental intrusions" (*wuru* 誤入).[12] These kinds of "intrusions" are typically made by wood-cutters or fishermen. For others, such as Daoist practitioners, entry to such sacred realms is granted only after periods of fasting and other liturgies.[13]

The concept of "accidental intrusion" into an otherworld became a literary motif and often acquired an element of romance. The theme of love in a

---

8   The classical Japanese legend of Urashimako's 浦島子 adventure to the dragon palace might have been influenced by the Liu-Ruan tale and its closest descendent, the *You xianku* 遊仙窟 (*Roaming to the Grotto of the Transcendents*) by Zhang Zhuo 張鷟 (d. early 8th c.) as well as other tales involving time dilation such as the Wang Zhi 王質 tale. For a study of Urashimako's adventure and its reliance on the *You xianku* in particular, see Hisamatsu Sen'ichi, *Man'yōshū no kenkyū* (*ichi*), 162.

9   In his definitive study of the Chinese concept of the grotto-heaven, Fransicsus Verellen defines the grotto as "a place of transcendental passage, of revelation, and interconnected with other supernatural realms." See Verellen, "The Beyond Within," 271. In addition to grottos, transcendent beings also live underground; see Ogawa Tamaki, *Chūgoku shosetsu no kenkyū*, 267.

10 See e.g., Sima Chengzhen 司馬承禎 (647–735), "Tiandi gongfu tu" 天地宮府圖, in *Yunji qiqian* (HY 1026), 27.1a–17b; Du Guangting 杜光庭 (850–933), *Dongtian fudi yuedu mingshan ji* (HY 599).

11 Lee Fong-mao, "*Shizhou ji* yanjiu," 294.

12 Lee Fong-mao, *Wuru yu zhejiang*, 15, 18.

13 Lee Fong-mao, "Dongtian yu neijing," 40, 48, 54.

grotto-heaven between a mortal man and a transcendent woman—or "grotto transcendent" (*dongxian* 洞仙)[14]—became an enduring influence on later literature. The Tang era saw this archetype of the transcendent lady assuming a triple role by merging *dongxian* with the Daoist priestess and the geisha (*ji* 妓) who resided in the entertainment quarters in Chang'an. Daoist priestesses were in constant association with intellectuals,[15] so it was natural for male writers to occasionally guise them as geisha and love objects. According to the Liu-Ruan topos, this inevitably resulted in frustrated romance, as mortal men must inevitably depart the transcendent realm.

A central concept ubiquitous in the cluster of texts descended from the Liu-Ruan tale is the Chinese term *xian* 仙, consistently translated as "transcendent" throughout this book. As Ying-shih Yü observes: "the idea of *hsien* (transcendence) became synonymous with concepts of supernatural longevity and 'no death.'"[16] For this reason, the two girls who received Liu and Ruan in the grotto later came to be known as the "two *xian*." The question about whether Liu and Ruan qualify for the appellation of *xian* became a topic of dispute. In Zhao Daoyi's 趙道一 (Yuan dyn.) efforts in putting together hagiographies of *xian* in history, Liu and Ruan occupy an entry in Zhao's book, while the nameless girls from the tale do not.[17] Despite the Song-dynasty disagreement on the men's *xian*-hood,[18] the term *xianlang* 仙郎 ("transcendent gentleman") is found passim in Tang–Five-dynasties texts and some of the occurrences refer directly to Liu and Ruan in some Song *ci*-poems.[19]

---

14   The "Dongxian ge" attributed to Lü Yan 呂巖 (b. 798) is on the pursuit of longevity. See *QTWDC*, "fubian," 3.1343. This poem has been proven to be a forgery and should be attributed to Lin Wai 林外 who lived in the Song. See ibid., 1344 ("kaobian"); *QSC*, 1767, 3869.

15   See Chen Yinke, *Yuan Bai shi jianzheng gao*, 107; Lee Fong-mao, "Xian, ji yu dongku," 476–89; Shi Zhecun, *Tangshi baihua*, 644. One recent study of the Tang literati, their relationship with these Daoist priestesses, and the roles of the latter, is Jia Jinhua, *Gender, Power, and Talent*, 11–17, et passim.

16   Yü, "Life and Immortality in the Mind of Han China," 108, 111. See also Joseph Needham, Ho Ping-yü, and Lu Gwei-djen, *Science and Civilisation in China, Vol. 5: Part III*, 93–96.

17   *Lidai zhenxian tidao tongjian* (HY 296), 7.11b–12a. The moral original of *xian* is seen in *Zhuangzi*, 12/31–32; trans., A. C. Graham, *Chuan-Tzŭ*, 179: "As for the sage, ... / When the empire lacks the Way / He cultivates the Power in the comfort of retirement. / A thousand years and he's weary of the world, / Departs and rises up as an immortal. / He rides upon those white clouds / All the way to the realm of God."

18   *Yixian zhuan* (HY 299), 2.9b.

19   A late Tang example is Zhang Ben 張賁, "He Ximei zuizhong xianqi ciyun" 和襲美醉中先起次韻. *QTS*, 631.7237. For other occurrences, see Chapter 4.

The term *xian* and our preferred English translation "transcendent" both imply an active process of going above or beyond. In this regard, Edward H. Schafer's discussion of the character *xian* 仙 offers some useful insights:

> This is a member of a word-family which connotes such things as light-stepping, walking on air, going about with one's head in the clouds, carefree and buoyant .... In Taoism the condition of a *hsien* (*xian*) is somewhat more etherealized, suggesting, beyond merely the magic power of flight, escape from the passions, attachments, filth, and illusions of the mortal condition.[20]

With these attributes assigned to the *xian*, Schafer translates it as "transcendents" or "sylphs" ... "because of their resemblance to the delicate, airy elementals of western tradition." In an earlier study, Schafer stresses the human basis of *xian* in his definition:

> 仙（僊）*syen sen hsien*
>
> transcendent, sylph (a being who, through alchemical, gymnastic and other disciplines, has achieved a refined and perhaps immortal body, able to fly like a bird beyond the trammels of the base material world into the realms of aether, and nourish himself on air and dew.[21]

The early form *xian* 僊 was replaced by *xian* 仙 as early as Han times.[22] Robert Ford Campany elaborates on Schafer's discussion and, focusing on the *xian*'s "upward movement," suggests "ascendant" as a more suitable rendering of the term in English.[23] In the present volume, we rely on "transcendent" because our *xian* exist in a realm that is concealed within our earthly plane, rather than high above.

As for Schafer's observation that the *xian* "escape from the passions, attachments, filth, and illusions of the mortal condition," the term "transcendent" accurately portrays the implied duality between those who suffer in the earthly plane and those who have escaped. But in our texts, we find the division is not so black and white. Indeed, in our core text, the Liu-Ruan tale, the protagonists experience both an earthly and a transcendent realm, and elect to return to

---

20 Schafer, *Mirages on the Sea of Time*, 21.
21 Schafer, "Thoughts about a Student's Dictionary of Classical Chinese," 204.
22 See *Shuowen jiezi gulin*, 8A.3622a–3263a, quoting various sources.
23 Campany, *Making Transcendents*, 34.

INTRODUCTION: FANTASY IN THE GROTTO

their earthly origins, with catastrophic results. This sets up an ambiguity and leads the reader to consider which realm is truly better under a variety of circumstances. Later allusions to the tale make liberal use of this ambiguity.

Xian-ship does not necessarily imply immortality. It is often portrayed as an impermanent state of being that requires that one "must constantly renew their vital powers."[24] Later writers played with the tenuousness of the transcendent. Objects of love may be portrayed as religiously *xian*-like, and then secularized and brought back down to earth, for poetic purposes.

We may consider the possibility of translating *xian* as "fairy." The latter is a term of some complexity. In his discussion of "The Longaevi," C. S. Lewis traces the concept to various origins:

> I take for them the name Longaevi from Martianus Capella, who mentions "dancing companies of Longaevi who haunt woods, glades, and groves, and lakes and springs and brooks; whose names are Pans, Funs ... Satyrs, Silvans, Nymphs. ..." Benardus Silvestris, without using the word Longaevi, describes similar creatures—"silvans, Pans, and Nerei"—as having "a longer life" (than ours), though they are not immortal. They are innocent—"of blameless conversation"—and have bodies of "elemental purity."[25]

Here again, we notice the attribute that "they are not immortal," which clearly distinguishes the "fairy" from the immortal being. Regarding "fairies" as "tarnished," Lewis painstakingly delved into relevant medieval literary texts and surveyed what the word fairy meant in these contexts. He sums up four definitions:

(1) That they are a third rational species distinct from angels and men.
(2) That they are angels, but a special class of angels who have been, in our jargon, "demoted."
(3) That they are the dead, or some special class of the dead.
(4) That they are fallen angels; in other words, devils.[26]

---

24 Schafer, *Mirages on the Sea of Time*, 21. In an earlier study of the word, however, Schafer defines *xian* as having "achieved a refined and perhaps immortal body." See his "Thoughts about a Student's Dictionary of Classical Chinese," 204. Campany also rejects this rendering as the *xian* are not "immortal," although "they live an extraordinarily long time." Campany, *Making Transcendents*, 33–34. Shawn Arthur opts for "immortal," which "does not necessitate a permanent existence, but indicates claims of life elongated far beyond the limits of the normal person." See Arthur, *Early Daoist Dietary Practices*, 128.
25 Lewis, *The Discarded Image*, 122.
26 See ibid., 123, 134–37.

The latter two apparently do not apply to the *xian* notion in early medieval Chinese contexts but may fit the ghosts or demons in *zhiguai* texts, whereas the *xian* in the Liu-Ruan tale seem to belong to the first two categories. They may be like "angels" in the Western sense, but more likely the "demoted" or "banished" ones due to some mistakes they made in the heavenly realm where they originally resided. A related concept of "banished transcendent" (*zhexian* 謫仙) had been prevalent since Han times; examples include Liu An 劉安 (179–122 BC), Hugong 壺公 ("Elder in the Flagon"; E. Han), and E Lühua 萼綠華 (mid-4th c.).[27]

One may, however, be troubled by a rendering of some of these figures as "fairies." Likely because of Wang Chong's 王充 (27–ca. 97) critical view of these kinds of "superstitious" thoughts, he calls Xiang Mandu 項曼都, who failed to achieve transcendence in his alleged journey to heaven, not a "banished transcendent" but one "rejected from transcendence seeking" (*chixian* 斥仙). Wang's assessment is that Xiang did not qualify for the former due to his human origins and his lies about his celestial journey (see Chapter 1).[28]

The two girls in the Liu-Ruan tale are not depicted as having descended from heaven. Their origins are unspecified, and therefore they fail to qualify as fairies, as per the C. S. Lewis etymology.[29] Also, the fact that they eat and live like humans further differentiates them from fairies. One might regard the Perfected Ones (*zhenren* 真人) who are recorded to have descended for Yang Xi's 楊羲 (330–386) séance, as fairies,[30] but one such perfected figure, Wei Huacun 魏華存 (252–334), for example, first completed her eighty-three years of mortal life before transcending.[31] Her mentor, Wang Pou 王褒 (whose sobriquet is Qingxu zhenren 清虛真人) was also of human origin but later transcended.[32] Therefore, the rendering of "transcendent" for these kinds of

---

27 Miyagawa Hisayuki, "Takusen kō," 1–12. Hugong and E Lühua are respectively recorded as "no one knows his name" and "a female *xian*" without previous record of living in the mortal world. See *TPGJ*, 12.80, 57.354.

28 *Lunheng jiaoshi*, 325–26.

29 For American readers, it should be pointed out that the term "fairy" is unsuitable because of its connotations of Tinkerbell and use as a derogative term for gay people.

30 See Michel Strickmann, "The Mao Shan Revelations," 3–15. Note that the notion of the *zhenren* (translated as "Perfected-Immortals") in these religious contexts was derived from the occurrence in *Zhuangzi*. See relevant discussion about the True Man in Michael Puett, *To Become a God*, 281–82; Nomura Takeo, "Shinjin ron," 1–12.

31 See *TPGJ*, 58.357–58; Yan Zhenqing 顏真卿 (709–785), "Jin Zixu yuanjun ling shangzhen siming Nanyue furen Wei furen xiantan beiming" 晉紫虛元君領上真司命南嶽夫人魏夫人仙壇碑銘, *Quan Tangwen*, 340.17a–18b.

32 See *Dongxuan Lingbao zhenling weiye tu* (HY 167), 4a.

individuals is more appropriate, and we adopt the general convention of "transcendent" for *xian* throughout the book.

Among the guises of grotto romance transcendents, one looms largest in metaphor and allegory in Tang times: the transcendent as a spiritually (religiously) perfected person. Schafer's pioneering work on the divine woman demonstrates how the images of the goddesses, shamankas, or nymphs underwent changes in pre-Tang and Tang literature.[33] In our case, we focus on only one source, the Liu-Ruan tale, to see how its descendent texts and thematic elements, especially those surrounding the two girls met by the two men, changed to serve new motifs. This treatment of one single lineage will enhance our understanding of its development. Chen Yinke's 陳寅恪 groundbreaking research elucidates the term "meeting with the Perfected" (*huizhen* 會真) as rendezvous of lovers with an erotic overtone.[34] This metaphor dominated texts such as Yuan Zhen's 元稹 (779–831) "Story of Yingying" ("Yingying zhuan" 鶯鶯傳), but is, in fact, also evident in Zhang Zhuo's 張鷟 (ca. 660–ca. 740) *Roaming to the Grotto of the Transcendents* (*You xianku* 遊仙窟). In Yuan Zhen and Bai Juyi's 白居易 (772–846) poetry exchange activities and discussion of Yuan's romantic experience, the Liu-Ruan tale became a repertoire metaphor (see Chapter 2). An interesting twist is seen in the writings of female poets. The Daoist priestess-poetesses Li Ye 李冶 (713–784) and Yu Xuanji 魚玄機 (844–871) identify themselves as "transcendents" (*xianzi* 仙子), playing the role of the lover left alone by *their* Liu and Ruan. This kind of appellation of *xianzi* or *xian* is also typical in amorous contexts in Tang lyrics. In these customary settings, the transcendent remains after her lover leaves the grotto, which becomes a kenning for the boudoir of a lady missing her absent lover in springtime in the secular world. These details of the secular presentation are not found in the original tale but are new developments augmented by Tang and later writers.

2   Research Questions and Chapter Synopses

The book is intended to present a qualitative analysis of grotto fantasy as an evolving cluster of literary themes, and to use this as a framework to better understand a selection of well-known works. The book comprises five chapters and one epilogue, synopses of which are as follows:

---

33   Schafer, *The Divine Woman*, passim.
34   See Chen Yinke, *Yuan Bai shi jianzheng gao*, 107; Gao Feng, *Huanjian ci yanjiu*, 105–6. See relevant discussion in Chapter 2.

Chapter 1 is an investigation of the literary device of time dilation in early Chinese texts. We focus on the Liu-Ruan tale and its literary, social and religious contexts. The tale and texts that precede it reveal a concern with the physical and emotional stress caused by time-dilation, and how certain foods facilitate prolonged sojourns under those conditions. The foods range from ambrosia to more typical mortal foodstuffs, and were portrayed consistently as key to surviving visits to realms where time elapses in a dilated manner. Themes of anxiety over unnatural passage of time; love that develops in time-dilated realms; and associated motifs of intrusion, detention, escape, nostalgia and trauma become core building blocks upon which later evolutions of grotto fantasy were constructed.

Chapter 2 introduces the use, in the Tang, of the Liu-Ruan tale in literary representation of extramarital love. We focus on how Yuan Zhen 元稹 (779–831) and Bai Juyi 白居易 (772–846) reference the Liu-Ruan tale in their occasional poems. In response to Yuan's poem "Dream of Spring Outing in Seventy Rhymes" ("Meng youchun qishi yun" 夢遊春七十韻), Bai Juyi assesses Yuan's romantic excursions and admonishes him for his skewed priorities. The Liu-Ruan tale becomes one of Bai's examples as he lectures Yuan on awakening and enlightenment. The chapter also includes a broader circle of work relevant to an understanding of this phase in the evolution of grotto fantasy. Several generations before Yuan and Bai, Zhang Zhuo may have been the first to use the Liu-Ruan tale as a metaphor for extramarital love. His narrative and poetic work, *Roaming to the Grotto of the Transcendents*, plays a pivotal role in expanding grotto fantasy beyond the genre of *zhiguai* into romance, and thereby paves the road for Yuan Zhen, anticipating, in particular, Yuan's "Story of Yingying."

Chapter 3 examines the poetic works of the mid-Tang statesman-poet Liu Yuxi 劉禹錫 (772–842) and how he adapts the two peach spring tales. Liu's poems alluding to Tao's tale were mainly dated to his ten-year banishment to the region of this legendary peach spring—Wuling 武陵 (in modern Hu'nan province); those alluding to the Liu-Ruan tale were political satires written upon his return to Chang'an from exile. In Liu's Wuling poems, the poet assumes the guise of the fisherman but refuses to tarry in the otherworldly realm he encounters because of his attachment to the political world. Another important figure in Liu's Wuling poetry is the Daoist transcendent Qu Boting 瞿柏庭. Liu shares quite a few similarities with Qu's life, and thus devotes a long section to Qu in his poem "Roaming the Peach Spring in One Hundred Rhymes" ("You Taoyuan yibai yun" 遊桃源一百韻). In the end, Liu can only admire Qu for having achieved transcendence. The pace of the passage of time naturally provides a prominent theme in his poems written on exile.

The theme of displacement anxiety is prominent in his two poems on the Mysterious Capital Abbey 玄都觀, one written upon his return to Chang'an in 815, which quickly brought him to another fourteen-year exile, and the other written upon his return in 828. Calling himself Gentleman Liu 劉郎, he plays with the adventure of Liu Chen in these satirical poems.

Chapter 4 shifts to a different genre: song lyrics of the Tang and Northern Song. We investigate tune-titles pertaining to the "transcendent" (*xian*) and the theme of romance in these lyrics. Relying on a long-established theory that the lyrics of most songs in their inceptive stage were composed in "tune-title of the original theme" (*diaoming benyi* 調名本意), we examine how lyrics discovered in Dunhuang manuscripts dated from the High to Late Tang (ca. mid-8th c. to early 10th c.) adapted the themes derived from the Liu-Ruan tale and their new developments. We focus on lyrics to tune-titles inclusive of the word *xian* or with relevant attributes of the *xian* persona, such as "Tianxianzi" 天仙子 ("The Celestial Transcendent"), "Bie xianzi" 別仙子 ("Farewell my Transcendent"), "Dongxian ge" 洞仙歌 ("Song of the Grotto Transcendent"), and "Linjiang xian" 臨江仙 ("The Transcendent by the River"). Another focus of this chapter concerns how Ouyang Xiu 歐陽修 (1007–1072), the most important *ci*-poet to leave traces of this tradition in his works, adopts the tune-titles related to the tale, such as "Gentleman Ruan Returning Home" ("Ruanlang gui" 阮郎歸) and "Reminiscing about an Acquaintance from the Peach Spring" ("Taoyuan yi guren" 桃源憶故人). To discuss the issue in a comprehensive manner, we survey related tune-titles by Northern Song poets, such as those by Liu Yong 柳永 (ca. 985–ca. 1053), Yan Shu 晏殊 (991–1055), and Su Shi 蘇軾 (1037–1101). The theory tying together "tune-title" with "the original tune" is applicable to most of these lyrics. They borrow traditional images and thematic elements from the Liu-Ruan archetype, but expound on new, secular amorous matters and assume a new literary life.

Chapter 5 moves on to Yuan–Ming times to explore how the political atmosphere under the Mongols shaped new representations of the Liu-Ruan tale. The scope of investigation extends from literary texts to visual and performance art. We select two drama scripts and one painting, namely, 1) a play entitled "Celestial Master Zhang's Conviction of Breeze, Flower, Snow, and Moon" 張天師斷風花雪月, attributed to Wu Changling 吳昌齡 (Yuan dyn.); 2) a play entitled "Liu Chen and Ruan Zhao's Straying to Mount Tiantai" 劉晨阮肇悞入天台, attributed to Wang Ziyi 王子一 (late Yuan to early Ming dyn.), and 3) a painting entitled "Liu Chen and Ruan Zhao Entering the Tiantai Mountains by Zhao Cangyun of the Yuan dynasty" 元趙蒼雲劉晨阮肇入天台山圖卷, along with the illustrative texts inscribed on the sections of the long scroll. In these works, the Liu-Ruan tale serves as a platform to satirize the political frustration and anxiety of the literati, and to emphasize the trauma experienced by Song loyalists after the downfall of the Song dynasty.

The Epilogue draws a conclusion through a comparative study through a comparative study of the Liu-Ruan tale along with its descendent texts with sections of the Greek classic, *The Odyssey*, with a focus on "romantic detention," a theme common to both groups of texts. The similar thematic element is that the divine ladies try to detain their lovers in their domains indefinitely but their "detainee(s)" insist(s) on leaving after a period of romance. The main motivation behind Odysseus's wish to depart stems from his heroic impulse to recover his kingdom, Ithaca, which was on the verge of being usurped by suitors of his wife, Penelope. Nonetheless, he does not want to "miss a thing—or a gift—on the way" home from the Trojan war,[35] resulting in years of sojourns on Kalypso's and Cerce's islands and nearly becoming the son-in-law of King Alkinoös. Liu and Ruan's sojourn and romantic detention serve different narrative purposes and yield a distinct moral. The weakness of human nature is a common theme in the comparison, while the irreversible spatiotemporal displacement imposed on Liu and Ruan upon their return to the human world becomes a unique device for delivering common motifs about values of family, ethical conduct, and religious beliefs. This comparative review consolidates our findings and emphasizes the significance of these issues in both literary traditions.

The *Youming lu* collection—and the Liu-Ruan tale in particular—have attracted insufficient scholarship relative to other early texts in the Chinese tradition.[36] The present book is the first transdisciplinary attempt to study the Liu-Ruan tale in the context of otherworldly adventure texts—both inside and outside of China—and to track the treatment of the Liu-Ruan grotto fantasy over time. This approach affords insights that may invite academic discussion among Chinese literary and religious scholars, contribute to the field of comparative literature, and serve as a valuable resource to anyone interested in literature dealing with the relationship between real and unreal as represented in such traditions as grotto fantasy.

---

35 See Howard W. Clarke, *The Art of* The Odyssey, 51.
36 In his "Tales of Strange Events," Robert Ford Campany provides a brief introduction to the *Youming lu* and scholarship on the text, asserting that "it has not received as much scholarly attention as some of its peer works have." One recent monograph-length study of the *Youming lu* in light of the Buddhist backgrounds of the time is Zhang Zhenjun, *Buddhism and Tales of the Supernatural in Early Medieval China*, but Zhang does not discuss the Liu-Ruan tale.

CHAPTER 1

Life-Prolonging Food and Its Magic in Early Chinese Narrative

1   Introduction

Many early medieval Chinese narratives feature a unique motif that certain special dietary practices support journeys to time-dilated realms. Unlike modern time travel fantasies, in which displacement may be triggered by eating petites madeleines, driving a car, going through a tunnel, sleeping, or using a machine,[1] "time displacement" in medieval Chinese texts runs behind the picture and its result is usually catastrophic. In these early Chinese narratives, the consumption of particular foods is treated as a crucial means by which the protagonist manages to survive the time displacement. This unique literary device plays an especially crucial role in narrative texts dated roughly from the second to the fifth centuries and became an established motif that persisted throughout Chinese literary history.

This chapter examines the inception and development of this motif by analyzing a selection of narrative texts involving time displacement. We focus on the tale of Liu Chen 劉晨 and Ruan Zhao's 阮肇 other-worldly adventure. With reference to manuals on magical diets dated from the same period, we will examine how time and space were seen in religious and literary writings and discuss how food consumption contributes to plot design and shapes rhetorical devices in early medieval China.

The adventure of Liu Chen and Ruan Zhao is the central text of our investigation on this topic and is the grotto fantasy archetype we return to throughout the book. Liu and Ruan's tale appears for the first time in the *Record of the Hidden and Manifested* (*Youming lu* 幽明錄),[2] an anthology of anomaly

---

[1] Examples of tunnel-like environments include: *Alice in Paradise*, *Rip Van Winkle*, *The Chronicles of Narnia*, and *Time Tunnel* (a TV series shown in 1966–67). The cakes called "petites madeleines" appear in Marcel Proust (1871–1922), *Remembrance of Things Past*, 48, 50, et passim. Using a machine as a means for time travel is first seen in H. G. Wells's 1895 novel, *The Time Machine*. Time travel adapted to Hollywood screenplays includes: *Somewhere in Time*, the *Back to the Future* series, *Narnia*, *Men in Black III*, etc. Paul Nahin provides a comprehensive introduction to relevant literary creations, but lists no classical Chinese work in his investigation. See Nahin, *Time Machines*, 16–52.

[2] For the meaning of the book title, see Li Jianguo, *Tangqian zhiguai xiaoshuo shi*, 357; Zhang Zhenjun, *Buddhism and Tales of the Supernatural in Early Medieval China*, 44–45.

accounts (*zhiguai* 志怪, lit., "recording the uncanny") traditionally attributed to Liu Yiqing 劉義慶 (403–444).[3] This tale is also attributed to Tao Qian 陶潛 (aka, Tao Yuanming 陶淵明, 365–427) but this attribution is less credible.[4] Here is my English translation followed by the Chinese original:[5]

> In the fifth year of the Yongping reign-period of Emperor Ming of the Han (AD 82), Liu Chen and Ruan Zhao of Shan District (in modern Zhejiang province) went into the mountains to gather the bark of paper mulberry trees.[6] They lost their way home. After thirteen days, they nearly died of starvation as their sustenance had been depleted. Coming into sight was a peach tree bearing large fruit, cut off by steep precipices and deep streams. They grabbed the vines and climbed up, each eating several peaches, satisfying their hunger and replenishing their energy before they started back downhill. With cups in their hands to fetch water for washing and rinsing, the men suddenly spotted some leaves of the rape-turnip flowing out from the middle of the mountain. Thereafter came cups containing grains of sesame and cooked rice. They said to one another, "There must be people dwelling close by." They then entered the river, swam upstream for some two or three *li* (i.e., about a mile), passed the

---

3 The first source that credits Liu for authorship of this book is *Suishu*, 33.980. Liu has also been referred to as the editor; see Lily Hsiao Hung Lee, "Shishou xinyu zuozhe wenti shangque," 14. Robert Ford Campany's translation of *zhiguai* is "accounts of anomalies." See Campany, *Strange Writing*, 29, n. 15, 151–52.

4 Wang Shaoying includes the tale in his *Soushen ji*, "yiwen," 250, but notes that it must have come from the *Soushen houji*, a book attributed to Tao Qian, because the story bears the year of 383, when Gan Bao 干寶 (fl. early 3rd c.), author of *Soushen ji*, had long since died. Yu Jiaxi dates the *Soushen houji* to the Liang dynasty (502–558); Li Jianguo renders Tao the author. See Yu, *Siku tiyao bianzheng*, 18.1144; Li, *Tangqian zhiguai xiaoshuo shi*, 344–46, 359. Li identifies two sources that bear a variant Taikang 太康 [reign-period, 281–290], rather than Taiyuan 太元 [376–397] as the time of Liu and Ruan's disappearance, i.e., *Mengqiu zhu* 蒙求注 and the entry on 'Liu Chen' in *juan* 7 of the *Lishi zhenxian tidao tongjian* (HY 296). This reign-period predates Gan Bao's time. See Li, *Xinji Soushen houji*, 718. Richard VanNess Simmons provides a comprehensive survey of views on the issue concerning the text and authorship of the *Soushen houji* and concludes that the extant text is "with no connection to Táo Qián." See Simmons, *The Sōushén hòujì*, 3–11, esp., 11.

5 Chan, "A Tale of Two Worlds," 213–14, with modification. The tale has also been translated in: DeWoskin and Crump, *In Search of the Supernatural*, 248–49; Campany, *A Garden of Marvels*, 108–9; and Zhang Zhenjun, *Hidden and Visible Realms*, 1–4.

6 "Paper mulberry" is *gusang* 穀桑, more commonly known as *chu* 楮, *broussonetia papyrifera*. See Bernard Read, *Chinese Medicinal Plants*, 192, no. 597. The bark of this plant is good material for paper-making and for textiles. Therefore, Liu and Ruan might have been involved in either of these crafts. See *Tangqian zhiguai xiaoshuo jishi*, 436, n. 3; Hu Zhengwu, "Liu Ruan yuxian gushi," 14–18.

mountain, and reached a large creek. Two beautiful maidens standing by the creek spoke to the two men holding cups: "Mr. Liu and Mr. Ruan, hand back the cups that we just lost." Wondering why the two girls they had never met were calling their surnames, they took pleasure as there seemed to be some acquaintance. The two girls asked, "What caused your late arrival?" and invited them to their home. The house was roofed with bronze tiles. There was one big bed by the south wall and one by the east wall, each curtained in crimson gauze. A bell hung at each corner, alternately in gold and silver colors. Ten maids stood by the bed. The two girls said: "Mr. Liu and Mr. Ruan have come from a hiking and swimming journey. Although they have just eaten some precious fruit, they are still weak. Go at once to prepare some food." The two men were served rice-in-sesame, goat jerky, and beef—it was all very delicious. After the feast, they were served wine. A bevy of girls, each with several peaches in hand, came to greet them with smiles: "We congratulate you on your wedding." When Liu and Ruan were half drunk, the music started, but their minds held mixed feelings of cheer and fear.

At nightfall, Liu and Ruan were made to rest behind two different curtains, each attended by one of the two maidens. The sweetness of the voices and words of these girls swept away the two men's worries.

Ten days later, the two men requested to return home. The maidens said, "You have come here by karmic blessings. Why do you still want to go back?" They stayed for half a year. Seasonal changes and plants heralded the advent of spring. Further agonized by the chirping of birds, the two unhappy men begged to return. "It is our fault for keeping you gentlemen here. What can be done?" said the two girls. They called in the thirty or forty girls who had come before. At the gathering, they performed music to bid farewell to Liu and Ruan and guided them to the exit leading to their homes.

After they returned to their hometown, they were treated as strangers because their relatives were all gone and all the villages and houses had changed. They asked around and found their descendants, who told them that their great-grandfathers from seven generations ago once got lost in the mountains and never returned.

In the eighth year of the Taiyuan reign-period (383), they suddenly left again. No one knew where they had gone.

漢明帝永平五年，剡縣劉晨、阮肇共入天台山取穀皮，迷不得返，經十三日，糧食乏盡，飢餒殆死。遙望山上有一桃樹，大有子實，而絕巖邃澗，永無登路。攀援藤葛，乃得至上。各噉數枚，而飢止體充。

復下山，持杯取水，欲盥漱，見蕪菁葉從山腹流出，甚鮮新，復一杯流出，有胡麻飯糝，相謂曰：「此知去人徑不遠。」便共沒水，逆流二三里，得度山出一大溪，溪邊有二女子，姿質妙絕，見二人持杯出，便笑曰：「劉阮二郎，捉向所失流杯來。」晨肇既不識之，緣二女便呼其姓，如似有舊，乃相見忻喜。問：「來何晚邪？」因邀還家。其家銅瓦屋，南壁及東壁下各有一大床，皆施絳羅帳，帳角懸鈴，金銀交錯，床頭各有十侍婢，敕云：「劉阮二郎，經涉山岨，向雖得瓊實，猶尚虛弊，可速作食。」食胡麻飯、山羊脯、牛肉，甚甘美。食畢行酒，有一群女來，各持三五桃子，笑而言：「賀汝壻來。」酒酣作樂，劉阮忻怖交并。至暮、令各就一帳宿，女往就之，言聲清婉，令人忘憂。十日後欲求還去，女云：「君已來是，宿福所牽，何復欲還邪？」遂停半年。氣候草木是春時，百鳥啼鳴，更懷悲思，求歸甚苦。女曰：「罪牽君當可如何？」遂呼前來女子有三四十人，集會奏樂，共送劉阮，指示還路。既出，親舊零落，邑屋改異，無復相識。問訊得七世孫，傳聞上世入山，迷不得歸。至晉太元八年，忽復去，不知何所。[7]

Thematically, this narrative features time, space, and eating. The time spans from AD 82 to AD 383, framing Liu and Ruan's round trip to a Shangri-La-like realm[8] where they enjoy a romance with two beautiful maidens. The plot device, which has the pair lost in the mountains, marks their transition from "this-world" to the "otherworld." During their transition, Liu and Ruan nearly starve to death. This leads to their discovery of the first magical food item: peaches. Their next discovery is leftover food on utensils afloat on a stream, which sparks hope for survival for the two men, who thereupon swim upstream and accidentally enter the transcendent realm where their romantic encounters take place. In this realm, Liu and Ruan are served a special meal consisting of sesame grains, goat jerky, beef, and more peaches. They stay there for six months before returning home, only to find that seven human generations have passed.

The plot design invites a question from the empirical reader: Why has so much time passed upon their return? The only explanation, it seems, is that time dilates, or passes more slowly during their stay in the transcendent realm relative to normal, mundane time. The theme of time dilation in a special realm is not unique to the Liu-Ruan tale, nor even to the Chinese tradition. In the early Christian tale of the Seven Sleepers, we find a similar time-dilated displacement where faith, rather than magical eating, enables the protagonists

---

7 *Youming lu*, in *Guxiaoshuo gouchen*, 205–6; *Tangqian zhiguai xiaoshuo jishi*, 462–63.
8 "Shangri-La" refers to an "enclosed paradise," and is a neologism in James Hilton's 1933 novel, *Lost Horizon*, 103, 110, et passim. The paradise described in this novel is not enclosed as it is up in the mountains of Nepal.

to endure 372 years in the cave of Mount Celion in Ephesus, a city in ancient Greece.[9] Although one sleeper named Malchus is said to have bought loaves before the seven young men fell asleep and after they woke up, bread was not implied to have factored into their survival. An earlier example is the tale of Epimenides of Crete who slept for fifteen years, but like the sleepers in Ephesus, food did not factor into the duration of his sleep nor his wellness upon waking.[10] Like Liu and Ruan, all these sleepers have avoided aging, and upon their return to the human world they are no older than when they fell asleep. However, the author of the Chinese tale demonstrates an awareness for making his narrative more physiologically accountable.[11] This medieval Chinese concern with sustenance on magical journeys is not an isolated case but, as we shall see in later chapters of this book, endures throughout much of China's literary history.

These questions of magical sustenance, time, and plot form a point of departure for this chapter.[12] In the pages that follow, we explore the early Daoist tradition for related storylines, and find magical power endowed to the mountains and their resident ladies. We also study the literary tradition that predates the Liu-Ruan tale for clues about how this theme might have formed.

2   Eating and Journeying in Early China

Eating has been an important consideration in writings pertaining to journeying since the earliest strata of Chinese literary history, where the details of sustenance are framed as important concerns of a gentleman.[13]

---

9   See Jacobus de Voragine (ca. 1229–1298), *The Golden Legend*, 401–4. The translator points out that "the saints must have slept only 195 years," because "Decius reigned in 252 and his reign lasted only fifteen months" and they arose in 448. Ibid., 404.
10   See William Hansen, *The Book of Greek and Roman Folktales*, 132–33, in which Apollonios' (15–100) and Diogenes Laertios' (180–240) versions of the tale are included. I acknowledge Tyler Pike for suggesting these tales (along with their sources) for comparison. Another work for comparison is Irving Washington (1783–1859), *Rip Van Winkle*, in idem., *Rip Van Winkle and Other Stories*, 17.
11   In his study of "unnatural narratology," Biwu Shang identifies the "unnatural temporality" and "nonactualizable elements" in the Liu-Ruan tale, but he does not explore the essential role of magical food. Shang, *Unnatural Narrative across Borders*, 57–61.
12   Livia Kohn's (ed.) volumes *Time in Daoist Practice* and *Dao and Time* are not concerned with time as a literary feature (and do not cover the primary texts that form the focus of the current study), but rather explore temporality as a core concern in the Daoist religious worldview.
13   Hunger is always made an ordeal for upholding righteousness and the repayment of kindness. One would rather starve to death than eat food given in a humiliating manner; another example of Confucius' food being cut off. See *Lunyu*, 15/2 and *Shiji*, 92.2609.

Our first example is a passage from the *Zhuangzi* in which the sustenance required for a certain travel distance is calculated. This consideration of food, space, and time reflects a narrative preoccupation that predates China's importation of Buddhism. In response to the cicada and the turtle dove's ridicule of the great *peng* bird for flying so high, the text explains:

> Someone off to the green of the woods with enough for three meals will be home with his belly still full; someone going a hundred *li* pounds grain for the days he will be away; someone going a thousand *li* gathers grain to last three months.
>
> 適莽蒼者，三餐而反，腹猶果然；適百里者，宿舂糧；適千里者，三月聚糧。[14]

The sustenance calculation reinforces the moral import of this *Zhuangzi* chapter on "Carefree Roaming." Guo Xiang's 郭象 (252–312) gloss focuses on this theme: "The farther one goes, the more grain one should amass. Therefore, the bigger its (i.e., the *peng* bird's) wings, the more air is needed."[15] Surviving a journey requires not heroic courage or prescient foresight, but attention to practical detail. The journeys implied in the parable do not, however, involve any voyage from one realm to another, nor is time a primary concern.

The *Chuci*, on the other hand, does embody a conception of how to survive travel to a realm in which time passes differently. Shih-hsiang Chen argues that the *Chuci* is the first poetry in the Chinese tradition to feature an awareness of the passage of time.[16] In the "Lisao," the protagonist's *itineraria* to otherworldly realms is triggered by his frustration on earth.[17] Anxious over time passing in mundane reality, he pursues eternity. The following episode takes place upon the protagonist's consultation with Lingfen 靈氛, the diviner. Aware that his destinations will include mythological realms such as Mount Kunlun 崑崙 and Mount Buzhou 不周, the protagonist knows what to prepare:

The latter is seen in Han Xin's 韓信 (231–196 BC) repayment for the laundry lady. See *Liji zhengyi*, 10.86c.

14 *Zhuangzi*, 1/9–10; trans., Graham, *Chuang-tzǔ*, 44, modified.
15 See *Zhuangzi jishi*, 1A.10, n. 2, quoting Guo Xiang's commentary.
16 Chen, "The Genesis of Poetic Time," 1–44. In fact, there are quite a few poems in the *Shijing* that express concerns about the passage of time. See, e.g., Mao 20, 26, 114, and 167. Traditionally, the *Shijing* was thought to predate the *Chuci*. Debates about the validity of this assumption are outside of the scope of this study.
17 David Hawkes, "The Quest of the Goddess," 59–63.

333	靈氛既告余以吉占兮	According to Spirit Aura's fine augury for me—,
334	歷吉日乎吾將行	on that fortunate day I prepare to depart.
335	折瓊枝以為羞兮	I snap off a carnelian branch to serve as my dried meat,
336	精瓊爢以為粻[18]	distil the splintered carnelian to serve as my victuals.

Wang Yi's 王逸 (fl. 120) commentary explores the intention behind these material preparations (I have italicized the key phrase for emphasis):

> This means: The poet was about to journey. He then broke branches of carnelian as dried meat and distilled splintered carnelian as provisions. His drinking and eating were fragrant and pure—*he wished to prolong his life.*
>
> 言我將行，乃折取瓊枝，以為脯腊，精鑿玉屑，以為儲糧，飲食香潔，冀以延年也。[19]

While Wang Yi's overriding hermeneutic concern involves identification of the metaphoric dimension to the "Lisao,"[20] here we may simply note that this gloss reflects the prevalent belief that otherworldly travel is possible and that one must make special dietary preparations for such journeys. The "Yuanyou" ("Far-off Roaming")—an imitation of "Lisao"—reinforces this idea. In this poem, the protagonist prepares magical foodstuffs such as the "Six Pneumas" (*liuqi* 六氣), "damps of coldest midnights" (*hangxie* 沆瀣), "aurora of dawn" (*zhaoxia* 朝霞), "essence and vitality" (*jingqi* 精氣), "tenuous liquor of the Flying Springs" (*feiquan zhi weiye* 飛泉之微液), "floriated blooms of gorgeous gemstones" (*wanyan zhi huaying* 琬琰之華英), etc.[21] Consumption of these items will result in physical and spiritual resilience:

83	玉色頩以脕顏兮	The suffusion of a jade sheen therewith imbued my features—

---

18 *CCBZ*, 1.42; trans., Williams, *Elegies of Chu*, 13, modified. For jade consumption in ancient China, see Ye Shuxian, "Shiyu xinyang," 4–12.
19 *CCBZ*, 1.42; my translation, my italics.
20 This strategy is central to Wang Yi's exegesis on the "Lisao." See his postface to the "Lisao," in *CCBZ*, 1.48. Pauline Yu, however, uses her terms "substitutive method" and "imagery of replacement" in reading the poem and Wang Yi's theory. See Yu, *The Reading of Imagery*, 85, 89, 92–98, 116–17, et passim. Yu's translation and discussion of Wang's postface is in op. cit., 105–6.
21 *CCBZ*, 5.165, 168; trans., Kroll, "On Far Roaming," 661, 662.

84	精醇粹而始壯	My essence, becoming whole and unmixed, now took on strength.
85	質銷鑠以汋約兮	As body, weakening and wasting, turned tender and listless—
86	神要眇以淫放[22]	Spirit, growing fine and subtle, was released, unrestrained.

These special foodstuffs seem to function as a spiritual weight loss tonic so the protagonist is ready for ascension.[23] The consumption of "essence and vitality" reflects the common belief that one would unite one's body with its macrocosmic counterpart, the universe.[24] The end of the poem depicts the protagonist's success in ascension.

In the *Chuci* textual circle, we find the following lines that enable us to see a full picture of what we shall be referring to as a "time-dilated journey," by which we mean a journey during which time passes more slowly for the traveler than for contemporaries left behind. The poet of "Crossing the River" ("Shejiang" 涉江) is evidently interested in how to survive such a journey:

9	吾與重華遊兮瑤之圃	Along with Chonghua I visit—the Pleasance of Jasper.
10	登崑崙兮食玉英	We climb up Mount Kunlun—and sup on blossoms of jade,
11	與天地兮比壽	I equal Heaven and Earth—in longevity,
12	與日月兮齊光[25]	and match the Sun and Moon—in radiance.

Here, the protagonist roams with Chonghua (lit., "Double Blossom," name of the legendary Emperor Shun).[26] Putting aside Wang Yi's "substitutive method" and focusing instead on the surface meaning of the verse, we observe in order

---

22 *CCBZ*, 5.168; Kroll, "On Far Roaming," 661.
23 Loss of weight is a basic "requirement" for transcendence. See Chan, "Lu Ji 'Lingxiao fu,'" 319–20. It prepares one for ascension from earth, as evidenced in the phrase "lightly ascending and far-off roaming" 輕舉遠遊. See, e.g., "Yuanyou," *CCBZ*, 5.163. Paul Kroll has proposed a reading of this poem from a Daoist perspective. See Kroll, "On Far Roaming," 653–69. The idea became an equivalent of transcendence. See e.g.: *Zhouyi cantongqi* (HY 998), 1.32b; *Wushang biyao* (HY 1130), 65.6b. Ge Hong 葛洪 (284–364) describes the result of consuming jade and mercury as "lightly ascending" (*qingju*). See *Baopuzi neipian jiaoshi*, 11.204, 11.210.
24 See Mark Edward Lewis, *The Construction of Space in Early China*, 43–45.
25 *CCBZ*, 4.128–29; Williams, *Elegies of Chu*, 54, modified.
26 Shun is recorded to have had double pupils in each of his eyeballs. See *Shiji*, 1.31, n. 1, Zhang Shoujie's 張守節 (d. 1075) commentary.

to roam in paradise with the sage-king for whom time passes on the scale of the lifespans of "heaven and earth," our protagonist consumes the "blossoms of jade" to prolong his life accordingly.

This poetic interest in food and transcendent journeying remained a marked feature in the *Chuci* poetic descendants in Han times. Later poets followed suit in their writing about the same topic. In Yang Xiong's 揚雄 (53 BC–AD 18) "counter-Lisao" ("Fan 'Lisao'" 反離騷), for instance, the poet might have intended to read *qiongzhi* 瓊枝 as chrysanthemum and make this flower and carnelian two life-prolonging foods. He writes: "Distilling the splintered carnelian and the fragrance of autumn chrysanthemum, / I will use them as a means to prolong my natural life span" 精瓊靡與秋菊芳，將以延夫天年.[27] This feature is also illustrated in Zhang Heng's 張衡 (78–139) preparation for his celestial journey. In his "*Fu* on Contemplation on the Mysterious" ("Sixuan fu" 思玄賦), Zhang relates that his protagonist takes a life-prolonging elixir before traveling to heaven: "I sip the flowing liquid of gushing springs, / Chew the fallen petals of stone mushrooms" 漱飛泉之瀝液兮，咀石菌之流英.[28] All these pieces reflect the theme that surviving travel through time-dilated realms requires magical foods.[29]

As with many other elements in the "Lisao" and its auxiliary texts, this theme finds its roots in early Daoist thought.[30] One such practice that appears in texts that predate the "Lisao," such as the Mawangdui manuscript and the *Daode jing*, is the consumption of *qi*, for example,[31] but we may observe that this practice was not portrayed as a precondition for otherworldly, time-dilated travel; therefore the *Chuci* family of texts appears to be foundational for our purposes.

---

27   Yang Xiong, "Fan Lisao," quoted in *CCBZ*, 1.42. The translation of the first few words of the couplet, borrowed from the "Lisao," is Nicholas Morrow Williams's. See *Elegies of Chu*, 13.
28   *WX*, 15.5b; trans., David R. Knechtges, *Wen xuan*, 3: 115.
29   In her discussion of "Yuanyou" and "Sixuan fu," Zornica Kirkova observes that "the maintenance of an ethereal diet and absorption of elixir substances, association with the animating essence of the sun, the successive exploration of all the coordinates of the universe and thus the acquisition of power over their divinities … exalted the hero to the highest spheres." See Kirkova, *Roaming into the Beyond*, 201–13, esp., 212.
30   See Hawkes, *Songs of the South*, 28–38; Chan, "The *Jing/zhuan* Structure of the *Chuci* Anthology," 293–327.
31   Robert Ford Campany, "The Meanings of Cuisines of Transcendence," 29–32. For the meaning and function of *qi* see Paul R. Goldin, "What is *Qi* 氣 and Why Was It a Good Idea?" 229–44; "Qi de hanyi jiqi jiji yiyi," 305–39.

3   Eating and Spatiotemporal Dimensions in Early Texts

There is no convincing evidence that concepts of time-dilated travel were imported into China, but it is enlightening to note that such ideas are in evidence in other early cultures around the world. In addition to the tale of the sleepers of Epheseus discussed above (an example of time-dilated sleep rather than travel, to be precise), we find relevant examples in early Hindu texts. The *Bhāgavata Purana*, a medieval Hindi work,[32] records a time-dilation episode about King Kakudmi who took his daughter to see Brahma the creator, who told the king: "Child, twenty-seven *chaturyugas* (4.32 million solar years) have passed since you entered my *sabha* (assembly), for time in my realm is very different from on the earth."[33] The concept of time revealed in this episode shares similarity with its Chinese counterparts, in which the mortal and immortal worlds are demarcated and time runs at a different pace in each. The calculation of time in ancient India is: "A year (of human beings) is equal to a day and night of the gods."[34]

There is a clear difference between passages like this in the Hindu tradition and their counterparts in the Chinese tradition. Unlike King Kakudmi, the protagonist of the *Chuci* texts worries about how he might survive to bear witness to a realm in which time is dilated to such a significant extent. He rationalizes that he must live long, if not eternally, to do so.

While the *Chuci* texts contain evidence for the inception of time-dilated travel in Chinese poetry, their advent in narrative form may be traced to the Eastern Han period. As in the *Chuci*, these early narratives frame magical eating as the crucial enabler of time-dilated travel. One such text was written by Wang Chong 王充 (27–97), an iconoclastic thinker-writer who cites the following tale as part of his attack on superstition:

> [Xiang] Mandu was fond of the *dao* on how to become a transcendent. He left his home and sojourned for three years before returning. [Upon his return] his family asked about his experience. Mandu said: "Upon

---

32   Different theories date this work to the third century, the sixth century, the ninth century, and the tenth century. See Sheo Shanker Prasad, *The Bhāgavata Purāṇa*, 37–49; Sindhu S. Dange, *The Bhāgavata Purāṇa*, 2–6.

33   *Bhagavata Purana*, trans., Ramesh Menon, Skandha 9, p. 603. Calculation of *chaturyuga* is based on S. V. Gupta, *Units of Measurement Past, Present and Future*, 3. A brief introduction to Hindi cosmology and cosmogony, on *kalpa* and *yuga*, is in Wendy Doniger, *Hindu Myths*, 43.

34   Kisari Mohan Ganguli, trans., *Mahabharata of Krishna-Dwaipayana Vyasa*, vol. 3, "Santi Parva," section 231, p. 155.

departure I did not know what happened to me but suddenly felt as though I was lying down. A number of transcendent beings came to carry me to the sky. They stopped at a point located several *li* away from the moon. I saw but obscurity and dimness above and below the moon and could not tell the directions of east and west. I stayed beside the moon, feeling cold and sad. I starved and wanted to eat. A transcendent at times fed me a cup of fluid aurora.[35] Each cup of the drink would quench my hunger for several months. I did not realize how many months and years had passed and did not know by what means I passed [the timespan]. Suddenly I felt as though reclining again and found myself down here." In Hedong he was given a sobriquet "expelled transcendent." When the empiricists heard this, they knew that it could not have happened as described.

[項]曼都好道學仙，委家亡去，三年而返。家問其狀，曼都曰：「去時不能自知，忽見若臥形，有仙人數人，將我上天，離月數里而止。見月上下幽冥，幽冥不知東西。居月之旁，其寒悽愴。口饑欲食，仙人輒飲我以流霞一杯。每飲一杯，數月不饑。不知去幾何年月，不知以何為過，忽然若臥，復下至此。」河東號之曰斥仙。實論者聞之，乃知不然。[36]

Despite Wang Chong's discrediting of the tale, we can treat this passage as a received text worthy of analysis. In the narrative, Xiang Mandu, who plays a double role of protagonist and narrator, is aware of his need for magical sustenance during his stay in the otherworldly realm. In the course of the narrative, although we are not informed of the precise ratio of the time difference between heaven and earth, Mandu implies that a greatly expanded time has passed during his trip, or at least it felt to him like dilated time. We also find in this tale an early example of the otherworldly traveler as not only an aspirant for *xian*-ship (Daoist transcendence), but also an accidental "intruder."[37] This example of Mandu's adventure together with a few other fragments suggests a

---

35 For "fluid aurora," see Kroll, "Li Po's Transcendent Diction," 104.
36 *Lunheng jiaoshi*, 325–26. Wang Jia in his *Shiyiji* (1.5) reports: "At that time, there were fleeting clouds sprinkling drops, which were called 'aurora nectar.' After drinking it, one would attain the *dao* and become old at a time later than one's natural life span."
37 Ying-shih Yü argues that this new "cult of *hsien* (*xian*) immortality" became popular among common people around the beginning of the Eastern Han. See Yü, "Life and Immortality in the Mind of Han China," 107–8, 110, 114. The text Yü refers to is "Xianren Tang Gongfang bei" 仙人唐公房碑 in *Lishi*, 3.

larger body of similar material probably existed before Wang Chong's time but has been lost.[38]

This brings us to a second narrative written during the Six dynasties period. A tale from *Bieguo dongming ji* 別國洞冥記 attributed to Guo Xian 郭憲 (E. Han)[39] describes a celestial journey undertaken by Dongfang Shuo 東方朔 (ca. 160–93 BC) in his childhood:

> When Dongfang Shuo was three years old, he always pointed in the air and talked to himself, gesturing in that direction. Once, his stepmother spanked him for his sudden, mysterious disappearance which lasted several months. On another occasion, he disappeared again for a whole year before returning. His stepmother saw him and said in great astonishment, "You have been away a year. How can you comfort me?" The boy replied: "I went to the Sea of Purple Mud, where my clothes were tainted by the purple water. Then I washed them at Yu Gulf. I set out in the morning and returned at noon. Why do you say it has been a whole year?" His stepmother asked: "Which state did you go to?" The boy replied: "When I finished washing my clothes, I rested at the Towering Terrace at Dark City. The Lord fed me some cinnabar chestnut rosy aurora nectar. I ate too much and was so stuffed that I nearly died. After drinking one half *he* of Yellow Dew of the Mysterious Sky, I sobered up at once. On my way back, I saw a green tiger resting by the road. I rode on its back to return home but was bitten by it because I hit it too hard." His stepmother felt sad and sighed and wrapped his wounds with a piece of blue cloth torn from her dress.

> 東方朔。……年三歲，……恒指揮天上空中獨語。隣母忽失朔，累月暫歸。母笞之。後復去，經年乃歸。母見之大驚曰：「汝行經年一歸，何以慰吾？」朔曰：「兒暫之紫泥之海，有紫水汙衣，仍過虞泉

---

38 Stephen R. Bokenkamp argues, "The scope of our loss [of literature on grotto passages] is apparent not only from the bibliographic record, but also from the abundant unofficial literature cited in Taoist texts—stele inscriptions, temple records, accounts of holy mountains, and the like." See Bokenkamp, "The Peach Flower Font and the Grotto Passage," 74. The article is an important case study of the belief in the existence of such a "land paradise" (pp. 65–77).

39 Some anachronistic elements prove this traditional attribution wrong. David Knechtges concludes: "Although there is far from unanimity among scholars, the evidence favors a Six Dynasties provenance for the work." See Knechtges, "Hanwu Dongming ji 漢武洞冥記 (Account of Emperor Wu of Han's delving into arcana)," in *Ancient and Early Medieval Chinese Literature*, ed. Knechtges and Taiping Chang, 347.

湔浣。朝發中還，何言經年乎？」母又問曰：「汝悉經何國？」朔曰：「兒湔衣竟，暫息冥都崇臺。一窹眠。王公啗兒以丹栗霞漿。兒食之既多，飽悶幾死。乃飲玄天黃露半合，即醒。還遇一蒼虎息於路。初兒騎虎而還，打捶過痛，虎嚙兒腳傷。」母便悲嗟，乃裂青布裳裹之。[40]

The narrative mode of this tale is similar to the Mandu story, although it portrays the boy as an accidental traveler. Even so, the mythological place-names indicate he travels to Heaven and the underworld. The Yu Gulf, for instance, is a locale where the sun sets.[41]

The most marked similarity in both tales is the consumption of magical foods. The young Dongfang Shuo and Mandu both ate "fluid aurora" and its equivalent "aurora nectar." The Dongfang Shuo tale also involves a buffet of other magic foodstuffs, which anticipates similar descriptions of magical feasts in the Liu-Ruan tale. Indeed, the concept that transcendent, time-dilated journeys require magical foods became well established by the end of the Eastern Han.[42] These tales and poems also reflect the fascination with the pursuit of carnal immortality during this period. We might also observe that magical eating was considered a prerequisite to the pursuit of transcendence.

4   Eating as a Means to Transcend Time

The conception, practice, and study of eating magical food were reactions to the problem of mortality and attempts to achieve a kind of immortality that was possible within the natural world. This aligned with the general Chinese expectation of, in Joseph Needham's words, "a perpetuation of existence within the natural world under the sun, whether on earth, or in the sky among the constellations."[43] Daoists took this one step further and conceived of physical

---

40 *TPGJ*, 6.39, quoting *Dongming ji* and *Shuo biezhuan* 朔別傳.
41 *Shanhai jing jiaozhu*, 381–82, n. 5, quoting Guo Pu's 郭璞 (276–324) commentary; *CCBZ*, 1.27, Wang Yi's commentary. Yuquan 虞泉, instead of Yuyuan 淵, is used is a result of avoiding the taboo word Yuan, given name of Emperor Gaozu of the Tang (r. 618–626).
42 Cao Cao 曹操 (155–220) in his "Qichu chang" #1 (*XQHWJ*, 345) says that he took "jade nectar" on his journey to Mount Penglai, a transcendent realm. Zornica Kirkova observes that "the protagonist is then given a draught of the jade liquor, which strengthens him for his subsequent journey to Penglai and eventually to the Gates of Heaven." See Kirkova, *Roaming into the Beyond*, 165.
43 Needham et al. continue: "... there had not been, and until the seeping in of Buddhism there would not be, ... other-worldly heavens and hells. .... Immortality, therefore, like

transcendence in more practical terms. In his study of the dietary practices of the *Wufu xu*, an esoteric cult in Daoist tradition prevailing in the second to the fifth centuries, Shawn Arthur observes that food was thought to enhance travel, enabling adherents to transcend mortal speed and physical space.[44] This cultural belief still holds true after the arrival of Buddhism. Although the concept of the "Wheel of Time" originated in Hinduism[45] and was therefore foreign and novel when first encountered in China, the Chinese had a pre-existing spiritual conceptualization of and concern for the passage of time. The idea of "transcending the world" (*du shi* 度世), frequently found in Han and post-Han texts, concerns mainly how one may stay in the mortal world without dying.[46] The Eastern Han, in particular, marks the advent of time-dilation fantasy in literary works.[47] While the rise of the cult of alchemists in the Eastern Han was a direct reaction to political and cultural anxiety, the invention of the earthly paradise is another means by which people sought to transcend.

The *Zhouyi cantong qi* 周易參同契 is one such representative alchemical text. One of its prefaces dated from the twelfth century illuminates the motive of transcending time:

> As for the open-minded aspirant-scholars with a pure and harmonious temperament, they regard worldly affairs as putting their hands in boiling water and can abandon their wife and children as though taking off their shoes. They realize the rapidness of one's fleeting lifetime and the enduring eternalness of the great *dao*. ... When they succeed in studying [this scripture], they will be able to witness the sea turning into hills and regard human life as amassed foams. They can fly and leap up to Grand Tenuity and roam freely with the Creator-Fashioner. These are not the deeds of Heaven and Earth, but the power of the returning elixir.

> 若有清虛志士，立性淳和。見世務如探湯，棄妻子如脫屣，覩浮生之遄速，知大道之攸長。……一成之後，看海水為丘陵，覩人生如聚

---

everything else in true Chinese thought-style, was 'this-worldly.'" See Needham, et al., *Science and Civilisation in China, Vol. 5: Part III*: 114.

44 Arthur, *Early Daoist Dietary Practices*, 112. The *Wufu xu* is *Taishang Lingbao wufu xu* (HY 388).

45 See John Newman, "Eschatology in the Wheel of Time Tantra," 284–85.

46 *Taiping jing*, 72.282–83, 287–88; 96.410–11; 98.438–39, 411, et passim; *Hanwudi neizhuan*, in TPGJ, 3.19–22. Wang Chong criticizes the superstition in *du shi*. See *Lunheng*, 7.329–38.

47 See Yang Yi's discussion in his Zhongguo xushixue, 214–225, quoting Qian Zhongshu 錢鍾書 in agreement. Yang treats time-dilation as a narrative device and terms it "hallucinated time" (*shijian huanhua* 時間幻化).

沫，飛騰於太虛之上，逍遙於造化之中。此非天地之功，實為還丹之力。⁴⁸

The *Zhouyi cantong qi* is a manual for making an elixir, written in cryptic language. The "returning elixir" is said to have magical efficacies of freeing the mortal from the temporal restraints of the human world. The idea of ascension, as in the *Chuci* texts quoted above, marks the achievement of transcending time through creating physical distance from the human world and its soil that ages the people who remain behind.⁴⁹

From a literary point of view, one may observe that the concepts of magical food, elixirs, and transcendence may be described as nested metaphors. Nathan Sivin's theory of alchemy as a means of manipulating time offers a picture of how alchemists approached their concerns about mortality. He points out that "almost every alchemical treatise used its manipulations as a concrete metaphor for cosmic and spiritual processes." Within this macro- and micro-cosmic correlative system, continues Sivin, "it was the nested and intermeshed cycles of the celestial bodies that governed the seasonal rhythms and, through them, the vast symphony of individual life courses." The elixir refining furnace is, therefore, "a model of the Tao, to reproduce in a limited space on a shortened time scale the cyclical energetics of the cosmos." The prevalent thoughts of escapism and transcendence in the Later Han may be construed from a different angle: "The idea that to grasp the unchanging reality that underlies the chaos of experience is to rise above that chaos, to be freed at least from the moment from the limits of personal mortality."⁵⁰ The examples of Mandu and Dongfang Shuo, among others, also lend themselves to a metaphorical interpretation, whereby the nature of accidental or intentional roaming can be couched as an escape from unnamed hardship in the real world. Likewise, magical eating would have served as an appealing panacea to catalyze this escape.

---

48 *Zhouyi cantongqi* (HY 998), "xu," 3b. The metaphor of "amassed foams" (*jumo* 聚沫) for the fleeting human life is a common Buddhist notion. The occurrence here in this Eastern Han text predates any Buddhist sutra known to have been imported to China. The earliest one should be *Lalitavistara* (*Fo shuo Puyao jing* 佛說普曜經), T 186, trans. Dharmarakṣa 竺法護 (233–310) in 308. See *Lalitavistara* (*Fo shuo Puyao jing*), T 186, 3.506a14.

49 An idea first found in *Zhuangzi*, 6/24, 11/42–44; trans. respectively, Graham, *Chuang-Tzŭ*, 86, Victor Mair, *Wandering on the Way*, 96–97. See my discussion in Chan, "Engulfing and Embracing the Vast Earth," 50–54.

50 Sivin, "Chinese Alchemy and the Manipulation of Time," 512, 514, 521–24. I thank Paul R. Goldin for referring me to this article.

There is, of course, a longstanding differentiation between "Eastern" and "Western" cultural concepts of eternity, but these types of contrasts tend to be reductive in nature. In his discussion of the idea of an "escape from time," Paul Davies poses a question: "Can a human being really escape time and glimpse eternity?" "As happens so often in reports from Westerners, the experience came totally out of the blue," continues Davies, "but Eastern mystics have perfect special techniques that allegedly can induce such timeless rapture." Quoting a Tibetan monk and an Indian philosopher, Davies only traces the Eastern tradition to the teaching of "Sankara, the exponent of Advaita Vedanta," dated from the eighth century,[51] without mentioning any examples from the Chinese tradition, which, of course, has a well-formed and complex textual heritage concerned with human access to the eternal.

Alongside the Eastern Han fascination with immortality is, perhaps, a parallel acknowledgment of—and reaction to—the unavoidable aging and dying of mortals. Failure to achieve immortality gave rise to carpe diem, a prominent theme in late Han poetry.[52] Failure to transcend also gave rise to competition among alchemists. Wei Boyang 魏伯陽, the reputed author of the *Cantong qi*, outlines a picture of the competition among different schools of the time, which were frantic to win trust from people.[53] Time was not the only concern for those who studied life-prolonging techniques in early medieval China; another alchemical technique aimed at manipulating spatial restriction. This technique was called "shrinking the earth's veins" (*suo dimai* 縮地脈). Fei Changfang 費長房 (E. Han) was known to possess this magic. The earliest such record is found in the *Lieyi zhuan* 列異傳, attributed to Cao Pi 曹丕 (187–226):

> Fei Changfang could also shrink the earth's veins. When he was receiving some guests at home, he went to the market to buy salted fish. Within one day, people saw him in several places located a thousand *li* away.
>
> 費長房又能縮地脈，坐客在家，至市買鮓，一日之間，人見之千里外者數處。[54]

An empirical reader such as Wang Chong might have questioned: how would people from a thousand *li* away see Fei on the same day? After all, there was

---

51 Davies, *About Time*, 25–26.
52 See, e.g., "Ancient poems" #13, WX, 29.6b: "If consuming an elixir in pursuit of transcendence / In most cases one is deceived by the drugs" 服食求神仙，多爲藥所誤.
53 Lu-Chiang Wu and Tenney L. Davis, "An Ancient Chinese Treatise on Alchemy," 278–79.
54 YWLJ, 72.1243, quoting *Lieyi zhuan*.

no instant messaging back then. Fei's alleged technique was also cited in Ge Hong's *Shenxian zhuan* 神仙傳:

> Fang possessed a magical technique. He could shrink the earth's veins. He could manifest a thousand *li* of distance, as though it were before his eyes. When he released it, it would be unfurled just like before.
>
> 房有神術，能縮地脉，千里存在，目前宛然，放之復舒如舊也。[55]

Ge Hong couches Fei's "ability" (*neng*) as a meditative method peculiar to the Shangqing Daoist tradition called *cun* 存 or *cunsi* 思, usually rendered as "visualizing" or "actualizing."[56] The mechanism of this method is quite self-explanatory in Ge's description and, as we see here, the result of this process is a vivid image in motion. Some therefore call the process "retentive meditation."[57] According to this line of thinking, rather than physically traveling a thousand *li* in a day, the technique of "shrinking the earth's veins" produces an illusion. Fan Ye 范曄 (398–445) must have followed Cao Pi's tale in his elaborated versions in which he provides the episode of Fei's death:

> On the same day, people saw him in several places a thousand *li* away and therefore regarded him as being proficient at the technique of "shrinking the earth." Later, as he lost his tally, he was killed by ghosts.
>
> 一日之間，人見其在千里之外者數處，因稱其有縮地術。後因失其符，為眾鬼所殺。[58]

Fan Ye's version of Fei's adventures contains a new element. Instead of eating, Fei's extraordinary travel is enabled by the tally (proof of official authorization), which also protects his person. Although eating does not play the role, we find here more evidence that unnatural journeys require a catalyzing aid.

In addition to the two versions of the Fei Changfang tale quoted above (which we will return to later in this chapter), we find several thematically similar tales dated from roughly the same period as our central tale featuring Liu Chen and Ruan Zhao. These narratives all explore how time dilates in special sites, and how magical eating enables survival along the journey there. In

---

55   *TPGJ*, 12.82, quoting *Shenxian zhuan*.
56   For a summary of studies and renderings of *cunsi* see Chan, "Yixiang feixiang," 231–33; Edward H. Schafer, "The Jade Woman of Greatest Mystery," 387.
57   Bokenkamp, *Early Daoist Scriptures*, 288.
58   *HHS*, 82B.2744.

Table 1, we endeavor not to present a single paradigm, but rather a variety of similar narrative themes and motifs.

Most of these narratives describe magical eating as a survival aid in time-dilated travel. The foodstuffs also enable the protagonist to feel no hunger during his stay in the otherworldly realm. As seen in the Dongfang Shuo narrative, the highest level of transcendence requires the consumption of *qi*.[59] This range of edibles for transcendent beings is reflected in the poetry about transcendence written during the period through the sixth century.[60] Some narratives featuring time dilation do not require eating at all. Others, such as the Mandu tale, involve magical eating and transcendent journeying (or at least journeys or stays of duration that would otherwise strain human physiology) but do not involve time-dilated travel.[61] The best-known example of a transcendent but not time-dilated journey is Tao Qian's Peach Blossom Spring.[62]

Here is another, fifth-century example of temporal displacement that does not involve eating, taken from the *Yiyuan* 異苑 (*Garden of Anomalies*):

> In the past, there was a man who rode his horse to the mountains. From a distance he saw two old men playing dice games inside a cave. He dismounted and approached them. He planted his whip on the ground and watched them playing. He thought only a short moment had passed, but then found his whip already dilapidated. Turning around, he found only a rotten saddle and a decayed skeleton of his horse. Upon returning home, he found none of his family members. He felt a spasm of agony and died.

> 昔有人乘馬山行，遙望岫裡有二老翁相對樗蒲，遂下馬造焉，以策注地而觀之。自謂俄頃，視其馬鞭，摧然已爛。顧瞻其馬，鞍骸枯朽。既還至家，無復親屬，一慟而絕。[63]

---

59   Campany, "The Meanings of Cuisines," 27–33.
60   See, e.g., Yu Xin 庾信 (513–581), "Xianshan" 仙山, no. 2; "Yan'ge xing" 燕歌行, in *Yu Zishan jizhu*, 4.373, 5.407. For other examples of poetry in this tradition, see Yen Chin-hsiung, *Liuchao fushi fengqi yu wenxue*, 179–218.
61   There are two tales where the protagonist falls into a cave and stays alive by consuming jade nectar 玉漿 and stone marrow 石髓, but does not experience time-dilated travel. See *Youming lu*, in *Guxiaoshuo gouchen*, 214; *Soushen hou ji*, 1.2.
62   See *Tao Yuanming ji*, 6.165–66. For an English translation with commentary see Hightower, *The Poetry of T'ao Ch'ien*, 254–58. Hightower's translation (with modification) is in the beginning of Chapter 3 of the present book.
63   *Yiyuan*, 5.4a.

TABLE 1   Eating and time dilation in works dated from the 1st to 5th centuries

#	Protagonist	Source	Food eaten	Timespan in otherworld vs. human world[a]
1	Dongfang Shuo 東方朔	*Dongming ji* 洞冥記; ca. 30	Cinnabar chestnut rosy aurora nectar 丹栗霞漿 and Yellow dew from the dark sky 玄天黃露	1 morning = 1 year
2	Lü Gong 呂恭	*Shenxian zhuan* 神仙傳; early 4th c.[b]	[Not recorded]	2 days = over 200 years
3	Herb gatherer 採藥人	*Shiyi ji* 拾遺記; ca. 350[c]	Jade and gold nectar 瓊漿金液	A short visit = 300 years
4	Wang Zhi 王質	*Zhilin* 志林; ca. 350[d]	[Not recorded]	[Home changed beyond recognition]
5	Fei Changfang 費長房	*Hou Han shu* 後漢書; ca. 440[e]	[Not recorded]	10 days = more than 10 years
6	Wang Zhi	*Dongyang ji* 東陽記; ca. 440[f]	Something like jujube seed 棗核	A short time = several decades
7	Wang Zhi	*Shuyi ji* 述異記; ca. 500[g]	Something like jujube seed	[Home changed beyond recognition]
8	Queen Mother of the West	*Hanwudi neizhuan*; ca. 400	"Numinous melon" 靈瓜	"Not long from memory" = 7,000 years
9	Liu Chen & Ruan Zhao	*Youming lu* 幽明錄; ca. 440	Peach, sesame, etc.	6 months = 300 years

a   There is no fixed formula for the calculation of the passing of time in the mortal world as compared with that of the otherworldly realm. Qian Zhongshu includes a long list of examples of such comparisons in Chinese and Western literature. See Qian, *Guanzhui bian*, 670–73.
b   *TPGJ*, 9.64, quoting *Shenxian zhuan*.
c   *Shiyi ji*, 10.235.
d   *Zhilin*, 59.1b.
e   *HHS*, 82B.2744.
f   *TPYL*, 763.2b; *Hejiao Shuijing zhu*, 40.7a.
g   *Shuyi ji*, 1.13a/b.

In most cases discussed above, visitors to this kind of otherworld need not readjust to the temporal dimension in the mortal realm upon their return;[64] this fellow, on the other hand, apparently died as a result of the dramatic difference he could not bear. A connoisseur of such narratives might have assumed this horse-rider passed away because he did not have any magical food to survive the fleeting experience of time-dilated travel, but no markers in the text encourage this conclusion.[65] It is possible that texts such as these are simply illustrative of the dangers of time dilation.

Another problematic text is the narrative of Fei Changfang's ordeals and adventures (item #5 in Table 1 above), recorded in a Liu-Song record in the official history. This tale deserves special attention because it was produced around the same time as the Liu-Ruan tale. Fei was once Clerk of a marketplace, where he saw an elderly herb hawker known as Gourd Elder (Hugong 壺公), who hoisted a flagon at his stall and jumped into it when the market closed. In great astonishment, Fei sought out the old man, hoping to learn the *dao* from him. He followed him into the deep mountains to start his learning. He progressed through several teaching ordeals but failed the last challenge, which involved the consumption of excrement. After failing this final test, Fei bade farewell and returned home. He thought it had been twenty days since he left home, but in fact more than a decade had passed.[66] We are left with the implication that the excrement may have served to enable Fei's ultimate transcendence, or that perhaps the story was concocted as a parody. Either way, we are not told how he survived his time-dilated period of training in the mountains. No other magical eating is explicitly mentioned in the narrative, and it is glaring in its absence, particularly in contrast with the offering of excrement. This particular detail appears to be an inconsistency, in juxtaposition with many of the other similar narratives discussed above.

This kind of inconsistency may have been a result of repeated scribal or editorial adaptation over time. As Stephen R. Bokenkamp observes:

> Stories divorced from their original context lose their reason for being and, as a result, are subject to all manner of distortion. ... Those who sought to preserve these stories apparently felt no compunction to copy

---

64   See Lee Fong-mao, *Wuru yu zhejiang*, 112–19.
65   The story itself has been categorized in the same "mode" as the Wang Zhi story (items #4, #6, and #7 in Table 1). See Lee Fong-mao, *Wuru yu zhejiang*, 116–17.
66   *HHS*, 82B.2744. Rolf A. Stein has a detailed discussion of this tale, its descendent texts, its relationship with alchemy, as well as its variations in other regions in East Asia. See Stein, *The World in Miniature*, 58–91.

out the whole text; they seem rather to have summarized brutally and recast tales into their own language. ... Stories may have been rewritten to suit the editor's personal prejudices.[67]

In oral and written transmission, certain details of a tale are prone to alteration. The Wang Zhi story (#4, 6, and 7 in Table 1) best illustrates the volatile nature of textual transmission. The edible item resembling jujube seed is not mentioned in the earliest extant record but was included in the later version. Here is the most recent version of the Wang Zhi story, found in the *Shuyi ji*, attributed to Ren Fang:

> Stone Chamber Mountains, Xin'an Prefecture. In Jin times, Wang Zhi was once cutting timber when he saw several lads playing chess and singing. Zhi then listened to their songs. The lads gave Zhi a substance which looked like a jujube seed. Zhi put it in his mouth and felt no hunger. After a short moment, the lads asked Zhi, "Why do you not leave?" Zhi rose and discovered that the handle of his axe had completely decayed. When he returned home, he found no others from his own time.
>
> 信安郡石室山，晉時王質伐木，至見童子數人，棋而歌，質因聽之。童子以一物與質，如棗核，質含之不覺饑。俄頃，童子謂曰：「何不去？」，質起，視斧柯爛盡，既歸，無復時人。[68]

While it is possible that the eating part was a later interpolation, it seems likely that such discrepancies simply resulted from the compiler's different choices of details, drawn from what might have been a large oral and written body of variations of the same story. Unlike the horse rider, Wang Zhi did not die upon return to his homeland.[69] Considering the similar texts, we surmise that Wang's survival of the temporal dilation was due to his consumption of the magical substance.

It is interesting to note this edible resembling a jujube seed is likely borrowed from the *Dongming ji*, which records an exotic substance called *duyixiang* 都夷香. The description of this substance as "like a jujube seed" is seen two times in this text. Consumption of a mere slice of it prevents one from hunger for several months. This magical function, I believe, has something to

---

67　Bokenkamp, "The Peach Flower Font and the Grotto Passage," 74.
68　*Shuyi ji*, 1.13a/b.
69　In a Yuan-dynasty adaptation of this tale, Wang is said to have returned to the mountains and later achieved transcendence. See *Lishi zhenxian tidao tongjian* (HY 296), 28.11b.

do with its inflatable size, as it is said to expand after one consumes it.[70] The exotic nature of this substance enhances its mysterious attributes and magical efficacy in literary creative works. Wang Zhi held it in his mouth instead of eating it and thus managed to stay alive in the time-dilated realm shared with the "lads." By the Liu Song period, jujube had become a popular hunger-satiating food.[71] This magical function of the jujube might have been extrapolated from *duyixiang*, which were often likened to jujube.

5 The Blessed Land; Plums and Peaches

We identify one more related thematic feature that emerged in post-Han texts. As Ying-shih Yü points out, the pursuit of *xian* transcendence/immortality saw a "vulgarized" migration from the imperial house to the common people (this phenomenon is most evident in the *Taiping jing*).[72] Another, consequent change was that the food portrayed in these texts had devolved from mythological nectar to more recognizable material foods, which nevertheless carried certain exotic characteristics and were only found in isolated locations.[73]

This change was evident as the cult of the grotto-heaven prospered in post-Han times, when the land-paradise was commonly believed to yield magical food with life-prolonging power. The Daoist encyclopedia, *Zhen'gao* 真誥, compiled by Tao Hongjing 陶弘景 (456–536), is most typical in presenting this change. Its chapter "Investigation of the Divine Pivots" ("Ji shenshu" 稽神樞) gives details on the magical functions of grotto-heaven environments in the Maoshan 茅山 area (in modern Jurong/Gourong 句容, Jiangsu province), in which we find especially relevant information on eating and drinking. This area is called "land lungs" (*difei* 地肺), as "its soils are fertile and its waters pure"; one may live through generations and transcend the world without suffering from wars.[74] In its record of the Huayang 華陽 area, we learn that the soil of grotto-heavens yields life-prolonging plants such as white plums (*baili*

---

70   *Dongming ji*, 1.125; TPYL, 981.3a/b, where the term "a slice" 一片 has a variant of "a *jin* (catty)" 一斤 (3a). The text that depicts its "inflatability" reads: "If a piece of it the size of a grain is thrown into the clear water, it will fill up a large basin in a moment."
71   See *Youming lu*, in *Guxiaoshuo gouchen*, 247.
72   Yü, "Life and Immortality in the Mind of Han China," 108–19.
73   Campany observes that the exotic food is located in zones removed by geographic distance. With the art of *xingchu* 行廚, there is no need to travel to secure the foodstuffs. See Campany, "The Meanings of Cuisines," 46–47.
74   *Zhen'gao* (HY 1010), 11.2a/b. The graph of *fei* is written as *zi* 胏. For the structure and landscape of grotto-heavens, see Miura Kunio, "Dōten Fukuchi shōron," 3–11.

白李), small sour apples (*nai* 柰), and magic mushrooms.[75] The section on white plums touches on the issue of the passage of time in relation to eating:

> In the past, in Gaoxin's time,[76] there was a transcendent, Zhan the Superior Lord. He planted plum trees all over the land where the dragon once reclined. Mr. Zhan is now Right Guardian Manager of the Nine Palaces. He once told others: "Once in the past, I ate some white plums at the foot of Mount Huayang and found them unusually delicious. Upon brief recollection, three thousand years suddenly passed."
>
> 昔高辛時有仙人展上公者，於伏龍地植李，彌滿其地。展先生今為九宮內右司保，其常向人說：昔在華陽下食白李，味異美。憶之未久，而忽已三千年矣。[77]

As a transcendent himself, Zhan could transcend time without special foods, but the white plums appear to be a local fruit with magical power. This assumption finds support in the small sour apples that grew in the same place. This fruit has the function of exorcising calamities and plagues. In the Huayang Grotto and Mount Liangchang 良常山 are found different kinds of bright mushrooms. Consumption of forty-seven Glimmer Mushrooms 熒火芝 will enable one to live for 10,000 years.[78] In the Maoshan area where these kinds of grotto-heavens are located, the Lord Azure Lad 青童君 once buried 8,000 to 9,000 *jin* of gold and jade in order to enhance the water quality of grotto-heavens.[79] As a result, the water benefits human essence and may be used for making elixir. The water of Mount Leiping 雷平山 in the Huayang area has the efficacy of killing the three corpse worms (*shichong* 尸蟲) in the human body.[80] One section of the ridges of Mount Juqu 句曲山 (a variant name of Maoshan) was named Gold Amassment (Jijin shan 積金山) after gold

---

[75] The English translation of *nai* is Bernard E. Read's. The Latin name is *Malus pumila*. See Read, *Chinese Medicinal Plants*, 133 (#435).

[76] Gaoxin (located to the south of modern Shangqiu 商丘 in He'nan province) is where Di Ku 帝嚳 hailed from and became his eponym. Ku was one of the five thearchs (*wudi* 五帝) in prehistoric China.

[77] *Zhen'gao* (HY 1010), 13.8a.

[78] For Ge Hong's discussion of the magical effects of mushrooms, see Campany, *To Live as Long as Heaven and Earth*, 26–29.

[79] The translation of Qingtong jun as "Lord Azure Lad" is Paul Kroll's. See details in Kroll, "In the Halls of the Azure Lad," passim.

[80] *Zhen'gao* (HY 1010), 11.11a/b; 13.8b. The three corpse worms are "body parasites who live on decay and earth and who report everyone's behavior to the administration of the cosmos. ... One can also get rid of them by taking specific longevity drugs, which starve

was discovered there. The water there has the magical function of prolonging life.[81] All these fantastic details lend support to our understanding of the enchanted power of the grotto-heaven in our central tale. In particular, Mount Tongbo (Paulownia and Cypress 桐栢), located in the Tiantai area where Liu and Ruan entered, is said to have rich resources for live-prolonging materials.[82] As such, this myth-laden locale must have been designated as one such fantastic realm visited by the two men.[83]

The transition to thematic settings more recognizable to commoners is evident in Jin-dynasty narratives. The Liu-Ruan adventure has been seen as an adaptation of the herb gatherer story (item #3 in Table 1) with its own distinct features.[84] Although the luxurious settings in the otherworldly realm are similar in the two texts, the food served to Liu and Ruan is no longer the herb gatherer's "carnelian ambrosia and gold nectar" 瓊漿金液 but rather human food.

Another contrast may be drawn between Liu and Ruan's destination and Tao Qian's utopian realm, the Peach Blossom Spring. The realm portrayed in the latter text is simpler, while the former is more luxurious. Most significantly, the food Liu and Ruan were served in their utopia differs from that in Tao Qian's account, which features an ordinary meal of chicken and wine. Tao Qian's wonderland also does not feature dilated time, in contrast to the Liu-Ruan tale.[85] Differences like these lead critics to conclude that the Liu-Ruan tale was a fantasy circulating among lower-class readers of the time who were tired of wars and social turmoil, and saw in the tale an escape from their troubled time and circumstances.[86]

---

them so that they eventually have to leave and find another host." See Toshiaki Yamada, "Longevity Techniques and the Compilation of the *Lingbao Wufu xu*," 110.

81   *Zhen'gao* (HY 1010), 11.3a–4a.
82   Ibid., 14.19a/b. The earliest work fully devoted to Mount Tiantai is Sun Chuo 孫綽 (320–377), "You Tiantaishan fu" 遊天台山賦, *WX*, 11.4a–10a; trans. Knechtges, *Wen xuan*, 2: 243–53. A Tang-dynasty account of the Tiantai mountains, in which the magic and fantasy of the locale is recorded, is Xu Lingfu 徐靈府, "Tiantaishan ji" 天台山記, "Tangwen shiyi" 唐文拾遺 (appended to *Quan Tangwen*), 50.10b–23a.
83   Wei Bin argues that it was the Shangqing school of Daoism that created the Tiantai area as a transcendent realm; see Wei Bin, *"Shanzhong" de Liuchao shi*, 140–50.
84   Lee Fong-mao, *Wuru yu zhejiang*, 130.
85   Kadowaki Hirofumi compares adventurous grotto tales dated from the third to fifth centuries with Tao Yuanming's tale and identifies some main different features, such as: encountering transcendents vs. common peasants; eating special foodstuffs vs. peasants' ordinary food; a venue located far away vs. at an ordinary distance; time dilation vs. normal time speed; and transcendent realm vs. village. See Kadowaki, *Dōkutsu no naka no den'en*, 18–49, esp., 48 (table).
86   Lee Fong-mao, *Wuru yu zhejiang*, 126–34. Tsuzuki Akiko 都築晶子 bases her arguments on Kominami's in her discussion of how the family and social backgrounds of Xu Mi 許謐

One magical food the two tales have in common is the peach. We may trace the literary veneration of this fruit to the formation of the cult of Queen Mother of the West. The earliest reference in this context occurs in the *Shanhai jing* 山海經, in which the idea of "immortality" (*busi* 不死) is frequently associated with magical eating. Here is one such example:

> The Immortal People are to the east [of the State of Cross-shank people]. They are black in color, long-living, and never die. (Guo Pu's commentary: There is Mount Dome Hill, on top of it are never-dying trees. Consumption of it will render longevity. There is also a red spring. Drinking its water will prevent one from aging.)
>
> 不死民在其東，其為人黑色，壽，不死。（郭璞注：有員丘山，上有不死樹，食之乃壽；亦有赤泉，飲之不老。）[87]

The *Shanhai jing* also relates that Queen Mother of the West lived in the Jade Mountains and three blue birds collected food for her.[88] One naturally assumes that she eats magical food to keep her immortal. The foodstuff was turned into a peach in the text's adaptation during the fourth century. The following quotation from Zhang Hua's 張華 (232–300) *Bowu zhi* 博物志 tells an entertaining story of Emperor Wu of Han's (r. 141–187 BC) audience with Queen Mother of the West:

> The emperor was seated in the east facing the west. The Queen Mother took out seven peaches as big as pellets, gave five to the emperor, and herself ate two. As he ate, the emperor placed the peach stones before his knees. The Queen Mother asked: "For what purpose are you taking these stones?" "These peaches taste sweet and fine; I intend to plant some." The Queen Mother smiled and replied: "It takes three thousand years for this peach to yield fruit once." Only the emperor was seated with the Queen Mother; no one in the cortege was allowed to enter the room. At this point, Dongfang Shuo stealthily peeped at the Queen Mother from the Vermillion Bird Wing south of the basilica. The Queen Mother turned around and said to the emperor: "It is this lad who peeped from the

---

(305–376) and Yang Xi gave rise to the themes of ideal social order, salvation, etc. See Tsuzuki, "Nanjin kanmon, kanjin no shūkyō sōzōryoku," 259–62; Kominami, *Chūgoku no shinwa to monogatari*, 211, 222.

87 *Shanhai jing jiaozhu*, 196, n.3.
88 Ibid., 306.

window. He has come here three times to steal my peaches." The emperor found it very strange. Thereafter, people of the world regarded Dongfang as a transcendent.

帝東面西向，王母索七桃，大如彈丸，以五枚與帝，母食二枚。帝食桃輒以桃核著膝前，母曰：「取此核將何為？」帝曰：「此桃甘美，欲種之。」母笑曰：「此桃三千年一生實。」唯帝與母對坐，其從者皆不得進。時東方朔竊從殿南廂朱鳥牖中窺母，母顧之謂帝曰：「此窺牖小兒，嘗三來盜吾此桃。」帝乃大怪之。由此世人謂方朔神仙也。[89]

The magical function of peaches is one main emphasis of the tale. In the *Hanwu gushi* version, the emperor requested immortality drugs from the Queen Mother but she gave him these peaches instead.[90] The implication is that peaches do not grant immortality and serve instead to extend life.

In the *Bowu zhi* quotation above, Dongfang Shuo is seen by the world as a "transcendent" because, according to the narrative, he stole peaches from the Queen Mother on three occasions. In variations of the tale Dongfang is depicted as one who visited this realm and thereby managed to live out ages in the mortal world.[91] While the narrative does not specify it, we presume that the thefts took place during three separate harvests. As Suzanne E. Cahill points out, "the Queen Mother explains that he has already stolen her peaches three times; he must have lived nine thousand years or three peach cycles to do so." Concludes Cahill, "he, rather than Han Wu-ti, is the divine transcendent in the tale."[92]

Readers would have read this heritage of the peach into the Liu-Ruan tale. At the same time, the characters are not divinities, and their food offerings are not the exclusive rarities available only in divine courts. The maidens who

---

89 *Bowu zhi jiaozheng*, 8.97. In the *Hanwu gushi*, some other "drugs of deathlessness" are mentioned by the Queen Mother on Wudi's request. See Michael Loewe, *Ways to Paradise*, 117. Kominami Ichirō compares the three versions of the tale and points out that the one in *Hanwudi neizhuan* has more Daoist elements than the other two. See Kominami, "Seiōbo to tanabata denshō," 39–40. Kristofer M. Schipper for this reason dates the *Hanwudi neizhuan* to the late sixth century. See Schipper, *L'Empereur wou des Han dans la légende Taoiste*, 19. Schipper's translation of this episode is in op. cit., 14.
90 *Hanwu gushi*, in *Guxiaoshuo gouchen*, 300.
91 *TPGJ*, 3.14.
92 Cahill, *Transcendence and Divine Passion*, 55. The calculation of years is not necessarily nine thousand because it is also possible that Dongfang Shuo came to steal the peaches three times in the same harvest season rather than in three different ones. See also my discussion in Chan, "Zhongshen huxing, buxu Yujing," 681.

greet and entertain Liu and Ruan also eat, as testified by their leftovers floating on the stream—their dishes are washed away, inadvertently or intentionally, by the current.[93] Their foods include peaches, sesame, beef, and goat jerky, and they are equally effective at prolonging life for the transcendent maidens as for their mortal visitors. If the maidens are "transcendent beings" (*xian*), according to Edward Schafer, they are not "immortal" and "must constantly renew their vital powers."[94]

In other post-Han sources, the peach's literary reputation as a life-prolonging food for mortals and transcendents grew.[95] In the Liu-Ruan tale, peaches are mentioned twice. First, a peach tree on a hilltop is found by the two starving men. Second, peaches are served to them after dinner. Like Mandu, these protagonists seem to always reach the point of near-starvation before they discover or are offered the life-prolonging fruit.

In addition to satisfying hunger and prolonging life, the peach also provides access to an otherworldly paradise. In a recent study, Kominami Ichirō 小南一郎 points out the common practice of using peach wood to expel evils and misfortune. Most significantly, the plant works to transmit heaven's vital energy to the human world and leads the way to a wonderland. In Tao Qian's tale, for example, the fisherman was led by the peach forest to the Peach Blossom Spring.[96]

Accepting Kominami's theory, we detect in the Liu-Ruan narrative the peach's function as a medium for the transmission of energy. When the two men arrive in the otherworldly realm, the two maidens order their servant girls to serve them: "Mr. Liu and Mr. Ruan have come from a hiking and swimming journey. Although they have just eaten some precious fruit, they are

---

93   This became a derivation of the female persona seducing her potential lover in Tang poetry. See Chan, "A Tale of Two Worlds," 222–30.
94   See Schafer, *Mirages on the Sea of Time*, 21.
95   Derk Bodde gives "peach soup" as an example in his dating of the magical function of the peach fruit. See Bodde, *Festivals in Classical China*, 133. A Jin dynasty example of a "giant peach" as food of the transcendents is in Wang Jia's *Shiyiji*, 6. Wei Guangxia gives a series of sources attesting the peach's function in prolonging life. See Wei, "Xiwangmu yu daojiao xinyang," 944–47.
96   Kominami Ichirō, "Momo no densetsu," 69–72 (illustration on p. 72). In his discussion of the "World Tree," Mircea Eliade says, "On the one hand, it represents the universe in continual regeneration, the inexhaustible spring of cosmic life, the paramount reservoir of the sacred (because it is the "Center" for the reception of the celestial sacred, etc.); on the other, it symbolizes the sky or the planetary heavens." See Eliade, *Shamanism*, 271. Miura Kunio treats the mountain (grotto-heaven in particular) as a means by which the mortal may communicate with the universe and obtain energy through *cunsi* meditation. See Miura Kunio, "Dōten Fukuchi shōron," 12–17.

still weak. Go at once to prepare some food." Here the peach is called a "precious fruit"—*qiong shi* 瓊實 in Chinese, literally "carnelian fruit." The word *qiong* denotes the elegant quality of the fruit, which worked in re-energizing the starving, exhausted men.[97] However, the narrator is aware that one serving of peaches would not suffice; therefore, more peaches are provided after dinner. In addition to re-energizing them, the peaches serve as a prelude to their romance with the maidens, in addition to enabling their survival of the time dilation.

6 Sesame: Transcending Time and Space

The peach was not the only life-prolonging food served to Liu and Ruan. The two men first find leftover sesame grains floating on the stream, and sesame is also served at the dinner table as a staple.

Sesame (*huma* 胡麻) has a variant name *jusheng* 巨勝 (lit., "giant victory"), and has been used in China at least as early as the beginning of the Han dynasty.[98] According to Song Yingxing 宋應星 (1587–1666), "it would not be an exaggeration to say that it is the king of all grains. A few handfuls are sufficient to quell one's hunger for a long time."[99] This effect is exaggerated in most fantastic tales and menus in early texts. Early sources such as the *Shenxian zhuan* and *Liexian zhuan* record sesame as "hunger suppressant."[100]

Sesame has long been regarded as a life-prolonging food in numerous sources since early times. It is "the most prevalent ingredient in the *Wufu xu*

---

97 Two later uses of the phrase are found in Shen Yue's 沈約 (441–513) and Yan Zhitui's 顏之推 (531–591) respective writings. They both refer to the magical look and quality of the fruit, in Buddhist and Daoist contexts. See Shen, "Xiuxiang zan" 繡像贊, *Quan Liang wen*, QSGSD, 30.9a; Yan, "Shenxian shi" 神仙詩, XQHWJ, 2283.

98 Berthold Laufer on the one hand ascertains that it was introduced to China from Iranian regions, but on the other hand cites the *Bencao gangmu* and observes that *huma*, also known as *jusheng* "grow in the river-valley of Čuṅ-yüan 中原 (Ho-nan)" and that "the terms *hu ma* and *kü šeṅ* originally applied to an autochthonous plant of Šan-si and Ho-nan." See Laufer, *Sino-Iranica*, 291–92. Citing the findings of Li Fan 李璠 in *Zhongguo zaipei zhiwu fazhanshi*, H. T. Huang further confirms that "sesame could have been either indigenous or brought to China during the Neolithic Age." See Joseph Needham, *Science and Civilisation in China, Volume 6: Part V*, 30–31.

99 Song, *Tiangong kaiwu*, 1.19a; trans., H. T. Huang, in Needham, *Science and Civilisation in China, Volume 6: Part V*, 29.

100 Stephen Eskildsen's discussion. He continues with the *Shenxian zhuan*: "In most cases, fasting adepts were probably permitted to drink water." See Eskildsen, *Asceticism in Early Taoist Religion*, 22. Sesame is on the list of herbs for abstention from cereals in Henri Maspero, *Le taoïsme et les religions chinoises*, 369.

and is contained in fifteen of seventy recipes" and has various anti-aging efficacies.[101] One Jin-dynasty source, the *Shiyi ji*, relates:

> The [envoy of the] Kingdom Behind Brightness came to pay tribute: ... including *Ma* with Access to Brightness. Those who eat it need no candle walking at night. It is [in fact] *jusheng*. Consumption of it will render a prolonged life, delaying normal aging.

> 背明之國，來貢其方物。……有通明麻，食者夜行不持燭，苣藤也，食之延壽，後天而老。[102]

Here, the narrator equates this Brightness Accessing *Ma* to what the central kingdom called *jusheng*.[103] Note that this outlying kingdom is "behind brightness" and therefore finds the grain, which provides light when consumed, especially useful. Its life-prolonging function is stressed here, too.

The magical functions of sesame are evident in sources dated from as early as the Eastern Han. A pharmacographic work, the *Shennong bencao jing* 神農本草經 renders *huma*, also known as *jusheng*, as possessing some healing and revitalizing powers and "one's body will become light and will not age after long-term consumption of it."[104] The life-prolonging function is obviously a marked efficacy of *jusheng*, as also recorded in Eastern Han sources such as an apocryphal text, the *Xiaojing yuanshen qi* 孝經援神契, the *Zhouyi cantongqi*, and the *Guanyinzi* 關尹子.[105]

---

101   See Arthur, *Early Daoist Dietary Practices*, 160–63. Eskildsen quotes "The Perfected Man's Method for Abstaining Completely from Grains" (quoted in the *Wufu xu*): when one consumes a drug of sesame seeds and fagara (Chinese pepper, *zanthoxylum planispinum*), "Naturally, you will not hunger. During years of famine you can eat this medicine by itself and abstain completely from grains. If thirsty, drink only water. Do not eat anything else. If you eat anything else you will become hungry." See Eskildsen, *Asceticism in Early Taoist Religion*, 60.

102   *Shiyi ji*, 6.132.

103   Laufer draws a clear line to differentiate *huma* and *jusheng*. See Laufer, *Sino-Iranica*, 292–93. Su Shi 蘇軾 (1037–1101) specifies that the *huma* in black color is called *jusheng*. See his "Fu huma fu" 服胡麻賦, in *Su Shi wenji*, vol. 1, 1.4–5. Translation and discussion of the relevant part of this *fu* is in David R. Knechtges, "Tuchkahoe and Sesame," 8–11.

104   *Shennong bencao jing*, 1.53. Part of this passage is quoted in the *Bencao gangmu* as *Bielu* 別錄. See *Bencao gangmu*, 2a, 3a; trans. Laufer, *Sino-Iranica*, 292–93. The *Shennong bencao jing* is a book of mysterious origin but was likely put together in the Eastern Han. See Yu Jiaxi, *Siku tiyao bianzheng*, 12.682–91.

105   *Xiaojing yuanshen qi*, 984; *Zhouyi cantongqi* (HY 998), 1.36a; *Guanyinzi*, 26a. Ji Kang 嵇康 (223–262) mentions that Guanyinzi "consumed the seed of *jusheng*" and consequently disappeared from the world, implying transcendence. This reveals Ji's belief in the

On the other hand, as mentioned above and in other sources, sesame is a marginally less miraculous substance. Its function of prolonging life and delaying death has a long history in the Daoist diet. The *Esoteric Biography of Ziyang the Perfected* 紫陽真人內傳, records an instruction of the transcendent given to Zhou Yishan 周義山, who later became Ziyang the Perfected:

> You may first consume some kinds of herbs, such as sesame, tuckahoe, spiked millet, cinnamon, asparagus lucidus, golden thread, digitalis, rheum officinale, peach sugar and bark, of which you pick one. Although consumption of these herbs will enable you to attain strength, without the methods of nine-circle divine elixir and gold liquid one would not be able to fly up to become transcendent. They can prolong one's lifespan and benefit one's longevity but cannot help one to avoid death. Our lord followed the sequence and took spiked millet for five years. His body emitted radiance, which enabled him to see through his five viscera inside.
>
> 可先服食眾草，巨勝、茯苓、朮、桂、天門冬、黃連、地黃、大黃、桃糖及皮任擇焉。雖服此藥以得其力，不得九轉神丹金液之道，不能飛仙矣。為可延年益壽，不辟其死也。君按次為之，服食朮五年，身生光澤，徹視內見五藏。[106]

The efficacy of sesame in prolonging mortal life appears to be a common understanding of the Southern Dynasties period. For example, sesame is listed by Most High Lord of the Dao 太上道君 as a "low-graded herb" (*xiayao* 下藥), and its consumption does not result in immortality, but rather:

> Consumption of it [this "low herb" sesame] results in small benefit, not eternal extension [of life]. One may live up to seven hundred years, or at least three to four hundred. I am afraid there is no way to enjoy life without expiring or to ascend to the clear sky. But it does enable one's body to emit radiance, restore a youthful countenance from white, give order to a thousand deities, make one an earthly transcendent, facilitate travel over

---

substance's magical function. See Ji Kang, *Shengxian gaoshi zhuan* 聖賢高士傳, *Quan Sanguo wen*, QSGSD, 52.4a; TPYL, 509.3b, quoting Ji's *Gaoshi zhuan*. For studies of the authenticity of *Guanyinzi*, see Zhang Xincheng, *Weishu tongkao*, 690–94; Tay Lian Soo, *Xu Weishu tongkao*, 1322–25.

106   *Ziyang zhenren neizhuan* (HY 303), 5a. Henri Maspero dates this scripture to a time no later than February 22, 399. See Maspero, *Le taoïsme et les religions chinoises*, 349.

ground to the Five Sacred Marchmounts, and enable one to roam famous mountains.

服之為能小益，不能永申。高可七百年，下可三四百歲，恐不便長享無期，上昇清天也；亦能身生光澤，還白童顏，役使千神，得為地仙，陸行五嶽，遊浪名山。[107]

This notion of the benefits of sesame accords with two tales in the *Zhen'gao*:

> Wu Mu. ... The Master taught him esoteric methods. They gathered herbs and consumed sesame together. He intensively delved into the teaching of the scriptures and achieved 320 years [of longevity]. He took an elixir and ascended to heaven in broad daylight.

吳睦……先生受其道，俱採藥服食胡麻，精修經教，得三百二十年，服丹白日升天。[108]

> Zheng Jingshi and Zhang Chonghua were both taught the acroama by Meng Deran the transcendent in early Jin times. They entered the mountains and practiced the methods of "guarding the five viscera" and "summoning the sun," while consuming sesame and mystic cinnabar. After a while they abstained from eating. Their bodies became light but strong. Their physical form was completely changed.

鄭景世、張重華，並以晉初受仙人孟德然口訣，以入山行守五藏含日法，兼服胡麻，又服玄丹，久久不復飲食，而身體輕強，反易故形。[109]

In both quotations, sesame is an important ingredient in the life-prolonging diet. Likewise, in the Shangqing 上清 school's exoteric meditative methods, eating sesame is combined with "guarding the five viscera" and "summoning

---

107 *Wushang biyao* (HY 1130), 78.1b, quoting *Dongzhen Taishang zhihui jing* 洞真太上智慧經. Ge Hong also emphasizes the distinction between the kinds of magical foods that appear in the Liu-Ruan tale and foods that might grant true immortality: "If one does not obtain gold elixir but only takes medicinal herbs and practices minor tricks, one can prolong one's life but will not achieve transcendence." See *Baopuzi neipian jiaoshi*, 13.243.
108 *Zhen'gao* (HY 1010), 14.11b.
109 Ibid., 14.9a. In her mortal life, Wei Huacun 魏華存 (252–334; better known as Wei furen 夫人 in Daoist theogony) started consuming sesame at an early age when she resolved to become a transcendent. See *TPGJ*, 58.356, quoting *Jixian lu* 集仙錄 and "Benzhuan" 本傳.

the sun."[110] The effects accord with what we have seen in the passages discussed above, namely keeping one free from hunger, reducing one's weight,[111] and prolonging one's life by hundreds of years.

Sesame was thought to not only help transcend time, but also space. Here is a description given by an early Tang Daoist adept Sima Chengzhen 司馬承禎 (643–735), who writes in his "Transcendents' Methods of *Huma* Consumption" ("Shenxian fu huma fa" 神仙服胡麻法):

> Consumption of it [i.e., sesame] may cure all kinds of chronic diseases. One year of consumption will bring brilliance to one's face and one will be free from hunger. In the third year of consumption, one may not be harmed by fire and water, and travel as fast as a galloping horse. Taking it for a long time will increase longevity.
>
> 服之能除一切痼病，至一年面光澤不飢，三年水火不能害，行及奔馬，久服長生。[112]

The two-fold efficacy of sesame described here would make a mortal doubly fit to enter time-dilated dimensions. This consideration is also in evidence in an account of Lu Nüsheng 魯女生 (E. Han):

> Lu Nüsheng was a native of Changle. In the beginning he consumed sesame and spiked millet (*atratylis*).[113] For more than eighty years he abstained from grains and became even younger and stronger. His countenance was like peach flowers. He was able to travel three hundred *li* per day and catch up with red deer.
>
> 魯女生，長樂人。初餌胡麻及朮，絕穀八十餘年，日少壯，色如桃花，日能行三百里，走及頳鹿。[114]

---

110 See *Shangqing dadong zhenjing* (HY 6), 1.17a/b; Chan, "Yixiang feixiang," 217–48; Robinet, *Taoist Meditation*, 187–93, 60–62.

111 As the second *Zhen'gao* tale quoted above shows, consumption of sesame was thought to alleviate hunger. At this stage, one would consume *qi* and the result could be growing feathered wings on one's body. See Campany, "The Meanings of Cuisines," 48–52.

112 Sima Chengzhen, *Xiuzhen mizhi* 修真秘旨, quoted in *Zhenglei bencao*, 24.5a. The whole *juan* of this book is a collection of various recipes for preparing sesame. See ibid., 5.2a–6a.

113 G. A. Stuart, *Chinese Materia Medica*, 57.

114 *HHS*, 82B.2740, Li Xian's 李賢 (655–684) commentary quoting *Hanwu neizhuan* 漢武內傳. The second item of Lu's consumption, *shu*, reads *shu* 朮, *shui* 水, or *qiu* 求 in different sources with different attributions. See, e.g., *TPYL*, 39.3b, 989.5b, quoting *Wudi zhuan*

The consumption of sesame gifted Lu Nüsheng both longevity and speed. This ability is no longer like Fei Changfang's symbolic "shrinking the earth's veins" but is instead portrayed as genuine physical travel.

Liu and Ruan are not portrayed as quick runners, but perhaps their travel to a realm with dilated time requires similar superhuman physical attributes. It is clear, however, that the food serves as a key ingredient of their life-prolonging feast.

7 Time-Travel Fantasy in the Literary World

These accomplishments of Lu Nüsheng as well as those of Liu Chen and Ruan Zhao who survive their time-dilation adventure may be examined in light of some basic theories of modern science about time. J. Richard Gott begins his discussion of "Time Travel to the Future" with this:

> Do you want to visit Earth 1,000 years from now? Einstein showed you how to do it. All you have to do is get in a spaceship, go to a star a bit less than 500 light-years away, and return, traveling both ways at 99.995 percent of the speed of light. When you come back, Earth will be 1,000 years older, but you will be only 10 years older.[115]

Gott's time travel example depends on Albert Einstein's 1905 special theory of relativity. According to special relativity, the speed of light in a vacuum is the same for all observers, and the laws of physics are invariant in all inertial frames of reference.[116]

At non-relativistic speeds, the more common-sense laws of Newtonian physics apply. If person A moves faster than person B, person A arrives first, and will not live longer by virtue of traveling faster. But if person A can travel at relativistic velocities, person A will then live longer than B, at least from person B's point of view. Obviously, there was no understanding of special relativity in medieval times, and three hundred *li* per day falls orders of magnitude short of relativistic velocity. Nevertheless, there is an amusing parallel in both the Lu

---

武帝傳; *Lu Nüsheng biezhuan* 別傳, YWLJ, 95.1648; quoting *Shenxian zhuan*; *Xianyuan bianzhu* (HY 596), 2.14a.
115   Gott III, *Time Travel in Einstein's Universe*, 33.
116   Einstein, "Zur Elektrodynamik bewegter Körper," 891–921. I acknowledge Tyler Pike for providing this information, as well as his help in elucidating some relativistic ideas in the next paragraphs.

Nüsheng tale and in special relativity: high velocity is a stepping stone to time dilation.[117]

While any correspondence between time dilation in early narratives and special relativity is purely a coincidence, another physical phenomenon may have been intuited by early thinkers. In physics, Newton's second law of motion expresses this relationship in terms of force, mass, and acceleration; if a force is constant, the only way to increase the acceleration of a body is to decrease its mass. Unlike the theory of relativity, Newton's second law is intuitive, and apparent to anyone who tries to throw rocks. If you throw a lighter one, it goes farther than a heavy one.

Perhaps aware of the relationship between a body's weight and its capacity to move quickly and easily, the writer of an adaptation of the Liu-Ruan tale stresses the magical function of the peach by adding some details to the narrative: upon the threshold of transitioning into the transcendent realm, Liu and Ruan "saw the peach, ate it, and felt that their body grew lighter."[118] The depiction accords with the Daoist notion discussed above, namely: "rising lightly, roaming afar, and flying and ascending in broad daylight" 輕舉遠遊, 白日飛升. Although this version of the Liu-Ruan tale is dated from the Song dynasty, it is a reasonable elaboration on the process of transcending. This notion of ascension is crucial (as I discuss elsewhere) because one cannot avoid aging if one stays on the earth, as recorded in the *Zhuangzi*.[119] Perhaps with this understanding, the two men must first grow lighter to transcend age.

The small amount of sesame and peach consumed by the two men in the *Youming lu* version of the tale might have seemed insufficient to writers of later adaptations. When Cao Tang 曹唐 (*jinshi* mid-9th c.) rewrote the adventure of Liu and Ruan, he portrayed their imminent aging as a crisis from which they needed urgent rescue. The following is voiced by a divine lady character:

玉皇賜妾紫衣裳	The Jade Lord bestowed upon me purple apparel,
教向桃源嫁阮郎	Allowing me to marry Gentleman Ruan at the Peach Font.
爛煮瓊花勸君喫	I concoct carnelian blossoms and urge you to consume,

---

117 One other example is Ding Lingwei 丁令威, who returns to the human world after 1,000 years of absence when several generations had passed but Ding did not grow old. See *Soushen hou ji*, 1.1.
118 See *Yuding Peiwenzhai guang Qunfang pu*, 10, 24b, quoting *Tiantai zhi* 天台志; *Jiading Chicheng zhi*, 21.13a.
119 See Chan, "Engulfing and Embracing the Vast Earth," 49–54.

恐君毛鬢暗成霜[120]　　As I fear that your hair will turn frosty unnoticed.

As far as magical foodstuffs are concerned, carnelian harkens back to the *Chuci* and might have been considered more effective than sesame, in this kind of crucial setting. Also, for Liu and Ruan to have been provided magical food by a rescuer rather than via accidental discovery marks another elevation of scale and urgency that remained a feature in later adaptations of the tale.[121]

8   Other Magical Food Items

In addition to sesame and peaches, Liu and Ruan also feast on two kinds of meats, namely goat jerky and beef. There is no particular tradition relating goat or beef to longevity, but other types of meat would have been considered counterproductive. Sun Simiao's 孫思邈 (581–682) Daoist scripture *Zhenzhong ji* 枕中記 states: "In consumption of sesame: it is a taboo to eat pork and dog meat."[122] To strengthen his theory, at the end of the same book Sun wrote this incantation:

神仙真藥，體合自然，	The realized medicine of the divinity enables one's physical form to fit its natural counterpart.
服藥入腹，天地同年。	By taking this medicine [sesame] in one's stomach, one will obtain a lifespan of heaven and earth.

---

120   Cao Tang, "Xiao youxian shi" no. 23, *QTS*, 641.7347; trans. cf. Schafer, *Mirage on the Sea of Time*, 74–75.

121   This concept might have been exported to Japan as shown in one adaptation of the tale of Urashima, in which the princess said: In the morning I make him take gold elixir and stone marrow; in the evening I make him drink jade wine and carnelian nectar. [I offer] the recipe of magic mushrooms with nine brightnesses that would stop one from growing old; and calamus with a hundred nodes that would prolong one's lifespan. Still, I gradually see Urashima's countenance withering year by year and his body a mere skeleton. I am sure of the cause: despite his apparent enjoyment of roaming and banqueting in this transcendent palace, inside his heart is growing more attached and missing his old home. 朝服金丹石髓，暮飲玉酒瓊漿，九光芝草駐老之方，百節菖蒲延齡之術。妾漸見島子之容顏累年枯槁、逐日骨立。定知外雖成仙宮之遊宴，而內生舊鄉之戀慕。See *Koji dan*, no page number. The Urashima story is said to have been influenced by some fairyland adventure tales from China. See, e.g., Hisamatsu Sen'ichi, *Man'yōshū kenkyu* (*ichi*), 161–63. See also Shimode Sekiyo, *Shinsen Shisō*, 168–71, in which the author links the Urashima adventure (as in the *Man'yōshū* version) to the *You xianku* and points out that the "state of immortality" 常世国 is treated as equivalent to Penglai 蓬莱.

122   *Zhenzhong ji* (HY 836), 26a.

祝訖服藥，斷豬肉五辛，最切慎之。[123]	Upon completing chanting the incantation, take the medicine. Stop eating pork and the five spices—be most cautious about it!

This holistic, correlative dietary concept is typical in Daoist thought. As pork and dog meat must not be eaten when consuming sesame, we infer that this is why beef and goat jerky were instead served at Liu and Ruan's transcendent dinner table. The following quotation from the *Wufu xu* (HY 388) may bolster this hypothesis:

> The reason why one must abstain from eating pork and dog meat is because when one becomes old, it will cause forgetfulness, moles on the face, skinniness, rotten teeth and a husky voice.
>
> 忌食豬犬肉者，食之令人老則忘誤，面目黶瘦，齒敗聲壞。[124]

There is no reference to good results after eating beef or goat jerky, but the following record shows that beef is an important ingredient in a particular life-prolonging recipe:

> *Master Shi's manual for elixirs* says: Select some unfledged crows, feed them a mixture of realized cinnabar and beef. They will have feathers of a deep red color. Dry them in the shade before consuming. One will live up to five hundred years.
>
> 石先生丹法：取烏未生毛者，以真丹和牛肉飴之，長毛羽赤色煞，陰乾服之，壽五百歲。[125]

One other item of food, *wujing* 蕪菁, also known as *manjing* 蔓 (rape-turnip; *Brassica rapa-depressa*),[126] mentioned in the Liu-Ruan narrative is worth our attention. The two men are lost and suddenly find some leftover foods afloat on the stream, including leaves of rape-turnip. The reader assumes that they had been leftovers discarded by the maidens who lived inside the grotto. The *Bencao gangmu* says, "[The root and leaves of rape-turnip] are very delicious

---

123 Ibid., 27b.
124 *Taishang Lingbao Wufu xu*, 2.23a/b.
125 Ge Hong, *Baopuzi*, quoted in *Yilin* (HY 1252), 4.14b.
126 Variant name *feng* 葑. See Gao Mingqian, *Zhiwu gu Hanming tu kao*, 415, 351. Stuart, *Chinese Materia Medica*, 74–75.

if eaten together with lamb."¹²⁷ This immediately reminds us of the banquet in which goat jerky was served. Even in modern times, rape-turnip is ascribed anti-aging benefits.¹²⁸ In today's Xinjiang, the root of rape-turnip is called *qiamagu* 恰瑪古. It is regarded as a "holy fruit for long life" (*changshou shengguo* 長壽聖果) and said to have a magical healing power and the function of prolonging life.¹²⁹

9 Conclusion

Eating magical life-prolonging foodstuffs to survive time dilation as a motif in literary works became a prominent feature from the Eastern Han to the Southern Dynasties. Although some time dilation narratives omitted magical eating, these cases are in the minority. This feature is most typical in the Liu-Ruan tale, in which magical foods (peaches and sesame in particular) enable the two men to allay hunger and remain in the time-dilated transcendent otherworld without rapidly aging.

Although, as Lee Fong-mao notes, the Liu-Ruan tale is *not* mentioned in any record in the tradition of Daoism as a philosophical school or as a religion, nor is it found in the writing about or by "method practitioners" (*fangshi* 方士),¹³⁰ the tale is saturated with Daoist imagery and concepts. Therefore, while it is not religiously canonical, it reflects religious concepts that were current. The tale also, of course, reflects other contemporary concerns. Both the Liu Ruan tale and Tao Qian's "Record of the Peach Blossom Spring" are likely products of the social turmoil present in the Southern Dynasties period.¹³¹ The Liu-Ruan tale also reflects other strands of folk religion, which is hinted at in the pretext of the maidens who wanted to keep Liu and Ruan in the grotto: "You have come here by karmic blessings." This statement seems likely to be a product of the long-term influence of Buddhist doctrines.¹³²

---

127 *Bencao gangmu*, 26.22b.
128 See Zhao Guoping et al, comps., *Zhongyao dacidian*, 1457.
129 https://baike.baidu.com/item/%E6%81%B0%E7%91%AA%E5%8F%A4%E9%A3%9F%E7%99%82/1823208. Viewed December 3, 2024.
130 Lee Fong-mao, *Wuru yu zhejiang*, 129–30.
131 Chen Yinke points out that people fled the chaos of the Jin dynasty, opting for reclusion. See Chen, "'Taohuayuan ji' pangzheng," 188–200. Chen Zhiyuan argues that Huang Daozhen "discovered the Peach Blossom Spring" and exerted influence on Tao Qian. See Chen, "Cong Wuling gu fangzhi kan," 45–49.
132 Lee Fong-mao, *Wuru yu zhejiang*, 129–30. Zhang Zhenjun points out that the beef and goat jerky they enjoy in the grotto are "contrary to one of the 'Five Precepts' in Buddhism's

It is the impermanence of the benefits from special diets that is the key to the tale's narrative tension. This impermanence creates urgency and anxiety. Like the knight who guards the holy grail in *Indiana Jones and the Last Crusade*, Liu and Ruan fail to achieve true transcendence or immortality. In the film, neither the grail nor one who drinks from it may leave the grail's resting place, as "remaining here is the price of immortality."[133] Likewise, Liu and Ruan retain the benefits of peaches and sesame only if they choose to remain in the grotto; when they elect to return home, the normal aging processes reassert themselves.

In summary, in the earliest phases of grotto fantasy, we already find the key thematic ingredients that later writers would come to exploit. In emphasizing the perils of traversing between time-dilated and earthly realms, the Liu-Ruan tale establishes the symbolic potency of magical foods in a literary context. Later writers need only mention the peach in a grotto fantasy work to invite intensity of a particular flavor. Secondly, the essential tenuousness of Liu Chen and Ruan Zhao's transcendency lays the ground for the possibility of role fluidity in future works of grotto fantasy, in which any character of any gender can transition between mortal and transcendent, sometimes multiple times. Often, the roles are not clearly demarcated, and a transcendent may display attributes of a mortal, and vice versa. One manifestation of this role fluidity will be the trifurcation of the role of the grotto vamp/transcendent. This triple role serves as a focus of Chapter 2.

---

basic teachings—the forbiddance of killing." See Zhang, *Buddhism and Tales*, 14. Zhang also discusses various kinds of karmic retribution in the *Youming lu*, although he does not discuss the Liu-Ruan tale in this context. See op. cit., 89–106.

133   The relevant scenes are found in the film script. Rob MacGregor, *Indiana Jones and the Last Crusade*, 211.

CHAPTER 2

In and Out of the Transcendents' Grotto: from Zhang Zhuo to Yuan Zhen and Bai Juyi

1   Introduction

Rather than religion, it was the theme of love in the Liu Chen and Ruan Zhao tale that assumed prominence in its future adaptations (or more precisely, appropriations) in Tang romantic literature.[1] In this new development, Zhang Zhuo 張鷟 (ca. 660–ca. 740) was a pioneer.

In the early Tang, the Liu-Ruan tale was transmitted in two ways, namely: abridged quotation and creative adaptation. In addition to the version printed in the *Yiwen leiju*, the seventh-century Buddhist Monk, Shi Daoshi 釋道世, in his Buddhist encyclopedia, the *Fayuan zhulin* 法苑珠林, includes the tale. His version was, most likely, based on the *Youming lu* text, and he understood it as an example of the subtle interactions that may occur between the mortal world and the otherworld.[2] Shortly afterwards, Zhang Zhuo in his *Roaming to the Grotto of the Transcendents* tells of Zhang Wencheng's 文成 (the author's given name)[3] romantic encounter with transcendents in Mount Jishi 積石山 in present-day Gansu province on an envoy journey to the western region. The protagonist associated with Zhang Zhuo himself blurs the lines between fantasy and autobiography.[4] The Liu-Ruan tale was one of the prototypes of Zhang

---

1 Julie Sanders defines: "An adaptation most often signals a relationship with an informing source text either through its title or through more embedded references; … appropriation frequently effects a more decisive journey away from the informing text into a wholly new cultural product and domain, often through the actions of interpolation and critique as much as through the movement from one genre to others." See Sanders, *Adaptation and Appropriation*, 35.

2 *Fayuan zhulin*, T 2122, 53.521a5–28. Wu Fuxiu argues that Shi Daoshi emulated Gan Bao's motive behind his recording the supernatural, to "prove that matters about ghosts and gods are infallible" in his teaching of Buddhist dharma. See Wu, *Fayuan zhulin fenlei sixiang yanjiu*, 181.

3 The name Zhang Wencheng appears as the author of the book in the Japanese editions. At the end of the text, this name, Wencheng, is given in a pun referring to "completion of the woven pattern" and as the protagonist's name. See *Yūsenkutsu shō*, colophon; *YXKJZ*, 33.

4 *YXKJZ*, "qianyan," 3–9; Hatano Tarō, "Yūsenkutsu shin kō," 1–12; Rouzer, *Articulated Ladies*, 204.

Zhuo's work and initiates the practice of narrating romantic (often erotic) experience behind the veneer of an encounter with "transcendents."

Zhang Zhuo achieved novelty and creativity in his narrative and poetic work and occupies a key position in the grotto romance tradition. Although there is no mention of Zhang's work, *Roaming to the Grotto of the Transcendents* (*You xianku* 遊仙窟),[5] in any extant Tang writing,[6] Zhang in fact paved a road for Tang love poetry, which flourished in the hands of Yuan Zhen 元稹 (779–831) and Bai Juyi 白居易 (772–846), who were likewise indebted to the Liu-Ruan tale. Yuan Zhen's poetic interests include his romantic exploits and the passage of time in his political career. The poetic revelation of romantic experience became especially prominent in the ninth century. In the narrative tradition, Zhang Zhuo demonstrated a new mode of writing, one that incorporates poetry in the narrative text mainly written in parallel prose. Above all, the settings of the Liu-Ruan tale become a framework for the Tang fantasy of clandestine love affairs.

Zhang Zhuo was not the first writer to depict a tryst with a divine lady as a metaphor for an association with entertainers,[7] but his *You xianku* is the first known Tang-era work that relies upon the Liu-Ruan archetype in doing so. This text was lost soon after its completion. Since Yang Shoujing's 楊守敬 (1839–1915) re-introduction of this text from Japan to China in the late nineteenth century,[8] it has filled a lacuna in Tang erotic literature. Without this text there would be no way to reconstruct the early development of erotic fantasy in Tang narrative and poetic tradition.

---

5 The Romanization and translation of the title poses *xianku* as a locale where the protagonist roamed (*you*). Victor Mair proposed this translation in our discussion in February 2013 at the University of Pennsylvania. My translation reflects this verb-object structure, so does Paul Rouzer's, *Dalliance in the Immortals' Den*, in his *Articulated Ladies*, 204, et passim. Howard S. Levy and Stephen Owen translate it based on the modifier + modified structure, as *The Dwelling of Playful Goddesses* and "The Cave of Roving Immortals," respectively. See Levy, op. cit. and Owen, *The End of the Chinese 'Middle Ages'*, 134. For *xian* in Zhang's work as referring to beautiful ladies, see Hatano Tarō, "Yūsenkutsu shin kō (shita)," 21–32, quoting various sources (p. 26) and giving Yuan Zhen's "Dream of Spring Outing in Seventy Rhymes" ("Meng youchun qishi yun" 夢遊春七十韻) as an example (p. 31).
6 Quoting Arthur Waley and Chen Yinke, who both argue that Yuan Zhen's work could have been influenced by the *You xianku*, Ronald Egan argues that there is "no proof of such influence." See Egan, "On the Commentary of the *Yu hsien k'u* Commentary," 136, n. 5.
7 See Li Jianguo, *Tangqian zhiguai xiaoshuo shi*, 453–57; Wei Fengjuan, "Xianfan qingyuan gui hechu," 44–46. The examples discussed by Li and Wei are in *TPGJ*, 295.2352–33, 296.2355–56, 326.2587–88, 327.2595–96, quoting *Bachao qiongguai lu* 八朝窮怪錄 and *Bowu zhi* (or *Xu Bowuzhi* 續), respectively. Li Jianguo dates the *Bachao qiongguai lu* to the Sui dynasty. See Li, op. cit., 452.
8 Yang, *Riben fangshu zhi*, 8.27a–28b.

2   From Grotto to Chamber: Zhang Zhuo's *You xianku*

The rediscovery of the early Tang narrative *You xianku* enabled literary historians to reconstruct a key moment in the development of Tang erotic literature. In addition to Li Jianguo's identification of the tales from the *Bachao qiongguai lu* as its predecessors, recent scholarship has alternatively identified the *fu* tradition and folklore of the Tang as the text's provenance. Cao Zhi's 曹植 (192–232) "*Fu* on the Goddess of River Luo" ("Luoshen fu" 洛神賦), for example, may be seen as such a predecessor because of its theme of love between a human and the supernatural. If we follow some critics in reading Cao Zhi's poem allegorically, it can be interpreted as an autobiographical description of Cao's indecent love for Zhen Fu 甄宓, who had then become his sister-in-law.[9] Although it might have been inspired by this work and others similar to it, Zhang Zhuo's work marks an innovation and heralds a new trope for the literary depiction of illicit love affairs. It predates the literary peak of the treatment of fantasy romance in the time of Yuan Zhen.[10]

We shall begin our probe of the grotto fantasy themes at play in *You xianku* by looking at its rhetorical devices in comparison with the Liu-Ruan archetype. We look also at the textual descendants of the *You xianku* to reconstruct the genealogy of this tradition, which will lead to conclusions about the writings of Yuan Zhen.

Using the first-person point of view, the protagonist Zhang describes a romantic encounter with two girls, named Wusao 五嫂 (fifth sister-in-law) and Cui Shiniang 崔十娘, who receive him enthusiastically in a grotto of the transcendents. Written predominantly in parallel prose, the narrative also cites poems written in flirtatious exchange. Wusao plays the role of a go-between; the exchange poems she passes between Zhang and Cui ensure their sexual union. After a romantic night, Zhang bids farewell and departs the grotto.

One of the key features of Zhang Zhuo's reference to the Liu-Ruan tale is how he stripped away its otherworldly setting. In this regard, Ogawa Tamaki's 小川環樹 summary of eight formal features in otherworldly adventures written during the Six Dynasties provides a framework for our analysis. Ogawa

---

9   See *WX*, 11b–16a. Li Shan's commentary quoting a certain *Ji* 記. In addition to Cao's *fu*, the "Xia nü fu ci" 下女夫詞, "Chonglang fu" 寵郎賦, "Kuolang fu" 廓廊賦, the "Meiren fu" 美人賦 by Sima Xiangru 司馬相如 (ca. 179–117 BC), and the Liu-Ruan tale have been identified as *You xianku*'s provenances. See Li Zongwei, *Tangren chuanqi*, 16–17; Dong Shangde, "Luelun Zhongguo gudai yanyuxing," 41–44.

10   Chan, "A Tale of Two Worlds," 222–26.

includes for his analysis the Liu-Ruan tale and the stories of Yuan Xiang 袁相 and Gen Shuo 根碩.[11] His eight formal features are:

1. Sojourns in the mountains.
2. Grottos.
3. Transcendent elixir and foodstuffs.
4. Beautiful ladies and marriage.
5. Magical gifts.
6. Nostalgia and returning home.
7. Temporal displacement.
8. Unsuccessful attempts to return to the otherworld.[12]

Although most otherworldly adventurous tales of the Six Dynasties do not feature all eight items, Ogawa's summary makes a useful paradigm for our analysis of the two Tang texts in question.[13] As we shall see, Zhang's work diverges from this eight-feature scheme. Indeed, among Tang texts that contain significant references to the Liu-Ruan tale, only Cao Tang's 曹唐 (fl. mid-9th c.) poems, as I discuss elsewhere, are an exception, in that they contain all eight features.[14] The failure to return to the grotto may be seen as a purposeful plot design, which, in the Tang contexts, is in line with the autobiographical framework of the texts.

Through intensifying and elaborating on certain scenes, Zhang Zhuo makes a thematic shift from adventurous romance to eroticism in adapting the Liu-Ruan tale. Lee Fong-mao treats the accidental discovery of the otherworld and enjoyment of the sexual encounter in the Liu-Ruan tale as a reflection of the desire of the common people living in political turbulence.[15] This is a valid reading for a Southern-Dynasties romantic tale but can hardly be applied to the situation of Zhang Zhuo, who lived in the early Tang, a much more peaceful time. He did, however, satirize the corrupt politics of the time, including Empress Wu's (r. 690–705) regime.[16] According to Seo Tatsuhiko 妹尾達彦, Zhang's writings on visiting the entertainment quarters are autobiographical.[17]

---

11 *Xinji Soushen houji*, 1.467.
12 Ogawa, *Chūgoku Shōsetsushi no kenkyū*, 267–71.
13 Cf. Sarah M. Allen's "adventure formula," in her *Shifting Stories*, 119–47.
14 Chan, "A Tale of Two Worlds," 230–31; Edward H. Schafer, "Empyreal Powers and Chthonian Edens," 670–71; Stephen Owen, *The Late Tang*, 325–29. The Yuan drama *Xixiang ji* 西廂記 contains a "return" as Student Zhang succeeded in his *keju* examination and went back to marry Cui. See *Xixiang ji*, Act 4 of Book 5, in *Jiping jiaozhu Xixiang ji*, 195–201.
15 Lee, *Wuru yu zhejiang*, 128–30.
16 See, e.g., *Chaoye qianzai*, 4.89, 99, 5.117, 6.138–39, "buji" 補輯, 160–61, 175, et passim.
17 Seo, "Koi o suru otoko," 2002–3. A Chinese translation of this article is Seo, "'Caizi' yu 'jiaren,'" 695–722.

IN AND OUT OF THE TRANSCENDENTS' GROTTO   57

Zhang eroticizes his adaptation of the Liu-Ruan tale in his depiction of a commissioned journey to Heyuan. This culminates in his discovery of a grotto where he had romantic encounters with Cui Shiniang.[18]

Let us read the introductory lines of Zhang Zhuo's *You xianku*, in Paul Rouzer's translation (with modification):

> I then came upon a certain place with extraordinarily steep cliffs. To the top rose blue-green walls a myriad armspans high; down below lay an emerald tarn a thousand fathoms deep. Among the elders here there circulates a saying: "This is a grotto-residence of the transcendents. Human traces rarely reach it; the paths of birds can merely get through. Often fragrant fruit, branches of jade, divine garments, and monks' staffs and bowls come floating out, although on one knows whence they come."
>
> I then put myself in a serious frame of mind and observed three days of purifying. I clambered up slender vines and took a light skiff against the current. My body was as though in flight, my essence-soul in a dream. Before long I came upon a cliff of pines and cypresses and a brook of peach blossoms. A fragrant breeze brushed the ground, and a bright radiance pervaded the sky.
>
> I noticed a girl washing clothes at the edge of the water.
>
> "I have heard that there is a grotto-residence of the transcendents, so I have come for a visit with respects. However, the hills and streams have blocked my way, and I have grown rather fatigued. May I find lodging with you and rest for a bit. Would that you could bestow hospitality; I hope that you would grant me an approval."[19]

The three-day purification suggests the protagonist's awareness of the unusual nature of what (and whom) he would encounter in this setting.[20] Zhang sends his protagonist on a *purposeful* visit to a realm like that in the Liu-Ruan tale, where he finds peach blossoms and items such as fragrant fruit, branches of jade, etc. floating to the outside world from an unknown source. It is the clear similarity in setting that prompts Rouzer to assume that "it is more likely that

---

18   Heyuan (lit., source of the Yellow River) refers to the Military Prefecture of Heyuan (in modern Xining, Gansu). See YXKJZ, 40, n. 8. Zhang was then Commandant of Xiangle 襄樂尉 (in modern Gansu province near Ningxia). See Hatano Tarō, "Yūsenkutsu shin kō," 2.
19   YXKJZ, 1–2; Rouzer, *Articulated Ladies*, 314.
20   Lee Fong-mao stresses the importance of the purifying ritual before entering sacred mountains or grottos in the Southern Dynasties period. See Lee, "Dongtian yu neijing," 54.

Zhang means to invoke the adventures of Liu Chen 劉晨 and Ruan Zhao 阮肇 and their encounter with goddesses."[21]

This site for a romantic encounter is also innovative, relative to the settings for romance in the Six-Dynasties anomaly tales. The stable political environment of Zhang Zhuo's time, mainly during Empress Wu's reign, played a role in transforming the more rustic setting of these earlier romantic tales into a grotto of elaborate luxury.

In his elaborate display of prosodic skills, Zhang Zhuo adds a fantastic spin to the encounter by turning the girls into *xian*.[22] Most modern scholars' speculation on the allegorical import of the *You xianku* is owed largely to Chen Yinke, who identifies the transcendents in this and other subsequent texts as female entertainers.[23] Chen's analysis of the *You xianku* is not, however, detailed, and he does not explore the implications of the text's derivation from the Liu-Ruan tale.

After Zhang sets the scene, we find an erotic poetry exchange set in a garden, in which peach blossoms play a pivotal role. The male protagonist (also named Zhang) begins his poem by using a metaphor of picking the flower and viewing it in his palm. Understanding Zhang's dalliance, Cui Shiniang responds with a seductive pun by likening herself to a peach blossom:

即今無自在	Since now I have no freedom,
高下任渠攀	Pick as you wish, from high or low.[24]

Zhang thus becomes more seductive in his next poem:

何須杏樹嶺	Why needs Apricot Tree Ridge?
即是桃花源	*Here* it is the Peach Blossom Spring![25]

The scene enables us clearly to distinguish the sexual overtones. In this progressively escalating sensual flirting, Zhang uses the homophonous word *xing* 杏 as a substitute for "desiring" 幸, the metaphorical meaning of the "tree"

---

21 Rouzer, *Articulated Ladies*, 315, n. 3.
22 The two girls are called "maidens" 女子 in the quotations of the Liu-Ruan tale dated from the early Tang. See YWLJ, 7.138; *Fayuan zhulin*, T 2122, 53.521a5–28.
23 Chen, *Yuan Bai shi jianzheng gao*, 107. Sun Wang argues that *xian* used as a kenning for a beautiful lady occurs as early as in the *Hanwu gushi* and *Hanwudi waizhuan*. See Sun, "'Yingying zhuan' shiji kao," 94–96.
24 YXKJZ, 24, 336, n. 697; Levy translates *zizai* as "self-control," Rouzer as "restraint." See Levy, *The Dwelling of Playful Goddesses*, 42; Rouzer, *Articulated Ladies*, 342.
25 YXKJZ, 25.

as the male's sexual organ and the "peach blossom spring" as the female's. In response, Cui Shiniang writes in a more explicitly metaphorical way:

1	梅蹊命道士	The Plum Brook commands the Daoist adept,
2	桃潤佇神仙	By the Peach Blossom Brook transcendents are waiting;
3	舊魚成大劍	The fish of the past have assumed a great sword.
4	新龜類小錢	The new tortoise looks like a small coin.
5	水湄唯見柳	By the edge of water one only sees willows,
6	池曲且生蓮	At the pond's nook thus grow lotus blooms.
7	欲知賞心處	Wishing to find out where you can please your heart?
8	桃花落眼前	It is where the peach blossom falls before your eyes.[26]

This literal translation fails to bring out the overt sexual overtones of the original. The frequent uses of puns here require interpretation to decipher Shiniang's euphemistic invitation for Zhang to join the revel. As such, a more vivid rendering of the poem would be:

1. You who practice the Dao are mandated to Plum Creek;[27]
2. By this Peach Brook await the transcendent beings.[28]
3. The "fish" of the past has now turned into a large "sword";
4. The new girl at the boudoir is as ravishing as a small coin.[29]

---

26 *YXKJZ*, 25.
27 A note found in two Japanese editions, dated from the seventeenth century, reads: "The Plum Creek is where the Dao scholars of ancient times pursued transcendence. It refers to the Wuling Spring of our time." See *YXKJZ*, 339, n. 706. The Wuling Spring refers to where the fisherman explored as depicted in Tao Qian's "Record of the Peach Blossom Spring."
28 The 1671 edition of *You xianku* quotes two glosses on the line: "It refers to the Peach Blossom Spring"; "It refers to: Zhao Sheng 趙昇, disciple of Zhang Ling 張陵 (34–156), flew into a deep creek to pick divine peaches." See *Yūsenkutsu shō*, 4.20a.
29 I treat *gui* 龜 as a pun for *gui* 閨, boudoir. The coin, named "Kaiyuan tongbao" 開元通寶 (also read "Kaitong yuanbao"), with a square hole in the center, was in use from 621. See Wang Shengduo, *Zhongguo qianbi shi hua*, 117–18. The sexual overtones like these similes are found throughout the *You xianku*. See, e.g., Zhang's poem on the knife: "A shame that so sharp a thing / Should stay within its scabbard-hide." Shiniang's response is equally seductive: "After you have pulled it out, / What's to become of the empty sheath?" In their exchange poems on shooting arrows, Zhang replies: "A shrunken shaft can never reach— / But when its head is raised, it goes quite beyond. / If it should enter below the navel, / a hundred times would I hit that mark." *YXKJZ*, 19, 27; Rouzer, *Articulated Ladies*, 335, 344. This kind of overtly sexual content is most likely the reason for the work ceasing to be transmitted since Song China and being considered "unprintable" in pre-modern Japan. See Hatano Tarō, "Yūsenkutsu shin kō," 11, quoting Zheng Zhenduo 鄭振鐸.

5   By the riverbank you only see willow leaf-shaped eyebrows;[30]
6   Her paces along the winding pond are so charming and lovely.[31]
7   Should you like to explore further the heart-pleasing source,
8   Here standing before you are two peach-flower-like beauties.

This poetic exchange borrows themes and images from the two Peach Blossom Springs in Tao Qian and Liu-Ruan. The erotic theme is brought out by the allusive elements and, above all, one central image: the peach blossom.

One other significant aspect of the *You xianku* is, as mentioned above, that it is the earliest Tang work in the lineage of the Liu-Ruan tale that eroticizes the two ladies. One finds scant depiction of the two ladies' flirting and seductive acts in the original tale. Zhang Zhuo now presents a full picture of them in his version by incorporating the references to the Liu-Ruan tale and Tao Qian's Peach Blossom Spring as a vehicle for the representation of his own pleasure-seeking experience.

Zhang Zhuo's grotto romance marks the advent of Tang love tales by laying a foundation for Yuan Zhen's "Story of Yingying," written one century later. In his interpretation of Zhang's work as a literary depiction of a visit to a prostitute in the entertainment quarter, Seo Tatsuhiko cites the era-appropriate etiquette for such visits. Seo summarizes five steps of the procedure:

1. Acquaintance;
2. Poetry exchange;
3. Banquet;
4. Sharing the bed;
5. Parting.[32]

Seo goes on to apply this scheme to "The Story of Yingying" by speculating that Yuan's work "seems to have been influenced" by Zhang's. He continues:

> The comparison reveals: although "The Story of Yingying" is more complex than the *You xianku* in choreography; the number and types of roles, as well as the plot design, it is basically a repetition of the same narrative structure. Perhaps both authors base their respective writings on their own associations with singing geishas at brothels (entertainment

---

30   The character *mei* is a homophone of *mei* 眉, eyebrows. Willow leaf is a common simile for beautiful eyebrows.
31   The character *lian* is homophonous to *lian* 憐, loveliness. The phrase *quchi* also refers to one's attractive strolling. Yuan Zhen uses the term *quchi bu* 曲池步 in his description of his lover (l. 16 of his "Dream" poem discussed below).
32   Seo, "Koi o suru otoko," 54–55; "'Caizi' yu 'jiaren,'" 706; Lee Fong-mao, *You yu you*, 384.

quarters). They employed skillful poetic, narrative, and dialogic language to unfold the formula of the development from acquaintance to sexual relationship.[33]

Similar speculative analyses have been attempted for decades but a consensus is yet to be reached.[34]

Other innovative elements and alterations are remarkable in Tang adaptations of the Liu-Ruan tale. One is that the grotto becomes a kenning for a bed chamber (often a female entertainer's room) in which an erotic encounter takes place.[35] Also, in the Liu-Ruan archetype the rapture of romance evolves into ennui for the men and separation angst for the women. The pleasure of the revel in the *You xianku* turns into heartbreak in the departing scene. In Yuan Zhen's "Story of Yingying" and in his "Dream," that separation angst is magnified. At this level of secular representation, the effect serves to emphasize the grief of the female entertainer upon parting with her client.

3   Romance in Reminiscence: Yuan Zhen's "Story of Yingying"

Yuan Zhen's literary representation of his love with the lady guised as Cui Yingying 崔鶯鶯 owes much to the Liu-Ruan tale. The "Story of Yingying," which has been seen as Yuan's autobiography,[36] alters the inherited Liu-Ruan archetype most drastically in its approach to the women in the story.

Yuan Zhen's interest in grotto romance is evident in his poetic and narrative works, in which he incorporates certain elements from the Liu-Ruan tale mainly in an autobiographical manner. To better understand his motives and fondness for grotto fantasy, we study how the archetype was approached in the Tang and what kinds of adaptations were made by Yuan and his contemporaries. Although the exact time when the Liu-Ruan tale was first romanticized remains unknown, Yuan is undoubtedly the most significant contributor to this trend. In 794, at the age of sixteen *sui* (fifteen years old), when he was less

---

33   Seo, "Koi o suru otoko," 55; "'Caizi' yu 'jiaren,'" 708.
34   Dong Shangde, "Luelun Zhongguo gudai yanyuxing," 38, 50, n. 6.
35   Lee Fong-mao, "Xian, ji yu dongku," 481–87. Edward Schafer uses the Japanese term *geisha* as an equivalent to the Chinese term *ji* 妓. See Schafer, "Notes on T'ang Geisha."
36   James Robert Hightower argues that the story was based largely on Yuan Zhen's own life experience but not written as an exact "autobiography." See Hightower, "Yüan Chen and the Story of Ying-ying," 119–23. A full English translation of the "Yingying zhuan" is in ibid., pp. 93–103.

likely to have had romantic experience,[37] Yuan's use of the Liu-Ruan tale was limited to the theme of anxiety over the passage of time. In a poem written in that year, he expresses astonishment at the changes in Chang'an, assuming the voice of an elder of Qujiang 曲江老人. This elderly man lived in reclusion during the times of turmoil and now returns to his former residence:

夢寐平生在	In a dream, when I was in my youth,[38]
經過處所新	I passed by places that looked new.
阮郎迷舊巷	Gentleman Ruan is now lost in the old alleys;
遼鶴記城闉[39]	The Liaodong crane recalls the bailey portal.

Here, the allusion to Ruan Zhao is used as a parallel, in both meaning and syntax, to Ding Lingwei 丁令威, a mythical figure who transformed into a crane and revisited his former town.[40] These allusions feature anxiety over the passage of time in the capital, Chang'an, which is beyond recognition after the war.

In his writing on love themes, Yuan Zhen's later use of the Liu-Ruan reference focuses mainly on romance. Yuan Zhen and Bai Juyi's intimate relationship with Liu Yuxi 劉禹錫 (772–842) yields a new meaning of the appellation of "Gentleman Liu" (Liulang 劉郎) in their correspondence, in which the term always refers to Liu Yuxi. This appellation is also used by Liu Yuxi to refer to himself in his political satire (see Chapter 3).[41] Yuan Zhen takes a different approach and focuses on the romantic elements of the Liu-Ruan tale in telling his own love story. This practice is the main focus of the present chapter.

One of Yuan's innovations is that, unlike Zhang Zhuo who writes of his romance in favorable terms, Yuan presents his young love experiences with excitement but also draws moral lessons from them. He focuses in particular on his love with a girl named Cui Yingying, the subject of the "Story of Yingying," which, as Luo Manling argues, "tries to achieve an ambiguous balance between endorsing romance as a positive story subject and condemning

---

37 See Hanabusa Hideki and Maegawa Yukio, *Gen Shin kenkyū*, 11; Bian Xiaoxuan, *Yuan Zhen nianpu*, 36. Xie Siwei suggests that the poem was written in 810. See Xie, "Yuan Zhen 'Dai Qujiang laoren baiyun' shi zuonian zhiyi," 42–44.
38 The meaning of *pingsheng* as "youth" is according to Kong Anguo's 孔安國 (ca. 156–ca. 74 BC) commentary on the *Analects*. See *Lunyu zhushu*, 14.55a.
39 "Dai Qujiang laoren baiyun," *YZJJZ*, 10.276; *QTS*, 405.4516.
40 *Soushen hou ji*, 1.1.
41 See, e.g., "Zuizhong chongliu Mengde" 醉中重留夢得 and "Chou Liu Hezhou xizeng" 酬劉和州戲贈. See *BJYJJ*, 27.1910, 24.1648; *QTS*, 450.5084, 447.5026.

it as an immoral act."[42] This ambivalence forms the core of Yuan's ruminations. Sarah Allen's treatment of the tale as a variation of what she calls an "adventure formula" fits quite well in our discussion of Yuan's romance as an otherworldly adventure.[43]

We treat the *You xianku* as a "bridge" text between the Liu-Ruan tale and Yuan's "Story of Yingying." Established scholarship on the subject supports viewing Zhang Zhuo's text in this way. Yang Shoujing not only brought back the newly discovered *You xianku* to China from Japan but also speculated for the first time on the origins of the two Tang texts. He says:

> When [Zhang] Wencheng served as a commissioner to Heyuan, he exchanged poetry and spent the night with Cui Shiniang whom he met at a grotto of transcendents. The surnames of the male and female protagonists are identical to [those in] "The Story of Yingying." However, [the *You xianku*] has slightly less to do with love matters; [rather,] it depicts lascivious scenes in parallel, exquisite writing. This may truly be considered debauchery without restraint. Wencheng was a shallow and showy person. Compared with the theory that identifies Zhang Junrui as Yuan Zhen, this [i.e, the protagonist Zhang being Zhang Wencheng] is of higher credibility.
>
> 文成奉使河源，於仙窟遇崔十娘，與之倡酬夜合。男女姓氏並同《鶯鶯傳》，而情事稍疏，以駢麗之辭，寫猥褻之狀，真所謂儻蕩無檢。文成浮豔者；較之謂張君瑞即元微之所託名，尤為可信。[44]

Yang Shoujing was the first scholar to question the originality of Yuan Zhen's "Story of Yingying" after reading the *You xianku*. As early as the Northern Song, however, Zhao Lingzhi 趙令時 (1061–1134) is the first known scholar to assert the autobiographical nature of the Yingying story and the first to make a connection between the life of Yuan Zhen and Student Zhang. This theory remained dominant and was further strengthened by Chen Yinke and followed

---

42 Luo Manling, *Literati Storytelling in Late Medieval China*, 132.
43 Allen's "adventure formula ... requires two actors, the human traveler and the stranger" and has four functions: traveling and encountering, interaction, parting, and discovery (or revelation). She puts the *You xianku* in the formula and sees the "Story of Yingying" as a "variation." See Allen, *Shifting Stories*, 121–23, 141–42.
44 Yang, *Riben fangshu zhi*, 8.27a/b; Chen Yinke, *Yuan Bai shi jianzheng gao*, 108–9. Sun Wang disagrees by emphasizing the differences between the characters in *You xianku* and those in "Yingying zhuan." See Sun, "'Yingying zhuan' shiji kao," 93–98; also in Bian Xiaoxuan, *Yuan Zhen nianpu*, 51–53.

by many others.⁴⁵ This tradition does not necessarily contradict Yang's earlier argument. We look to the latter for the artistic rather than autobiographical provenance of Yuan's work.

It is necessary to give a synopsis of "The Story of Yingying" before further discussion. The variant title of this tale, "Record of Encountering the Perfected" 會真記, reflects the fantastical nature of the story. Student Zhang once stayed as a guest at the Pujiu Monastery 普救寺. He was invited to a banquet by the Zheng family because he had saved this family from a mutiny. There, he met Cui Yingying and, with the help of Cui's maid Hongniang 紅娘, they became secret lovers and enjoyed romantic pleasure for a month or so. Later, when Zhang failed the imperial examination in the capital, he remained there to "saunter," but they still wrote love letters to each other. In the end, Zhang changed his mind about the romance. In his conversations with his friends, he referred to Cui as a *youwu* 尤物 (lit., "fault-causing creature," see below for more discussion). A year later, they each got married to someone else. The text contains some seductive poems about the trysts, including "A Tryst with the Perfected, in Thirty Rhymes" 會真詩三十韻.⁴⁶

Rather than repeating existing scholarship on the relationship between Zhang Zhuo and Yuan Zhen's texts, our present focus is on how Zhang Zhuo adapted the Liu-Ruan tale in his romantic story.⁴⁷ This link makes the first part of the stemma of Yuan's provenances of his "The Story of Yingying" and the cluster of his poetic representations on his young love and its ensuing broodings.

As mentioned above, Zhao Lingzhi (as quoted by Wang Zhi 王銍 [fl. 1130s]) was the first to read "The Story of Yingying" as autobiography and to identify Yuan Zhen as Student Zhang.⁴⁸ This reading was further elucidated by Chen Yinke, who goes even further to identify Yingying as a geisha (*ji* 妓).⁴⁹ Accepting Hightower's theory about the "triple identification of the protagonist Chang [Zhang], the narrator Yüan Chen [Yuan Zhen], and the poet Yüan

---

45 Zhao, *Houqing lu*, 5.41–45. Chen Yinke, *Yuan Bai shi jianzheng gao*, 108–9; Wang Shiyi, *Yuan Zhen lun gao*, 150–54.
46 See *YZJJZ*, "buyi," 6.1513–20, 1518–19; *Tangren xiaoshuo*, 162–68; trans., Hightower, "Yüan Chen and the Story of Ying-ying," 93–103. Bian Xiaoxuan, *Yuan Zhen nianpu*, 56, 58.
47 Rouzer observes that the Liu-Ruan tale "and similar *zhiguai* were a likely influence on Zhang [Zhuo, my insertion] when he composed his own tale." See Rouzer, *Articulated Ladies*, 205–6.
48 See ibid., 107.
49 Chen, *Yuan Bai shi jianzheng gao*, 107.

Chen, who is the author,"[50] we shall look at the way this unity of three roles affects the Liu-Ruan allusion and how Yuan builds his own world of romance.

Stephen Owen compares the role of Yingying with the Goddess of Mount Wu but stresses that our reading of them is different because Yingying is not portrayed as a goddess.[51] Rendering the term *youwu* as "creature of bewitching beauty," Owen stresses "the compelling force of personality that makes them so engrossing and thus so dangerous." Invoking "Paradise Lost," Owen argues: "As with Milton's Satan, if we attempt to sustain the reading that supports public morality, we are forced to confront the true power of the dangerous alternative and discover a strong party in ourselves that would make the choice against public morality."[52] Yingying's two prominent attributes, divinity and beauty, reflect those of predecessors in the two earlier texts, the two "transcendents" in the Liu-Ruan tale and Cui Shiniang in *You xianku*. This three-stage development shows that the divinity of the grotto lady underwent a secularization process in the Tang, in which she descended from transcendent to prostitute. The theme of abandonment in each text reflects anxiety over the men's loss of the time and space to which they originally belonged (and, by extension, a loss of family and social connection); abandonment also applies to the anxiety felt by the lady missing her lover.

Lorraine Dong's discussion sheds light on our comparison of the role of Yuan Zhen's Yingying with the two maidens in the Liu-Ruan tale. She argues: "Finally, in her last letter to Zhang, she is further reduced to a state of self-pity when she sees no future in their relationship and releases him from any bond."[53] At this stage, the lovers have both realized that their relationship can no longer continued. For Zhang's part, he "represents society and who never shows any sense of moral conflict or regret throughout the course of the affairs." Dong continues:

> Yuan Zhen's characterization of Yingying also includes a rebellious woman who dares to break the rules, only to be defeated in the end by those very same rules. ... In the end she is no longer fighting against

---

50 Hightower, "Yüan Chen and the Story of Ying-ying," 122. The *pinyin* spellings are my insertions.
51 Owen, *The End of the Chinese 'Middle Ages'*, 160. The Goddess of Mount Wu is the divine woman met by King Xiang of Chu (r. 298–263 BC) with whom he had a romantic encounter in a dream. See Song Yu, "Gaotang fu," *WX*, 19.1b–6b; Knechtges, *Wen xuan*, 3: 325–39; Schafer, *The Divine Woman*, 35–37.
52 Owen, *The End of the Chinese 'Middle Ages'*, 151–52, 155–56, et passim.
53 Dong, "The Many Faces of Cui Yingying," 80.

society but has once more become a part of its moral standards and has returned to her earlier "proper" self, when she feels that what she has done is wrong and "forgives" Zhang for seducing and betraying her. ... Yingying can only find fault with herself and not with Zhang or society. ... she has justified her fate by blaming it all on herself.[54]

As *youwu* has long been a pejorative term for women who possess the power to seduce men and to "destroy a man's family, or overturn his state" (to borrow Glen Dudbrdige's words), Zhang's defense, absent of regret, would have been considered justified. As for Yingying, as Dudbridge argues: "Yüan is totally evasive about his heroine Ying-ying, her true moral stature and her fate."[55] In his discussion of the same topic, Kominami Ichirō identifies *youwu* as a main subject matter of the "discourse" 話 or casual chats amongst the authors and readers of Tang *chuanqi* narratives. It represents two opposite attitudes, namely criticism and sympathy, in the discourse of the young intellectuals.[56] Nonetheless, within this historical context and in light of Zhang's quibbling, at which his friends all heave a long sigh, Yingying accepts her fate.

The two maidens in the Liu-Ruan tale, on the other hand, *confess* that it is their *sin* (*zui* 罪) to have confined their lovers and finally agree to *release* them. They have a clear understanding that it is a violation of the social norms to keep the two married men for their own pleasure. While the consequences are borne by the two men in the Liu-Ruan tale, they fall on the women in Yuan's writing, as well as in other Tang-Song adaptations (see below and Chapter 4).

Despite the clear similarities among the three tales, it is fair to question whether we are confusing similarity with identity.[57] Surely there were many modes suited to the writing of fantasy on illicit love. The recurring images, setting, and plot in this circle of works can serve to overshadow the differences between three unique pieces of writing. Table 2 compares elements common to the three stories in question:

---

54 Ibid., 81–82.
55 Dudbridge, *The Tale of Li Wa*, 68–70, 72, quoting *Zuozhuan*, Zhao 28, and Bai Juyi, "Guzhong hu" 古冢狐 (*QTS*, 427.4709). Bai says that this poem is a "warning against beauties" 戒豔色也.
56 Kominami Ichirō, *Tōdai denki shōsetsuron*, 116, 119.
57 Kenneth Burke, *Permanence and Change*, 97.

TABLE 2 Characters, settings, and plot features in the three stories

	Liu-Ruan tale in Youming lu	*You xianku*	"Story of Yingying"
Protagonists (lovers), go-between	Liu Chen and Ruan Zhao; two ladies (with no go-between)	Zhang Wencheng; Cui Shiniang (with Wusao 五嫂 as go-between)	Student Zhang and Yingying (with Hongniang 紅娘 as go-between)
Site of romance	Grotto	Grotto	Chamber
Romantic circumstances	Accidental romance; ladies courting men	Accidental romance; reciprocal flirting	Accidental acquaintance; man courting lady
Time span	About one half year	One night (?)	Several months
Token, action	No gift given No poetry Renouncing due to homesickness	Gifts given Poetry exchange Parting due to Zhang's official duties	Gifts given Poetry exchange Zhang abandoning Cui due to pressure from social norms
Conclusion	7 human generations passed upon returning home	Heartbreaking parting	Man abandons lady
Presumed moral	It is better to remain where one belongs	Pursuit of the sensual results in sorrow	Mistakes may be corrected by abandoning the lover

The discrepancies appear to upset our supposition that the two Tang texts are modeled upon the Liu-Ruan tale. In his analysis of the text (discussed above), Hightower avoids identification of the literary antecedents of "The Story of Yingying." After all, Liu Chen and Ruan Zhao cannot transform themselves (or, be transformed) into Student Zhang, whereas the two transcendents in the Liu-Ruan tale do not closely resemble Yingying despite the similarities in the roles of these characters. In this regard, one is reminded of Northrop Frye's discussion of archetypes:

> In terms of narrative, myth is the imitation of actions near or at the conceivable limits of desire. ... The world of mythical imagery is usually represented by the conception of heaven or Paradise in religion, and it is

> apocalyptic, in the sense of that word already explained, a world of total metaphor, in which everything is potentially identical with everything else, as though it were all inside a single infinite body.[58]

Frye's "apocalyptic ... world of total metaphor" is a good illustration of the possibilities presented by the transcendent realm in the Liu-Ruan tale, as adapted in Yuan Zhen's work. Frye, thus, continues his discussion:

> The presence of a mythical structure in realistic fiction, however, poses certain technical problems for making it plausible, and the devices used in solving these problems may be given the general name of *displacement*. Myth, then, is one extreme of literary design; naturalism is the other, and in between lies the whole area of romance, ... to displace myth in a human direction and yet, in contrast to "realism," to conventionalize content in an idealized direction.[59]

The romance of Yuan is "displacement" at work.[60] This Freudian term does a good job of construing Yuan's efforts to find a means to represent his realistic sensual experiences through adaptation of the two inherited sources.

Parallels in the Greek classic, *The Odyssey* (see Epilogue), shed light on how the role of the "transcendent" evolves. As William G. Thalmann observes, the role and circumstances of Kalypso are characterized by the pristine nature in which she lives; Cerce is much more "civilized" because she lives in a house.[61] Later when the hero meets Nausikaa, princess of Scheria, we see that she is even more civilized. Of these ladies, however, Penelope is the most "civilized" and "human," as she is Odysseus's ultimate goal.

Similarly, we regard Yuan Zhen's version of grotto romance as a civilized one—we should not forget that his protagonist, Zhang, is driven by his desire for redemption after abandoning Yingying. With his set of characters and plot,

---

58 Frye, *Anatomy of Criticism*, 136.
59 Ibid., 136–37.
60 Although Frye defines "the essential element of plot in romance [as] adventure" and "we may call this major adventure, the element that gives literary form to the romance, the quest," his focus is on romantic depictions that lean toward the heroic, rather than the accidental romance we observe in the grotto romance tradition. See Frye, *Anatomy of Criticism*, 186–89. "Displacement" is derived from Sigmund Freud, *The Interpretation of Dreams*, 340–43, 602, 634–36, et passim.
61 Thalmann, *The Odyssey*, 76–78. Thalmann also defines Polyphemos as "uncivilized and impious." Polyphemos's behavior toward the stranger "systematically inverts the norms of hospitality as exemplified by Nestor, Menelaos, and the Phaiakians." Ibid., 82.

derived from and inspired by his two predecessors, Yuan aims to "transmit the unusual" (*chuanqi*) of his time—thus drawing a clear line between his story and the earlier ones. The grotto settings in the two early tales make a contrast by unveiling the luxury in the savage surroundings. The price of the affair in all three Chinese tales is the sacrifice of the possibility of living an ordinary human life. In this sense, all the protagonists choose to return from fantasy to reality, to the "human" world. Liu and Ruan's awakening takes place too late; in contrast, the two Zhangs choose to cut off the romance before their indulgence deepens to the extent that their deeds in the mortal world would be thwarted.

4   Liu Chen and Ruan Zhao in Yuan Zhen's Love Poetry

The autobiography theory proposed by Chen Yinke guides us to read the poems on or about Yuan's premarital love in the same light as Student Zhang's love with Yingying.[62] Additional support for this treatment may be found in the name of Yuan's lover, Shuangwen 雙文 (literally, "double graph") and Jiujiu 九九 as Yingying, because, according to Chen, all these names are reduplicated phrases and *jiujiu* (LMC: **kuw' kuw'*) onomatopoeically resembles the chirps of orioles.[63] As we have seen above, "The Story of Yingying" has its distinct literary features but owes much to the Liu-Ruan tale, which also influenced Yuan's poetic works.

Yuan Zhen's use of erotic elements is mainly self-referential. As commonly agreed, early Tang poets, especially Chen Ziang 陳子昂 (661–702), resumed the allegorical function of poetry in their poetic reforms against the poetic "decadence" they perceived in the poetry of the Southern Dynasties.[64] Thereafter, some love content in poetry began to be viewed as an expression of the poet's personal feelings or aspirations, which traditionally implied treating poetry as autobiography. Yuan used the love theme as a veneer for his own story. His correspondence with Bai Juyi on poetics promote realism in poetry.[65] This

---

62   Termed "reciprocal testimony of poetry and history" (*shi shi hu zheng* 詩史互證), this research method is Chen's most important contribution. See Wong Young-tsu, *Shijia Chen Yinke zhuan*, 151.

63   See Chen, *Yuan Bai shi jianzheng gao*, 85–105, 109–10, et passim. The name Shuangwen is found, e.g., in Yuan, "Zeng Shuangwen" 贈; "Dai Jiujiu" 代, in *YZJJZ*, "buyi," 1.1440, "xu buyi," 1.1537. The LMC (late middle Chinese) reconstruction is in E. G. Pulleyblank, *Lexicon of Reconstructed Pronunciation*, 161, q.v.

64   See Wu Fusheng, *The Poetics of Decadence*, 35–39. See Chan, "A Reevaluation of Chen Ziang's 'Manifesto of a Poetic Reform,'" for a different view.

65   Bai, "Yu Yuan Jiu shu" 與元九書, *BJYJJ*, 2790–95.

realistic poetic style encourages an autobiographical reading of the following two poems, which may be regarded as components of "The Story of Yingying."⁶⁶

古豔詩二首	"Two Amorous Poems in Ancient Style"
	Number 1
春來頻到宋家東	Since springtime I have frequented the east side of the Song household.
垂袖開懷待好風	With my sleeves lowered and lapels open, I wait for a fine breeze.
鶯藏柳闇無人語	The orioles hide in the shade of the willows, there is no human talk;
惟有牆花滿樹紅	Only flowers above the fence-walls, covering the trees in pink.
	Number 2
深院無人草樹光	In the deep courtyard there is no one, just lustrous trees and plants.
嬌鶯不語趁陰藏	The lovely orioles do not chirp but find themselves shade to hide under.
等閒弄水浮花片	Purposelessly I play with the water, setting flower petals afloat,
流出門前賺阮郎⁶⁷	Sending them to flow out to the gate to beckon Gentleman Ruan.

Traditionally dated to 800, one year before "The Story of Yingying" was written, the suite may be contextually read as a prelude to Yuan's "A Tryst with the

---

66 Chen Yinke asserts that most of the one hundred or so "Yanshi" were written for Yuan's lover, Cui Yingying. See Chen, *Yuan Bai shi jianzheng gao*, 81.

67 *QTS*, 422.4645. These poems were originally included in an anthology by Yuan Zhen's own hands, entitled *Yanshi juan* 豔詩卷 (*A Fascicle of Amorous Poems*). Poem 2 was anthologized in Wei Hu's 韋穀 (ca. mid-10th c.) *Caidiao ji* 才調集 under the title of "Chunci" 春詞. See *Tangren xuan Tangshi xinbian*, 5.817. Given its earlier occurrence, the variant title "Chunci" should prevail. For discussions of the *Yanshi juan*, see Yamamoto Kazuyoshi, "Gen Shin no Enshi oyobi Tōbōshi ni tsuite," 54–84; Hanabusa Hideki and Maegawa Yukio, *Gen Shin kenkyū*, 194–202, which contains a reconstruction of the anthology; Anna M. Shields, "Defining Experience," 61–78, which includes Du Mu's 杜牧 (803–52) condemnation of Yuan's "lascivious and wanton expressions" (pp. 71–72). A comprehensive picture of Yuan and Bai's fondness for and appraisals of the "yanshi" as well as the polemics in the Tang and beyond is in Yin Zhanhua, "Yuan Zhen pingzhuan," 662–67.

Perfected, in Thirty Rhymes." While the "Tryst" poem is a full account of the love story, these two quatrains focus on Yingying's quest for love. The "Song household" in Poem 1 (also in the "Tryst" poem) refers to the poet Song Yu 宋玉 (fl. late 3rd c. BC), a model "true lover" with whom Yuan Zhen draws a comparison when he introduces Student Zhang at the beginning of his narrative:

> [Student Zhang] was agreeable, refined, and good looking, but firm and self-contained, and capable of no improper act ... He explained, ... "Dengtuzi 登徒子 was no lover, but a lecher. I am the true lover—I just never happened to meet the right girl ..."[68]

This high-minded statement as Zhang's self-introduction not only anticipates the romance with Yingying but later becomes a pretext for abandoning her. The reference to "Dengtuzi haose fu" 好色賦 ("Master Dengtu the Lecher") is about the handsome young man Song Yu, the poet-persona who, after a full description of "the daughter of my eastern neighbor," says: "For three years this girl has been climbing the wall and peeping at me, but I have never given to her."[69] Yuan's quatrains quoted above are written in the voice of the girl who peeps at the handsome young man. According to Chen Yinke's euhemeristic theory, it was Yingying who wanted to start the romance. The hiding oriole (*ying*) is a vivid anthropomorphic representation of Yingying peeping at Zhang.[70]

The seductive scene in Poem 2, where the Liu-Ruan allusion occurs, is especially intriguing. Here, the poet assigns two roles to the girl, who is first in the disguise of the oriole but, as she hides herself in the shade, appears in her second role, the maiden in the Liu-Ruan tale, who now *purposefully* sends out petals, instead of leaves, to attract *her* Ruan Zhao from outside the courtyard. This picture reminds one of the grotto romance, as now the girl "inside" is eager to have her man to join her in a tryst. This poetic representation supplements "The Story of Yingying," with a more active role played by the girl, which perfectly construes her fluctuation in the tale, in which she first reproaches Zhang but later submits to her passion that has possessed her since the very beginning.

---

68   *YZJJZ*, "buyi," 6.1513; trans., Hightower, "Yüan Chen and the Story of Ying-ying," 93, with slight modification.
69   See *WX*, 19.10a; Knechtges, *Wen xuan*, 1: 351.
70   Edward Schafer reads the settings described in Poem 2 as a Daoist convent and asserts that "the oriole is an enchanting young priestess." See Schafer, "Empyreal Powers and Chthonian Edens," 668. This reading fits most poems on the Liu-Ruan story, as discussed below, but not this one.

A reading of Yuan's poetry in isolation from "The Story of Yingying" portrays a similar love story between the protagonist and a girl. We have seen the girl's name Shuangwen, which means "double graph," most likely a sobriquet of Yingying. Chen Yinke points out that many of the "Amorous Poems" ("Yanshi" 豔詩) were written for or about this girl whom Yuan courted in his youth.[71] Five hepta-syllabic quatrains titled "Zayi" 雜憶 ("Miscellaneous Remembrances") involve her. The third line of each poem has a formulaic structure beginning with "I remember Double Graph such and such" 憶得雙文 xxx.[72] The five-poem suite titled "Lisi" 離思 (Parting Thoughts) in "Yanshi" might well have been composed in response to "Zayi," because of the parallel structure of the titles and the content written in the voice of the lover-girl. Three of them may be read in relation to our central text, the Liu-Ruan tale, which might then be in Yuan's repository of stock diction:

其一	Poem 1
自愛殘妝曉鏡中	I cherish my remaining make-up in the morning mirror.
環釵謾篸綠雲叢	Rings and pins are disorderly clipped on my "green clouds."
須臾日射臙脂頰	In a while the sunlight shall shine upon my rouged cheeks;
一朵紅酥旋雨融	Like a rosy, tender blossom it shall quickly melt in the rain.
其二	Poem 2
山泉散漫繞階流	The mountain spring spills and splashes around the stairs.
萬樹桃花映小樓	Ten thousand peach blossoms reflect the small building.
閑讀道書慵未起	At leisure I read Daoist books, lolling and not getting up,
水晶簾下看梳頭	Beneath the crystal blinds, getting ready to comb my hair.

---

71 Chen, *Yuan Bai shi jianzheng gao*, 81. The "Yanshi" is one of the ten categories of poetry defined by Yuan when he compiled his own works. It contains love poems composed in his early years. See Shields, "Defining Experience," 62–66. Wang Jisi and Zhang Renhe compiled a collection of "poems related to the 'Huizhen ji' 會真記 by Yuan Zhen, Bai Juyi, and others," in their *Jiping jiaozhu Xixiang ji*, 265–73.

72 *YZJJZ*, "Buyi," 1.641.

其四	Poem 4
曾經滄海難為水	It was once the blue sea, but it can hardly form a river [now].
除卻巫山不是雲	Aside from those above the Wu Mountains, nothing can be called a cloud.
取次花叢懶回顧	Before any wreath of blossoms, I hesitate to look at them—
半緣修道半緣君[73]	Half because of my study of the *dao*, half because of you.

One finds some familiar scenes and images derived, if not borrowed from, the Liu-Ruan tale. The suite begins with a lone lady who keeps her makeup on overnight and cherishes the remaining vestiges of her beauty. One may contextualize the poem by presuming that, after a tryst, the lover of this girl-persona has just left her chamber. This presumption is bolstered by Poem 2, in which we see her abode located by a creek and in the midst of a peach blossom grove. Note that she reads Daoist books. Poem 4 starts with two allusions, one to Magu 麻姑 (Maiden Hemp), a transcendent who witnessed the East Sea turning into a mulberry field three times,[74] and the other to the romantic encounter between King Xiang of Chu and the goddess of Wu Mountains (discussed above). The protagonist likens herself to these transcendents. Playing with the spatiotemporal displacement established in the Liu-Ruan tale, the poet emphasizes that everything has changed: the sea has now been dried up, and the cloud (i.e., the Wushan goddess incarnate) is no longer a cloud after it has been displaced from Mount Wu. Her indifference to the blooming flowers implies her ambivalence: she misses her lover but is not permitted to meet him as she is now a Daoist priestess.[75]

Why has the persona become a Daoist priestess? What does this priestess have to do with the Liu-Ruan tale? These issues have been thoroughly discussed by scholars who have convincingly identified the origins of most Tang priestesses in the Liu-Ruan thematic cycle as the two girls in the *Youming lu* tale.[76] Li Ye 李冶 (mid to late 8th c.) plays one such role in her poem, "Sending Yan the Twenty-sixth to Shan District" ("Song Yan Ershiliu fu Shanxian" 送閻二

---

[73] *YZJJZ*, "Buyi," 1.640.

[74] *Yunji qiqian* (HY 1026), 109.12b–13a, quoting *Shenxian zhuan*; Schafer, *Mirages on the Sea of Time*, 92; Campany, *To Live as Heaven and Earth*, 267–70.

[75] Bian Xiaoxuan argues that some of the five poems in the suite are on "Yingying" and some on Wei Cong 韋叢 (784–809), wife of Yuan Zhen. He seems to suggest that Poem 4 is not on "Yingying." See Bian, *Yuan Zhen nianpu*, 189.

[76] See Chan "A Tale of Two Worlds," 238–43, quoting Chen Yinke, Lee Fong-mao, Edward Schafer, and Chang Yi-jen.

十六赴剡縣). The ending couplet is most revealing in decoding her triple role as Daoist priestess, lover, and transcendent. Here is the poem:

	送閻二十六赴剡縣	"Sending off Yan the Twenty-Sixth to Shan District"
1	流水閶門外	Currents flow beyond the Chang Portal—[77]
2	孤舟日復西	Since the solitary boat has gone, the sun goes westward again.
3	離情遍芳草	Our parting sentiments cover the fragrant grasses,
4	無處不萋萋	Nowhere are they not lush and green.[78]
5	妾夢經吳苑	In my dream I pass by the Wu Garden;[79]
6	君行到剡溪	Your journey brings you to Shan Creek.
7	歸來重相訪	When you come back, do come see me again.
8	莫學阮郎迷	Do not go astray as Gentleman Ruan did.[80]

The allusion in the final line of this poem tells us that Li Ye likens her lover, Mr. Yan, to Ruan Zhao. The poetess compares the romantic encounter of Ruan Zhao with her worries about her lover, who now travels outside and may repeat his romantic encounter with a new "transcendent" and neglect to return to visit *this* one. This kind of imaginary scene serves to cast doubt on her lover's loyalty. The last three characters also form a High Tang tune-title "Ruan lang mi" 阮郎迷, as found in the *Jiaofang ji* 教坊記; this reveals the Liu-Ruan tale's important role in High to late Tang poetry and songs.[81] Most poetic works about the *xian*, Daoist priestess, and her association with her lover are presented in this scenario: the husband or lover goes out (or exits the "grotto") and leaves behind his wife (or lover), who suffers from loneliness.

Yuan Zhen, who wrote his quatrains some fifty years after Li, situated himself within the same thematic lineage when he depicted his lover in the guise of a priestess returned to her convent. The allusion to the goddess of the Wu Mountains has a similar function as allusions to the Liu-Ruan tale; both recall

---

77 West of modern Suzhou.
78 An allusion to the "Zhao yinshi" 招隱士 ("Summons for a Recluse") in *CCBZ*, 12.233; trans., David Hawkes, *The Songs of the South*, 244: "A prince went wandering and did not return. / In spring the grass grows lush and green" 王孫遊兮不歸，春草生兮萋萋.
79 A garden built on an island on a river called Long Island (Changzhou 長洲). It was once owned by the King of Wu. See *Hanshu*, 51.2363, n. 7.
80 *QTS*, 805.9059; trans., Chan, "A Tale of Two Worlds," 232. See also Jia Jinhua, *Gender, Power, and Talent*, 144–45 (this poem), 140–54 (Li Jilan).
81 *Jiaofang ji jianding*, 93.

well-known sexual relationships in literature. These rhetorical elements serve common themes of transgression from and violation of certain norms. The excitement of this illicit romance, like that of the lovers in its precursory texts discussed above, preludes disastrous and heartbreaking consequences.

It is quite certain that Yuan Zhen often had the Liu-Ruan tale in his stock of references when writing about his young love. This practice is evident in two poems on the "wives" of Liu and Ruan, in which Yuan retells the romance in the voice of the two maidens.

劉阮妻二首	"Wives of Liu and Ruan," Two Poems
其一	Poem 1
仙洞千年一度閒	When the transcendent grotto opened at its thousand-year interval,
等閒偷入又偷迴	Inadvertently, [our lovers] sneaked in and out by stealth.
桃花飛盡東風起	When peach flowers finished scattering, an easterly wind arose,
何處消沈去不來	Where have they gone and submerged, never to return?
其二	Poem 2
芙蓉脂肉綠雲鬟	Like hibiscus, our buxom flesh and green-cloud hairbuns,
罨畫樓臺青黛山	On color-patterned tower-terraces, by green-kohl mountains,
千樹桃花萬年藥	With a thousand peach trees and myriad-year-old herbs—
不知何事憶人間[82]	We do not know their reason for missing the mortal realm.

These two quatrains also fit the love story between Zhang and Oriole, because the poet uses "stealth" (*tou*) for the male persona's visit to his lover's place. If we accept the year 810 as the composition date,[83] the two poems tell the same story as the last few poems on Yuan's romance with Shuangwen. Therefore, these poems are not necessarily about visiting the actual locale of the Liu-Ruan

---

82 YZJJZ, "xu buyi," 1.1540; QTS, 422.4640; trans. Chan "A Tale of Two Worlds," 225, with modification.
83 Bie Xiaoxuan, *Yuan Zhen nianpu*, 187; Yang Jun, *Yuan Zhen ji biannian jianzhu*, 353, 1021.

romance or merely an adaptation of the old tale but clearly depict the author's own romance in the guise of Liu Chen and Ruan Zhao's.[84]

This reading is supported by Yuan Zhen and Bai Juyi's frequent associations with courtesans, a common but socially unsanctioned practice in Tang elite culture.[85] In these poems, the "wives" have been jilted and are yearning for their lovers to come again from the "mortal realm." In narrating the meeting of the lovers, Yuan uses the word *tou* in addition to *dengxian*, "inadvertently"; on the one hand he follows the accidental discovery in the original story but, on the other hand, stresses the "stealthy" nature of the intrusion.[86] The description of the otherworldly realm matches that of the courtesan's dwelling, where there are beautiful ladies and elegant buildings; "immortality" becomes a metaphor for an enjoyable life.[87] But Liu and Ruan left. Their attachment to the social norms of the mortal realm was beyond the understanding of their temporary wives because they were not legally married. This return to the mortal world meant a return to the unexciting world of social order and discipline. We shall come back to this issue below.

5   Poetic Nostalgia of the Grotto: Bai Juyi's Remonstrance

Bai Juyi was the recipient of an occasional poem by Yuan and responded by penning an even longer poem, intended as an admonition. In both poems, the Liu-Ruan tale plays a significant role and is turned into a lesson in juxtaposition with Buddhist parables. These references become a means by which

---

84   Song Bangsui 宋邦綏 (d. 1779) also asserts: "The wives of Liu and Ruan stand for Shuangwen." See Song, *Caidiao ji buzhu*, 5.12a. These poems are quoted in a section on a locale called Liu-Ruan Grotto in a Song-dynasty gazetteer, *Jiading Chicheng zhi*, 21.15a.

85   See, e.g., Wang Shunu, *Zhongguo changji shi*, 88–90; Wang Shiyi, *Yuan Zhen lun gao*, 160–61, 169.

86   The same wording is seen in Cao Tang's poem on the Liu-Ruan story and is said to be "a violation of church rule." See Lee Fong-mao, *You yu you*, 147.

87   In his explanation of "Huizhen ji," a variant title of the "Yingying zhuan," Chen Yinke glosses *huizhen* as "meeting the transcendent being," a figure for a tryst with a beautiful girl. See Chen, *Yuan Bai shi jianzheng gao*, 107. See also Gao Feng, *Huajian ci yanjiu*, 105–6. Yuan Zhen's description of the courtesan's dwelling in his "Gui wan" 閨晚 (*YZJJZ*, "xu buyi," 1.1531–32; *QTS*, 422.4638) fits the one in Sun Qi's 孫棨 (late 9th c.) *Beili zhi* 北里志. See Wang Shiyi, *Yuan Zhen lun gao*, 168–69. For the location and study of Beili, aka Pingkang li 平康里 and Pingkang fang 坊 as entertaining quarter, see Hiraoka Takeo and Imai Kiyoshi, *Tōdai no Chōan to Rokuyō*, map 1, 5H; Victor Cunrui Xiong, *Sui-Tang Chang'an*, 189–90, 220.

the poets articulate how one goes through and eventually abandons spurious romance, evolving into a discourse on spiritual awakening. Our discussion of what kind of enlightenment is implied in these texts will rely largely on some parables in Chan Buddhist sutras, and we observe how Yuan and Bai deviate from Zhang Zhuo and transform the Liu-Ruan tale into an instructive parable on the virtue of refraining from indulgence in sensual pleasure.

Yuan Zhen's literary remembrance of his personal love story is always associated with the Liu-Ruan tale. This association is unmistakable, and is demonstrated by his frequent use of derivative images in combination, such as the grotto, peach blossoms, the season of spring, brooks, luxurious houses, and beautiful ladies. These images are inlaid in the Liu-Ruan thematic circle of adaptations in Tang times and patently adopted in Yuan's "Dream of Spring Roaming in Seventy Rhymes" ("Meng youchun qishi yun" 夢遊春七十韻). When these images are woven together with the themes of revel and dalliance, this poem may be identified, as Kominami Ichirō observes, as being under the influence of Zhang Zhuo's *You xianku*.[88]

Our point of departure concerns how the Liu-Ruan adventure is adapted. The Liu-Ruan tale is used as a haunting reference by the poet, who starts his "adventure" by relying on the Liu-Ruan archetype. This episode ends with a Chan meditative discourse. Here is what Yuan reminisces, in Hightower's translation with slight modification:

1	昔歲夢遊春	Years ago, I dreamed of an outing in spring
2	夢遊何所遇	An outing in spring, and what did I find?
3	夢入深洞中	I dreamed I entered a deep, deep grotto
4	果遂平生趣	And there achieved my lifelong desire.
5	清泠淺漫流	Clear and cool the shallow waters flow,
6	畫舫蘭篙渡	A painted boat with magnolia oars drifts by.
7	過盡萬株桃	I pass a myriad of peach trees in flower
8	盤旋竹林路	And stroll along the bamboo grove path.
	......	...
15	未敢上階行	I dare not climb the steps directly
16	頻移曲池步	But pace back and forth beside the pool.
17	烏龍不作聲	The black dog makes no sound;[89]
18	碧玉曾相慕	Green Jade is the one I always yearned for.
19	漸到簾幕間	I approach at length the curtained door

---

88 See Kominami, *Tōdai denki shōsetsuron*, 120, 129–30.
89 Wulong as a dog's name is first seen in *Soushen houji*, 9.59.

20	裴回意猶懼	And hesitate, feeling fearful still.
21	閑窺東西閣	I take time to peek in the rooms west and east—
22	奇玩參差布	Everywhere rare objects set out in view:
	......	...
29	簾開侍兒起	A curtain opens and the serving girl gets up,
30	見我遙相諭	Sees me and understands without a word.
31	不辨花貌人	I cannot make out the flower-like girl
32	空驚香若霧	And am only surprised at the fragrance-like mist.
33	身回夜合偏	Her body turns: a magnolia bloom aslant
34	態斂晨霞聚	Her form contracts: sunrise clouds cluster.
	......	...
43	紕頓鈿頭帬	Soft woven blouse of filigree
44	玲瓏合歡袴	Bright trousers with a shared-joy print.
45	鮮妍脂粉薄	But now her once fresh makeup is worn thin
46	闇澹衣裳故	Her faded clothes have grown old,
47	最似紅牡丹	Just like the red peony flower
48	雨來春欲暮	When the rains come at the end of spring.
49	夢魂良易驚	The dreaming soul is easily awakened
50	靈境難久寓	In the spirit world it is hard to stay long.
51	夜夜望天河	Every night I gaze at the Milky Way—
52	無由重沿泝	No way again to follow that stream.
53	結念心所期	My mind has been fixed on what my heart desires,
54	返如禪頓悟	Though my return is like Chan instantaneous enlightenment.
55	覺來八九年	During the eight or nine years after awakening
56	不向花迴顧	I did not turn again to look at the flowers.

Here, one finds some such elements as the realm, romance, and progress in the adventurous discourse almost identical to the narrative framework of the Liu-Ruan tale, with the addition of autobiographical and erotic details. From a synchronic point of view, the content of these verses may be seen as a poetic version of "The Story of Yingying," in which the interlude takes place in the western chamber where Zhang has his dream-like romance with his lover.[90] Thus, we make our way back to the "triple role" theory or the euhemeristic reading discussed above. The lover is now a "modish Tang lady" with the innocent attributes that render her unlike the goddess in the repertoire of transcendent

---

90 Yuan, "Yingying zhuan," YZJJZ, "buyi," 6.1515–16.

encounters.[91] Another difference is the nature of the encounter as a tryst, the most obvious indication of which is the servant girl who spots the protagonist, does not say a word, and expresses her understanding (ll. 29–30). This fits the similar scene in "The Story of Yingying."

The Chan enlightenment at the end of this episode (ll. 49–56) somewhat dovetails with the unhappy ending of "The Story of Yingying" but also forms some ironies. In the Liu-Ruan tale, the two men leave the grotto with reluctance but, ironically, the longer they enjoy the revel the keener they are to return to the mortal world of social norms; the protagonist in the poem, likewise, puts an "apparently involuntary end to the experience."[92] This reluctance is revealed by the protagonist's desire to return to "flowers," despite being prevented from looking back for eight to nine years since the "awakening" (ll. 55–56). One irony is the enlightenment that grows from the protagonist's reluctant renunciation of this love affair. Chen Yinke argues that Yuan was under pressure from the social norms of the time and, therefore, needed to restrain all his indecent behavior.[93] Another irony is the protagonist's self-discipline that rekindles memories of the romance, which creates the grounds for his confession. This discourse reflects both the remorse and enjoyment of the act of poetic exposition, as well as the degree to which the protagonist has been possessed by the unforgettable experience.

This reading finds evidence in Bai Juyi's preface to his poem, "Harmonizing 'Dream of Spring Roaming' in One Hundred Rhymes." Bai quotes Yuan's words:

> These words cannot be known by those who do not know me; and for those who know me, they cannot be kept unknown to them. You, Letian, know me; I dare not but let you know, my friend.
>
> 斯言也，不可使不知吾者知；知吾者亦不可使不知。樂天知吾也，吾不敢不使吾子知。[94]

Upon reading Yuan's poem, Bai expresses his understanding and starts preaching in response:

---

91 Anna Shields refers to the protagonist's departure from this grotto as an "escape" from romance. The description of the lover as a "modish Tang lady" is Shields's. See Shields, "Defining Experience," 74–75.
92 Ibid., 75.
93 Chen, *Yuan Bai shi jianzheng gao*, 89–90; Liu Kairong, *Taidai xiaoshuo yanjiu*, 110–12, 117–22.
94 *BJYJJ*, 14.863; trans., Shields, "Defining Experience," 73, modified.

If one's emotion is not profoundly moved, one's regret will not be matured. If one's emotional stirrings do not reach their ultimate, one's regret will not be deep. For this reason, I enlarge the length of your seventy rhymes to one hundred, to elaborate on the most profoundly moving parts of your dream journey and to account for the moving episodes in your marriage and taking office. I want to give a detailed picture of the absurdity and a comprehensive knowledge of the wrongdoing. Thereupon, we will recover genuineness and return to substantiation. This is just like the moral of the narrative about the residence on fire and the hymn on the conjured city in the *Lotus Sutra*,[95] and the episodes in the *Vimalakirti sutra* on entering the houses of prostitution and visiting the taverns.[96] Weizhi, Weizhi: This composition of mine cannot be made known to those who do not know us. I hope you keep it to yourself. It reads as follows.

夫感不甚則悔不熟；感不至則悔不深，故廣足下七十韻為一百韻，重為足下陳夢遊之中所以甚感者，敘婚仕之際所以至感者。欲使曲盡其妄，周知其非，然後返乎眞，歸乎實，亦猶《法華經》序火宅、偈化城，《維摩經》入婬舍、過酒肆之義也。微之微之，予斯文也，尤不可使不知吾者知，幸藏之，爾云。[97]

Hightower observes distinct motives behind the respective compositions. He interprets Yuan's "Spring Roaming in a Dream" as "self-congratulatory" while he views Bai's response as a didactic lesson via a comparison between Yuan's romance and the two Buddhist sutras.[98] Kominami Ichirō shares similar views but focuses more on the phrase "the time of marriage and taking office" (*hunshi zhiji* 婚仕之際). The phrase most typically depicts a dilemma faced by most young scholar-aspirants, many of whom had a love affair with a lady but were forced to abandon her upon taking office in order to marry a lady of higher

---

95   The tale of the residence on fire is about how the father persuaded his young children, who indulged in playing with their favorite toys and did not realize the danger, to flee the blazing house by promising to give them their favorite items after the escape. The tale of the conjured city is about a nāyaka (spiritual guide) taking a group of people to a cache of jewels. Midway into the journey the people became exhausted and scared of the dangerous road, and the nāyaka conjured up a city to let them rest. When the people wanted to settle there, he destroyed it and urged them to continue the journey. See *Saddharma-puṇḍarīka-sūtra* (*Miaofa Lianhua jing*), T 262, 9.12b14–12c18, 9.25c27; *BJYSJ*, 14.1135, 1145–46.
96   Vimalakirti's visits show the sin of sexual desire and establish his high aspiration. See *Vimalakīrti-sutra* (*Weimojie suoshuo jing*), T 475, 14.539a29–539b1.
97   *BJYJJ*, 14.863–64; my translation.
98   Hightower, "Yüan Chen and the Story of Yingying," 118.

social status. Bai Juyi does not explicitly acknowledge this side of Yuan Zhen's dilemma in this preface.[99] In our reading of these works, however, we may temporarily set aside "The Story of Yingying" to simplify what Hightower defines as the "triple identification" of the protagonist, narrator, and poet, and read the exchange poems together.[100]

Interestingly, Bai Juyi, in his harmonizing poem, vies to persuade Yuan to change his ways and elevate his mind. He does this through a more detailed and refined representation of the same topics Yuan employs. What is Bai's motive behind his retelling of Yuan's story if he aims only to preach on his Buddhist perspective? Bai begins his poem with the following lines:

1	昔君夢遊春	In the past you dreamed of an outing in spring
2	夢遊仙山曲	An outing to the transcendent mountainous nooks.
3	悅若有所遇	It was as though you had some encounter,
4	似愜平生欲	Which seemed to have fulfilled the desire of your lifetime.
5	因尋菖蒲水	Thereupon you went along the streams filled with calamus,
6	漸入桃花谷	Gradually entering the valley of the Peach Blossom [Spring],
7	到一紅樓家	Arriving at a red mansion, a residence,
8	愛之看不足	Loving it so much, feeling insatiable looking at it.
	……	…
15	烏龍臥不驚	The lying black dog was not startled [by your visit];
16	青鳥飛相逐	The blue birds in flight chased after each other.
17	漸聞玉珮響	As the jingles of jade pendants lingered,
18	始辨珠履躅	She recognized the paces of your pearl shoes.
19	遙見窗下人	From a distance you saw her by the window,
20	娉婷十五六	Pretty and comely, at the age of fifteen or sixteen—
21	霞光抱明月	Like aurora light embracing the bright moon,
22	蓮豔開初旭	And water lilies blooming in morning sunlight,
23	縹緲雲雨仙	Now hiding, now looming, a transcendent of cloud and rain,
24	氛氳蘭麝馥	Fragrant and redolent, like thoroughwort and musk.
	……	…

---

99 Kominami Ichirō, *Tōdai denki shōsetsuron*, 123.
100 Hightower discusses "the identity of the narrator" in the works in question and points out that "the author and narrator are the same person, the poet-friend of Bai Juyi." Ibid., 119–23.

39	秀色似堪餐	Her beautiful face served to satisfy your appetite;
40	穠華如可掬	The blooming flowers seemed to be for your embrace.
41	半卷錦頭席	Half rolled were the damask-woven bed linens;
42	斜鋪繡腰褥	Spread out askew was the embroidered mattress.
43	朱脣素指匀	Her red lips and natural-colored fingers were so fine;
44	粉汗紅觢撲	Her makeup and rouge mixed with sweat.
45	心驚睡易覺	With a vigilant heart, your sleep was easily disturbed;
46	夢斷魂難續	Your dream was halted, your soul reluctant—
47	籠委獨棲禽	Just like a cage confining the bird to perch alone;
48	劒分連理木	Just like a sword severing the double-trunk tree.
49	存誠期有感	You preserved your integrity, hoping to hold the passion;
50	誓志貞無黷	You swore your chastity, having no intent to abuse it.
51	京洛八九春	For the eight or night years in the capital and Luoyang,
52	未曾花裏宿	You never spent one single night among flowers.[101]

The elaborate depiction of the luxurious scene and the romantic encounter is intended to serve as a foil for Bai's discourse on enlightenment. Both poets set the scene of Yuan's romance at the peach blossom spring in the Liu-Ruan tale with an obvious intent to romanticize Yuan's secular love story. Bai seems to repeat what Yuan told him, but his distinct motive is revealed in some keywords. If Yuan's poem is a confession through reminiscence, Bai's, which keeps the same title of "Dream" in response, may be seen as a sermon on the fleeting, transient value of human affairs. This goal is achieved by the construction of illusory scenes through the use of carefully chosen verbs such as *huang, si, ru* (ll. 3, 4, 39, 40; meaning "seem"), and the adjective *piaomiao* ("now hiding, now looming") as a modifier of the symbolic images of "cloud and rain" (l. 23) and "dream" (l. 46), all of which are laden with sexual overtones.[102] These elements contribute to the illusory nature of love and sexual relationships to draw a picture of delusion. In addition to "clouds and rain," this sense of delusion is continued in the evocative images such as the black dog ("wulong" 烏龍, which also appears in Yuan's poem and carries an overtone of adultery found in its

---

101 *BJYJJ*, 14.864. My translation of Bai's poem borrows from Hightower's translation of Yuan's poem quoted above so as to maintain the cohesive relationship between the two poems, as Bai likewise borrows certain images and diction from Yuan's poem.

102 An allusion to the Goddess of Mount Wu, who turned herself into clouds and rain and shared the bed of King Xiang of Chu in the latter's dream. The image of "clouds and rain" thereafter became a euphemism for a sexual relationship. See Song Yu, "Gaotang fu," *WX*, 19.2a/b.

source *Soushen houji*),[103] blue birds (messengers of love),[104] and the feminine and sensual descriptions of the scene and the girl. This is Bai's strategy. His elaborate retelling of Yuan's romance is a custom-made parable for his friend. Like the Buddhist lore he quotes in the preface, the common moral is that one must first go through the transience of prosperity to reach decay before one may attain enlightenment.

6 A New Discourse on Enlightenment

Bai Juyi and Yuan Zhen customarily wrote in response to each other's poems in the same rhyme scheme and corresponding content,[105] but in "Spring Roaming in a Dream" Bai does not follow this practice. First, he changes the rhyme to entering tone. Second, he evens up the weight of each episode (in terms of the number of lines devoted to each). Third, he adds a fourth part as a lesson for Yuan. Clearly, Bai has a goal to achieve in this unconventional response. In this respect, we may look to Saint Augustine's (354–430) discussion of confession as a way to frame Bai's motives:

> Between temporal and eternal things there is this difference: a temporal thing is loved more before we have it, and it begins to grow worthless when we gain it for it does not satisfy the soul, whose true and certain rest is eternity; but the eternal is more ardently loved when it is acquired than when it is merely desired.[106]

Bai seems to see through the "temporal" nature of Yuan's young love. To remind Yuan to consider the "eternal," and enlighten him about the ultimate goal of the Great Vehicle, Bai includes a series of Buddhist parables in his responding poem. In so doing, he contributes to the Buddhist parabolic repertoire a new iteration of the Liu-Ruan tale.

Here, Yuan Zhen's "dream" illustrates his alleged "instantaneous enlightenment" (l. 54). He *seems* to have derived this idea from the *Vimalakirti sutra*,

---

103 *Soushen houji*, 9.59. See also *Yuan Zhen ji biannian jianzhu*, 340, n. 5.
104 The three blue birds were first depicted as food-deliverers for Queen Mother of the West. See *Shanhai jing jiaozhu*, 306. They later became messengers for Queen Mother of the West in her meeting with Emperor Wu of the Han. See *YWLJ*, 91.1577–78, quoting *Hanwu gushi*. These birds became a metaphor for the go-between of lovers.
105 See Maegawa Yukio, "Chiteki yūgi no bungaku," 117–57.
106 Saint Augustine, *On Christian Doctrine*, p. 32, Book one, XXXVIII.42.

in which a dream is one of the ten analogies for mortal life and arises from fantasy.[107] Bai responds accordingly:

173	請思遊春夢	Please brood upon your dream of spring roaming—
174	此夢何閃倏	How flickering and fleeting is this dream!
175	豔色即空花	The colorful guise is the same as flowers of vanity.
176	浮生乃焦穀	One's mortal life is nothing but singed grains.

Chen Yinke's reading of Yuan's literary creations as a romantic autobiography sheds light on our understanding of the two "Dream" poems. If the Liu and Ruan characters in Yuan's poem are used to illustrate Yuan's enlightenment, the moral would involve his detachment from love affairs; however, his "enlightenment" turns out to be a justification for his departure from this "grotto." Ironically, the protagonist is eager to return to the "grotto." His love makes him stay away from *other* flowers for eight to nine years (ll. 55–56). He admits how painful it is to bury this sweet memory (ll. 63–64). Bai exaggerates the nature of the force that separated the lovers, referring to a cage that separates the paired birds and a sword that severed the double-trunk tree (ll. 47–48). Yuan expresses a desire for reviewing the pleasure in having attained the "temporal," but suggests that the "eternal" nature of the *Dao* is strengthened, and has ultimately superseded the "temporal."

In response, Bai juxtaposes a series of Buddhist tales as parallels to Yuan's vicissitudes in his discussion of the fleeting nature of the affair. He tells his friend:

169	欲除憂惱病	To be rid of the ailments of worries and anxieties,
170	當取禪經讀	You should obtain some Chan sutras and study them.
171	須悟事皆空	Do realize that all secular matters are but vanity;
172	無令念將屬	Do not let those thoughts linger and fester.

Bai turns Yuan's reluctant separation into a lesson: "The evil must be slain by a sword of Wisdom" 魔須慧刀戮 (l. 196).

Bai expresses his disagreement with Yuan's interest in "instantaneous enlightenment" (l. 54 in Yuan's poem), likely in favor of Bai's preferred northern Chan doctrine on "gradual enlightenment." By this time, Bai had already

---

107 *Vimalakīrti-sutra* (*Weimojie suoshuo jing*), *T* 475, 14.539b19: "One's person is like a dream, which is a false vision" 是身如夢為虛妄見.

been exposed to the southern Chan school of Buddhism.[108] In his preface to the harmonizing poem (translated above), his examples include "the house on fire," the conjured city, and Vimalakīrti entering the "house of prostitution" and "tavern" (i.e., drinking establishment). These tales are most typical in illustrating the "Three Vehicles"—how one achieves Buddhahood through arduous ordeals,[109] although they hardly correspond to the three stages of Yuan's life. Bai's juxtaposition of these tales side by side with the Liu-Ruan tale metaphorically forms a paradigm of lessons on Yuan's wrongdoings in his early life, whereby Bai turns Yuan's alleged "instantaneous enlightenment" into "gradual enlightenment" as his clever switches of the three stages of Yuan's life illustrate Yuan's gradual realization of the Truth. To further enhance this gradual process, Bai aligns his references from the Liu-Ruan tale with Yuan's young love, his marriage, and his career path, in an attempt to help Yuan transcend mundanity and achieve a higher level of enlightenment.

Bai's discourse on "gradual enlightenment" is typical in the two turning points between the three episodes of Yuan's ordeal. In a comparison between the length of each episode (see appendix), we see two different treatments:

TABLE 3   Sections in Yuan's and Bai's poems[a]

Episode	Couplet numbers in Yuan's poem (number of couplets)	Couplet numbers in Bai's poem (number of couplets)
1. Young love	1–32 (32)	1–28 (28)
2. Marriage	33–48 (15)	29–54 (25)
3. Career	49–70 (21)	55–82 (28)
4. Reflection		83–100 (17)

a   The Chinese texts of these two poems are in the appendix to this chapter.

The statistics show that Yuan's interest is mainly in the first three episodes (of which "young love" is a main focus); Bai, in his harmonizing poem, evens up the emphasis on the three episodes and adds a fourth part on "reflection."

The Liu-Ruan tale as a new parable in Bai's preaching on enlightenment, as pointed out above, deserves further discussion. In transiting to the second

---

108   Xie Siwei argues that Bai's exposure to the southern Chan school started in the early Yuanhe period (which began in 806). See Xie, *Bai Juyi ji zonglun*, 268.
109   Chan, *Considering the End*, 150.

episode, Bai employs the term "Liu-Ruan" as a metonymy for the illicit love, as antithetic in content and parallel in syntax to "Pan-Yang":

| 63 | 劉阮心漸忘 | As your Liu-Ruan romantic thought is gradually forgotten, |
| 64 | 潘楊意方睦 | Your Pan-Yang happiness becomes harmonious. |

This second episode in Bai's poem is on Yuan's marriage. Derived from Pan Yue's 潘岳 (247–300) marriage with Lady Yang, the term "Pan-Yang" becomes a synecdoche of happy married life. But Pan's happiness soon ended with the death of Yang; the same tragedy happened in Yuan's life when his wife Wei Cong passed away in 809.[110]

Bai uses the word *jian* (gradually) to scorn Yuan's reluctance to learn his first "lesson" from his romantic relationship with the girl, just as Liu and Ruan learned too late of their mistake in the grotto. In so doing, Bai refutes Yuan's claim that he gained "instantaneous enlightenment" from his young love. In the next few couplets, Bai writes about the prosperous and pleasant scene of Yuan's married life (ll. 65–76), which quickly ended upon his wife's death. The third episode relates to Yuan's official life, which begins with an ambitious statesman (Yuan) who aspired to "repay the emperor" by performing duties at court (ll. 121–22). This "dream" was smashed by slanderers and ended with a series of banishments to the remote, uncivilized south.

By converting Yuan's tragic life and grievances to the three-stage tale in the Buddhist mode, Bai consoles his friend with these conclusions:

| 181 | 合者離之始 | Coming together is the beginning of parting;[111] |
| 182 | 樂兮憂所伏 | Happiness is where worry crouches.[112] |

---

110 Chen Yinke argues that Yuan abandoned Yingying and married Wei Cong because the former was from a low class. Chen, *Yuan Bai shi jianzheng gao*, 95, 111. Pan Yue's works on his deceased wife Lady Yang include: "Daowang shi" 悼亡詩 (3 poems), "Ai yongshi wen" 哀永逝文, and "Daowang fu." See *WX*, 23.18a–20b; 57.24b–26a; *YWLJ*, 34.602–3. For the backgrounds of Pan and his wife, along with translations of these works, see C. M. Lai, "The Art of Lamentation in the Works of Pan Yue," 409–25.

111 An allusion to *Zhuangzi* 20/8: "… for those who are concerned with the circumstances of the myriad things and the teachings on human relationships: no sooner do they join than they are sundered; no sooner do they succeed than they are ruined" 若夫萬物之情, 人倫之傳, …… 合則離, 成則毀. Translation (with minor changes to punctuation and layout) is by Victor H. Mair, *Wandering on the Way*, 187.

112 Zhan Fangsheng's 湛方生 (E. Jin) "Beisou zan" 北叟贊: "Joy is the root of worry; bliss is the inception of disaster" 樂為憂根, 福為禍始. *BJYSJ*, 14.1145. An earlier source is *Laozi* 58: "It is on disaster that good fortune perches; / It is beneath good fortune that disaster crouches" 禍兮福之所倚, 福兮禍之所伏. Trans., D. C. Lau, *Lao Tzu*, 119.

183	愁恨僧祇長	Sorrow and remorse are as long as asaṃkhya;
184	歡榮剎那促	Pleasure and honor are as transient as a *kṣaṇa*.
185	覺悟因傍喻	Awakening and enlightenment are reliant on metaphors;
186	迷執由當局	Perplexity and obstinacy stem from being trapped within.
187	膏明誘闇蛾	The lamp oil's brightness lures the benighted moth;[113]
188	陽焰奔癡鹿	The mirage in solar blazes makes the possessed deer gallop.[114]
189	貪爲苦聚落	Greed compels the settlement of bitterness;[115]
190	愛是悲林麓	Passion is the forest-foothill of sorrow.
191	水蕩無明波	Water churns ripples of ignorance.[116]
192	輪迴死生輻	The reincarnation wheel is made of spokes of life and death.
193	塵應甘露灑	The dust ought to be sprinkled with sweet dew.[117]
194	垢待醍醐浴	The stain needs to be bathed with ghee.[118]
195	障要智燈燒	Barricades must be burned by the lamp of intelligence.
196	魔須慧刀戮	Evil needs to be slain by a sword of Wisdom.[119]
197	外熏性易染	When exposed, one's inner nature is easily contaminated.[120]
198	內戰心難馴	Battling inside, one's heart is not easily subdued.

---

113 A flying moth rushing towards lamps and candles. *BJYSJ*, 14.1145, quoting *Abhiniṣkramaṇa-sūtra* (*Fo benxing ji jing*), *T* 190, 3.729a22–23.

114 A flock of deer driven by thirst running towards the mirage of water. *BJYSJ*, 14.1145, quoting *Laṅkâvatāra-sūtra* (*Lengqieabaduoluo baojing*), *T* 670, 16.491a8–10.

115 *BJYSJ*, 14.1145–46, quoting *Saṃyuktâgama-sūtra* (*Za Ahan jing*), *T* 99, 2.33c28–34a1 and *Avataṃsaka-sūtra* (*Dafang guang fo Huayan jing*), *T* 278, 9.546b20–23.

116 The term *wuming* 無明 ("ignorance"; Sanskrit: *avidyā*) is the first of the twelve *nidānas* 十二因緣 ("the twelve links in the chain of existence"). It is the root of confusion that exists in one's past life. It represents the fundamental ignorance underlying our existence, the inability to recognize the cause of the suffering of birth, aging, illness, and death. See Nakamura Hajime, ed., *Bukkyōgo daijiten*, 1346, qv.; William Edward Soothill and Lewis Hodous, *A Dictionary of Chinese Buddhist Terms*, 379–80, 42–43, qvv.

117 Dharma of sweet dew 甘露法 is a method of purification. See, e.g., *Saddharma-puṇḍarīka-sūtra* (*Zheng Fahua jing*), *T* 263, 9.81a20, 9.93b7.

118 *Tihu* (Sanskrit: *maṇḍa*) is refined milk of the highest quality, which becomes a metaphor for the most sublime form of the Buddhist teachings.

119 The "knife of wisdom" is a means by which one may cut off the "various views" 諸見 and achieve "liberation" 解脫. Bai Juyi here may have borrowed the term and relevant theory from *Fo wei Xinwang pusa shuo Toutuo jing* 佛為心王菩薩說頭陀經, 286. The sutra has long been regarded as apocrypha. See Fang Guangchang's introduction and discussion in pp. 251–52; 318–28.

120 A common metaphor in Buddhism. See, e.g., *Vijñaptimātratāsiddhi-śāstra* (*Cheng weishi lun*), *T* 1585, 31.12a24–28.

| 199 | 法句與心王 | The *Dharma-phrase* and *Mind-king* sutras,[121] |
| 200 | 期君日三復 | I hope you can review them thrice a day. |

Bai starts his discussion with Daoist relativism and moves to Buddhist parabolic preaching. His reference, in the ending couplet, to the two sutras creates a multifold metaphorical entity,[122] the tenor of which relies upon vehicles drawn from some Buddhist tales as well as from the Liu-Ruan tale.[123] His inclusion of the Liu-Ruan tale in his parable circle was guided by Yuan Zhen, in front of whom he styles himself as a doyen wishing to enlighten an acolyte. The tale is now used in a Buddhist context in the fashion of Shi Daoshi in the early Tang Buddhist encyclopedia, *Fayuan zhulin*.[124] Liu and Ruan adapts well to this new context.

Bai's introspective preaching views Yuan's early romantic life as a deception. To Bai, Yuan's claim to have attained enlightenment is but self-deceit. His use of the Buddhist tales may be read in light of Augustinian discussions of the Christian Scripture, in which the road is a metaphor:

> But anyone who understands in the Scriptures something other than that intended by them is deceived, although they do not lie …, he is deceived in the same way as a man who leaves a road by mistake but passes through a field to the same place toward which the road itself leads. But he is to be corrected and shown that it is more useful not to leave the road, lest the habit of deviating force him to take a crossroad or a perverse way.[125]

Yuan has taken the wrong road and has been confounded by conflicting values. Bai juxtaposes these examples and points to the correct road to enlightenment. His Chan references imply a unique interpretation of the Liu-Ruan tale, the protagonists of which left the correct road. This same mistake is repeated by Yuan. Bai also observes that Yuan has recognized himself in Liu Chen and

---

121 Chen Yinke identifies these sutras as: *Fo wei Xinwang pusa shuo Toutuo jing* and *Dharmapada* (*Fo shuo Faju jing*), T 2901. He also regards these sutras as apocrypha and their content vulgar and shallow. He therefore considers Yuan and Bai's study of Buddhism rather superficial. See Chen Yinke, *Yuan Bai shi jianzheng gao*, 99.
122 Chen Yinke points out that Yuan and Bai were both apprentices of Buddhism because they allude to these "vulgar" sutras. See Chen, *Yuan Bai shi jianzheng gao*, 99. Zhu Jincheng disagrees with Chen's denigrating comments. See *BJYJJ*, 14.868.
123 Here, I refer to the "vehicle" first discussed by I. A. Richards, rather than the Buddhist term. See his *The Philosophy of Rhetoric*, 96, et passim.
124 *Fayuan zhulin*, T 2122, 53.521a5–28.
125 Saint Augustine, *On Christian Doctrine*, Book one, p. 31, XXXVI.41.

Ruan Zhao, and renounced his romantic yearnings. After abandoning fanciful nostalgia, Bai advises Yuan to eliminate the Liu-Ruan tale from his emotional repertoire.

The ambivalence between "instantaneous" and "gradual" enlightenment in Bai Juyi's poetic discourse was likely a result of his apprenticeship in Buddhist learning.[126] In his juxtaposition of parables and inclusion of Yuan's three episodes, Bai proposes a gateway to enlightenment through life experience and reading. Above all, the Liu-Ruan tale referenced by Yuan and included in Bai's response contributes to a new discourse. It serves as a multivalent model for the retelling of Yuan's unforgettable love story and in support of Buddhist doctrines on enlightenment through overcoming mundane entanglements. Bai asked Yuan to review the Buddhist parables, one after another, and apply them to his life in order to transcend secular trouble and cultivate his heart-mind. This is reinforced by his admonition at the end: "Read *Dharma-phrase* and *Mind-king* sutras thrice a day." This instruction would seem to violate the doctrinal practice of Southern Chan. In fact, these two sutras contain contradictory doctrines, as the *Mind-king* sutra advocates "instantaneous" enlightenment while the *Dharma-phrase* sutra (*T* 210) preaches "gradual" enlightenment.[127] Bai was not a writer of Wang Wei's 王維 (701–761) leanings but rather perceived Buddhist doctrines in a loosened and secular sense by synthesizing them with Confucianism and Daoism.[128] This secularization of Buddhism would likely have contributed to his practical poetics, as seen in his "Letter to Yuan Zhen the Ninth" written in 815, in which he claims that the very functions of writing are to "remedy and observe current politics" and "direct and vent people's feelings."[129]

---

126 Chen Yinke, *Yuan Bai shi jianzheng gao*, 99. The two doctrines were not exclusive to each other but were instead considered reciprocal and complementary in Tang times. See Ge Zhaoguang, *Zhongguo Chan sixiang shi*, 198–200; Chan Wing-tsit, *A Source Book in Chinese Philosophy*, 426; Peter N. Gregory, *Inquiry into the Origin of Humanity*, 185–88. The famous dispute between the two doctrines by Shenxiu and Huineng is recorded in *Fozu tongji*, *T* 2035, 49.292a20–21; trans, Kenneth Ch'en, *Buddhism in China*, 355; Wing-tsit Chan, *A Source Book in Chinese Philosophy*; A. F. Prince and Wong Mou-Lam, trans. *The Sutra of Hui Neng*, 15, 18.

127 See, respectively, *Fo wei Xinwang pusa shuo toutuo jing*, 292; *Dharmapada* (*Faju jing*), *T* 210, 4.568b20–23.

128 See Sun Changwu, "Tangdai wenren de Weimo xinyang," 103–6.

129 Bai, "Yu Yuan Jiu shu," *BJYJJ*, 45.2790 (text), 2796 (dating).

7 Conclusion

Tracing the roots of Yuan Zhen's writings about his young love is more than just an exercise in poetic biography; through the lens of grotto fantasy, we are in a better position to appreciate the aesthetic range of some of his best-known work. We have positioned the *You xianku* as a precedent for Yuan's complex poetic representation of his love story and its aftermath. In his hands, the theme of trysting with a transcendent evolves into multilayered depictions of erotic fantasy.

This evolution in grotto fantasy focuses on the figurative possibilities of the female role. While Zhang Zhuo's adaptation is the first known source to turn the two maidens into "transcendent beings" (a euphemism for entertainers in Tang times), Yuan Zhen should be considered the poet who consummates the maidens' "triple role" in his poetic and narrative works as the entertainer, Daoist priestess, and the transcendent. The role proliferation of grotto maidens was in vogue in the literature of the day.[130] The time dilation motif in the Liu-Ruan tale is less prominent in these works. In its place, nostalgia over the passage of time and the intensity of lovesickness and remorse become prominent motifs.

Chen Yinke's approach to "Spring Roaming in a Dream" as an autobiographical depiction of Yuan Zhen's love affair with Yingying remains essential. We also observe that the Liu-Ruan tale contributes to the portrayal of this love story across Yuan's works. This observation finds evidence in Yuan's "staying away from 'flowers' for eight or nine years" after the love affair, as claimed in his and Bai Juyi's poems. This autobiographical reading is further bolstered by Bai's metonymic use of "Liu-Ruan romantic thought" to demarcate Yuan's amorous life before he was married. Bai Juyi responded to Yuan's 70-couplet poem in 100 couplets to remonstrate Yuan's attachment to his romance, a lesson that carries the same weight as the Buddhist tales cited in the poem. Bai shows his friend that he should rather undergo a "gradual enlightenment" process through the study of Buddhist parables in sutras (irrespective of which Chan "school") as well as reflecting on Yuan's own love story, insofar as it resembles

---

130 An early example of a different double role is the protagonist of Wang Lingfei 王靈妃, a lover of Li Rong 李榮 (mid 7th c.), a Daoist master. Wang is a Daoist priestess and calls herself "banished transcendent" (*chudi* 黜帝). See Luo Binwang 駱賓王 (627?–684?), "Dai nüdaoshi Wang Lingfei zeng daoshi Li Rong" 代女道士王靈妃贈道士李榮 ("Presented to Daoist Adept Li Rong, written on Behalf of Daoist Priestess Wang Lingfei"). See my discussion and translation of this poem in Chan, "Amorous Adventure in the Capital," 1–54.

that of Liu and Ruan. The Liu-Ruan tale becomes a metaphor that serves as a common reference point in their poetry exchange.

Appendix

Chinese Texts of Yuan Zhen's and Bai Juyi's Poems on "Spring Roaming in a Dream".[131]

元稹《夢遊春七十韻》

…… 斯言也，不可使不知吾者知；知吾者亦不可使不知。樂天知吾也，吾不敢不使吾子知。……

白居易《和夢遊春詩一百韻并序》

　　微之既到江陵，又以夢遊春詩七十韻寄予。且題其序曰：「斯言也，不可使不知吾者知；知吾者亦不可使不知。樂天知吾也，吾不敢不使吾子知。」予辱斯言，三復其旨，大抵悔既往而悟將來也。然予以為苟不悔不寤則已，若悔於此，則宜悟於彼也；反於彼而悟於妄，則宜歸於真也。況與足下外服儒風，內宗梵行者有日矣。而今而後，非覺路之返也，非空門之歸也，將安返乎？將安歸乎？今所和者，其卒章指歸於此。夫感不甚則悔不熟；感不至則悔不深，故廣足下七十韻為一百韻，重為足下陳夢遊之中，所以甚感者；敘婚仕之際，所以至感者。欲使曲盡其妄，周知其非，然後返乎眞，歸乎實。亦猶《法華經》序火宅、偈化城，《維摩經》入淫舍、過酒肆之義也。微之，微之，予斯文也，尤不可使不知吾者知，幸藏之爾云。

(1)

1　昔歲夢遊春，夢遊何所遇？夢入深洞中，果遂平生趣。
5　清泠淺漫流，畫舫蘭篙渡。過盡萬株桃，盤旋竹林路。
9　長廊抱小樓，門牖相回互。樓下雜花叢，叢邊繞鴛鷺。
13　池光漾霞影，曉日初明煦。未敢上階行，頻移曲池步。

(1)

1　昔君夢遊春，夢遊仙山曲。悅若有所遇，似愜平生欲。
5　因尋菖蒲水，漸入桃花谷。到一紅樓家，愛之看不足。
9　池流渡清泚，草嫩蹋綠蓐。門柳闇全低，檐櫻紅半熟。
13　轉行深深院，過盡重重屋。烏龍臥不驚，青鳥飛相逐。

131　The layouts and numbering of the texts show the corresponding sections of the two poems, i.e., how Bai addresses Yuan's ideas and responds to them.

17	烏龍不作聲，碧玉曾相慕。漸到簾幕間，裴回意猶懼。	17	漸聞玉珮響，始辨珠履躅。遙見窗下人，娉婷十五六。
21	閑窺東西閤，奇玩參差布。隔子碧油糊，駝鉤紫金鍍。	21	霞光抱明月，蓮豔開初旭。縹緲雲雨仙，氛氳蘭麝馥。
25	逡巡日漸高，影響人將寤。鸚鵡饑亂鳴，嬌娃睡猶怒。	25	風流薄梳洗，時世寬妝束。袖頓異文綾，裾輕單絲縠。
29	簾開侍兒起，見我遙相諭。鋪設繡紅茵，施張鈿妝具。	29	裙腰銀線壓，梳掌金筐蹙。帶襯紫蒲萄，袴花紅石竹。
33	潛褰翡翠帷，瞥見珊瑚樹。不辨花貌人，空驚香若霧。	33	凝情都未語，付意微相矚。眉斂遠山青，鬟低片雲綠。
37	身回夜合偏，態斂晨霞聚。睡臉桃破風，汗妝蓮委露。	37	帳牽翡翠帶，被解鴛鴦襆。秀色似堪餐，穠華如可掬。
41	叢梳百葉髻，金蹙重臺屨。紕頓鈿頭冪，玲瓏合歡袴。	41	半卷錦頭席，斜鋪繡腰褥。朱唇素指勻，粉汗紅餘撲。
45	鮮妍脂粉薄，闇澹衣裳故。最似紅牡丹，雨來春欲暮。	45	心驚睡易覺，夢斷魂難續。籠委獨棲禽，劍分連理木。
49	夢魂良易驚，靈境難久寓。夜夜望天河，無由重沿泝。	49	存誠期有感，誓志貞無黷。京洛八九春，未曾花裏宿。
53	結念心所期，返如禪頓悟。覺來八九年，不向花迴顧。	53	壯年徒自棄，佳會應無復。鸞歌不重聞，鳳兆從茲卜。
57	雜合兩京春，喧闐眾禽護。我到看花時，但作懷仙句。		
61	浮生轉經歷，道性尤堅固。近作夢仙詩，亦知勞肺腑。		
	(2)		(2)
65	一夢何足云，良時事婚娶。當年二紀初，嘉節三星度。	57	韋門女清貴，裴氏甥賢淑。羅扇夾花燈，金鞍攢繡縠。
69	朝騶玉佩迎，高松女蘿附。韋門正全盛，出入多歡裕。	61	既傾南國貌，遂坦東牀腹。劉阮心漸忘，潘楊意方睦。
73	甲第漲清池，鳴騶引朱轂。廣榭舞霓裳，長筵賓雜遝。	65	新修履信第，初食尚書祿。九醞備聖賢，八珍窮水陸。
77	青春詎幾日，華實潛幽蠹。秋月照潘郎，空山懷謝傅。	69	秦家重蕭史，彥輔憐衛叔。朝饌饋獨盤，夜醪傾百斛。
81	紅樓嗟壞壁，金谷迷荒戍。石壓破闌干，門摧舊栘栭。	73	親賓盛輝赫，妓樂紛曄煜。宿醉纔解酲，朝歡俄枕麴。
85	雖云覺夢殊，同是終難駐。悵緒竟何如，夢絲不成絇。	77	飲過君子爭，令甚將軍酷。酩酊歌鷓鴣，顛狂舞鸜鵒。
89	卓女白頭吟，阿嬌金屋賦。重璧盛姬臺，青冢明妃墓。	81	月流春夜短，日下秋天速。謝傅隙過駒，蕭娘風過燭。

93	盡委窮塵骨，皆隨流波注。幸有古如今，何勞縑比素。	85	全凋薜花折，半死梧桐禿。闇鏡對孤鸞，哀弦留寡鵠。
		89	凄凄隔幽顯，冉冉移寒燠。萬事此時休，百身何處贖。
		93	提攜小兒女，將領舊姻族。再入朱門行，一傍青樓哭。
		97	櫪空無廐馬，水涸失池鶩。搖落廢井梧，荒涼故籬菊。
		101	莓苔上几閣，塵土生琴筑。舞榭綴蠨蛸，歌梁聚蝙蝠。
		105	嫁分紅粉妾，賣散蒼頭僕。門客思徬徨，家人泣呼噢。
	(3)		(3)
97	況余當盛時，早歲諧如務。詔冊冠賢良，諫垣陳好惡。	109	心期正蕭索，宦序仍拘跼。懷策入崎函，驅車辭鄒鄏。
101	三十再登朝，一登還一仆。寵榮非不早，邅迴亦云屢。	113	逢時念既濟，聚學思大畜。端詳筮仕著，磨拭穿楊鏃。
105	直氣在膏肓，氛氳日沈痼。不言意不快，快意言多忤。	117	始從讐校職，首中賢良目。一拔侍瑤墀，再升紆繡服。
109	忤誠人所賊，性亦天之付。乍可沈爲香，不能浮作瓠。	121	誓酬君王寵，願使朝廷肅。密勿奏封章，清明操憲牘。
113	誠爲堅所守，未爲明所措。事事身已經，營營計何誤。	125	鷹鞲中病下，豸角當邪觸。糾謬靜東周，申冤動南蜀。
117	美玉琢文珪，良金填武庫。徒謂自堅貞，安知受磨鑄。	129	危言詆閹寺，直氣忤鈞軸。不忍曲作鉤，乍能折爲玉。
121	長絲羈野馬，密網羅陰兔。物外各迢迢，誰能遠相錮。	133	捫心無愧畏，騰口有謗讟。只要明是非，何曾虞禍福。
125	時來既若飛，禍速當如鶩。曩意自未精，此行何所訴。	137	車摧太行路，劍落酆城獄。襄漢問修途，荊蠻指殊俗。
129	努力去江陵，笑言誰與晤。江花縱可憐，奈非心所慕。	141	謫爲江府掾，遣事荊州牧。趨走謁麾幢，喧煩視鞭朴。
133	石竹逞奸黠，蔓青誇畝數。一種薄地生，淺深何足妒。	145	簿書常自領，縲囚每親鞫。竟日坐官曹，經旬曠休沐。
137	荷葉水上生，團團水中住。瀉水置葉中，君看不相污。	149	宅荒渚宮草，馬瘦畬田粟。薄俸等涓毫，微官同桎梏。
		153	月中照形影，天際辭骨肉。鶴病翅羽垂，獸窮爪牙縮。
		157	行看鬢間白，誰勸杯中綠。時傷大野麟，命問長沙鵩。

161 夏梅山雨漬，秋瘴江雲毒。巴水白茫茫，楚山青簇簇。

(4)

165 吟君七十韻，是我心所蓄。既去誠莫追，將來幸前勗。

169 欲除憂惱病，當取禪經讀。須悟事皆空，無令念將屬。

173 請思遊春夢，此夢何閃倏。豔色即空花，浮生乃焦穀。

177 良姻在嘉偶，頃剋爲單獨。入仕欲榮身，須臾成黜辱。

181 合者離之始，樂兮憂所伏。愁恨僧衹長，歡榮刹那促。

185 覺悟因傍喻，迷執由當局。膏明誘闇蛾，陽焰奔癡鹿。

189 貪爲苦聚落，愛是悲林麓。水蕩無明波，輪迴死生輻。

193 塵應甘露灑，垢待醍醐浴。障要智燈燒，魔須慧刀戮。

197 外熏性易染，內戰心難刟。法句與心王，期君日三復。

CHAPTER 3

Roaming, Roleplay, and Rhetoric in Liu Yuxi's Peach Spring Adventures

1   Introduction

During the mid-sixth to early seventh century, Tao Qian's "Record of the Peach Blossom Spring" became a synecdoche for transcendence or withdrawal from the dusty world. Examples of this practice abound and are particularly well attested among the writings of court poets and the recluse poet Wang Ji 王績 (ca. 585–644).[1] As we have demonstrated earlier, Tao's "Record" was often recalled together with the Liu-Ruan tale, despite the thematic differences. Bai Juyi and Liu Yuxi were among the earliest poets to combine references to both narratives.[2] Liu Yuxi lived in the same period as Yuan Zhen and Bai Juyi, and the three were members of an elite caste that shared the same literary tradition. Still, Liu's grotto fantasy took a different turn. For him, the Liu-Ruan tale is pivotal in enabling grotto fantasy to communicate political satire.

Friendship, politics, and geographic reference are the focuses of recent studies of mid-Tang intellectual culture and literature, and Liu Yuxi plays a central role in this scholarship. Both Anna Shields and Stephen Owen deal with how the Liu-Ruan tale functions in Liu Yuxi's writing (citations below). Other scholars frame their readings of these works around geographic elements, such as the location of Tao Yuanming's peach spring.[3] The present chapter departs from existing scholarship by drawing upon mid-Tang lore to investigate how

---

1 See, e.g., Xu Ling 徐陵 (507–583), "Shanzhai shi" 山齋詩; Yu Xin 庾信 (513–581), "Yong huapingfeng shi" 詠畫屏風詩, no. 5, "Fengbao Zhaowang huijiu shi" 奉報趙王惠酒詩; Shen Junyou 沈君攸 (6th c.), "Fude linshui shi" 賦得臨水詩; Wang Ji, "Youxian shi" 遊仙詩, no. 3; Chen Ziliang 陳子良 (d. 632), "Xiawan xun Yu Zhengshi zhijiu fuyun" 夏晚尋于政世置酒賦韻, etc. See *XQHW*, 2530, 2395, 2111; *QTS*, 37.483, 39.496.
2 See Bai, "Zeng Xue Tao" 贈薛濤, *BJYJJ*, "waiji," 1.3828. Zhang Jianwei identifies Liu Zhangqing 劉長卿 (709–785) as one such early poet to initiate this trend. See Zhang, "Lun Tangshi zhong Taoyuan diangu," 73. Liu's poem is "Guo Baihe guan xun Cen xiucai buyu" 過白鶴觀尋岑秀才不遇, *QTS*, 147.1481. Nonetheless, the abbey visited by Liu is in Mount Lu; one finds it hard to read the peach blossom spring as Tao Qian's. See *Liu Zhangqing shiji biannian jianzhu*, 229.
3 See Mark Meulenbeld, "The Peach Blossom Spring's Long History"; Ao Wang, *Spatial Imaginaries in Mid-Tang China*, which discusses Liu Yuxi's thought of the "map-guide" and his sojourning life (e.g., pp. 154–56, 160–62, 164–65, 225–28).

the peach springs (of both Tao Yuanming and the *Youming lu*) operate in Liu Yuxi's writing. We focus, in particular, on how he adopts and recasts these two peach springs to construct a paradise of his own.

We have read the Liu-Ruan tale in Chapter 1; let us now have a closer look at Tao's "Record of the Peach Blossom Spring" with Hightower's translation (with slight modification) here:[4]

> During the Taiyuan period of the Jin dynasty a fisherman of Wuling once rowed upstream, unmindful of the distance he had gone, when he suddenly came to a grove of peach trees in bloom. For several hundred paces on both banks of the stream there was no other kind of tree. The fragrant flowers growing under them were fresh and lovely, and fallen petals were in profusion. It made a great impression on the fisherman. He went on for a way with the idea of finding out how far the grove extended. It came to an end at the foot of a mountain whence issued the spring that supplied the stream. There was a small opening in the mountain and it seemed as though light was coming through it. The fisherman left his boat and entered the cave through the opening. At first it was extremely narrow, barely admitting his body; after a few dozen steps it suddenly opened out onto a broad and level plain, where well-built houses were surrounded by rich fields and pretty ponds. Mulberry, bamboo and other trees and plants grew there, and criss-cross paths skirted the fields. The sounds of cocks crowing and dogs barking could be heard from one courtyard to the next. Men and women were coming and going about their work in the fields. The clothes they wore were like those of ordinary people. Old men and boys were carefree and happy.
>
> When they caught sight of the fisherman, they asked in great surprise how he had got there. The fisherman answered all their questions and was invited to go to their house, where he was served wine while they killed a chicken for a feast. When the other villagers heard about the fisherman's arrival they all came to pay him a visit. They told him that their ancestors had fled the disorder of Qin times and, having taken refuge here with wives and children and neighbors, had never ventured out again; consequently, they had lost all contact with the outside world. They asked what the present ruling dynasty was, for they had never heard of the Han, let alone the Wei and Jin. They sighed unhappily as the fisherman

---

4 Hightower, *The Poetry of T'ao Ch'ien*, 254–55. For the convenience of reading, I have changed the Wade-Giles romanization to *pinyin*. The Chinese text is based on *Tao Yuanming ji*, 6.165–66, while the punctuations are based on *Tao Yuanming ji jianzhu*, 6.479–80.

enumerated the dynasties one by one and recounted the vicissitudes of each. The visitors all asked him to come to their houses in turn and served him wine and food. He stayed several days. As he was about to go away, the people said, "There's no need to mention our existence to outsiders."

After the fisherman had gone out and recovered his boat, he carefully marked the route. On reaching the city, he reported what he had found to the magistrate, who at once sent a crew of men to follow him back to the place. They proceeded according to the marks he had made, but went astray and were unable to find the cave again.

A high-minded gentleman of Nanyang named Liu Ziji heard the story and happily made preparations to go there, but before he could leave he fell sick and died. Since then there has been no one interested in trying to find such a place.

晉太元中，武陵人捕魚為業。緣溪行，忘路之遠近。忽逢桃花林，夾岸數百步，中無雜樹，芳華鮮美，落英繽紛。漁人甚異之。復前行，欲窮其林。林盡水源，便得一山。山有小口，髣髴若有光。便捨船從口入。初極狹，纔通人，復行數十步，豁然開朗。土地平曠，屋舍儼然，有良田、美池、桑竹之屬。阡陌交通，雞犬相聞。其中往來種作，男女衣著，悉如外人。黃髮垂髫，並怡然自樂。見漁人乃大驚。問所從來，具答之。便要還家，為設酒殺雞作食。村中聞有此人，咸來問訊。自云先世避秦時亂，率妻子邑人來此絕境，不復出焉，遂與外人間隔。問今是何世，乃不知有漢，無論魏晉。此人一一為具言所聞，皆歎惋。餘人各復延至其家，皆出酒食。停數日，辭去。此中人語云：「不足為外人道也。」既出，得其船，便扶向路，處處誌之。及郡下，詣太守說如此。太守即遣人隨其往，尋向所誌，遂迷不復得路。南陽劉子驥，高尚士也。聞之，欣然規往，未果，尋病終。後遂無問津者。

Liu Yuxi's poetic representation of the two tales tracks the ups and downs in his political career and serves to express his reluctance to abscond in seclusion. In the year 805, the political reform led by Liu's political patron Wang Shuwen 王叔文 (753–806) was crushed in a coup. The consequences included Wang's being put to death the next year and the banishment of his adherents to a political backwater in southern China.[5] Liu Yuxi would spend over two decades in exile,

---

5 See *Zizhi tongjian*, 236.7609–23; Michael T. Dalby, "Court Politics in Late T'ang Times," 601–4. The eight Adjutants and their respective destination of banishment are: 1) Wei Zhiyi 韋執誼 (769–814), Yazhou 崖州 (in modern Hainan); 2) Han Tai 韓泰 (d. ca. 831), Qianzhou 虔州 (modern Ganzhou, Jiangxi); 3) Chen Jian 陳諫, Taizhou 台州 (modern Taizhou, Zhejiang); 4) Liu Zongyuan 柳宗元 (773–819), Yongzhou 永州 (southern part of modern Hu'nan);

first for ten years in Lianzhou 連州 (in modern Guangdong) and soon after for fourteen years in Langzhou 朗 (in modern Hu'nan),[6] where the peach blossom spring described by Tao Qian was located. This old, myth-laden locale sparked new inspiration for the unhappy poet. Although it vanishes at the end of Tao Qian's narrative, the paradise formed a new fantasy for Liu Yuxi upon his visit to the reputed site. Far and unrelated to Langzhou, which was the site of the *Youming lu* tale, the locale of Tao Qian's spring played no role in Liu's decade-long sojourn away from the capital, but it became a major vehicle for Liu's satirical views, which directly caused him a second, even longer banishment. In his poetic depictions of adventures to Tao Qian's peach spring, Liu Yuxi assumes three roles: the fisherman, the Daoist lad Qu Boting 瞿柏庭 (755–773), and Liu Chen. The fisherman appears quite frequently in Liu's writing on the Wuling region. Chenzhou 辰州, located in the vicinity of Wuling, is also where Qu Boting became a Daoist apprentice and finally transcended in broad daylight, according to legend. Our central text in this present book—the Liu-Ruan tale—is not geographically related to the legends of Wuling. Nevertheless, Liu Yuxi inserts himself into the Liu-Ruan tale, makes use of its device of time displacement, and borrows the image of the peach blossom to playfully assume the conceit of "Gentleman Liu" 劉郎. In the guise of this character, he makes his return to the political arena after a long absence.

Liu Yuxi tends to avoid the erotic and sensual branch of the grotto-romance literary tree. Instead, we examine how Liu immerses himself in the contextual worlds of the Wuling peach spring, Qu Boting, and Liu Chen. In this chapter, we shall see how Liu Yuxi plays these three roles in establishing a complex self-portrait as a statesman who had undergone political turbulence with a positive attitude and an unbending sense of political righteousness.

2 The Homesick Fisherman

When Liu Yuxi arrived in Langzhou in the winter of 805, he started portraying himself as "the fisherman." He had just arrived in the supposed location of Tao Qian's peach blossom spring as an unhappy poet. Unlike in the Tao Qian tale, Liu's discovery of his metaphoric paradise is saturated with homesickness rather than pleasant surprise. For this reason, Liu's version of the peach

---

5) Liu Yuxi, Langzhou; 6) Han Ye 韓曄, Raozhou 饒州 (modern Boyang district, Jiangxi); 7) Ling Zhun 凌準, Lianzhou 連州 (northern part of modern Guangdong); 8) Cheng Yi 程异, Chenzhou 郴州 (southeastern part of modern Hu'nan).

6 See Bian Xiaoxuan, *Liu Yuxi nianpu*, 41–46.

blossom spring tale is tinted with sadness and a wish to return to the capital. His wish was not to be granted for ten years.

This theme of homesickness is expressed in his "Ballad of the Peach Blossom Spring," in which the poet assumes the conceit of Tao Qian's fisherman.

	桃源行	"Ballad on the Peach Blossom Spring"
1	漁舟何招招	On the fishing boat, drifting and jolting,
2	浮在武陵水	He stayed afloat on the waters of Wuling—
3	拖綸擲餌信流去	Dropping a baited line, following the currents
4	誤入桃源行數里	For several *li*, straying to the Peach Blossom Spring.
	***	***
5	清源尋盡花綿綿	He reached the pure source filled with flourishing flowers.
6	踏花覓徑至洞前	Stepping on petals, probing the trails, reaching the grotto mouth,
	***	***
7	洞門蒼黑煙霧生	He saw a dark-green entrance where mist and fog arose.
8	暗行數步逢虛明	After walking some steps in the dark he saw a flickering light.
	***	***
9	俗人毛骨驚仙子	His mortal hair and bones startled the transcendents,
10	爭來致詞何至此	Who vied to come and ask: "How have you come here?"
	***	***
11	須臾皆破冰雪顏	Shortly after, they all broke their icy facial expressions,
12	笑言委曲問人間	With a smile inquiring about details of the outside world.
	***	***
13	因嗟隱身來種玉	They then sighed at having secluded themselves and come to plant jade here,[7]

---

[7] Planting jade: Yang Boyong 楊伯雍 lived in a mourning hut on the mountain where his parents were buried. He once offered water to a certain traveler, who gave Yang a picul of stone seeds in gratitude and told Yang to plant them on the summit of the mountain. Yang ended up harvesting jade, by means of which he married a good wife. The place where he planted jade was called the Jade Field. See *Soushen ji*, 11.137; the paraphrased translation is based on Kenneth DeWoskin and J. I. Crump, Jr., *In Search of the Supernatural*, 133–34.

14	不知人世如風燭	Not knowing the human world was like a candle in the wind.
15	筵羞石髓勸客餐	They banqueted their guest with stalactite as a delicacy.
16	燈熱松脂留客宿	Lighting resin lamps they had the guest stay for the night.
	***	***
17	雞聲犬聲遙相聞	When roosters and dogs were mutually heard from afar,
18	曉色蔥蘢開五雲	In colorful dawn hues the five spectra of clouds were displayed,
19	漁人振衣起出戶	The fisherman put on his clothes, set out, and exited the door.
20	滿庭無路花紛紛	No path was in the courtyard blanketed completely by petals.
	***	***
21	翻然恐迷鄉縣處	Suddenly worried about losing his way back to his home district,
22	一息不肯桃源住	He refused to live in the Peach Blossom Spring for an instant.
23	桃花滿溪水似鏡	Peach blossoms piled up on the creek that resembled a mirror.
24	塵心如垢洗不去	His dusty mind was like a stain, which could not be washed away.
	***	***
25	仙家一出尋無蹤	Once he left the transcendents' home, it was nowhere to be found again.
26	至今水流山重重	Still today, the water flows to the mountains, ridge upon ridge.[8]

Liu Yuxi's poetic representation of the fisherman's adventure becomes a figure for his political saga, which ends in banishment. Unlike other Tang poems on the peach blossom spring of the Tao Qian and Liu-Ruan tales,[9] Liu's work tells of the poet's unwillingness to linger in this "paradise" despite its promises of transcendence. In lines 13–15, Liu posits a temporal contrast between "the human world" which is temporary "like a candle in the wind" and the

---

8 *LYXJ*, 26.819; *QTS*, 356.3995.
9 See, e.g., Wang Wei, "Taoyuan xing," in *Wang Wei ji jiaozhu*, 1.16–17; *QTS*, 125.1257–58; *Yuefu shiji*, 19.1269–70.

eternal transcendence of the mythical paradise. To reinforce this contrast, the poet relates that the fisherman was fed with stalactite, or "stone marrow," a life-prolonging foodstuff.[10] The life-prolonging feature of the peach blossom spring, paradoxically, forms a dilemma for the fisherman, who is "worried about losing his way back to his home district" and thus "refused to live in the Peach Blossom Spring for an instant" (ll. 21–22). In the fisherman's guise, the poet-persona expresses his reluctance to be naturalized in this transcendent realm, lest he fade from the political world because of his long absence.[11]

Liu enhances his poem's philosophical content with Chan Buddhist thought. This element is not surprising given the poet's associations with Chan Buddhist monks during his decade-long stay in Langzhou.[12] The barrier between this-world and the otherworld is demarcated by the dark passage (ll. 7–8), going through which may be seen as a process of purification, or an unburdening of one's mundane troubles. Possibly with this in mind, the fisherman, who deems himself unable to successfully unburden himself, eventually decides to leave this realm of Chan meditation. The description in ll. 23–24 reminds us of the famous gathas about the mirror as a metaphor for one's mind, respectively by Shenxiu 神秀 (606–706) and Huineng 慧能 (638–713), who later became respective patriarchs of the Northern and Southern schools of Chan Buddhism.[13] The poet, who might have borrowed this Chan idea, turns this transcendent realm into a mirror, on which the fisherman sees his "stain" that stubbornly remains (ll. 23–24).

The concern about political alienation over time is a main theme in Liu Yuxi's poetic representation. In the circle of tales about grotto romance, as we have seen in Chapter 1, social and family values in the mundane world are a major force drawing the archetypical sojourners Liu Chen and Ruan Zhao back to the mortal world. A similar mechanism is at work in Liu's fisherman's discourse: his fear of losing his political status forms the same power that pulls him out of the transcendent realm. This observation finds support in our discussion of Liu Yuxi's allusion to the Liu-Ruan tale below. It is also reinforced by Liu Yuxi's identification with the family name he shared with Liu Chen and Liu Ziji 劉子驥, two key figures who explored the "otherworld" and eventually

---

10 This substance has been said to have a life-prolonging function since at least the third century. See *TPGJ*, 9.62, quoting *Shenxian zhuan*; Chan, "Ruan Ji and Xi Kang's Visits to Two 'Immortals,'" 147–51.
11 Long deprivation of political status drains one's potential to perform heroic deeds, as we will see in the Epilogue of this book.
12 For the names of these monks and relevant poems, see *LYXJ*, 22.615, 29.942, 949–50, 953, 954; *QTS*, 357.4020, 4014–15, 359.4057–58, 357.4028, 359.4048.
13 *Liuzu dashi fabao Tanjing*, T 2008, 48.348b24–25; 48.349a7–8.

returned (more below). In this personalized representation, therefore, Liu's anxiety over the passing of time becomes a new element grafted into this rewritten version of Tao Qian's tale. Surprisingly, the paradise forms an obstacle for the poet's deeds in the human world. He is well aware of the lag in time and space and is therefore worried about losing his way back.

The poet writes about the exotic geography of the region through a juxtaposition of references. An example of this is his long poem, "Writing My Inner Feelings in Wuling in Fifty Rhymes" ("Wuling shuhuai wushi yun" 武陵書懷五十韻), written when the poet first took the post of local governor of Langzhou in 806.[14] The poet tends to write extensively on the region from the perspective of a stranger, who has not come of his own initiative. For this reason, the poem may be seen as a gazetteer-like poetic exposition made of exotic allusive scenes; it seems the poet has been highly selective of the local history in order to reconstruct an emotional landscape. As if to ensure this poetic landscape is received as a "mythical space," to borrow Yi-fu Tuan's term,[15] the poet appends an informative preface and his own commentary on the verse. In the preface, he highlights two historical figures from the local region: the wronged "righteous ruler" 義帝 (i.e., Xiang Ji 項籍 [232–202 BC]) and Qu Yuan. Upon arrival in the region, Liu looked into the local history and interviewed local people in his study of these historical figures, and reflected "thereupon I present all I have heard and seen and compose this poem, detailing the causes of my services and retreat. For this reason, I entitle it 'writing my inner feelings.'" In his discussion of mythical space, Yi-fu Tuan argues: "Worlds of fantasy have been built on meager knowledge and much yearning."[16] Despite the details provided in the poem and the preface, Liu's main interest is, paradoxically, to write about his yearning for getting out of this place.

The poem begins with the development of the prefecture in the Western Han and, upon citing historical figures and tales related to the locale, it proceeds with the poet's disclosure of "inner feelings." Through constructing a misty and foggy atmosphere, the poet aims to unfold scenes of the political turmoil of the Chu state by juxtaposing the sacrificial rituals for Grand Lord of the East 東皇太一, the local songs on the wronged "righteous ruler," and the

---

14 Bian Xiaoxuan, *Liu Yuxi nianpu*, 53; LYXJ, 22.605–7; QTS, 362.4087–88. See my discussion below.

15 Tuan distinguishes "two principal kinds of mythical space": "In the one, mythical space is a fuzzy area of defective knowledge surrounding the empirically known; it frames pragmatic space. In the other it is the spatial component of a world view, a conception of localized values within which people carry on their practical activities." See Tuan, *Space and Place*, 85.

16 Ibid., 86.

"loyal spirit" of Qu Yuan. In his description of local people's means of livelihood, he mentions the bullying by evil "rural magnates." Looking around, in history and in reality, the poet realizes that his neighbors are all "banished strangers" (*qianke* 遷客) just like him. As time passes, their children all speak the local language, which the poet calls "left talk" (*zuoyan* 左言), a pejorative term based on his perception of the region as uncultivated.[17] He fears that he will devolve into the uncultured people that they have become.

In the next stanza through the end of the poem, the poet shifts to focus on himself, the main generic component of "writing my inner feelings." This autobiographical mode of representation is customary in his longer compositions in Langzhou. The political path he has gone through in the capital often becomes a focus in this poem. It haunts the poet throughout his banishment. The ending lines of the poem most typically and directly tell of his eagerness to return to the capital:

就日秦京遠	It is far to the sun in the Qin capital.
臨風楚奏煩	Against the wind, I am troubled by the Chu music.
南登無灞岸	To the south I can ascend no riverbank by Baling.
旦夕上高原	In the evening I can only hike up to the high hills.[18]

The imagery and references here emphasize his spatiotemporal distance from the capital. The Qin capital and the sun refer to the Tang emperor in Chang'an, who is now impossible to "get close to" (*jiu* 就) not because of the spatial distance but the banishment that has brought the poet here. The Chu music allusion stresses his attachment to where he feels he belongs, despite dislocation, just as Zhong Yi 鍾儀 (6th c. BC), a native of Chu who was captured and jailed in the Jin state, continued to play the music of his native land.[19] The final couplet expresses the sorrow of separation through a fantasy of ascending the Ba Mausoleum, where Emperor Wen of the Han (r. 180–157 BC) was buried. Skillfully borrowing Wang Can's 王粲 (177–217) ending lines from his "Seven Sorrows" ("Qiai shi" 七哀詩),[20] Liu writes about his ascension to the *wrong*

---

17   Liu Yuxi's attitude towards the local Man people is typically reflected in his "Song of the Manzi" 蠻子歌, which begins with a couplet: "The Speech of the Man is a *kou-chou* sound, / The dress of the Man is a *pan-lan* linen" 蠻語鉤輈音，蠻衣斑斕布. *LYXJ*, 26.813; *QTS*, 354.3963; trans., Edward H. Schafer, *The Vermilion Bird*, 54. Schafer's discussion of the Man people recorded by these Tang literati is in ibid., 48–61.
18   *LYXJ*, 22.607; *QTS*, 362.4088.
19   *Zuozhuan*, Cheng 9.9.
20   *XQHWJ*, 365.

height and thereby stresses his great (spatial and temporal) displacement from Chang'an, as, unlike Wang Can, he now cannot gaze at the capital.

In earlier versions of adventures to the peach blossom spring, all visitors ended up departing from the grotto; Liu Yuxi follows this convention but for a different reason. In Tao Qian's version, the grotto is depicted as a utopia-like realm that could no longer be found. When Tao Qian's protagonist, Liu Ziji of Nanyang, tried to find it, he ended up dying before he could take the trip.[21] Liu Yuxi had no interest in finding Tao Qian's Peach Blossom Spring; what is more, he never wanted to be there.

3 The Interlocutory and Introspective Peach Blossom Spring

In addition to his banishment to Langzhou, there is another, more specific milieu that must have played a role in the formation of Liu Yuxi's attitude towards the peach blossom spring. His refusal to stay in this transcendent realm contradicts his ideas expressed in a poem entitled "An Excursion to the Peach Blossom Spring, in One Hundred Rhymes" (a full translation of which is in the appendix).[22] The last stanza of the poem tells of the poet's plan to settle there as a commoner. While there is no direct evidence for my hypothesis that this poem and the one just discussed above were written in response to each other, Liu's "Hundred Rhymes" was obviously written on a special occasion involving some exchanges of views among Liu's friends. This socio-poetical function of literary creation becomes our guideline for looking at a particular case in which the peach blossom spring becomes a central topic. These cultural backgrounds and settings tune the poem to a descriptive and lyrical mode, aimed at its target readers, one of whom was Han Yu 韓愈 (768–824).

The occasion-subject that initiated this poetic exchange was a painting. A certain "Governor of Wuling District" (Wuling taishou 武陵太守) sent a painting to the head of the "south palace" (nangong 南宮), a general term for "ministry" (shangshu 尚書).[23] Upon viewing this painting, Han Yu wrote a poem

---

21   Liu Ziji's name is Liu Linzhi 劉驎之, who is recorded as a high-minded recluse in *Shishuo xinyu* and, according to the *Jinji* 晉紀 quoted in Liu Xiaobiao's 劉孝標 (462–521) commentary, "died of old age." See *Shishuo xinyu jianshu*, 18/8 (pp. 654–65), 23/38 (p. 749); trans., Richard Mather, *Shih-shuo Hsin-yü*, 335–36; 384–85. The *Soushen houji* also contains an entry on Liu, which recounts his adventures. See *Soushen houji*, 1.6.
22   *LYXJ*, 23.653–55; *QTS*, 355.3980–81.
23   Chen Jingyuan 陳景元 (1035–1094) identifies the "Governor of Wuling District" (l. 5 of Han's poem below) as Dou Chang 竇常 (746–825), and the head of the "south palace" (l. 7

titled "Painting of the Peach Spring" ("Taoyuan tu" 桃源圖).[24] It is unknown whether Han Yu wrote his poem before or after Liu's "Hundred Rhymes," although Chen Jingyuan asserts that Han "must have written this to accompany one by a certain Gentleman."[25] This hypothesis is in fact attested in lines 7–10 of Han's poem (quoted and translated below). Without mentioning the painting, however, Liu seems to be responding to Han's views about transcendence and reclusion. In any case, the painting and the two poems formed a poetic discussion on the peach blossom spring around 813 when Liu Yuxi was in Langzhou.[26]

Han Yu depicts the otherworldly realm not as a land of the transcendents but as a place to which one should not sojourn.[27] He begins with a criticism of fantasy, followed by a discussion of what he sees and feels from viewing the painting, as follows:

1	神仙有無何眇芒	How obscure and unfathomable are questions about the existence of transcendent beings.
2	桃源之說誠荒唐	The discourse about the Peach Blossom Spring is indeed absurd and unsound.
3	流水盤迴山百轉	Flowing currents meander and circle around the mountains a hundred times—
4	生綃數幅垂中堂	All these are on several pieces of raw silk, hung in the middle of the hall.
	***	
5	武陵太守好事者	The Grand Protector of Wuling district, one who is fond of the matter
6	題封遠寄南宮下	Penned an inscription on it, sealed it, and sent it to the southern palace far away.
	***	
7	南宮先生忻得之	At the southern palace the master was so pleased upon receiving it.

---

of Han's poem below) as Lu Ting 盧汀. The former was governor of Wuling in 810 and the latter had frequent poetic exchanges with Han Yu in this period. See HCLS, 8.912, n. 1.

24 Painters of the time present the scene as a transcendent realm. See, e.g., Quan Deyu 權德輿 (759–818), "Taoyuan pian" 桃源篇; Shu Yuanyu 舒元輿 (791–835), "Lu Taoyuan hua ji" 錄桃源畫記. See QTS, 329.3679; Quan Tangwen, 727.19a–20a.
25 HCLS, 8.914, n. 8.
26 Qian Zhonglian, who dates Han's poem to 813, assumes that Han wrote the poem in response to the "absurd" content about Qu Boting in Liu's poem. See HCLS, 8.913, n. 1.
27 Sun Changwu suggests that it was the atheistic thought of Han Yu that set the tone of the poem. See Sun, Han Yu shiwen xuanping, 131–32.

8	波濤入筆驅文辭	Waves and billows from the tip of the writing brush prompt literary expression.
9	文工畫妙各臻極	The literary craftsmanship and drawing skills each reach a supreme level.
10	異境怳惚移於斯	The vague and veiled otherworldly realm has been transported here.

***

11	架巖鑿谷開宮室	These people piled up boulders, dug caves, and constructed chambers and rooms,
12	接屋連墻千萬日	Living for a myriad of days under adjacent roofs and within continuous walls.
13	嬴顛劉蹶了不聞	They were completely uninformed of the downfall of the Yings and the collapse of the Lius,
14	地坼天分非所恤	And unconcerned about the earth falling apart and heaven being divided.

***

15	種桃處處惟開花	They planted peach trees everywhere, which burst in full bloom—
16	川原近遠烝紅霞	Near and far from rivers and plains they look like steaming rosy aurora.
17	初來猶自念鄉邑	When they first came, they still missed their own hometown;
18	歲久此地還成家	But as years went by, this land became their home.

***

19	漁舟之子來何所	The man of the fishing boat, whence has he arrived?
20	物色相猜更問語	His guise arouses their curiosity and questions swarm in.
21	大蛇中斷喪前王	"The giant serpent was severed in the middle and the former ruler died."[28]
22	羣馬南渡開新主	"As a flock of 'horses' went to the south, a new ruler ascended the throne."[29]

***

---

[28] An allusion to the story of Liu Bang's 劉邦 (posth., Emperor Gaozu of the Han, r. 206–195 BC) killing a serpent blocking the road. The serpent was the son of White Thearch 白帝子 and Liu was the son of Red Thearch 赤帝. See *Hanshu*, 1A.7.

[29] An allusion to a prophetic song: "Five horses crossed the river. / One horse became a dragon." It refers to the story of how five Kings of the Western Jin, surnamed Sima 司馬, moved to the south and one of them became Emperor Yuan of the Eastern Jin (r. 318–323). See *Jinshu*, 6.157.

23	聽終辭絕共悽然	When the telling and hearing were completed everyone felt sorrowful.
24	自說經今六百年	They then told their own story: "It has been six hundred years.
25	當時萬事皆眼見	"At that time, everything was eye-witnessed by everyone;
26	不知幾許猶流傳	"No one would know how many of them are still in circulation."

***

27	爭持酒食來相饋	They vied to bring wine and food as gifts for the fisherman.
28	禮數不同罇俎異	Their rites were not the same, and their flagons and plates were different.
29	月明伴宿玉堂空	The bright moon accompanied him as he stayed at the empty jade hall.
30	骨冷魂清無夢寐	He felt cold in his bones, and lucid in his soul, but dreamt about nothing.

***

31	夜半金雞喁唽鳴	In the middle of the night, the gold rooster heralded and crowed.
32	火輪飛出客心驚	As the fiery wheel flew out the visitor felt startled in his heart.[30]
33	人間有累不可住	He had entanglements in the human realm and should not live here,
34	依然離別難為情	Reluctantly, he took leave and found it hard to cut off this attachment.

***

35	船開櫂進一迴顧	As his boat set off and his oar rowed, he looked back
36	萬里蒼蒼烟水暮	At a thousand *li* of the blue-green mist water of the dusk.

***

37	世俗寧知偽與真	How would the secular world distinguish the fake from the genuine?
38	至今傳者武陵人[31]	Even today, the transmitters of the legend are the men in Wuling.

---

30   The "fiery wheel" is a kenning for the sun.
31   *HCLS*, 8.911–12.

Han Yu seems to have Liu Yuxi as his interlocutor in this poetic exercise written in 813.[32] Han skillfully blends the tale of the peach blossom spring told by Tao Qian with the recent political turmoil and thereby adds a new layer of meaning and allegorizes Tao's tale. There are at least two adaptations in Han's rewriting of the tale. First, he changes "Qin and Han" to "Ying and Liu" (l. 13) when referring to the downfall of the two dynasties. In doing so, Han Yu may have intended to embed the surname of Liu Yuxi in the text. Second, he adds the allusion to Liu Bang slaying the serpent (l. 21) to recall the havoc in history and, more importantly, the political havoc in his own time. The emphasis here is on Liu Bang becoming the new ruler. We might relate the death of the *wang* to Shunzong's 順宗 (761–806; r. 805) death, who was replaced by Xianzong 憲宗 (778–820; r. 805–20). It may also refer to the two leaders of the reform movement—Wang Shuwen and Wang Pi 王伾 (d. 806)—as their surname was also Wang and they both died soon after the failure of the attempted reform and their subsequent banishment to the south. This latter reading is bolstered by Han Yu's pun on the "flock of horses" (*qun ma* 羣馬; l. 22), which may refer to the eight adjutants (sima 司馬) who were banished to the south at the same time, one of whom was Liu Yuxi. In light of these implicit references, we may sum up the figurative correspondences between some images in Han's poem and the political climate during Han and Liu's time. Han and his colleagues bore witness to the political turmoil in Chang'an. Liu Yuxi is the fisherman who has now sojourned to the hidden grotto near the peach blossom spring, where it would have been impossible to learn of the demise of the current political regime. He visits the "grotto" before the others at the poetry gathering and remains to report to them what has happened.

One further reason to read Liu Yuxi into Han Yu's poem involves the opening couplet. Han asserts that it is "absurd" (*huangtang* 荒唐) to believe in transcendent fantasies. His worries about distortions of the witnessed "truth" (ll. 25–26, 37) form a contradiction because no *mortal* dweller at the peach blossom spring would have personally witnessed six hundred years of history. Instead, Han Yu's concern could only have been about what had recently happened in the capital, which was "witnessed" by Liu Yuxi (who paid the price for his role), and which would likely be distorted or misunderstood over time. Han's message in his poem is clear: although the human realm is full of entanglements, you (Liu Yuxi, now in Wuling) should come back, as you are the only one who can tell the truth.[33]

---

32 *Han Yu quanji jiaozhu*, 630–31, n. 1.
33 Han Yu had already been back in Chang'an since 810 and, according to Charles Hartman, "There is no doubt Han Yü felt ideologically and politically at home in this group." Despite

We invert the order of the exchange poems, as suggested by Qian Zhonglian,[34] and hypothesize that Liu's "Hundred Rhymes" is a response to Han's poem. Liu writes similarly to personalize the images and references to fit them in the contemporary political landscape. Liu's poem begins as a third-person narration, *not* disguising himself as the fisherman, but rather in first-person (a full translation of the poem is in the appendix). Likely corresponding to the painting about Tao Qian's fisherman, in the first section the poet recounts the fisherman's adventure, but then asserts that character's reluctance to stay (ll. 21–24). This fisherman is not Liu himself, who holds a view apparently opposite to what the poet-persona preaches in the later stanzas. We may reconstruct a conversational setting: Liu is now detailing his excursion accompanied by the painting of "Taoyuan tu," which was sent to the south palace master by a certain "Fisherman of Wuling, a *haoshizhe* (i.e., one who is fond of the matter [of Liu's banishment, in this case])" 武陵漁人好事者. Liu's composition is meant to give details to Han Yu's poem as both elaboration on and defense of his Wuling adventure. On a hiking trip portrayed in the poem, Liu strives to represent the scene as a figure of his political life:

51	夤緣且忘疲	Creeping and scaling, for now I forgot about tiredness.
52	耽玩近成癖	Indulging myself in playing, I am almost inveterate.
53	清猿伺曉發	Gibbons waited for dawn to cry out clear growls;
54	瑤草凌寒圻	Carnelian plants had overcome cracking coldness.

The poet's enjoyment of ascending to the heights, combined with the images of animals and plants, may be read figuratively as his reflections on his recent career path. This reading is supported by other self-referencing representations in other parts of the poem, which will be discussed presently.

The lines about transcendence in Liu's poem seem to imply a debate with Han Yu. As the poet-persona reaches the historic site of the legendary peach blossom realm, some transcendent beings invite him to stay (ll. 57–78). In this transcendent realm, he now finds solace for his recent failure in political life. This may be read as Liu's deliberate protest against Han Yu's line, "The

---

their different political stances and misfortunes, as well as Han's "scathing satirical" views of Wang Shuwen (in 803), in 805 when the large-scale exiles happened, Han should "have dispelled any suspicions and hostility he may have harbored concerning the role of the two Lius in his own exile of 803." See Hartman, *Han Yü and the T'ang Search for Unity*, 53–57, 67, 77. He Zhuo 何焯 (1661–1722) glosses the term "Wuling ren" in the last line as "also including the governor." See *HCLS*, 8.916, n. 24.

34   *HCLS*, 8.912–13, n. 1.

discourse about the Peach Blossom Spring is indeed absurd and unsound." Liu Yuxi finds relevance in the tale and solace in his metaphorical absorption in it.

4   Encountering the Daoist Lad Transcendent

In his poem, "Hundred Rhymes," Liu Yuxi adds a new element to serve a purpose in response to Han Yu. Above the Tao Qian version of the fisherman's adventure, Liu layers a tale about a Daoist lad. This tale was set in the same geographic area and was established as local lore not long before Liu's residency. When the poet arrives at the temple of Qu Boting, built by the Tang royal house (ll. 29–36), he finds a new vehicle for telling his own story and wishes. It is noteworthy that Han Yu criticizes the "absurd and unsound" in his poem (ll. 1–2, quoted above). Liu Yuxi, who is known to be a rationalist,[35] devotes a long, twenty-line stanza to the legend of this Daoist transcendent. Why did the tale draw Liu's attention? Let us first look at this stanza:

81	乃言瞿氏子	Thereupon, I was told about a lad from the Qu family:
82	骨狀非凡格	His bone structure and bearing were not those of a mortal.
83	往事黃先生	At that time when he served as a disciple of Master Huang,
84	羣兒多侮劇	Other children always bullied and tricked him,
85	謷然不屑意	Yet he maintained his high-mindedness and not worrying,
86	元氣貯肝鬲	Keeping his primordial breath in his liver and diaphragm.
87	往往遊不歸	Occasionally, he roamed and did not return on time.
88	洞中觀博弈	Inside a grotto he watched others playing chess.
89	言高未易信	His language was so pretentious that it was hard to believe.
90	尤復加訶責	And yet, they heaped scorn and blame on him.
91	一旦前致辭	One morning, he gave a speech,
92	自云仙期迫	Saying: "My time of transcendence is approaching."
93	言師有道骨	He told his teacher: "I have bones of the transcendents,
94	前事常被謫	"But because of some matters in my past I was once banished.
95	如今三山上	"Now, on the Three Mountains of Transcendents,
96	名字在真籍	"My name is on the register of the Perfected Beings."
97	悠然謝主人	At ease, he bade farewell to his patron:

---

35   For a detailed discussion of Liu's political thought, see Anthony DeBlasi, *Reform in the Balance*, 86–91.

98	後歲當來覲	"In a few years I shall come back to see you."
99	言畢依庭樹	This said, he went towards a tree in the courtyard,
100	如煙去無跡	Leaving without a trace, like a wisp of smoke.
101	觀者皆失次	All those who witnessed this became disorderly,
102	驚追紛絡繹	Amazed and astonished, chasing in all directions.
103	日莫山逕窮	At sunset, they searched the mountain trails.
104	松風自蕭槭	Winds on pine trees were soughing and sweeping.
105	適逢修蛇見	At that very moment, a long snake was spotted.
106	瞋目光激射	The glare of its gazing eyes was sharp and shining,
107	如嚴三清居	As though on guard for the Three Clarities palaces,
108	不使恣搜索	Not allowing anyone to haphazardly search and seek.
109	唯餘步綱勢	There only remained the phalanxes of Star Pacing—
110	八趾在沙礫	Eight footprints were on the sand and pebbles.
111	至今東北隅	Nowadays, at the northeast corner [of the site],
112	表以壇上石	A stone slab at the altar records the incident.
113	列仙徒有名	The roster of transcendents merely lists their names;
114	世人非目擊	People of the world did not see this in their eyes.
115	如何庭廡際	How would it have happened in that courtyard?
116	白日振飛翮	Under broad sunlight he flapped his soaring wings;
117	洞天豈幽遠	How obscure and distant was the grotto-heaven?
118	得道如咫尺	His attainment of the Way was scarcely an inch away.
119	一氣無死生	The one prime breath, be it for the dead or living,
120	三光自遷易	With the Three Brightnesses they mutated on their own.

A self-referencing, allegorical reading of this lore may be established on the basis of the similar life stories of Qu Boting and the poet. These similarities include that they were both gifted figures who once studied with a great master, they offended people with their eloquence, and they were estranged from the powerful majority.[36] The text of the Qu Boting story, according to Liu's poem, was inscribed on a stone slab at the site (ll. 112–13). This version must have been based on Fu Zai's, in which the episode on Qu being bullied (l. 84) is not mentioned. Liu might have personalized his version of the tale in order to fit his own situation; otherwise, it would have been a variant of the received version seen only by Liu.

---

36 The earlier version of the Qu Boting story is Fu Zai 符載 (fl. 780), "Huang xianshi Qu Tong ji" 黃仙師瞿童記, in *Wenyuan yinghua*, 822.8b–10b; *Quan Tangwen*, 689.9a–11b. Other important sources about the life of Qu Boting include: Wen Zao 溫造 (766–835), "Qu Tong shu" 瞿童述, in Wu Shu 吳淑 (10th c.), *Jiang-Huai yiren lu* 江淮異人錄 (HY 595), 21b–25b; Lu Zhao 盧肇, "Qu daoshi" 瞿道士, in *TPGJ*, 45.281–82, quoting *Yishi* 逸史. In this latter account, Qu is recorded to be lazy and was often whipped by his teacher, Huang. A general, comprehensive study of Qu Boting is Bai Zhaojie, "Qu Boting."

Liu Yuxi taking Qu as his model justifies allegorization of the peach blossom spring adventures. Fu Zai relates that Qu Boting often roamed by himself to the brooks and grotto in this very region, where Tao Qian's tale was set, and did not return until a few days later.[37] He was chided by his master, Huang Dongyuan 黃洞元 (d. 802), but replied: "By chance I visited a nice place where I met the divinities and saw the cloud pneuma, grasses and trees, houses, and food and drink. These made me feel calm and forget about other feelings, and no longer enjoy where I formerly stayed."[38] In Liu's poetic version, this extraordinary capability of Qu did not attract public admiration but rather distrust and blame (ll. 89–90). Without being recognized in his mortal life, Qu ended up achieving transcendence. Only then did people believe in the lad's divine status. Liu Yuxi asserts: "People of the world would not see this in [the transcendents'] eyes" (l. 114, *muji* 目擊). This statement might have been intended as a direct response to Han Yu, who also posts a question about what was "witnessed" (*yanjian* 眼見) at that time (l. 25 of Han's poem, quoted above). If this is the case, Liu may intend to show Han another example of the unreliability of "eyewitnesses" in matters of character. Nonetheless, the two merged personae, Liu and Qu, bifurcate again in this particular context: the poet has now "returned" to reality, as he cannot match Qu Boting in his divinity and transcendence, despite his eagerness to do so.

In Liu's poem, the image of the "long snake" (l. 105) may have been intended as another response to Han Yu. Instead of referring to the Liu Bang story, Liu depicts the scene after Qu transcended, when a serpent blocked people from chasing after Qu. This treatment, again, reflects Liu's interest in what Han Yu would regard as "absurd and unsound," but Liu enjoys telling the wonder of Qu Boting, which becomes a vehicle for his autobiographical poetics.

Although not referred to explicitly in the poem, the following episode on Qu Boting in Fu Zai's record might have been a key motive for Liu to liken himself to Qu.

> Later, [Huang Dongyuan, teacher of Qu] took [Qu] to a marketplace in Xiangyang. Amidst the hustle and bustle of the crowd, Qu closed his eyes and would not look at anything. His appearance was as though he was badly drunk. When they returned to the hostel, he sobered up after the night passed. Huang then asked for the reason. Qu cupped his hands as he replied, "The Grand Simplicity has long scattered and decayed. People of today wear round hats and square shoes but vie to deceive each other

---

37 For details of this locale and other related information on Qu Boting, see Mark Meulenbeld, "The Peach Blossom Spring's Long History," 32–34.
38 Fu Zai, "Huang xianshi Qu Tong ji," 8b–9a.

and to make profit from each other. These are what I cannot tolerate." Huang was then greatly astonished by what he just said and dared not treat him as an ordinary servant.

[黃洞元]後領[瞿童]至襄陽市闤闠之下，齊人浩擾，則瞑目不視。神氣醉泥。返至逆旅，通宵而後醒。問其故，捧手對曰：「太樸散壞者久矣。今之人圓冠方履，以詐相尚，以利相市，余所不堪。」方大駭其說，不敢以常僕僕之。[39]

When Qu Boting told people at the Daoist abbey that his time for transcendence was approaching, no one would believe him. Zhu Lingbian 朱靈辨, a Daoist adept there, was especially suspicious and said, "This lad looks frightened. He must have been assaulted by some evils." He then planned to exorcise them with tallies of cinnabar writing.[40] The final transcendence of Qu Boting dumbfounded everyone who witnessed it. There are no direct parallels between Qu Boting's and Liu Yuxi's social circumstances, but Qu's distaste with widespread deception was likely a feeling Liu identified with. Why else would Liu bother to give such a full account of Qu with emphasis on the onlookers' astonishment?[41] The poet, in weaving Qu's story into his autobiographical poem, invites his reader to compare him to Qu.

This reading of the narrative about Qu Boting as a reflection of the poet himself finds further support in the next stanza, which begins with a line: "Thereupon, I brood upon the human world" (l. 121). This kind of transition is not necessarily allegorical, but this reading may find support in that allegory and metaphor are dominant features in his songs on various subjects such as mosquitos, kite, bush warblers (*baishe* 百舌), fireflies, cranes, etc. dated from his ten-year stay in Langzhou.[42] His discovery that Qu Boting's fantastic biography resembled his own would have presented an irresistible poetic inspiration. Liu's contemplation on life is positioned at the transition between his Qu Boting account and a narration of his own predicament:

127	性靜本同和	Their inner nature was at first balanced and harmonious.
128	物牽成阻厄	Entangled by things, there were obstacles and disasters.
129	是非鬥方寸	Right and wrong battle in the square-inch heart;

---

39 Fu Zai, "Huang xianshi Qu Tong ji," 9a.
40 Ibid., 9a/b.
41 Sunayama Minoru argues that the incident must have come as a shock for Liu, who had long believed in "facts." See Sunayama, "Ku Dō tōsen kō," 11.
42 Bian Xiaoxuan, *Liu Yuxi nianpu*, 78. These songs include: "Juwen yao," "Baishe yin," "Feiyuan cao," and "Qiuying yin," *LYXJ*, 21.579–84.

130	葷血昏精魄	Meat and blood bewildered the essential *po*-soul.
131	遂令多夭傷	Consequently, many die young and many are harmed;
132	猶喜見斑白	One would feel glad to see one's own hoary, white hair.
133	喧喧車馬馳	Clamorous and tumultuous, the rushing chariots and horses;
134	苒苒桑榆夕	Luxuriant and exuberant are mulberry and elm trees of dusk.
135	共安緹繡榮	People all enjoy the honor of brown silk embroidery;
136	不悟泥途適	But do not understand the comfort of the muddy path.

The secular picture of Liu's rumination on his political struggles marks a smooth transition from Qu Boting's story to the poet's. Like Qu, who disdains the filth of the world and the loss of its simplicity, the poet ascribes his struggles to the same causes (ll. 122–24). Liu's placement of Qu Boting's story immediately before a review of his early life suggests that he takes Qu as his model. This long section (ll. 137–74) on Liu's early life, noble-mindedness, and his political goals marks a sharp contrast to the realm of transcendence and forms an irony: an able statesman has now met with misfortune. This irony unveils to the reader the absurdity of the human world and, in fact, supplements the comparison of himself and Qu Boting. With no surprise, Qu Yuan, again, becomes a phantom representation of his lamentation and fear (l. 163). In the closing section, the poet-persona again claims to emulate Qu Boting in his transcendence. This fluctuation confuses readers in identifying his real "paradise": the poem ends with a plan to stay in the peach blossom spring, a resolution in contrast to the fisherman's choice of returning to the mortal world. The poet-persona realizes how helpless he is, as his return to the political world has now become impossible.

His pledge to remain in the transcendent realm (i.e., remain away from the capital) appears to go against Han Yu's poetic advice that Liu should re-enter the mortal (political) world. Liu's fluctuation between wishing to leave and to stay reflects his intense introspection about his career, a process leading the poet to new enlightenment: when he finds himself unable to transcend like Qu Boting, the peach blossom spring becomes an unwanted "paradise." Then, when he finds himself stranded in this undesired fantasy realm he begins constructing his own customized paradise. Here, he is free from anxiety as he is not involved in politics; he may teach here and enjoy roaming with and learning from Daoist figures. This kind of contentment finds its parallel in the writings of Han Yu and Liu Zongyuan, two outcasts from the same background.[43]

---

43 See Madeline Spring, "T'ang Landscapes of Exile," 319–20.

Han and Liu's method of enjoying the awe-inspiring yet threatening landscape is to appropriate it in their writing and alter its meaning to suit their purposes. Liu Yuxi constructs his own paradise by building some structures in Wuling, including a bower called North Pavilion of Wuling, and a vihāra, where he can teach and enjoy life through reliance on Daoist philosophy and alchemical practice (ll. 181–82).[44] In addition to alluding to the classics such as the *Zuozhuan* and *Zhuangzi*, Liu addresses Tao Qian's reclusive poetry by borrowing Tao's imagery, namely the clamorous chariots and the mulberry and elm trees (ll. 133–34).[45]

Although the painting entitled "Taoyuan tu" is no longer extant, Han Yu's poem by the same title yields hints at its likeness and its intended meaning as a portrait of "the one in Wuling." In Liu Yuxi's "Hundred Rhymes," the poet seems to address some of Han's views and to echo some of his expressions and allusions, leading us to read Liu's "Hundred Rhymes" as a response to Han Yu's poem. The two poems may be read as a conversation. Liu's poem presents a complete picture of how the banished poet struggles, reminiscences about his painful experience by comparing it with those in the life of Qu Boting, and his resolution to stay in this ironical wonderland as he realizes that, at least for the time being, there is no way to get out of it.

5 The Frustrated Fisherman

Liu Yuxi's feigned contentment during his stay in Langzhou may thus be seen as the result of a psychological compromise. In his poems on the peach blossom spring, the role of the fisherman differs from that in other works inspired by the same legend. The fisherman character, with its rich political undertones, is ubiquitous in early to medieval literature as well as in Tang literature. In most of these literary references, the literary role of the peach blossom spring fisherman corresponds to a mode I refer to as "fishermanism," and always carries specific political undertones.[46] The portrayed high-mindedness of the fisherman in these works derives principally from the *Chuci*, in which he appears as a paradoxical recluse eager to be known by others. Literary references to the fisherman also invoke Lü Shang 呂尚 (12th c.–11th c. BC), also known as Jiang Ziya 姜子牙. In mid-Tang times, the fisherman is a common character in

---

44 See Liu, "Wuling Beiting ji" 武陵北亭記, *LYXJ*, 9.232–34, in which he details the use of construction materials allegorically referring to how his "talents" (*cai* 才), a pun on "timber" 材, were misused and are now reused in his quiet life in Wuling.
45 See Tao Qian, "Yinjiu" no. 5, "Gui yuantian ju" nos. 1 and 2, in *Tao Yuanming ji*, 3.89, 2.40.
46 Chan, *Considering the End*, 187–207.

the exile poems of Liu Zongyuan, who uses this prototype fisherman Jiang to express a wish to be promoted, just as Jiang was awaiting his patron King Wen of the Zhou Kingdom (12th–11th c. BC).[47]

While Liu Yuxi's fisherman conceit is like that in the *Chuci*, it clearly incorporates new elements. Liu's expression of frustration through the fisherman conceit is catalyzed by Tao Qian's peach blossom spring fantasy. The following poem well exemplifies his attitude towards the fisherman reference. This piece was also written during his exile in Wuling.

	晚歲登武陵城顧望水陸悵然有作	"At Year's End, I Ascended the Walls of Wuling, Looked around at the Waters and Lands, Felt the Onset of Melancholy, and Composed This"[48]
1	星象承烏翼	The starry simulacra sustain the Crow's Wings;[49]
2	蠻陬想犬牙	This corner of the Man region reminds me of dog's teeth.[50]
3	俚人祠竹節	The local people worship the God of Bamboo Nodes.[51]
4	仙洞閉桃花	The grotto of transcendence is shrouded by peach blossoms.
5	城基歷漢魏	The foundations of these walls survived the Han and Wei.
6	江源自賨巴	Its river's source flows from the regions of Cong and Ba.
7	華表廖王墓	A splendid monument marks the tomb of King Liao;[52]
8	菜地黃瓊家	The vegetable field used to be the residence of Huang Qiong.[53]
9	霜輕菊秀晚	The frost is light and chrysanthemums bloom late.

---

47 See William Nienhauser, jr., "Floating Clouds and Dreams," 174–75.
48 *LYXJ*, 25.757–58; *QTS*, 362.4089.
49 The locale of Wuling is within the "apportioned champaign" (*fenye* 分野) of Crow's Wing (Yi 翼), one of the twenty-eight constellations. See *Liu Yuxi quanji biannian jiaozhu*, 178, n. 2. For Yi and the English translation of *fenye*, see Edward Schafer, *Pacing the Void*, 75; a table of "Important Starry Chronograms" is in ibid., 76–77. For a diagram and theories of Yi, see Gustave Schlegel, *Uranographie chinoise*, 466–69.
50 The "dog's teeth" is a description of the terrain, which forms a zigzag pattern. The phrase was first used in *Shiji*, 10.413: the feudal kings of Emperor Gaozu were placed in fiefs arrayed like dog's teeth so they could restrain each other.
51 An ancient ruler of Yelang 夜郎 (in modern southwestern China), named God of Bamboo King the Third 竹王三郎神. When he was a baby, he was wrapped inside the bamboo nodes and sent to a laundry lady by the river. See *HHS*, 86.2844.
52 Liao Li 廖立, a native of Wuling, served the Shu Kingdom during the Three Kingdoms era.
53 This figure may be Huang Xie 黃歇 (d. 238 BC), who is better known as Lord Chenshen 春申君 and was buried in Wuling. See *Liu Yuxi quanji biannian jiaozhu*, 178–79, n. 9.

10	石淺水紋斜	Pebbles are under shallow water and ripples angle away.
11	樵音繞故壘	The woodcutters' singing circles the old ramparts.
12	汲路明寒沙	The road to fetch water turns clear in cold sands.
13	清風稍改葉	Pure breezes slightly change the color of leaves;
14	盧橘始含葩	The Lu tangerine trees have just begun blossoming.
15	野橋過驛騎	On the wild bridge, a postal horseman passes.
16	叢祠發迴笳	In the shrine echoes pipe music from afar.
17	跳鱗避舉網	The jumping fins flee the raised nets.
18	倦鳥寄行槎	The weary birds perch on moving boats.
19	路塵高出樹	Dust on the road rises higher than treetops.
20	山火遠連霞	Hill fire stretches far to join the auroras.
21	夕曛轉赤岸	Evening sun rays go around the red banks.
22	浮靄起蒼葭	Floating mists loom in the greenish reeds.
23	軋軋渡水槳	Slap slap go the ferrying oars.
24	連連赴林鴉	Countless crows flock ceaselessly to the woods.
25	叫閽道非遠	The road to call at the palace gate is not too far away,
26	賜環期自賒	The time of bestowing a circular jade-disc is itself belated.[54]
27	孤臣本危涕	The forlorn subject has long been shedding tears,
28	喬木在天涯	And the tall trees are now on the edge of the sky.[55]

Just like the poet's selection of certain historical references in his "Writing My Inner Feelings in Wuling in Fifty Rhymes" (discussed above) to represent his frustration, this poem shares this same feature but plays more with the evocative natural imagery. The natural scene, passage of time, and the tears identify the poem as a "reminiscence of the past" (*huaigu* 懷古).[56] The poem's tension comes mainly from the interplay of the poet's self-pity with elements of grotto fantasy, signaled clearly in the peach blossom spring reference in line four. This interplay pushes the poet to travel to the past and back to the present. The grotto enables passage to Qin times, symbolizing a respite from politics (as discussed above), but the poet refuses to stay there. The historical relics (ll. 1–8)

---

54 The word *huan* 環 is a homophonic pun for *huan* 還, return. The bestowal of a *huan* disc refers to a decree summoning back an official who has been away. Its opposite is the *jue* 玦 disc, which has a segment cut to indicate "separation" (*jue* 訣). See *Xunzi*, 17.322, Yang Liang's 楊倞 (fl. early 9th c.) commentary.

55 The tall trees are a kenning for the loyal subject. See *Mengzi*, 1B.7; trans., D. C. Lau, *Mencius*, 67.

56 Hans Frankel sums up "six topoi" that are "associated with the evocation of the past in other T'ang poems." See Frankel, "Contemplation of the past in T'ang poetry," 347–53, et passim.

are all but history. From line thirteen on, the seasonal changes and gazing provoke the poet's emotional attachment to the capital. The fish and birds are images laden with rich, symbolic meanings that owe much to Tao Qian's use of them; they now take a leap from history to Liu's own time. These provocative images retain their symbolism because Liu, like Tao, met with misfortune in his career and "retreated" from the outside world.

The poem's theme of involuntary retreat interplays with the natural landscapes. The point of view in the poet's gazing starts from high and far, to treetops, hills, mist, and finally lands upon the boat. The boat crossing the river (l. 23) does not take the fisherman to roam the river or to the peach blossom spring, but rather it returns him to the capital. The poet jumps from natural landscape to textual allusion and uses two poetic images that intensify his eagerness to return. The first one is the circular jade disc (l. 26). The Chinese term *huan* is homophonous with "return" and is traditionally used as a token by the emperor to summon the banished subject. The second image is the tall trees. It refers to one's home state, i.e., the capital.[57]

The historic peach blossom spring in Liu's representation intensifies the poet's concerns about his displacement in both time and space. The seasonal changes just discussed and the movements of the sun, auroras, trees, and animals create a vivid scene colored by the poet's sense of the passing of time. His poetic tour of local history and legend calls attention to their presence and immediacy, but in his references to the "Ballad of the Peach Blossom Spring" the effect is reversed, serving to communicate a great depth of anxiety over his estrangement from the political center for so long. The phrase "calling at the imperial gate" (*jiao hun* 叫閽; l. 25) is not merely a borrowed phrase from the "Lisao,"[58] it merges the poet-persona's concerns with those of Qu Yuan. This allusion triggers imaginary flights in search of a model in history: the protagonist in the "Lisao" calls at the imperial gate in heaven after failed attempts on earth; Liu's flight to this legendary locale would only further distance him, in time and space, because he envisions no fixed date for his return to the capital. Liu's sentiment undergoes a catalysis because Qu Yuan was in exile to this same region for the very same reason. The poet combines his fantasy with Qu Yuan's frustration in this expression of his eagerness to return to *his* iconic paradise from *this* ironic paradise.

---

57 The image of tall trees as a synecdoche for one's hometown is earlier seen in Jiang Yan 江淹 (444–505), "Bie fu" 別賦, *WX*, 16.29b.
58 See *CCBZ*, 1.29; trans., David Hawkes, *The Songs of the South*, 74.

6   Gentleman Liu's Travel in Time and Space

Liu Yuxi's self-pity over his displacement from the capital caused him great anxiety during his sojourns in Wuling, and this sentiment continued to haunt him even after his exile was revoked and he returned to the capital. This entire period of banishment to the Peach Blossom Spring embodies sarcasm. To most others, it is a locale of fantasy; Liu may treat it as an asylum but an unwanted one. His identification with the fisherman visiting the peach blossom spring was partly triggered by the poet's physical proximity to this legendary location. In his post-Wuling life, Liu's identification with Liu Chen, the main character in the Liu-Ruan tale, continued as did his poetic reliance on the peach blossom spring, but the effect of these allusions changed significantly. In the pages below we shall follow the poet as he is reprieved from his banishment and leaves Wuling, and we consider how he turns his references to the Liu-Ruan tale into political satire.

Let us first look at the transition from his decade-long stay in Wuling, when an imperial order was announced to call back the eight adjutants.[59] In a poem written on this occasion, Liu expressed excitement about his long-desired return to the capital:

元和甲午歲詔書盡徵江湘逐客，余自武陵赴京，宿於都亭，有懷續來諸君子。	In the Jiawu Year of the Yuanhe Reign-period (815), an Edict was Issued to Summon back all the Banished Officials. On My Way to the Capital from Wuling, I Stayed at a Municipal Hostel, Thinking of the Other Gentlemen who Would Continuously Arrive.
雲雨江湘起臥龍	Amidst clouds and rain on the Jiang and Xiang Rivers the reposing dragons rise.
武陵樵客躡仙蹤	The firewood gatherer of Wuling has been tracing the whereabouts of the transcendents.
十年楚水楓林下	For ten years, I have lived by the Chu Rivers and under maple groves.
今夜初聞長樂鐘	This evening, for the first time I hear the bell tolling at the Palace of Everlasting Joy.[60]

---

59   See note 5 above for details about the eight, including the rationale behind their banishment.
60   *LYXJ*, 24.698, *QTS*, 365.4116.

The Peach Blossom Spring tale is told as a pleasant fantasy in the hands of Tao Qian and Wang Wei, but as a figure of bitter experience by Liu Yuxi. This poem removes the disguise of contentment the poet wore in "Hundred Rhymes." The "reposing dragon" (l. 1) is a sobriquet of Zhuge Liang 諸葛亮 (181–234), the famous statesman of late Han times, who is now singled out as a model of Liu Yuxi and his banished colleagues, as he had been living in reclusion until he was invited and promoted by Liu Bei 劉備 (161–223) to act as his assistant and later as Prime Minister of the Shu Han Kingdom. The term "clouds and rain" in this kind of context usually refers to the showering down of imperial favor.[61] In the next line, the poet plays with "tracing the whereabouts of the transcendents" because it marks a shift from his pursuit of the mythological realm of an ideal society—a solace for the setbacks he had experienced back in the capital—to a return to a real political life after a decade of absence. If the poem is read on its literal level, the term "clouds and rain" describes the gloominess of the South and the emotion of being banished. The "tracing" refers only to Liu Yuxi's sauntering in this homeland of the transcendents. Now he will have finally managed to leave this unwanted false paradise, Wuling, as he has his own transcendent realm to pursue. The allusion to Zhuge Liang also reveals the poet's view of the current Tang court. When Liu Bei visited Zhuge at his thatched hut, the warlord cast the political situation in stark terms: "The Han royal house has been collapsing. Disloyal officials have stolen the mandate and our superior ruler has been covered by dust."[62] Zhuge's acceptance of the offer means that he has resolved to restore the order to the legitimate regime and to eradicate the usurpers. To Liu Yuxi, the rise of his former colleagues in this group of "reposing dragons" has the same goals he hopes to achieve. They are now ready for the mission.

As the poet journeyed away from Wuling, he found a new grove of peach trees at the Mysterious Capital Abbey (Xuandu guan 玄都觀), which he treats as a mirage of the peach blossom spring. This particular abbey, located in "a locale of great royal significance," according to Victor Xiong, served "to suppress potential challenges to the throne" since it was relocated and renamed in 582.[63] In addition, the paradoxical notion of the capital as a paradise is evident in this poem,[64] in which the poet again plays the role of Liu Chen, but with a satirical effect.

---

61   See *HHS*, 16.613, quoting Deng Zhi's 鄧騭 (d. 121) memorial.
62   *Sanguo zhi*, 35.912.
63   See Xiong, *Sui-Tang Chang'an*, 235, 250, 297.
64   The capital symbolizes career success, which in turn has been often represented in terms of achievements in religious transcendence since the early and high Tang times. See Chan,

元和十一年自朗州召至京戲贈看花諸君子	"To the Gentlemen who Viewed the Flowers, Written in a Playful Manner in the Eleventh Year of the Yuanhe Reign-period (816) when I was Summoned by an Imperial Command back to the Capital from Langzhou"
紫陌紅塵拂面來	On the purple country paths, red dust caresses the faces.
無人不道看花回	No one says that they did not return from seeing flowers.
玄都觀裏桃千樹	The one thousand peach trees at Mysterious Capital Abbey
盡是劉郎去後栽	Were all planted after Gentleman Liu was gone.[65]

Two images—the peach trees and the fellow named Liu—strongly suggest the *Youming lu* tale of Liu Chen and Ruan Zhao as the archetype of this poem. In this adaptation, however, this Gentleman Liu makes his way back not to a mundane reality, but rather to a realm of immortals marked by metaphorical peach trees.[66] This reversal of the spatiotemporal displacement theme in the Liu-Ruan tale relies on the poet's obsession with *his* paradise, namely the capital to which he has long hoped to return. Ironically, in this center of political power, Gentleman Liu only finds newly cultivated politicians. This is the realization of the worries of the fisherman of Wuling: getting trapped in the Wuling peach blossom spring for too long, resulting in the loss of the real paradise he longs for. The sarcastic tone in the last line is ominous. This poem has been said to be responsible for Liu's ensuing banishment shortly after his return because it offended some powerful officials who saw themselves criticized as the "tree planters."[67]

Fourteen years later, Liu again returned from another banishment, visited the Mysterious Capital Abbey again, and wrote another quatrain, which is preceded by a preface:

"Yujingshan Chaohui," 18–23; "The Transcendent of Poetry's Quest for Transcendence," 218–19.

65 *LYXJ*, 24.702; *QTS*, 365.4116.
66 See Stephen Owen, *The Late Tang*, 76.
67 *Benshi shi*, 12; trans., Howard S. Levy, "The Original Incidents of Poems," 23. See also Graham Senders' translation and discussion in his *Words Well Put*, 234–35.

余貞元二十一年為屯田員外郎時，此觀未有花。是歲出牧連州，尋貶朗州司馬。居十年，召至京師，人人言，有道士手植仙桃，滿觀如紅霞，遂有前篇以志一時事。旋又出牧，今十有四年，復為主客郎中。重遊玄都觀，蕩然無復一樹，唯兔葵燕麥動搖於春風耳。因再題二十八字，以俟後遊，時大和二年三月。	In the twenty-first year of the Zhenyuan reign-period (805), when I was Vice Director of the State Farms Bureau, there were no flowers in this abbey. In that year I went out to become Prefect of Lianzhou, but was later demoted to be Adjutant of Langzhou. I stayed there for ten years before I was summoned back to the capital. Everyone said that a Daoist priest planted transcendent peach trees and the entire abbey seemed to have been tinted in auroral hues. So, I wrote that previous poem to record what happened then. Soon after that, I became a regional prefect again. Fourteen years later, I returned as Director of the Bureau of Reception. When I revisited the Mysterious Capital Abbey, I found not a single [peach] tree but only hare mallow and oat waving in spring breezes. Thus, I wrote another 28-word poem for my new visit. The time now is the third month of the second year of the Dahe reign-period (828).
百畝庭中半是苔	In the hundred-acre courtyard half is covered by moss.
桃花淨盡菜花開	Peach flowers are completely gone, while rapeseed flowers bloom.
種桃道士歸何處	Where is the Daoist adept who planted the peach trees?
前度劉郎今又來	Gentleman Liu of the past has returned.[68]

In this sequel poem, our poet Liu, again, personalizes the Liu-Ruan tale. These changes in the capital he describes are so drastic that most commentators do not bother tracing the allusion but instead pay attention to the surface meaning of the poem as political satire.[69] The "Daoist adept" is not found in the *Youming lu* narrative but now plays a pivotal role in the poem. The metaphorical site of this Daoist abbey needs a character such as the planter of the peach blossoms. The preface relates that the trees were planted when Liu returned to the capital from Langzhou. Then, as these peach blossoms flourished and

---

68 *LYXJ*, 24.703–4; *QTS*, 365.4116.
69 See, e.g., Chen Bohai, *Tangshi huiping*, 1842–43, quoting various sources; Shang Yongliang, *Tang Wudai zhuchen*, 355–56.

as Liu was so outspoken about them (as seen in the last poem just quoted), his enemies took it as an offense and quickly removed him. But now, in the new political landscape, the blossoms are all gone and there are rapeseeed flowers instead, while the Daoist adept is nowhere to be found. His fourteen years of banishment had changed things beyond recognition. Unlike Liu Chen and Ruan Zhao who returned to their home, the poet now makes a return to *his former paradise*, but the peach blossoms had undergone the process of being planted, blooming, and disappearing. This process outlines Liu's reaction to the political changes he experienced.

The political turmoil of the early ninth century was traumatic for this generation of literati, and Liu Yuxi was not an exception. In the same year of 828 when he wrote his second poem on the Mysterious Capital Abbey, Liu, who by then had assumed the sobriquet of Gentleman Liu 劉郎,[70] joined a gathering at Apricot Garden 杏園 in Chang'an organized by Bai Juyi. Bai starts with his gift poem for Liu Yuxi:

杏園花下贈劉郎中	"Beneath the Flowers in Apricot Garden, Presented to Gentleman Liu"
怪君把酒偏惆悵	How strange that you look troubled even with a cup of wine in hand.
曾是貞元花下人	You were one of those under the flowers of the Zhenyuan era.
自別花來多少事	Since you left those flowers how many events have taken place?
東風二十四迴春	The east wind has returned for twenty-four spring seasons.[71]

Bai's poem is a painful reminder of Liu Yuxi's twenty-four years of banishment discussed in this chapter. This kind of poetic representation reminds one of Demodokos's singing of Odysseus's years of his wandering life when the hero was in Scheria and, upon hearing his own sad stories, he "melted, and from under his eyes the tears ran down, drenching his cheeks."[72] Likewise, Liu must have been overwhelmed by this kind of review of his bitter life experience.

---

[70] This sobriquet is seen in Bai Juyi's poem written in 825 in Liyang 歷陽 (in modern Anhui province) in response to Liu's, in which Bai alludes to Liu Chen's adventure to Mount Tiantai. See Bai, "Chou Liu Hezhou xizeng" 酬劉和州戲贈, *BJYJJ*, 27.1910, 24.1648; *QTS*, 447.5026.

[71] *BJYJJ*, 1756.

[72] Lattimore, *The Odyssey of Homer*, 8.520–22 (p. 134).

Bai's mention of the flowers of the apricot tree becomes a reminder of Liu's suffering and a tally of the years of Liu's absence.

During the same gathering, only Yuan Zhen' poetic contribution also refers to a Gentlemen Liu, flowers (not peach blossoms, though), the passage of time, and the season of spring. The other contributions written at the gathering all deal with the same images surrounding the Gentleman Liu, but do so without invoking the full resonance of the Liu-Ruan tale.[73] Yuan plays with Liu's official title ("Liu Langzhong") in Bai's poem and shortens it to "Liulang." His poem reads:

酬白樂天杏花園	"In Response to Bai Letian's Poem, The Garden of Apricot Blossoms"
劉郎不用閑惆悵	Gentleman Liu needs not feel lonely and troubled,
且作花間共醉人	For now, just join the tipsy ones among the flowers.
算得貞元舊朝士	Adding up the old officials of the Zhenyuan reign,
幾人同見太和春	How many can together see the Taihe era's spring?[74]

Yuan's poem continues Bai's sympathy and takes an optimistic turn to celebrate Liu Yuxi's survival of his twenty-four-year ordeal. Unlike Liu Chen, however, this Gentleman Liu has traveled on a normal, mortal timeline on which he has been politically and geographically displaced for twenty-four years. In addition, this Gentleman Liu has returned from the grotto to find a happy ending rather than tragedy. Yuan implies that Liu Yuxi has survived his displacement, returned to find friends, and therefore should enjoy drinking with them under the flowers at *this* moment. As a lover of the Liu-Ruan tale (see Chapter 2), Yuan has thus incorporated his own vicissitudes into his sympathy of Liu Yuxi in this gathering of middle-aged colleagues.[75]

---

73   See Bian Xiaoxuan, *Liu Yuxi nianpu*, 145–46. Liu's responsive poem is titled "Xingyuan huaxia chou Letian jianzeng" 杏園花下酬樂天見贈, in *LYXJ*, "waiji," 1.1081; *QTS*, 365.4122. Other poems in response to Bai's by Zhang Ji 張籍 (766–830) and Linghu Chu 令狐楚 (766–837) respectively are in *QTS*, 386.4358, 334.3751.

74   *YZJJZ*, xu buyi, 2.1597.

75   Anna Shields points out that Yuan "responds to Bai's poem more wryly, with a contrast between the promise of the Zhenyuan era, when all four men had passed the *jinshi* or the *mingjing* examinations, and the changed world of the Taihe reign." See Shields, *One Who Knows Me*, 136.

7 Conclusion

Liu Yuxi's political banishment from "home" spurred him to identify with Liu Chen, the fisherman, and Qu Boting. In so doing, Liu Yuxi succeeds in creating an idiosyncratic self-image. The painting of Wuling provided him and Han Yu with a platform for poetic compositions on the legendary transcendent realm first created by Tao Qian. Han and Liu each enhance the realm with new, personal elements in this conversation. The two men had different views on exile, but both referred to the same historical events that brought Liu into disfavor and caused his banishment to Wuling. In the eyes of these poet-officials, the Wuling peach blossom spring symbolizes but a temporary haven, not a long-term residence.

The ways Liu Yuxi recast the peach spring represent a formative contribution to the evolution of the Liu-Ruan tale. The grotto fantasy tradition he inherited emphasized the mythical and romantic/erotic themes of the Liu-Ruan tale, as well as the didactic implications, as represented in the poetry of Yuan Zhen and Bai Juyi. Liu Yuxi's adaptations embody the sense of alienation and isolation that came from a turbulent political life. In his versions of Gentleman Liu's adventures, written upon his return to the capital from exile, political satire is the most important layer of the stratum of grotto romance themes. In this context, the Tao Qian grotto adventure finds no place to exert its influence. In adapting the Liu-Ruan tale, however, Liu's interests sublimate the amorous themes, and the lady protagonist and her various alternate roles is not prominent in Liu's work. Instead, he plays with the motif of time displacement in his satirical poetics on the changes in the political landscape in the capital, fashioning a highly personal image within the political picture of the time.

Appendix

劉禹錫：遊桃源一百韻	Liu Yuxi, "An Excursion to the Peach Blossom Spring, in One Hundred Rhymes"[76]
1　沅江清悠悠	The Yuan River is limpid and flowing freely
2　連山鬱岑寂[77]	Along the exuberant ridges, silently and serenely.
3　回流抱絕巘	The whirling currents embrace the towering peaks.
4　皎鏡含虛碧	The lustrous mirror envelops hues of tenuous cyan.

76　*LYXJ*, 23.653–55; *QTS*, 355.3980–81.
77　*LYXJ* has 日 for 山; I adopt the latter, according to *Liu Mengde wenji*, 1.6a.

5	昏旦遞明媚	Dusk and dawn take turns in brilliance and coquetry.
6	煙嵐分委積	Mist and vapor separately assemble and accumulate.
7	香蔓垂綠潭	Fragrant vines droop alongside the Green Tarn.
8	暴龍照孤磧	The Ferocious Dragon is refracted in the lone gravel.[78]
9	淵明著前志	Tao Yuanming narrated in a record of the past:
10	子驥思遠蹠	Liu Ziji wanted to set his far-roaming feet herein.
11	寂寂無何鄉	Desolate and isolated, this realm of Nothingwhatsoever—[79]
12	密爾天地隔	So concealed and cut off from heaven and earth.
13	金行太元歲	In the Taiyuan year of the Metal-phase Jin Dynasty,[80]
14	漁者偶探賾	A fisherman accidentally fathomed its profundity.
15	尋花得幽蹤	Following the flowers, he located the obscure trail;
16	窺洞穿闇隙	Peeping at the grotto he went through the dim gaps,
17	依微聞雞犬	He heard faint, faded sounds of roosters and dogs.
18	豁達值阡陌	Then he was faced with the outspread crisscross paths.
19	居人互將迎	The local residents came to receive him.
20	笑語如平昔	Their smiles and colloquies were just like before.
21	廣樂雖交奏	Although extraordinary music was played in unison,
22	海禽心不懌	Like a seabird he felt no pleasure in his heart.[81]
23	揮手一來歸	Waving his hand, resolving to return home,
24	故溪無處覓	This creek of his last visit was nowhere to be found.
25	駸駸五百載	So long since then, five hundred years have passed.
26	市朝幾遷革	Markets and courts have undergone numerous changes.
27	有路在壺中	There is a road leading there inside the magic flagon,[82]
28	無人知地脈	But no one knows how the earthly veins would work.[83]
	***	***
29	皇家感至道	Unto our august royal house was revealed the Ultimate Way,
30	聖祚自天錫	With its sacred sovereignty bestowed by Heaven.
31	金闕傳本枝	Within the gold pylons, they inherited it from root to branches.

---

78   According to the note to the text, Ferocious Dragon is the name of the rock.
79   An allusion to *Zhuangzi*, 1/46: 无何有之鄉; cf. trans., Graham, *Chuang-tzǔ*, 47.
80   February 7, 376–February 12, 397.
81   An allusion to *Zhuangzi*, 18/33–35. The marquis of the state of Lu worshipped a visiting seabird and treated it with fine wine and delicacies. The bird dared not eat or drink and died after three days.
82   An allusion to Fei Changfang's 費長房 acquaintance with Gourd Elder 壺公. See HHS, 82B.2743 and the relevant discussion in Chapter 1 of the present book.
83   Fei Changfang was known to be proficient at this magic called "shrinking the earth's veins" (*suo dimai* 縮地脈). See YWLJ, 72.1243, quoting *Lieyi zhuan*; TPGJ, 12.82, quoting *Shenxian zhuan*. See Chapter 1 of the present book.

32	玉函留寶曆	In the jade casket were preserved the precious almanacs.
33	禁山開祕宇	In these restricted mountains, a mystic structure was built.
34	復戶潔靈宅	The households exempt from tax clean this numinous abode.
35	藥檢香氛氳	The fragrance of flowery book-covers profusely prevails;
36	醮壇煙羃羃	Mist around the sacrificial ritual altar flows and spreads.
	***	***
37	我來塵外躅	I have now set my feet in this realm beyond the dust,
38	瑩若朝醒析	Brilliant as the clearing of a morning hangover.
39	崖轉對翠屏	The cliffs meander, facing cyan-screen peaks,
40	水窮留畫鷁	At the river's source I moored my osprey-patterned boat.
41	三休俯喬木	Hiking with three rests, I then overlooked tall trees;
42	千級攀峭壁	Climbing one thousand steps, I scaled a steep escarpment.
43	旭日聞撞鐘	At twilight, I heard tolling bells;
44	綵雲迎躡屐	Colorful clouds welcomed my hiking shoes.
45	遂登最高頂	Thereupon, I ascended the highest summit,
46	縱目還楚澤	Extending my vision around the Chu Marshes.
47	平湖見草青	By a lucid lake were revealed grasses in their verdancy,
48	遠岸連霞赤	The distant banks were covered with expanses of auroral red.
49	幽尋如夢想	My probes for the hidden were like fantasies and dreams.
50	緜思屬空闃	My endless thoughts were inspired by void and silence.
51	夤緣且忘疲	Creeping and scaling, for now I forgot about tiredness.
52	耽玩近成癖	Indulging myself in playing, I was almost inveterate.
53	清猿伺曉發	Gibbons waited for the dawn to cry out clear jabbers;
54	瑤草凌寒坼	Carnelian plants had overcome cracking coldness.
55	祥禽舞蔥蘢	Propitious birds danced in verdure and vigor.
56	珠樹搖的皪	Pearl trees swayed in glitters and glows.
57	羽人顧我笑	The feathered beings looked back at me and smiled,[84]
58	勸我稅歸軛	Admonishing me to untie my returning carriage's yoke bar.
59	霓裳何飄颻	Their rainbow robes were wavering and fluttering;
60	童顏潔白皙	Their childish countenance, so white and fair.
61	重巖是藩屏	Layered rocks formed their fences and screens.
62	馴鹿受羈靮	Tamed deer were reined and harnessed.
63	樓居邇清霄	Their terrace abodes were near the pure ethereal.
64	蘿蔦成翠帟	Dodder and mulberry air plants made cyan drapes.
65	仙翁遺竹杖	The transcendent elder left behind a bamboo cane.[85]

---

84 The feathered beings are transcendents. See *CCBZ*, 5.167.
85 An allusion to Fei Changfang's adventure. Fei wanted to learn magic from Elder Flagon but worried about his family missing him. The elder gave him a bamboo stick and asked him to hang it at home, symbolizing Fei's body after he was to have hanged himself. When

66	王母留桃核	The Queen Mother of the West kept the peach seed.[86]
67	姹女飛丹砂	The Pretty Girls fly in cinnabar powder;[87]
68	青童護金液	The Azure Lad safeguards the gold nectar.[88]
69	寶氣浮鼎耳	Precious vipers spewed from the cauldron's ears.
70	神光生劍脊	Divine radiance appeared from sword blades.
71	虛無天樂來	From tenuous emptiness, celestial music approached,
72	偠窣鬼兵役	Quietly and secretly, commanding the divine soldiers.
73	丹丘肅朝禮	On the Cinnabar Hills, solemn was the pilgrimage liturgy.
74	玉札工紬繹	The Jade Scriptures were skillfully analyzed and structured.
75	枕中淮南方	Hidden in the pillow were prescriptions by Master Huainan;[89]
76	牀下阜鄉舄	Beneath the bed were the shoes of Anqi sheng from Fuxiang.[90]
77	明燈坐遙夜	Under a bright lamp I reposed through the long night,
78	幽籟聽淅瀝	Listening to profound pipe music, pitter patter.
	***	***
79	因話近世仙	Thereupon we talked about the recent transcendent beings.
80	聳然心神愓	I was startled, alerted in my mind and spirit.
81	乃言瞿氏子	Thereupon, I was told about a lad from the Qu family:[91]
82	骨狀非凡格	His bone structure and bearing were not those of a mortal.
83	往事黃先生	At that time, when he served as a disciple of Master Huang,
84	羣兒多侮劇	Other children always bullied and tricked him,
85	警然不屑意	Yet he maintained his high-mindedness and did not worry,
86	元氣貯肝鬲	Keeping his primordial breath in his liver and diaphragm.
87	往往遊不歸	Occasionally, he roamed and did not return on time.

    Fei completed his learning in the mountains, the elder gave him another bamboo stick and asked Fei to ride on it to return home. When Fei arrived home he cast the stick on the floor and it turned into a dragon. See *HHS*, 82B.2743–44.

86 When Emperor Wu of the Han visited Queen Mother of the West, he was treated to some magic peaches and wanted to save some seeds of the fruit and plant them in the mortal realm. See *Bowu zhi jiaozheng*, 8.97.

87 Pretty Girl is a cryptonym for mercury, an ingredient for refining elixir.

88 The Azure Lad is a god in the Daoist theogony. See Paul W. Kroll, "In the Hall of the Azure Lad."

89 Master Huainan is Liu An 劉安 (179–122 BC), uncle of Emperor Wudi, who was fond of the study of Daoist transcendence and known as the editor of the *Huainanzi*.

90 Anqi sheng 安期生 was said to have lived for a thousand years. The First Emperor of Qin (r. 221–210 BC) once requested an audience with him and bestowed on him thousands of gold discs, but was given a letter and a pair of shoes and was asked to meet him in the mythological Penglai Mountains. The audience took place in Fuxiang. See *Liexian zhuan*, 1.14b–15a.

91 For Qu Boting, see discussion above.

88	洞中觀博弈	Inside a grotto he watched others playing chess.
89	言高未易信	His language was so pretentious that it was hard to believe.
90	尤復加訶責	And so they heaped scorn and blame on him.
91	一旦前致辭	One morning, he gave a speech,
92	自云仙期迫	Saying: "My time of transcendence is approaching."
93	言師有道骨	He told his teacher: "I have bones of the transcendents,
94	前事常被謫	"But, because of some matters in my past, I was once banished.
95	如今三山上	"Now, on the Three Mountains of Transcendents,
96	名字在真籍	"My name is on the register of the Perfected Beings."
97	悠然謝主人	At ease, he bade farewell to his patron:
98	後歲當來覿	"In a few years I shall come back to see you."
99	言畢依庭樹	This said, he went towards a tree in the courtyard,
100	如煙去無跡	Leaving without a trace, like a wisp of smoke.
101	觀者皆失次	All those who witnessed this became disorderly,
102	驚追紛絡繹	Amazed and astonished, chasing in all directions.
103	日莫山逕窮	At sunset, they searched the mountain trails.
104	松風自蕭槭	Winds on pine trees were soughing and sweeping.
105	適逢修蛇見	At that very moment, a long snake was spotted.
106	瞋目光激射	The glare of its gazing eyes was sharp and shining,
107	如嚴三清居	As though on guard for the Three Clarities palaces,
108	不使恣搜索	Not allowing anyone to haphazardly search and seek.
109	唯餘步綱勢	There only remained the phalanxes of Star Pacing—[92]
110	八趾在沙礫	Eight footprints were on the sand and pebbles.
111	至今東北隅	Nowadays at the northeast corner [of the site],
112	表以壇上石	A stone slab at the altar records the incident.
113	列仙徒有名	The roster of transcendents merely lists their names;
114	世人非目擊	People of the world did not see this in their eyes.
115	如何庭廡際	How would it have happened in that courtyard?
116	白日振飛翮	Under broad sunlight he flapped his soaring wings;
117	洞天豈幽遠	How obscure and distant was the grotto-heaven?
118	得道如咫尺	His attainment of the Way was scarcely an inch away.
119	一氣無死生	The one prime breath, be it for the dead or living,
120	三光自遷易	With the Three Brightnesses they mutated on their own.[93]

---

92 *LYXJ* has *bujiang* 步江 ("pacing by the river") instead of *bugang* 綱; I follow *Liu Mengde wenji*, 1.7b, as Pacing the Stars (also written as *bugang* 罡) is a Daoist ritual first known as "paces of Yu" 禹步 transmitted by the mythological king Yu of the Xia dynasty. See *Yunji qiqian* (HY 1026), 61.4b; Edward Schafer, *Pacing the Void*, 239–42.

93 The three brightnesses are the sun, moon, and stars.

	***	***
121	因思人閒世	Thereupon, I brood upon the human world—
122	前路何湫窄	How muddy and narrow is the road ahead.
123	瞥然此生中	So transiently we live within this span of life,
124	善祝期滿百	With good blessings one may live up to a full century.
125	大方播羣類	The Great Square disseminates various kinds of lives.
126	秀氣尚翕闢	Their fluorescent breath resembles shutting and opening.
127	性靜本同和	Their inner nature was originally alike and harmonious.
128	物牽成阻阨	Entangled by things, there were obstacles and mishaps.
129	是非鬭方寸	Right and wrong battle in the square-inch heart;
130	葷血昏精魄	Meat and blood bewilder the essential *po*-soul.
131	遂令多夭傷	Consequently, many die young and many are harmed;
132	猶喜見斑白	One would feel glad to see one's own hoary, white hair.
133	喧喧車馬馳	Clamorously and tumultuously rush the chariots and horses;
134	苒苒桑榆夕	Progressively there come mulberry and elm trees of dusk.
135	共安緹繡榮	People all enjoy the honor of brown silk embroidery,
136	不悟泥途適	But do not understand the comfort of the muddy path.[94]
	***	***
137	紛吾本孤賤	In this world of complexity, I have been alone and lowly.
138	世業在逢掖	My inherited career was in loosened sleeves—Confucianism.
139	九流宗指歸	The Nine Streams of doctrines, I absorbed their main ideas;
140	百氏旁攎摭	The Hundred Schools, I gathered their related learning.
141	公卿偶慰薦	By chance, ministers and chamberlains recommended me;
142	鄉曲謬推擇	By mistake, my home village selected and promoted me.
143	居安白社貧	I lived in poverty at the White Temple but felt contented,[95]
144	志傲玄纁辟	Aspiring to receive black and pink cloth for appointment.
145	功名希自取	Deeds and renown; rarely had I craved them myself;
146	簪組俟揚歷	Hairpins and ribbons were won in recognition of excellence.
147	書府早懷鉛	At the Archive Office, with a lead-pen in hand since an early age;[96]
148	射宮曾發的	At the Archery Hall, I once launched a shot and hit the target.[97]

---

[94] An allusion to *Zhuangzi*, 17/81–84; trans. A. C. Graham, *Chuang-Tzǔ*, 122. The tortoise "alive and dragging its tail in the mud" stands for Zhuangzi's pursuit of freedom.

[95] An allusion to Dong Jing 董京 (W. Jin), who was a beggar when he first arrived in Luoyang and resided in White Temple. See *Jinshu*, 94.2426.

[96] An allusion to Yang Xiong 揚雄 (53 BC–AD 18), who brought with him a lead-pen and wood-pads and followed the clerks to various places to record dialects. See *Xijing zaji*, 3.1a.

[97] Archery Hall is a kenning for the Ministry of Rites.

149	起草香生帳	I drafted official documents and fragrance rose from the drapes;[98]
150	坐曹烏集柏	Working at the bureau where crows gather on cypress trees.[99]
151	賜宴聆簫韶	Invited to imperial banquets, listening to the Shao flute tunes,[100]
152	侍祠閱琮璧	Serving at sacrificial rituals, I inspected jade tubes and discs.[101]
153	嘗聞履忠信	I had heard: as long as one practices loyalty and fidelity,
154	可以行蠻貊	One might apply them to the Man and Mo ethnic groups.[102]
155	自述希古心	To myself I expressed admiration for the ancients,
156	妄恃干時畫	And hastily relied on [their wisdom] in my dealings with current affairs.
157	巧言忽成錦	As crafty words suddenly formed embroidered brocade,
158	苦志徒食蘗	My bitter ambition vainly turned into eating cork tree leaves.
159	平地生峯巒	On a flat land there arose peaks and ridges;
160	深心有矛戟	Deep inside one's heart were lances and glaives.
161	曾波一震蕩	Layers of waves, should they shake and quake,
162	弱植忽淪溺	The frail plants would thus be down and drown.[103]
163	北渚弔靈均	On the North Island I mourned for Lingjun.[104]
164	長岑思亭伯	On the Long Hills I thought of Tingbo.[105]
165	禍來昧幾兆	When misfortune occurred, I was unaware of the omen;
166	事去空歎惜	When the matter passed, I sighed and felt sorry in vain.
167	塵累與時深	Dusty entanglements were deepened as time went by;
168	流年隨漏滴	The fleeting years drift away with the clepsydra's drips.
169	才能疑木雁	Judging talent, I am confused by the timber and wild goose.[106]

---

98   Referring to the year 791 when Liu worked at the office of Du You 杜佑 (715–812). See *Liu Yuxi quanji biannian jiaozhu*, 171, n. 12, 13, n. 1.

99   A kenning for the Censorate (*Yushi tai* 御史臺), where crows gathered on the cypress trees. See *Hanshu*, 83.3404.

100 The music is said to be dated to the time of Shun 舜, the mythological sage-ruler (trad., r. ?–2184 BC).

101 Inspection of these objects for the court's ritual refers to Liu's status as Censor cum Investigating Commissioner (*jiancha shi* 監察史) when he was adhered to Wang Shuwen.

102 An allusion to *Lunyu*, 15/6.

103 Referring to Liu himself, who was without any powerful patron who would protect him.

104 Lingjun is the byname of Qu Yuan, who was banished to and eventually ended his life in the same area.

105 Tingbo is the byname of Cui Yin 崔駰 (d. 92), who was banished to Long Hills (a toponym of Changcen in northeastern China) after his frequent protests against the powerful yet corrupt marshal, Dou Xian 竇憲 (d. 92). See *HHS*, 52.1721.

106 An allusion to *Zhuangzi*, 20/1–5; trans., Graham, *Chuang-Tzǔ*, 121: Zhuangzi's disciple asked: "Yesterday, because its time was good for nothing, the tree in the mountains could last out Heaven's term for it. Today, because the stuff it's made of is good for nothing,

170	報施迷夷跖	In rewarding others, people confound Prince Boyi and Brigand Zhi.[107]
171	楚奏繫鍾儀	Chu music was played when Zhong Yi was captured,[108]
172	商歌勞甯戚	Songs of sorrow were sung when Ning Qi was laboring.[109]
173	稟生非懸解	My reception of life is not about setting free from fetter.
174	對鏡方感激	In front of the mirror, now I am moved and agitated.
	***	***
175	自從嬰網羅	Since I was first entangled in nets and snares,
176	每事問龜策	On every matter I consulted turtle shells and milfoils.
177	王正降雷雨	In the first month were sent down thunder and rain.
178	環玦賜遷斥	A circular or notched jade disc commanded my banishment.[110]
179	倘復夷平人	Now I have become the same as a commoner again,
180	誓將依羽客	I will then follow the feathered transcendent beings.
181	買山構精舍	I will purchase a mountain plot and build a vihāra,
182	領徒開講席	Recruiting disciples, opening my lecture seat.
183	冀無身外憂	I hope there will be no worries beyond my physical form;
184	自有閑中益	And there will naturally be benefits from being idle.
185	道芽期日就	As the Daoist alchemical sprouts will be duly ready,
186	塵慮乃冰釋	My mundane worries will thereupon melt like ice.
187	且欲遺姓名	As I am about to leave behind my surname and given name,
188	安能慕竹帛	Why bother having my name inscribed on bamboo and silk?[111]
189	長生尚學致	While longevity may be achieved through learning,
190	一溉豈虛擲	How would daily irrigation be practiced in vain?
191	芝朮資糇糧	Mushrooms and spiked millet are my sustenance.[112]
192	煙霞拂巾幘	Mists and auroras brush my scarf and hood.

---

our host's goose is dead. Which side are you going to settle for, sir?" Zhuangzi replied: "I should be inclined to settle midway between being food for something and being good for nothing."

107 Bo Yi 伯夷 is an icon of integrity as he and his younger brother Shu Qi 叔齊 starved to death on Mount Shouyang after the founding of the Zhou dynasty in the early 12th century BC, which they resolved not to serve. Brigand Zhi 盜跖 is an icon for the most evil people.

108 When Zhong Yi was captured and jailed in the state of Jin, he played the music of the south, his native land, on his *qin* zither. See *Zuozhuan*, Cheng 9.9.

109 Ning Qi sang in sorrowful tunes to draw the attention of Duke Huan of Qi 齊桓公 (r. 685–643 BC) and was promoted after his talent was recognized by the duke.

110 See note 54.

111 Referring to achievement of great deeds and being remembered.

112 The two edibles are said to have the magical efficacy of prolonging one's life.

193	黃石履看墮	Seeing Senior Yellow Rock's shoes being dropped,[113]
194	洪崖肩可拍	I shall pat the shoulders of Master Grand Cliffs.[114]
195	聊復嗟蜉蝣	For the time being, I heave a sigh for mayflies,[115]
196	何煩哀虺蜴	Why bother lamenting over snakes and lizards?[116]
197	青囊既深味	I have savored the blue bag of books on prognostication,
198	瓊葩亦屢摘	And, time after time, plucked carnelian flowers.
199	縱無西山資	Although I lack the potential of the Western Mountains,[117]
200	猶免長戚戚	I am still free from lasting anxiety and anguish.

---

113   The Senior, known as Huangshi gong 黃石公, was met by Zhang Liang 張良 (262–186 BC) when he was in his teens. The Senior gave a book of military tactics. At the meeting, Zhang went through the tasks assigned by the senior, including arriving at the meeting place earlier than the senior, picking up the shoe the latter threw down to the bridge base, and putting it onto his feet. See *Shiji*, 25.2034.

114   Master Grand Cliffs is a transcendent. One tradition says that he was Ling Lun 伶倫, a minister of the Yellow Emperor. He had lived for three thousand years by the time of Yao 堯. He has a sobriquet of Perfected Man of Mount Qingcheng 青城真人 according to the *Zhen'gao*, a fifth-century Daoist encyclopedia. See *Lishi zhenxian tidao tongjian* (HY 296), 4.2b–3a.

115   These insects live a very short life.

116   The snakes and lizards are a kenning for the common people who suffer from oppression. See *Shijing* 192.

117   The western Mountains are a kenning for achieving transcendence. See Cao Pi, "Zhe yangliu xing" 折楊柳行, in *Yuefu shiji*, 37.547.

CHAPTER 4

The Transcendent by the River Sending Off Gentleman Ruan: Grotto Romance in Tang–Song Lyrics

1   Introduction

In previous chapters, we have looked at early to mid-Tang *shi* poetry and narrative; this chapter will examine the legacy of the grotto romance tradition in the poetic genre of *ci* (lyrics).[1] We cover works from the genre's inception through to its peak of popularity in the Tang–Song era. Of the various tune-titles, the "Linjiang xian" 臨江仙 ("The Transcendent by the River") and "Ruanlang gui" 阮郎歸 ("Gentleman Ruan Returns Home") most typically present vivid pictures of some such episodes in the Liu-Ruan tale. These tunes, along with the image of a transcendent by the river and that of the mortal visitor to the grotto, become a focus of our investigation in this chapter.

In early *ci*-poetry, the content of a song was largely determined by its tune-title. This rubric is discussed by Huang Sheng 黃昇 (S. Song), who gives the archetype of the transcendent as an example. Here are the relevant lines in his *Hua'an cixuan* 花庵詞選:

> The *ci*-poems of the Tang dynasty were mostly composed in line with [the literal meaning of] their respective titles. [For example,] "The Transcendent by the River" is about matters of the transcendents; "The Capelined Priestess" tells of love affairs of the Daoist priestess;[2] "The God of the River Ditch" is a panegyric on the bethel or temple. In general, they would not deviate from the meaning of the original title. Afterwards this practice underwent gradual changes and [the theme and content of a poem] became detached far from the title's meaning.

---

1   The works in the genre in Tang times are known retrospectively as *quzici* 曲子詞 (lit., "lyrics to tune"), a term first coined by Wang Zhongmin 王重民. See Wang, *Dunhuang quzici ji*. Ren Bantang 任半塘 calls these songs "Dunhuang geci" 敦煌歌辭. See DHGC. See also Kim Hyun Choo and Lee Eun Ju, "Guanyu Dunhuang quzici," 91; Zhou Yao, "Cong Wudai wenxian shitan," 158–60. Ren Bantang opposes the use of the term "Tang ci" 唐詞; Jao Tsung-i proposes a flexible attitude. See Jao, "'Tang ci' bianzheng," 1098–1108.

2   The translation of this tune-title is Edward H. Schafer's. See Schafer, "The Capeline Cantos," 5–65.

唐詞多緣題所賦，《臨江仙》則言仙事，《女冠子》則述道情，
《河瀆神》則詠祠廟，大概不失本題之意。爾後漸變，去題遠矣。[3]

This theory laid a principal foundation in the scholarship of Chinese *ci*-poetic history. Huang Sheng's prominent example is Li Xun's 李珣 (early 10th c.) "Wushan yiduan yun" 巫山一段雲 ("A Section of Clouds in the Witch Mountains"), a poem "composed on the title's meaning" 緣題所賦.[4] In his anthology of Dunhuang song lyrics, Ren Bantang divides the chapters by "types of tunes" and "form and style." In addition, each chapter is assigned to a certain theme, such as "boudoir grievances" (*yuansi* 怨思), "love and romance" (*lianqing* 戀情), "journey and sojourn" (*xinglü* 行旅), etc. Some tunes are footnoted with a rubric "tune-title of the original theme" (*diaoming benyi* 調名本意) as a "subtitle."[5] This subtitle is assigned according to the content of the song. This assignment helps the reader easily identify the theme of the song, but also limits one's reading to relying on Ren's reconstructed subtitles to gauge the original theme of a given song. These subtitles, it must be noted, were created by Ren rather than adopted from generally-accepted precedent. Some questions are thus raised: is Ren's rubric of "tune-title of the original theme" the same as Huang Sheng's "written on the title's theme"? To what extent would the lyricists of early times (i.e., mid-eighth to early ninth centuries) faithfully adhere to the "original theme," which inspired the nomenclature of a given tune-title in their respective compositions? What kinds of changes were made by these early lyricists to the allegedly original source in these new songs? Above all, what conclusions can we draw about the evolution of grotto romance themes?

The present chapter is devoted to answering these questions through examination of the archetypical and stereotypical significance of the poetic role of *xian* 仙 ("transcendents") and that of their mortal lovers in Tang–Song lyrics. The chapter is divided into two parts.

The first part discusses lyricists' personalized compositions to "tune-title of the original theme" as they expand the range of their meanings to current

---

3 Huang Sheng, *Hua'an cixuan*, 1.24b. Shen Jifei 沈際飛 (fl. 1621–1634) argues: the reason for Tang *ci*-poems mainly writing on their original content is because only the lyrics, not the title, were then available. See *Yuxuan Lidai shiyu*, 112.19a.

4 The Goddess of Mount Wu could change between a cloud and a human form and once had a romantic relationship with King Xiang of Chu (r. 298–263 BC). See Song Yu 宋玉 (late to mid-3rd c. BC), "Gaotang fu," *WX*, 19.1b–6b.

5 *DHGC*, 324, 452, et passim. Ren's original name was Ren Ne 任訥 but he was commonly known by his byname, Zhongmin 中敏. He later published works by the names of Ren Bantang and Ren Erbei 二北. In this present book, his work is cited by the name he uses in the respective publications.

events and the expression of emotion. The Dunhuang lyrics under investigation in this chapter are dated roughly from the middle of the eighth century to the early tenth century, a period when *ci*-poetry was in its burgeoning stage. The style of these works differs from later works that feature more rhetorical ornamentation and more use of allusion.[6] We also expect a closer adherence to the specific meaning of the tune-title. However, from a critical point of view, we risk reading in a reductive and shallow way if we limit our attention to the "tune-title of the original theme," as the historical and personal background of the poet may be overshadowed.[7] Although the content of Dunhuang lyrics on "the transcendent" share narrative and dramatic features with other popular songs,[8] the rubric of "tune-title of the original theme" still serves as an important guideline. This reading strategy aims to convey the rich aesthetic appeal of these lyrics. We apply this strategy in analyzing the *ci*-poems collected in the *Yunyao ji* 雲謠集 (*Anthology of Tunes from the Clouds*).[9] Jia Jinhua's monograph on the priestess-poets of Tang times marks a new level of sophistication in the study of this peculiar category of women writers of this period,[10] but here, our attention is on the female persona as a literary disguise. Gender flexibility in poetic point of view enables the expression of our familiar grotto romance theme: the abandoned transcendent.

The second part of the chapter deals with lyrics within the paradigm of the Liu-Ruan tale dated to the Northern Song, with a focus on the works of Ouyang Xiu 歐陽修 (1007–1072). By Tang times, the popularity of grotto fantasy led to the establishment of an encyclopedic repertoire of themes universally known to the literati. From the second half of the Tang (by the ninth century), this grotto romance repertoire had expanded to express a variety of amorous themes in early *ci* lyrics. The developments of the genre in the hands of lyricists collected in *Poems Gathered from among Flowers* (*Huajian ji* 花間集) and early Song *ci* poets continued to expand the literary possibilities of the grotto romance to the expression of more secular themes. In the Northern Song, Ouyang Xiu inherited this legacy and appears to have been especially fond of drawing from the Liu-Ruan tale in his *ci*-poems.

---

6   Sun Qifang, "Ci (fu Foqu)," 197.
7   Ibid., 199.
8   See Kang-i Sun Chang, *The Evolution of Chinese Tz'u Poetry*, 19.
9   For a brief introduction to this anthology, see Owen, *Just a Song*, 49. The *Yunyao ji* has attracted less scholarly attention than other manuscripts preserved in the Dunhuang collections. For a study of another Dunhuang anthology, namely the *Yaochi xin yong ji* 瑤池新詠集 (*Anthology of New Poetry from the Turquoise Pond*); see Jia Jinhua, "New Poetry from the Turquoise Pond."
10 See Jia Jinhua. *Gender, Power, and Talent*.

The versatility of Ouyang Xiu, as a great statesman, an artist, and a poet par excellence, has long inspired scholarship in various fields such as political history, historiography, intellectual history, music, and literature. Still, relatively little attention has been given to the considerable number of amorous *ci*-poems attributed to him. This oversight was mainly motivated by conservative efforts to protect Ouyang's posthumous image as a paragon of virtue. These efforts resulted in the winnowing of many amorous works. In the years and centuries following his death, this editorial purification was conducted in accordance with two related, tautological criteria: works of dubious authorship and those with erotic elements. Several works of erotic nature were disassociated from Ouyang Xiu to prevent any defiling of the noble reputation of this great Confucian scholar.[11] We endeavor to revisit these lyrics and draw a fuller picture of how the amorous *ci* took shape in the Northern Song.

2   Part 1

2.1   *In Search of the Transcendent in Tang Songs*

As discussed in previous chapters, the courtesans portrayed in the grotto romance works of the Tang are often euphemistically endowed with perfected (*zhen* 真) qualities, a depiction typically applied to supernatural beings in the Daoist tradition. This multilayered presentation of a courtesan is relevant to our reading of the Dunhuang songs selected for investigation. As we have seen in previous chapters, the notion of *xian* came to refer to the female protagonists in the *You xianku* as well as to Yuan Zhen's casting of Cui Yingying, both of whom have been identified as characters drawn from lower social stratum in the Tang, most likely serving as geisha. In the lyrics selected for discussion below, we shall look at these fantastic encounters from the point of view of the "transcendent" maiden and that of her mortal lover.

In doing so, we must remember that not all transcendents in Dunhuang lyrics may be identified as courtesans or female Daoist adepts. In the Dunhuang songs discussed below, the characterization of the *xian* persona is often ambiguous. Examples of this ambiguity include lyrics to the tune-title of "Nüguanzi"

---

11   Stephen Owen argues: "It was believed that an unknown number of lyrics were composed by Ouyang Xiu's enemies to discredit him around the time of the great examination scandal, and Luo Bi 羅泌 (1131–1189), the editor of *Jinti yuefu* 近體樂府, is explicit about omitting these." See Owen, "Who Wrote That?" 212–13. The dates and Chinese characters are my insertions. The issue of Ouyang's authorship is analyzed further in Owen, *Just a Song*, 32–35, 125–49.

("The Capelined Priestess"), in which the male poet uses the female transcendent, rather than the male adventurers, as a voice through which to express his own feelings. In the illusory otherworld conjured in this kind of poetic creation, it is often difficult to precisely identify the role(s) played by the transcendent persona.

Despite the creative ambiguity involved in this characterization, we still observe in these works the standard recurrence of language, themes, and images inherited from the grotto romance tradition, with a focus on the term *xian* and its layered resonances. This phenomenon may be contrasted with Stephen Owen's discussion of pastiche in the Music Bureau (*yuefu*) poetry tradition. This kind of poem, according to Owen, is composed of "thematic segments," such that "what we see in the poems are not stories but pieces, yet enough pieces to construct the variables."[12] In our case, there are complete works alluding to or being derived from a common, traceable source; the Liu-Ruan tale. Here, we reconstruct the "pieces" that work, in aggregate, to reflect established grotto fantasy themes, and thereby explore the artistic purposes of the individual lyric.

2.2   The "Celestial Transcendent"

In the extant Dunhuang lyrics, three tune-titles most typically pertain to "the transcendent," namely, "Tianxianzi" 天仙子 ("The Celestial Transcendent"), "Bie xianzi" 別仙子 ("Farewell My Transcendent"), and "Dongxian ge" 洞仙歌 ("Song of the Grotto Transcendent").[13] The lyrics to these three tunes apparently adhere to the rubric of "tune-titles of the original theme," although they also communicate real-life stories of the respective lyricists.

Who is this *xian* in this new context? We start our probe with two songs entitled "The Celestial Transcendent" anthologized in the *Yunyao ji*, the first of which reads:[14]

| 1 | 燕語鶯啼三月半 | Swallows twitter and orioles chatter halfway through the third month. |
| 2 | 煙蘸柳條金線亂 | Mist dampens willow branches; gold threads are in disarray. |

---

12   Owen, *The Making of Early Chinese Classical Poetry*, 110–20, esp. 118–19.
13   The two songs under this tune-title are in *DHGC*, 1.150, 1.157. As the content of these songs is not directly related to the Liu-Ruan tale although traces can still be detected, they will not be discussed in the present chapter.
14   The customary, bipartite structure of a *ci*-poem was established at the inception stage of the genre. In the lyrics quoted in this book, three asterisks mark the break of a song made of two parts.

3	五陵原上有仙娥	On the Wuling Height there is a transcendent maiden,
4	攜歌扇	With a singing fan in hand,
5	香爛漫	My fragrance, pervading in profusion,
6	留住九華雲一片	Makes a cloud of Mount Nine Efflorescences tarry.
	***	***
7	犀玉滿頭花滿面	Rhino horns and jade richly deck out my coiffure, flowers cover my face.
8	負妾一雙偷淚眼	Your betrayal of me has resulted in a pair of eyes in covert tears.
9	淚珠若得似真珠	If the teardrops are like pearls,
10	拈不散	They cannot be dispersed by hand.
11	如何恨	What are my grievances like?
12	串向紅絲應百萬[15]	If strung on a red thread, the pearls would number a million.

Ren Bantang's remarks are of importance to our discussion. He reconstructs the background of the song as "a chasing scene, or even a 'market,' of the amorous lady and the noble scion." He reasons that the term "transcendent maiden" (*xian'e* 仙娥) refers to the "celestial transcendent" (*tianxian* 天仙). Ren also asserts that "these lyrics make the first tune of this title," and, judging by the line "on the Wuling Heights," Ren dates the creation of this tune to the time of Kaiyuan and Tianbao eras (712–756).[16]

The scene immediately recalls the Liu-Ruan romantic encounter. As we have seen in the *You xianku* and in Yuan Zhen's and Bai Juyi's poems (Chapter 2), the pleasure-seeking activities of the Tang are often provided with the metaphorical disguise of a romantic encounter with a divine lady in a grotto. However, the depictions of the lady's dressing and makeup are not found in the Liu-Ruan tale, and thus lovesickness and crying after her lover has departed register as new elements that attract the reader's attention. The *xian* in the song refers to the "voluptuous lady" or, more specifically, an entertainer, as she has "a singing fan in hand" (l. 4). According to Sun Qifang, Wuling refers to the Tang entertainment quarters filled with singing and dancing, and the lyrics relate "the noble young man's flirting and the entertainer's coquetry."[17]

---

[15] DHGC, 1.121; QTWDC, "zhengbian," 4.803. "The Celestial Transcendent" was in the Kuchean 龜茲 collection of tunes and was in the Tang Music Office. See *Jiaofang ji*, 16; *Yuefu zalu*, 45.

[16] DHGC, 1.122.

[17] Sun Qifang, "*Yunyao ji zaquzi* jiaozhu," 275; DHGC, 1.123–26.

A description of the seasonal scene of "Swallows twittering and orioles chattering" is found in both songs titled "The Celestial Transcendent." This element might well be a formulaic feature of the tunes of this tradition. Apart from the musical arrangement, which determines the tonal pattern, it is not a requirement to write about a specific season or scene for lyrics about the entertainment quarters and the grievances derived from the love stories that happen therein. If we assign the Liu-Ruan tale to these songs as their archetypal framework, these references to the season and theme of involuntary separation may be plausibly read as archetypal elements. The next song under the same title further bolsters these associations with the Liu-Ruan tale:

1	燕語鶯啼驚覺夢	Swallows' twitter and Orioles' chatter startle and wake me from a dream.
2	羞見鸞臺雙舞鳳	I am ashamed to see the paired phoenixes dancing on Simurgh Terrace.
3	天仙別後信難通	Since the celestial transcendent parted [with him] it is hard to get news of him.
4	無人共	No one remains with me
5	桃花洞	In this peach blossom grotto.
6	羞把同心千徧弄	Coyly, I tie thousands of "heart-sharing knots."
	***	***
7	叵耐不知何處去	Regretfully, I don't know where he has gone.
8	正值花開誰是主	As flowers are just blooming, who is their lord?
9	滿樓明月夜三更	The moonlight-drenched building at the third watch—
10	無人語	With no one to talk to,
11	淚如雨	And tears like rain,
12	便是思君腸斷處[18]	—Is where I miss you, a heartbreaking place.

The fragmentary nature and rhyming inconsistency of this song form some obstacles in understanding its lyrics. For this reason, some scholars treat it as two separate pieces, while some remain loyal to the received text.[19] Here, we follow Wang Zhongmin and treat it as a single song. Further, we take it as a complement to the first song translated above. The two songs combine to make a complete story: after the romantic encounter and the man's departure,

---

18   *DHGC*, 127–28; *QTWDC*, "zhengbian," 4.803.
19   Ren Bantang holds that "these two songs in different rhymes share the same theme"; Wang Zhongmin treats it as a song composed of two stanzas. See Wang Zhongmin, *Dunhuang quzici ji*, 2.71; *Dunhuang Yunyao ji xin jiaoding*, 36.

the maiden—in the guise of a celestial transcendent—declares her longing for her absent lover. The inspiration, if not a direct borrowing, from the framework of the Liu-Ruan tale is tantalizing, as the romance takes place in the very locale of the "peach blossom grotto" (l. 5); the tune-title refers to the women encountered by Liu Chen and Ruan Zhao, and the roles, imagery, and theme are familiar. The second half of the song supplements the romance with the lone maiden's sadness aroused by the blooming flowers and the empty chamber, which have no "master" now. These images figuratively point to her loneliness after the excitement of the romance, which took place in this "heartbreaking place" (l. 12).

Although the phrase "swallows' twitter and orioles' chatter" became a cliche in mid-Tang literature to describe spring scenes,[20] in "The Celestial Transcendent" the bird calls serve to "wake me up from a dream." This recalls the onset of Liu and Ruan's homesickness and their eagerness to return home. This sentimental scene may have been inherited from the *Youming lu*, in which we read: "Seasonal changes and plants heralded the advent of spring. Further agonized by the chirping of birds, the two unhappy men begged to return" (see Chapter 1). In the lyrics here, however, the lady plays the key role in this springtime melancholy after her man has left the "peach blossom grotto" (ll. 4–5). Her reminiscence of the romantic encounter has become like a dream. The double metaphor of putting the Liu-Ruan tale in a dream setting has its precedent in Yuan Zhen's poem "Dream of Spring Roaming in Seventy Rhymes" and Bai Juyi's responsive poem (see Chapter 2).[21] These examples in the Dunhuang lyrics further illustrate that the motifs, images, and plot elements derived from the Liu-Ruan tale had become popular metaphors for or symbols of love affairs by mid-Tang times. We find more examples of the Liu-Ruan tale transformed into dreaming poems by Yuan Zhen and Bai Juyi, such as "I recently composed a poem on dreaming about the *xian*" 近作夢仙詩 (note, in particular, l. 63 of Yuan's poem) and "An outing to the transcendent mountainous nooks" 夢遊仙山曲 (note l. 2 of Bai's poem). Liu and Ruan, no matter whom they represent in these adapted contexts, have been turned into "putative lovers" of the ladies in the grotto.[22]

Thus, the grotto romance repertoire is broadened to include the declarations of longing by courtesans in the *ci* format. This additional poetic possibility

---

20 See, e.g., Meng Jiao 孟郊 (751–814), "Shangchun" 傷春, Huangfu Ran 皇甫冉 (716–769), "Chunsi" 春思. *QTS*, 374.4199; 250.2834. The latter poem is also attributed to Liu Zhangqing 劉長卿 (709–785).
21 *QTS*, 422.4635–36; 437.4856–58.
22 Schafer, "The Capeline Cantos," 25; Lee Fong-mao, "Xian, ji yu dongku," 486–87.

would blossom in the late Tang to Five Dynasties period, an issue to be dealt with in Part 2 of this chapter. The prescriptive meaning of this tune-title, "The Celestial Transcendent," becomes clear: it is a song sung by a forlorn lady disguised as a transcendent in the manner of the grotto romance tradition. We might also conclude that grotto fantasy underwent a process of secularization during Tang times, i.e., the transcendent became a euphemism for a mortal geisha—an object of (male) literati infatuation.

Other mid-Tang poets write within the same topos and from the same point of view, namely, in the voice of the bereft lady. Most likely in her own voice, the female poet Yu Xuanji 魚玄機 (ca. 844–ca. 868) addresses the following poem to Li Ying 李郢 (*jinshi* 856):

無限荷香染暑衣	The endless fragrance of the lotus flowers scents my summer clothes;
阮郎何處弄船歸	My gentleman Ruan makes ready his returning boat somewhere.
自慙不及鴛鴦侶	I feel not as privileged as the mandarin ducks in pairs,
猶得雙雙近釣磯	Which have a chance to get closer to their fishing islet.[23]

The setting is familiar: a female "celestial transcendent" stands alone expressing her melancholy resulting from having sent off her lover, guised as Ruan Zhao. The poetess, who plays a triple role of the Daoist priestess, a courtesan, and the grotto *xian*, adds some personal sentiments, envying the mandarin ducks roaming in pairs, as a contrast to her lonely self. These birds, which are always seen in pairs, symbolize lovers in Chinese literature. They can swim side by side to where her lover would now be fishing. Thus, her Ruan Zhao has turned into a fisherman, the visitor to Tao Qian's peach spring (see Chapter 3).[24]

This mode of writing in the voice of a forlorn woman continued in later works under the "Celestial Transcendent" tune, as Ren Bantang points out:

> The lyrics of "The Celestial Transcendent" written by Huangfu Song 皇甫松 (early 9th c.) and those in the Dunhuang collection are no exception to the original meaning (*benyi* 本意) of the tune-title. In the lyrics,

---

23 Yu, "Wen Li Duangong chuidiao hui jizeng" 聞李端公垂釣回寄贈, *QTS*, 804.9051. Cf. Jia Jinhua's remark on this poem in Jia, *Gender, Power, and Talent*, 171.

24 See Chan, "A Tale of Two Worlds," 232–33, for Yu's life and her other poem, "Muchun jishi" 暮春即事 (*QTS*, 804.9053), in which she analogizes her lover Yan Bojun as Ruan Zhao.

each song contains terms such as "celestial transcendent" (*tianxian* 天仙), "transcendent" (*xianzi* 仙子), or "transcendent maiden" (*xian'e* 仙娥).[25]

Although Ren does not specify the "original meaning" of this tune, a verse in the Huangfu Song lyrics mentioned by Ren reveals some clues. The verse reads: "On this day Gentleman Liu bade farewell to the celestial transcendent" 劉郎此日別天仙.[26] This combines with other elements of Huangfu's work, leading it to be read as an expression of the springtime loneliness of the *xian* after her lover has left the grotto. Thus "the original meaning" of this lyric is the same as others under the title of "The Celestial Transcendent."

The following two songs with the same title, respectively by Wei Zhuang and He Ning, like that of Huangfu, explicitly blame Liu and/or Ruan as the lover responsible for the lovesickness of the female transcendent character:

1	金似衣裳玉似身	Gold resembles my clothing and jade resembles my person;
2	眼如秋水鬢如雲	My eyes are like autumn water and my earlocks are like clouds.
3	霞裙月帔一群群	In an aurora skirt and moon scarf, following one flock after another,
4	來洞口，望烟分	I have gone to the grotto's mouth, gazing at the dispersing mist.
5	劉阮不歸春日曛[27]	Liu and Ruan have not returned, the spring sun has turned dark.
1	洞口春紅飛蔌蔌	At the grotto's mouth, vernal red petals fly and fall.
2	仙子含愁眉黛綠	The transcendent's sadness is enveloped in her kohl-green eyebrows.
3	阮郎何事不歸來	Gentleman Ruan, for what reason have you not come back?
4	懶燒金，慵篆玉	Lazy to refine gold elixir and lethargic to carve jade seals—

25　*Jiaofang ji jianding*, 128. With this argument, Ren refutes Duan Anjie's 段安節 (late 9th c.) argument that "the 'Wansinian qu' 萬斯年曲 presented by Li Deyu 李德裕 (747–849) is 'Tianxianzi.'" See *Yuefu zalu*, 14.

26　See the "Tianxianzi" songs respectively by Huangfu, Wei Zhuang 韋莊 (ca. 836–ca. 910), and He Ning 和凝 (898–955), in *HJJJ*, 26, 44 (no. 5), 110 (no. 2).

27　*HJJJ*, 44.

5   流水桃花空斷續²⁸   The currents and peach blossoms, in vain, now running, now stopping.

The images of the grotto and the peach blossoms here became customary elements in the grotto romance genre. This practice continued to grow in the Song dynasty, when a new tune-title, "The Celestial Transcendent of Tiantai" ("Tiantai xianzi" 天台仙子), emerged. As Tiantai is the name of the mountains where the classic Liu-Ruan romance took place, this new tune-title may be seen as a further confirmation of the linkage between "The Celestial Transcendent" and the Liu-Ruan tale.²⁹ The *xian* persona in the songs is by no means a replica of the maiden in the original tale; rather, she now assumes a triple role that includes transcendent, Daoist priestess, and a courtesan in love with a Tang intellectual. Her guise as a Daoist priestess is evident in Wei Zhuang's song just quoted, in which the persona's outfit resembles that worn by Daoist priestesses. In He Ning's song, the lovelorn persona is so troubled by the spring season having aroused her longings for her Gentleman Ruan that she pays no attention to her quotidian work of making an elixir and carving Daoist seals, two typical tasks for a Daoist adept.³⁰

2.3 *"Farewell My Transcendent" in the Secular Realm*

The folk songs of the time saw a new development in the grotto romance tradition and resulted in the further secularized representation of love episodes. In this trend, the role of the *xian* in these songs continues to blend that of the two maidens in the Liu-Ruan tale with the Daoist priestess and Tang courtesan, despite the earlier convention limiting lyrics to the surface meaning of their tune-title. In this light, we shall explore how the literal meaning of the tune title, "Farewell My Transcendent," is used and adapted.

"Farewell My Transcendent," No. 1

1   此時模樣   The atmosphere of this season—
2   算來似   I reckon, it is like
3   秋天月   The moon of autumn.

---

28   Ibid., 110.
29   *Jiaofang ji jianding*, 237. Shen Jifei asserts that "the tune of 'Tianxian zi' writes about the transcendents of Mount Tiantai." See *Yuxuan lidai shiyu*, 112.19a. The tune-title "Tiantai xianzi" is not found in representative anthologies of *ci*-poetry, such as QTWDC and QSC.
30   See Schafer's discussion of the image of this persona in early *ci*-poems in Schafer, "The Capeline Cantos," 26–34.

SENDING OFF GENTLEMAN RUAN

4	無一事	I have not a single matter
5	堪惆悵	That my melancholy can bear.
6	須圓闕	I wait for its wax and wane;
7	穿窗牖	[Its beams] penetrate the window.
8	人寂靜	When others have become silent,
9	滿面蟾光如雪	My face is full of toad light resembling snow,[31]
10	照淚痕	Shining on my tears.
11	何似兩眉雙結	How is it like my two eyebrows knitted in a frown?
	***	***
12	曉樓鐘動	When the bell tower heralds the morning,
13	執纖手	You hold my delicate hands.
14	看看別	Realizing that it is time to part,
15	移銀燭	I remove the silver candle,
16	猥身泣	Lean my body against you, sobbing
17	聲哽噎	In a choking whimper.
18	家私事	[You have] family matters,
19	頻付囑	You repeatedly bade me.
20	上馬臨行說	Mounting the horseback, before leaving, I say:
21	長相憶	Remember me for ever
22	莫負少年時節[32]	And don't waste your adolescence.

"Farewell My Transcendent," No. 4

1	曾來不信	Never had I believed in
2	人說道	What others said:
3	相思苦	"Missing one's lover is agonizing."
4	如今現	Now it happens [to me].
5	嗔交（叫）我	Anguish makes me
6	勞情與	Exhausted with my sentiments.
7	贊（攢）眉立	I frown with raised eyebrows
8	欹枕川（臥？）	When I lie on the pillow.
9	日夜懸腸各（割）肚	Day and night, as though my viscera were hanging and my stomach severed.
10	隨（垂）玉柱（筯）	In falling jade-like tears,

---

31 Toad light is a kenning for moonlight. According to legend, a toad lives on the moon.
32 Dunhuang manuscript S.7111; *DHGC*, 2.324; *QTWDC*, "zhengbian," 4.860. Lee Fong-mao argues that these songs are on the farewell of the young man and his lover (the *xianzi* or *tianxianzi* 天仙子) in Chang'an. See Lee, "Xian, ji yu dongku," 478.

11	直代（待）寄（綺）門朱戶	I await you at the vermilion gate all the time.
	***	***
12	憶君直得	I miss you so much
13	如痴醉	As though I'm possessed and drunk
14	容言語	As reflected in my utterances.
15	胸裙上	On my upper garment,
16	紅羅帶上	On my red gauze sash,
17	啼恨紆	Crying and grievances linger on.
18	過然得	When this [waiting] is through,
19	從（重）相見	We shall see each other again.
20	于（依？）舊還同一處	Just like before, we shall stay at the same place,
21	歸羅帳	Returning to our gauzy curtains
22	特地再論心蘇[33]	And chatting especially about our heart['s feelings].

The fragmentary, corrupt condition of the texts and their uncertain meaning do not prevent our comprehending the basic content of these two songs, which outline the early status and evolution of the tune. At a glimpse one notes the expected theme of a lovelorn lady missing her lover.[34]

This "suite" of songs randomly put together demarcates a change from "tune-title of the original theme" to tune-title divorced from its original theme. The more corrupt status of songs 2 and 3 hinders our understanding of them; fortunately, song 3 clearly repeats the content of song 4. The content of song 2 is a celebration of Zhang Chengfeng's 張承奉 founding of the Jinshan 金山 Kingdom in the Western region in the year of 910 after he defected from the Tang empire. In terms of literary genre, according to Tang Jun, this piece may be seen as a changed mode of "Farewell My Transcendent," from song to parallel prose style.[35] More importantly, this song 2 illustrates its being delinked from its original theme, "farewell my transcendent." This change is clearly observable in a comparison of two songs written at two points in time at least one century apart. Songs 1 and 4 were created around the Tianbao reign-period

---

33. Chai Jianhong and Xu Jun, "Dunhuang ci jijiao sitan," 54. The graphs in parentheses are reconstructed from the ones preceding each of them, provided by the article authors.
34. Tang Jun observes: "These two songs relate two aspects of one same story"; they were "originally in one suite" and "should be songs created at the Music Bureau of the High Tang palace." See Tang, *Dunhuang quzici diyu wenhua yanjiu*, 117–24.
35. Ibid., 119, 124–25.

(742–755),[36] a time close to the presumptive inception of the tune-title. Their lyrics are related to the theme of "Farewell My Transcendent" but are also related to the cultural milieu of their times of composition. In these songs, the metaphorical meaning of the *xian* as a "voluptuous lady" or a geisha remains the same as in the other Tang poems discussed above. This common referent may be attested through a paradigmatic analysis. In this regard, Tang Jun's discussion yields some useful hints: "Song 1 depicts the parting scene of a couple in which the agonized lady incessantly talks to her husband. ... Song 4 continues this by portraying the lone lady, who leans against the door, shedding tears, frantically missing her husband."[37] This reading, however, neglects the content surrounding the *xian* in the tune-title, which provides a story framework of two lovers from two different realms missing each other.

This framework involves the theme of humans in love with the supernatural. These literary conventions of human/divine love guide us to read the song about the joyful tryst of the two lovers. More significantly, the "transcendent" in the song speaks in a first-person narrator's voice about her parting with her lover and her subsequent lovesickness. This kind of episodic presentation in retelling a story is most typically seen in Cao Tang's 曹唐 (fl. 860–871) rewriting of the Liu-Ruan tale in regulated verse. His "Greater Poems on Roaming in Transcendence" 大遊仙詩 and "Lesser Poems on Roaming in Transcendence" 小遊仙詩 each take a perspective of the "transcendent" in depicting the scenes of her acquaintance and falling in love with Liu and Ruan, and the scene of her parting with them.[38]

Comparatively, the tenor of the metaphor of the transcendent in love with a mortal in Dunhuang songs mainly refers to the lone wife missing her husband who is away on a military campaign. In his analysis of the meaning of the "grotto" in Cao Tang's poems adapting the Liu-Ruan romance, Edward Schafer points out:

> The mouth of the grotto is a place of assignation—a limbo waiting for a definite commitment by the outsider. It is also a boundary: the decision to cross it, once made, especially out into the mundane world, is fateful.[39]

This view is well attested in the "boundary crossing" practiced by the role of Cui Yingying in Yuan Zhen's "Story of Yingying" (see Chapter 2). In the

---

36   Ren Bantang assigns Song 1 to "tune-title of the original theme." *DHGC*, 2.325.
37   Tang Jun, *Dunhuang quzici diyu wenhua yanjiu*, 117.
38   See *QTS*, 640.7337–38, 641.7347, 7349.
39   Schafer, "The World Between," 6; *Mirage on the Sea of Time*, 43.

Dunhuang songs in question, however, one finds a more secularized theme on the romance of the "young husband" and his lover in the disguise of the fantasy about the *xian*. In these kinds of contexts, the man "exiting the grotto" is a figure for the husband away from home and on sojourn. Since he is gone, the *xian* is left in the "grotto" on her own—"day and night, as though my viscera are hung and my stomach severed" (l. 9 of Song 4).

The prototypical grotto seductress character type provides a conventional story framework for the content of the Dunhuang songs with similar themes. The secular scene in these works is realistic but is also enriched through the mythology of the original Liu-Ruan tale. This kind of adaptation colors the secular love with the fantasy of a mortal falling in love with a divine being. When the young couple, who may have just wedded, first experience such excitement and ecstasy, but then suddenly encounter separation, the result is tremendous pain and trauma.

2.4 *The Transcendent by the River*

How much does the tune-title's original meaning matter in our reading of Dunhuang songs? Our discussion of "The Celestial Transcendent" and "Farewell My Transcendent" above demonstrates a strategy for striking a balance between the tune-title and the unique secular content of the lyrics. The latter often reflects the author's time and life; therefore, the tune-title and its prescribed elements provide a vehicle for the expression of a metaphorical layer of meaning.[40] Unlike poetry composed by the elite class, these folk songs contain far fewer allusions; but in this early development period of the genre, the rubric of "tune-title of the original theme" plays an important role in delivering the intended meaning.

The tune-title of "The Transcendent by the River" ("Linjiang xian"), which contains another vivid image relevant to our present discussion, came from the entertainment quarters collection. Let us look at the lyrics of this "Linjiang xian" song to see the relationship between the tune-title and its content.[41]

---

40 Sun Qifang argues that the first "Tianxianzi" was written by a male intellectual. See Sun, *Yunyao ji zaquzi jiaozhu*, 268. Lily Hsiao Hung Lee, however, argues that the majority of songs in the *Yunyao ji* were created by women or by men who wrote in the voice of women. See Lee, "Hypothesis Regarding the Gender of the Creator," 894–917.

41 The song has a variant title of "Linjiang shan" 山 ("Overlooking the River and Mountains"), which implies a very different picture (see the lyrics below) and has nothing to do with *xian*. Ren Erbei argues that *shan* should not be changed to *xian*, that changing *shan* to *xian* would be "a violation of the convention," and that this song has nothing to do with "the transcendent" or "the mountain" but is about the persona longing to return home. See Ren Erbei, *Dunhuang qu chutan*, 105–6. Nonetheless, the so-called "variant" title "Lin

SENDING OFF GENTLEMAN RUAN 149

	臨江仙	"The Transcendent by the River"
1	岸闊臨江帝宅賒	Shores wide apart, overlooking the river: the emperor's residence is far away.
2	東風吹柳西斜	East winds blow on the willow branches towards the west.
3	春光催綻後園花	The spring scenes urge the blossoms in the backyard to bloom.
4	鶯啼燕語撩亂	Orioles' twitters and swallows' chatters trouble me—
5	爭忍不思家	How can I bear not thinking of my home?
	***	***
6	每恨經年離別苦	Often I grieve for the bitterness of years of separation.
7	等閒拋棄生涯	I thoughtlessly abandoned my livelihood.
8	如今時世已參差	Now the time and generation are different.
9	不如歸去	Nothing can compare with going home.
10	歸去也	Going home—
11	沉醉臥煙霞[42]	I will recline amidst mist and auroras.

The theme of this and other lyrics under the same title has long been understood as the homesickness of the sojourner, which has nothing to do with the meaning of the tune-title. Ren Bantang, for example, assumes that this song "is

---

jiangshan" in fact only existed as an error. First noted in Wang Zhongmin's edition, this mistaken "variant" was later corrected and changed back to "Linjing xian" by Wang himself. See *Dunhuang quzici ji*, 1. 12. Ren's version, which was based on Wang's 1950 edition, was erroneously transmitted by Pan Chung-kwei 潘重規, who in turn relied on Ren's version as his master copy, and thereafter this alleged "variant" of "Lin jiangshan" has been in circulation. See *Dunhuang quzici ji (xiuding ben)*, 1. 39; Pan Chung-kwei, "Ren Erbei Dunhuang qu jiaolu bujiao" 任二北敦煌曲校錄補校, in Pan, *Dunhuang ci hua*, 79; Xu Jun, "Bo 2506 quzici chao," 941, n. 1. Jao Tsung-i bases his redaction on S.2607 and entitles the song "quzi Linjiang xian" 曲子臨江仙. See Jao, *Dunhuang qu*, 834; S.2607 (p. 114).

These inaccuracies and unnecessary disputes could have been avoided had the Dunhuang manuscript, P.2506, been consulted more carefully. P.2506 is reproduced in Pan Chung-kwei, *Dunhuang ci hua* (no page number), "Bo 2506 hao (1)." Wang Zhongmin's mistake in his first redaction, it must be noted, is not completely groundless. In addition to his reliance on the lyrics themselves, he might also have been inspired by later compositions under the tune-title of "Lin jiangshan." Examples include the two pieces by He Shouqian 何守謙 (early 14th c.), which also invoke the peach blossom grotto. See *QSC*, 1137.

42 *DHGC*, 2.406–407, a recension based on P.2506, S.2607, and one manuscript in the Stein collection without number.

most likely a product of the later part of the High Tang in transition to the time of decline and chaos" by providing relevant backgrounds of the disillusioned aspirant who wishes to return home after his failure to pursue deeds and fame but sojourning in the Tang capital.[43] This reading finds support in some motifs in the song, such as: "overlooking the river," "spring scenes," "orioles' chirps," homesickness, "years of separation," a different "time and generation," "going home," etc., which, when put together, present a full picture of a sojourner's life and feelings. It would make sense for this sojourner, who wishes to return from the capital to a reclusive life at his home.

The findings of our discussion above concerning the relationship between the literal meaning of a tune-title and its theme and content may also inspire a different interpretation. As the tune-title indicates, there must logically be a "transcendent by the riverbank," but she is absent from the surface meaning of the lyrics. We also do not find any indication of what this "transcendent" does. Without altogether abandoning Ren's interpretation, we may still read this quasi-adaptation as a metaphor for a sojourner missing his home. To achieve this, we bring the song back to its possible provenance. In the *Youming lu* tale of Liu Chen and Ruan Zhao, the two maidens are encountered "by the riverbank," and at that time, they call the men's names. The "orioles' twitters and swallows' chatters" indicate the advent of spring, which also fits the Liu-Ruan tale. The same phrases describing the same scene are customarily found in the two songs of "The Celestial Transcendent" quoted above, forming a provocative image prompting the nostalgia derived from the rapid passage of time and the lively springtime. In the first half of the song, the protagonist gazes at the river and the "emperor's residence" (i.e., the capital) from afar and is suddenly startled by his prolonged sojourn in this "otherworld"; thus, he realizes that it is time for him to return to the "human realm."

As we follow the storyline of the Liu-Ruan tale, the song makes perfect sense all the way through to the end. The second half of the song expresses the protagonist's sentiments after he exits the grotto—he finally decides to return to the otherworldly realm. The "bitterness of years of separation" (l. 6) refers to his previous life in the "mortal realm": when he entered the mountains he abandoned his family and career; now as he "gets out of the grotto" he suddenly finds out that the "time and generation are different" (l. 8) and therefore wants to return to the "otherworld"—"amidst mist and auroras"—rather than living in the imperfect secular world.

An adaptation is by no means a simple rewriting of the original story but must carry a new meaning or message that the author means to deliver. It is,

---

43   DHGC, 2.407. Similar interpretations can be found in, e.g., Zhang Jian, *Dunhuang quzici baishou yizhu*, 70; Gao Guofan, *Dunhuang quzici xinshang*, 97–102.

according to Linda Hutcheon, "*a process of creation*," as "the act of adaptation always involves both (re-)interpretation and then (re-)creation; this has been called both appropriation and salvaging, depending on your perspective."[44] The creative tension in the Liu-Ruan tale is generated by a pervasive dissatisfaction with mundane reality. This kind of reaction, as we shall see in Chapter 5, is particularly prominent in Yuan and Ming grotto fantasy. After Liu and Ruan leave the mountains and return home, as the *Youming lu* version relates, "they became strangers because their relatives were all gone and all the villages and houses had changed. ... They suddenly left again. No one knew where they had gone." This can be viewed as a reaction of the literati to oppressive or poorly administered rule. The same level of political discontent may have been present among the literati during the period in which the "Linjiang xian" song was composed (we recall Ren Bantang's assertion that the lyric was "a product of the later part of the High Tang in transition to the time of decline and chaos").[45] The line the "time and generation are different" marks the awakening of the protagonist bearing witness to the decline of the Tang in the Kaiyuan reign-period (712–742). The unique intrigue of spatiotemporal displacement in the *Youming lu* tale is now at work in this text, yet in a different way. Although this new adventure does not trigger a displacement of seven generations, the time intrigue becomes a means by which the persona expresses his wish to renounce the world that has undergone changes beyond his expectations.

2.5   *The Transcendent Seeking Transcendence in the Grotto*

The transcendent persona in the lyrics of the songs entitled "The Transcendent by the River" and "The Celestial Transcendent" descended from a tradition in which she had transformed from a grotto transcendent to a mortal lover or wife. But in a song (discussed below), we observe a contradictory phenomenon as the persona tells us that she "seeks transcendence." This expression prompts us to investigate the vestiges of the secularization process of relevant tales. The early stages in the formation of the tune-title may, in turn, help us explore the stemmatic relationship between the provenance and its adaptations. The foremost task is to identify the transcendent who originally belongs to the early context of "The Transcendent by the River." This process may not result in a definitive answer but shall help us better understand the songs descended from, related to, or inspired by the same tradition.

As discussed above, the lyrics under the tune-titles of "The Celestial Transcendent" and "The Transcendent by the River" invoke the maidens encountered by Liu Chen and Ruan Zhao. This claim may be contradicted

---

44   Hutcheon, *A Theory of Adaptation*, 8.
45   DHGC, 2.407.

TABLE 4   Protagonist *xian* in "The Transcendent by the River" songs anthologized in *Poems Gathered from Among Flowers*

Protagonist *xian* / Lyricist	Gaotang goddess 高唐神女[a]	Xiang consort 湘妃	Maiden Xie 謝女	Goddess of the Luo River 洛神	Playing girl of Han'gao 漢皋遊女	Nongyu 弄玉
Niu Xiji 牛希濟	✓	✓	✓	✓	✓	✓
Sun Guangxian 孫光憲	✓				✓	
Yan Xuan 嚴選	✓					
Feng Yansi 馮延巳	✓					
Mao Wenxi 毛文錫		✓				
Zhang Bi 張泌		✓				

a   For the Gaotang goddess, see *HJJJ*, 93, 149, 173; *QTWDC*, "zhengbian" 正編, 3.668; Xiang Consort: *HJJJ*, 95, 192, 73; Maiden Xie: *HJJJ*, 93; Goddess of the Luo River: *HJJJ*, 94; Playing girls of Han'gao: *HJJJ*, 95, 149; Nongyu: *HJJJ*, 93.

by the fact that none of the songs included under the latter tune-title ("The Transcendent by the River") anthologized in the *Poems Gathered from Among Flowers*—an early collection put together in 940—concerns the Liu-Ruan tale. In her analysis of "The Transcendent by the River" songs in this anthology, Suzanne E. Cahill argues that the tune-title and the song theme are closely related. She identifies the sexual encounter between the Goddess of Mount Wu and King Xiang of Chu 頃襄王 (r. 298–263 C), first found in Song Yu's "Gaotang fu," as the prototypical element in all these songs.[46] The statistics in Table 4, however, do not support this observation. Only four of the twelve such songs include definite references to, or explicitly mention, the Gaotang goddess.

As the Five Dynasties of the tenth century were geographically based in the southern part of China, one may surmise: the lyricists active at that time tended to use references to local history. Therefore, the Gaotang goddess, Xiang consort, and the playing girl of Han'gao would naturally comprise this repertoire of local references in these songs.

None of these divine ladies, however, are related in any way to the image of "The Transcendent by the River." The Gaotang goddess, for example, has never

---

46   Cahill, "Sex and the Supernatural in Medieval China," 199–203.

been referred to as a *xian* but as a "maiden of Mount Wu" 巫山之女 or "goddess" 神女,⁴⁷ nor is she related to any river (*jiang*). Although the Xiang Consort (Xiang furen 湘夫人) is by the Xiang River in the *Chuci* and other related contexts,⁴⁸ she has never been called a *xian* throughout Chinese poetic history. The temple where Maiden Xie practiced transcendent skills is not located next to any river but is at the South Sea of Guangdong province.⁴⁹ The Goddess of the Luo River is Luoshen 神 or Consort Fu (Fu fei 宓妃), not a *xian*, who resides in Luo River 洛水, which is not called a *jiang*. The playing girl of Han'gao is by the nook of a mountain named Han'gao Terrace 臺.⁵⁰ Although Nongyu did attain transcendence (*xian*-ship), she was never recorded to have been called a *xian* "by the river." Despite this incompatibility, most of these songs have been defined by Yang Jinglong as "lyrics on their original tune" 詞詠本調,⁵¹ which presents a contradiction. We should be more cautious about this treatment and note that these Five-dynasties lyricists liked showing off their erudition by cultivating allusions in their compositions.

The "transcendents" found in *Poems Gathered from Among Flowers* just discussed are, in fact, rarely found in Tang songs; the Liu-Ruan romance, on the other hand, had remained a repertoire theme in these erotic songs since early times. In the original tale, the "transcendents" acquainted with Liu and Ruan, after all, were "by the river" in their debut when receiving the two starving men upon their accidental visit to the peach spring. We have seen how the images and plot elements work in the songs in the former tune; the same reading strategy may be employed in interpreting the following "The Transcendent by the River":

臨江仙 其三	"The Transcendent by the River," no. 3
1　不處囂塵千百年	Not staying in the dusty world for hundreds of years,
2　我於此洞求仙	I seek transcendence in this grotto—
3　坐□行遊策杖	Sitting on [?], strolling, roving, with a staff in hand.
4　策杖也	With a staff in hand,
5　尋溪聽流泉	I explore the brook while listening to the flowing streams.
***	***

47　See Song Yu, "Gaotang fu" and "Shennü fu," *WX*, 19.2, 19.7a/b.
48　See *CCBZ*, 2.64–68, text of "Xiang furen" and Wang Yi's commentary quoting Liu Xiang's 劉向 (77–6 BC) *Lienü zhuan* 列女傳 (2.64).
49　*Huajian ji jiaozhu*, 5.789, n. 1.
50　See Zhang Heng, "Nandu fu" 南都賦, *WX*, 4.2b; trans., Knechtges, *Wen xuan*, 1: 314, quoting *Shuijing zhu*.
51　*Huajian ji jiaozhu*, 5.778, 785, 789, 795, 801.

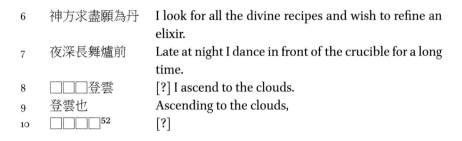

The phrase "hundreds of years" in the first line originally read "thousands and myriads of years" 千万年. These are both hyperboles, according to Xiang Chu, and "it was the lyricist's original intent and should not be altered."[53] Xiang's insightful point needs further elucidation. Contextual support may be found through a reading of the lyrics with reference to the tradition of grotto romance. As discussed in Chapter 1, Liu and Ruan experience "time dilation" in their adventure to the grotto, whereas the transcendents manage to live through "thousands and myriads of years" by "staying away from the dusty world."

But there is a complication in this song: now the persona is a *xian*, so why does she still "seek *xian*-ship"? Paradoxically, this testifies to the common view in the field about the triple identity of the *xian* who simultaneously plays the roles of the transcendent maiden, the entertainer, and the Daoist priestess. In this song, the grotto setting is still a trope for the secular scene of the lone lady who has been separated from her lover. This kind of grievance is customary in the writings by Tang literati and Daoist priestesses alike. This literary tradition lends support to our reading of "The Transcendent by the River" as well as other songs about the transcendent. There is one difference, however, in the Dunhuang songs: the grievance is often softened, and the focus is on how to transcend the agony that stemmed from being separated from her lover. In this song, the role of this triple persona determines that her lover will leave the grotto and return to the mortal realm, which has passed through seven human generations. The "transcendent" "stays away from the dusty world" but turns to the crucible to refine an elixir to attain transcendence. All these fit well with the characteristics of a prototypical Tang Daoist priestess, who had a double identity, namely a religious practitioner and a courtesan in constant association with the literati.[54] This phenomenon is reflected in quite a number of songs in the *Poems Gathered from Among Flowers* that portray a Daoist priestess

---

52 *DHGC*, 2.521.
53 Xiang Chu, *Dunhuang geci zongbian kuangbu*, 39.
54 Liao Mei-yun, *Tangji yanjiu*, 201–4; Chang Yi-jen, "Wen Tingyun liangshou 'Nüguanzi,'" 178–82; Jia Jinhua, *Gender, Power, and Talent*, 191–92.

missing her lover named Liu and/or Ruan.[55] These songs support our reading of the Dunhuang "The Transcendent by the River" songs. In the one just quoted, the lady strolls with a staff in her hand to overcome her loneliness. The place she visits is the riverbank. These details supplement the Liu-Ruan tale so well that they make a "sequel": the forlorn lady reminisces by the river, the very scene of her acquaintance with her lover. Now she can only listen to the murmurs of the currents, which seem to remind her of the past. In the middle of the night, this lone Daoist lady begins dancing before the crucible to refine an elixir, but who will appreciate her graceful appearance again? These scenes and activities serve to bring out the loneliness of this jilted lady. Therefore, seeking transcendence has become an irony of her love: she now lives alone in this timelessness; ageless but always struggling to evade lovesickness.

This traditional poetics on the combination of transcendence-seeking and love affairs is evident in some of the monologues of the Daoist priestess created by Wen Tingyun 溫庭筠 (812–870). Wen wrote two songs to the tune "The Capelined Priestess" on the beauty and loneliness of the priestess and ended with lines on the "early quest for transcendence" and "sooner or later I shall ride on the simurgh."[56] The theme of pursuing transcendence is a figure for the female persona's craving for love and venting her loneliness.

The following two songs, one to the tune of "The Transcendent by the River" and one to "The Capelined Priestess" written by Zhang Bi illustrate the fusion of these literary themes:

	臨江仙	"The Transcendent by the River"
1	煙收湘渚秋江靜	As mist clears over the Xiang and Zhu streams, the autumn rivers turn silent.
2	蕉花露泣愁紅	Banana flowers in dew weep in sorrowful red colors.
3	五雲雙鶴去無蹤	The five-color clouds and the paired cranes are gone, leaving no trace.
4	幾回魂斷	How many times has my cloud-soul been broken?—
5	凝望向長空	Gazing fixedly at the immense sky.
	***	***
6	翠竹暗留珠淚怨	On halcyon colored bamboo I secretly leave pearl teardrops and grievances.

---

55 Schafer, "The Capeline Cantos," 25–26; Shields, *Crafting a Collection*, 320–21. Chang Yi-jen, "Cong Lu Qianyi," 272–75.
56 *HJJJ*, 16.

7	閑調寶瑟波中	In my leisure time, I tune my precious psaltery strings by the ripples.
8	花鬟月鬢綠雲重	My flowery round-braided hair and moonlight earlocks amidst the dense green clouds,[57]
9	古祠深殿	In this ancient temple and deep basilica,
10	香冷雨和風[58]	Fragrance and chills are mixed with rain and wind.

	女冠子	"The Capelined Priestess"
1	露花煙草	Dewy flowers and grass in mists,
2	寂寞五雲三島	Serene and solitary are the five-color clouds and the three [transcendent] islands.
3	正春深	In the depth of spring,
4	貌減潛消玉	My appearance has decayed, like jade losing luster unnoticed.
5	香殘尚惹襟 ***	Some fragrance remains and still provokes my lapel. ***
6	竹疏虛檻靜	The bamboo grove is sparse, keeping the empty balustrade quiet;
7	松密醮壇陰	The pines are dense, providing shade for the ritual altar.
8	何事劉郎去	For what reason has gentleman Liu gone?—
9	信沉沉[59]	No news of him but silence.

One sees such familiar images and scenes in these songs, which lead an informed reader into the realm of grotto fantasy. The protagonist in both songs is a Daoist priestess of the triple role made of the transcendent, the entertainer, and the priestess. She is positioned alone at the "ancient temple" and "ritual altar," in the transcendent realm of "three islands" in springtime after her Gentleman Liu has left. Troubled by the vestiges of romance evident in objects such as tears on the bamboo and the lingering fragrance, the persona cannot concentrate on her Daoist practice in this "otherworld," so she stands facing the river (l. 1 in song 1). These kinds of representations form a repertoire in the circle of lyricists of the *Poems Gathered from Among Flowers* and offer support for our reading of the Dunhuang song "The Transcendent by the River" no. 3 (quoted above) in which the persona is also located at a temple. This prevalence of adapting the elements of grotto romance from mid to late Tang times perfectly construes the persona who "seeks transcendence in this

---

57   "Green cloud" is a kenning for dense black hair.
58   *HJJJ*, 73.
59   Ibid., 73–74.

grotto," "listens to the flowing streams," and is "late at night dancing in front of the crucible for a long time."

3 Part 2

3.1 Ruan Zhao Returning Home: an Amorous Poet Unveiled

As lyrics evolved to assume a matured genre of *ci*-poetry in the Northern Song, vestiges of the Liu-Ruan tale are still evident in the works of Ouyang Xiu. Scholars of his works have, however, rarely heeded Ouyang's poetic nods to the grotto romance tradition. In dealing with the female personae in Ouyang's *ci*, one may be even more hesitant to correlate the poem to the poet's life. This interpretive uncertainty is not new to scholars of earlier amorous songs, such as those collected in the *Poems Gathered from Among Flowers*. The practice of male poets writing in female voices had been common since the advent of the *yuefu* tradition, and it was more fully embraced by *ci* lyricists.

Of Ouyang Xiu's extant lyrics, his works to the tune "Gentleman Ruan Returning Home" rely most heavily on the Liu-Ruan tale. Here is one such example:

	阮郎歸	"Gentleman Ruan Returning Home"
1	濃香搓粉細腰枝	Profound fragrance, cosmetic powder and my slender waist;
2	青螺深畫眉	Beneath my spiral-shell chignon, deep color highlights my eyebrows.
3	玉釵撩亂挽人衣	My jade hairpins are askew, catching our clothes.
4	嬌多常睡遲	My coquetry is such that we always go to bed late.
	***	***
5	繡簾角	By the corner of the embroidered curtains,
6	月痕低	The moon tracks low.
7	仙郎東路歸	My transcendent gentleman's homeward road to the east—
8	淚紅滿面溼臙脂	My tears run red down my face from dampened rouge.
9	蘭房怨別離[60]	In my eupatory chamber I lament his parting.[61]

---

60 *QSC*, 153.
61 I follow Nicholas Morrow Williams in translating *lan* 蘭 as "eupatory." See Williams, *Chinese Poetry as Soul Summoning*, passim. Paul W. Kroll lists "thoroughwort, agrimony, eupatorium" in his *A Student's Dictionary of Classical and Medieval Chinese*, 252, q.v.

This poem describes a scene common to other lyrics under the title "Gentleman Ruan Returning Home." Although the term "transcendent gentleman" (l. 7) is found passim in Tang-Song poetry and has various possible referents, one finds it hard to disassociate this one from Ruan Zhao because of the tune-title adopted by the poet. In this thematic cycle, we recall that this male persona is usually the client/lover of a geisha in the entertainment quarters. The poet adopts the perspective and tone of this lovesick lady, who reminisces about the scene of her romantic encounters with her lover. The second half of the lyric is a transition from sweet memory to cruel reality, in which the lady is deeply saddened by her lover's absence.

In his description of the romantic encounter, Ouyang Xiu adds several provocative new elements, such as the hairpins caught in the clothing of the entangled lovers (l. 3), the late hour the lovers retire (l. 4), and the tear-stained makeup (l. 8). The curtains and the moon further intensify her grief witnessed from a "eupatory chamber" (rather than the grotto chamber in the Liu-Ruan tale).

The erotic scene in the first half of Ouyang's poem is a marked feature and, like other Northern Song boudoir poems, has been read as an inheritance from the *Among Flowers* poetic tradition, but otherwise left generally unelaborated. In the context of the title, which recalls the Liu-Ruan tale, we may propose that Ouyang's erotic scene portrays Ruan Zhao's lover and their love-making in the grotto. Accordingly, the second half of the poem imagines a scene after Ruan's transcendent maiden has bid farewell to her lover and sent him back to the mortal realm.

3.2 *Liu and Ruan's Transcendence and Return to the Mortal Realm*

In its development, the tune-title, "Gentleman Ruan Returning Home," has several variant titles. In each case, the title refers to an episode of or elaboration on the Liu-Ruan romance, as well as some typical imagery and scenes in the grotto settings. These variant titles include:

1. "Fine Brooks and Mountains" ("Hao xishan" 好溪山)
2. "Banqueting at the Peach Spring" ("Yan Taoyuan" 宴桃源)
3. "Banqueting at the Peach Garden" ("Yan Taoyuan" 宴桃園)
4. "Going Home upon Attainment of the *Dao*" ("Dao cheng gui" 道成歸)
5. "Spring Season of the Emerald Peaches" ("Bitao chun" 碧桃春)
6. "Spring Season of the Emerald Clouds" ("Biyun chun" 碧雲春)
7. "Getting Drunk at the Peach Spring" ("Zui Taoyuan" 醉桃源)[62]

---

[62] See Wu Outing and Wu Xiaoting, *Cidiaoming cidian*, 279.

The earliest extant lyrics to "Gentleman Ruan Returning Home" are dated before the Song, and include level-tone rhymes depicting a lady missing her absent lover.[63] A poem written under the variant title, "Getting Drunk at the Peach Spring," is most revealing in its connection with the Liu-Ruan tale.[64] Likewise, lyrics written under the other seven variant titles listed above consistently reflect grotto romance themes. For this particular tune-title, "Gentleman Ruan Returning Home," the theme and imagery generally adhere to the grotto romance tradition until the Northern Song.[65] But when poets like Cai Nan 蔡栩 (d. 1170) wrote his two songs under the title, "Enhanced Version of Telling of My Sincere Feelings" ("Tanpo Su zhongqing" 攤破訴衷情), a tune-title often identified as a variant of "Gentleman Ruan Returning Home" because it shared the same music scheme, we find no reference to the Liu-Ruan tale.[66] We shall return to this issue in the next section.

The development of another tune-title closely related to the Liu-Ruan tale, "The Capelined Priestess" ("Nüguanzi"), also set a model for Ouyang Xiu's *ci* composition. This collection of lyrics written during the late Tang to the Five Dynasties period marks the same overlaying of Daoist themes and racy secular romance with the Liu-Ruan tale seen in *Poems Gathered from Among Flowers*. According to Mao Xianshu, Xue Zhaoyun 薛昭蘊 (mid-10th c.) was the first poet to write in this tune.[67] In the voice of the priestess, Xue mentions that she "seeks transcendence" (*qiuxian* 求仙) in the grotto (no. 1) and that she met a "Gentleman Liu the envoy" 劉郎使 (no. 2).[68] The first poem is reminiscent of the Dunhuang songs, "Transcendent by the River" ("I seek transcendence in this grotto") discussed above; the second one makes Liu an envoy, recalling

---

63   Of these, the original song is attributed to a range of different people, including Li Yu 李煜 (937–978; last emperor of the Southern Tang dynasty), Feng Yansi 馮延巳 (903–960), Ouyang Xiu, and Yan Shu 晏殊 (991–1055), but is agreed to be either by Feng or Li. See *QTWDC*, "zhengbian," 3.757–58.

64   Ibid., 3.757, n. 1.

65   Sima Guang's 司馬光 (1019–1086) "Ruanlang gui" is on the Liu-Ruan story; Zhang Xian's "Zui Taoyuan" and Yan Jidao's 晏幾道 (ca. 1030–ca. 1106) "Ruanlang gui" (5 poems) are all on boudoir grievances of the lone lady. These works may have taken the maiden in love with Liu and Ruan as an archetype. See *QSC*, 72, 199, 237–38.

66   The musical scheme includes the length of the song and each verse, caesuras, *ping-ze* (level-toned 平 and deflected-toned 仄 characters) patterns, etc. See Wu Outing and Wu Xiaoting, *Cidiaoming cidian*, 279. Cai's poem is in *QSC*, 989. Two other variant titles of the tune carry meanings unrelated to the Liu-Ruan tale, namely, "Washing My Hat Tassel" ("Zhuoying qu" 濯纓曲) and "The Crane Soaring to the Sky" ("He chongtian" 鶴沖天). See ibid., 279.

67   Mao, *Tianciming jie*, 1.12a.

68   *HJJJ*, 55.

Zhang Wencheng in the *You xianku* (see Chapter 2). These "The Capelined Priestess" songs in *Among Flowers* all depict Daoist priestesses, with a focus on their romantic life. In some cases, one finds vestiges of their source, such as the images of peach blossoms and the grotto.[69] Most (but not all) invoke the Liu-Ruan tale. As Chang Yi-jen 張以仁 points out, "in [those poems] writing about the love feelings of the Daoist priestesses, the gentleman Liu allusion almost became a must."[70] Examples include the three songs of "The Capelined Priestess" by Liu Yong 柳永 (ca. 985–ca. 1053), which demonstrate the familiar framework of a lady (though not a priestess, in his poems) thinking of her lover.[71]

This development of the tune-title "The Capelined Priestess" outlines how a tune was created and what changes it underwent by poets of different social backgrounds. It supports our observation of other tunes, which underwent similar developments in dealing with the archetypal elements in Northern Song *ci*. The image of the transcendent, along with the grotto settings, also plays a role in Yan Shu's lyrics in his two songs "Changsheng le" 長生樂 ("Joy of Living Long"), in which one finds the grotto-residence, crucible, transcendent, singing, banqueting, and so forth.[72] These images from the repertoire of the Liu-Ruan tale contribute to Yan's representation of the literal meaning of the tune-title, "the joy of living long." It is noteworthy that the tune-title becomes the title of a Qing-dynasty play adapted to the Liu-Ruan tale.[73] This phenomenon suggests that the connotation of the term *changsheng le* was derived directly from the Liu-Ruan tale, at least in the Qing playwright's understanding.

In his new versions of amorous poems to the tune of "Gentleman Ruan Returning Home," Ouyang Xiu further intensifies the maiden's sadness by enriching the original Liu-Ruan tale—the framework of these poems—by means of a large variety of rhetorical devices and provocative images.

"Gentleman Ruan Returning Home," no. 1

1	劉郎何日是來時	Gentleman Liu, which day are you coming?
2	無心雲勝伊	Even the heartless clouds outdo you:
3	行雲猶解傍山飛	The roaming clouds would understand me and hover by the mountains,

---

69 See, e.g., Wen Tingyun's and Lu Qianyi's poems, in ibid., 17, 152.
70 Chang Yi-jen, "Cong Lu Qianyi," 272; Edward Schafer, "The Capeline Cantos," 25.
71 Liu Yong, "Nüguanzi" (3 poems), *QSC*, 19, 45, 54; translations of the second and third poems are in James Robert Hightower, "The Songwriter Liu Yung, Part II," 48, 59.
72 *QSC*, 103.
73 See "Changsheng le," attributed to Yuan Yuling 袁于令 (1599–1674) or Zhang Yun 張勻 (fl. late 17th c.).

4	郎行去不歸	But my gentleman, you left and did not return.
	***	***
5	強勻畫	I push myself to apply makeup and draw my eyebrows.
6	又芳菲	Again, blossoms and grasses are in bloom.
7	春深輕薄衣	In deep spring I am in light and thin clothes.
8	桃花無語伴相思	Only the speechless peach blossoms are with me missing my lover,
9	陰陰月上時	Cloudy and gloomy when the moon rises.

"Gentleman Ruan Returning Home," no. 2

1	落花浮水樹臨池	Falling petals afloat on water, trees overlooking the pond—
2	年前心眼期	Since last year my heart-eyes have been expecting your return.
3	見來無事去還思	Seeing you there was no trouble, but I have missed you since you left.
4	而今花又飛	Now the petals fly again.
	***	***
5	淺螺黛	In light spiral-shell kohl,
6	淡燕脂	And sheer rouge,
7	閒妝取次宜	In simple makeup, I take it easy.
8	隔簾風雨閉門時	As curtains keep out winds and rain and with my doors shut,
9	此情風月知[74]	My feelings ... only the winds and the moon understand.

Despite Hou Wencan's 侯文燦 attribution of these poems to Zhang Xian, it is commonly agreed that they were written by Ouyang Xiu.[75] Hou's attribution was most likely motivated by his intent to disassociate Ouyang from the erotic content and feminine imagery in the poems. The familiar images and settings in the poems prompt one to read them as poetic elaborations on the Liu-Ruan tale. The first one begins with Gentleman Liu, who has left the scene of romance where his lover now misses him. In addition to the newly added images such as the clouds and the moon, the key image of peach blossoms (l. 8, poem 1) in springtime still remains as a physical reminder of their love. These blossoms, in the beginning and line 4 of the second poem, likewise serve to

---

74 *QSC*, 125.
75 *Ouyang Xiu ci jianzhu*, 28–29.

call the lone lady's attention to the year that has passed without the return of her lover. She puts on makeup only for the wind and the moon. Although the second poem does not have a Gentleman Liu, the theme of missing her lover conforms to the literal meaning of the tune-title, "Gentleman Ruan Returning Home."

The content and style of these poems do not set them apart from the *Among Flowers* poems except for the absence of the Daoist priestess. The stereotype of a Daoist priestess—so common in poetry of the Tang and Five-dynasties periods—was not as prevalent in Ouyang's time, which might explain her absence in these poems. Even so, the grotto romance remains as the framework for these and many other *ci* lyrics of Song times.

3.3 How to "Remember the Transcendent's Beauty"

Xu Qiu 徐釚 (1636–1708) argued that "Tang *ci* were mainly written on the title's meaning,"[76] but the Song witnessed a new vogue of writing *ci* according mainly to the author's own feelings rather than strictly following the music and theme prescribed by the tune-title.[77] Su Shi is such a poet, for which he became a target of Li Qingzhao's 李清照 (1084–1155) criticism as a result of his violation of the basic rules for *ci* writing.[78] As part of this unconventional new approach to *ci*, how were the Liu-Ruan-related tunes changed? Why was Ouyang Xiu so fond of writing so rigidly on the conventional theme, rather than extemporizing like Su Shi? To answer these questions, we first discuss how secular themes in songs on transcendents are handled by Song writers.

In addition to the songs of "The Capelined Priestess" discussed above, the following song attributed to Li Cunxu 李存勗 (posth., Emperor Zhuang of the Later Tang [r. 923–926]) maintains the framework of the grotto romance:[79]

	憶仙姿	"Remembering the Beauty of the Transcendent"
1	曾宴桃源深洞	We once banqueted in the deep grotto of the Peach Spring,

---

76 Xu, *Ciyuan congtan*, 1.27b, quoting *Cipin* 詞品. Ren Bantang says that it is partly true only in certain cases. See Ren, *Tang shengshi*, 76–77.

77 Long Yusheng, "Tianci yu xuandiao," 177. Li wrote most of her *ci*, especially at an early age, in compliance with the theme and content that came with the tune-title.

78 See Li, "Ci lun" 詞論, in *Li Qingzhao ji jianzhu*, 3.267. See English translation and discussion by Ronald Egan in his *The Burden of Female Talent*, 77, 80–83; *The Problem of Beauty*, 310–14.

79 A Song record relates that the emperor found a broken stele in his garden, on which the lyrics were inscribed. He ordered some musicians to compose music for the performance of the song. See *Gujin cihua*, 19.

2	一曲舞鸞歌鳳	Serenaded by a song of dancing simurghs and singing phoenixes.
3	長記別伊時	For long I remember the moment I bade farewell to you—
4	和淚出門相送	In tears, I passed through the door and we parted.
5	如夢，如夢	Like a dream, like a dream—
6	殘月落花煙重[80]	The setting moon, the falling petals, the dense mist.

The tune-title and the familiar images and scenes lead us to make a connection with the banquet and farewell episodes in the original Liu-Ruan tale. However, there are several differences. First, instead of sending off her lover through the grotto mouth, the transcendent sends him to a "door," which marks a civilizing move in line with the secularization of grotto romance at the time. Second, the romance is likened to a dream, a grotto romance innovation of Yuan Zhen, followed by Li Yu or Feng Yansi in the Five-dynasties work, "Gentleman Ruan Returning Home."[81] Third, the female protagonist's sentiment is intensified by the newly added provocative images in line 6: "The setting moon, the falling petals, the dense mist."

The work thus conforms to the image of the transcendent maiden, revised to fit in the new context of the time. The lyrics relate the banquet and farewell scenes of the Liu-Ruan tale without openly stating who is remembering whom. The tune-title leads us to read the work as an erstwhile grotto visitor reminiscing about the beauty of the transcendent he once met in the "deep grotto of the Peach Spring," but this reading does not accord with the content, which takes the point of view of the grotto transcendent missing her lover who had once visited her there. One resolution for this contradiction is to turn the visiting lover into a transcendent as well. In fact, the term *xianlang* ("transcendent gentleman"), as seen in Ouyang Xiu's "Gentleman Ruan Returning Home," denotes the grotto visitor. This characterization helps us understand Li Cunxu's song more accurately: the song may be read as a (female) grotto transcendent missing her "transcendent gentleman." This correlative reading is also conducive to a hypothesis that this male lover is an avatar of Ruan Zhao.

The comparison of the romance with a dream sees the advent of a new tune-title, which, along with other variant titles, reflects the growing diversity of the grotto romance tradition. According to Su Shi, this "Remembering the Beauty of the Transcendent" was the original title, but Li Cunxu found it inelegant and changed it to "A Dreamlike Ditty" ("Rumeng ling" 如夢令) because

---

80 *QTWDC*, "zhengbian," 3.445.
81 Ibid., 3.757.

of the repeated phrase *rumeng* found near the end of the song.[82] This change might also have been motivated by Li's reading of the Liu-Ruan romance as a dream. After Li made this change, the new title "A Dreamlike Ditty" was born. Later compositions to this tune mainly expanded on the new keyword ("like a dream") with a large variety of themes, many of which veer away from the Liu-Ruan archetype despite the continued reliance on stock images and diction derived from this source.[83] Although He Zhu 賀鑄 (1052–1125) and Hong Hao 洪皓 (1088–1155) later wrote lyrics to the tune of "Remembering the Beauty of the Transcendent," there is no trace of a reference to the Liu-Ruan tale.[84] Other variant titles of this tune each depict a certain aspect of the grotto adventure and might also have triggered the thematic digression from the source text in later compositions. For example, the title "Banqueting at the Peach Blossom Spring" ("Yan Taoyuan") captures only the banquet scene but contains nothing about how the adventure and romance began and no details on the farewell scene. This narrow thematic focus is also found in the other variant titles, such as "A Ditty on Fulfilling My Intent" ("Ruyi ling" 如意令), "Not Seeing" ("Bujian" 不見), "Comparing with the Plum Blossoms" ("Bimei" 比梅), and "Ancient Record" ("Guji" 古記).[85]

In sum, the proliferation of variant titles accelerated the divorce of tune-titles from their originally prescribed content. Thus liberated, the *ci* lyricist began to compose songs to grotto-romance-themed titles that did not directly recall the original Liu-Ruan tale. This kind of flexibility is at work even in the "Dreamlike Ditty" by Li Qingzhao, who is quite conservative in her own creations. Her two songs under this title have nothing to do with the grotto romance tradition.[86]

---

82 See *Gujin cihua*, 19; *Tiaoxi yuyin conghua houji*, 39.326, both quoting Su Shi.
83 The tune became very popular in the Song and the notion of romance "being like a dream" was widely borrowed. In the *Quan Songci*, some 180 poems are under this title; 15 under "Remembering the Beauty of the Transcendent" ("Yi xianzi" 憶仙姿) and 8 under variant titles listed in the main text above. See Gao Xitian and Kou Qi, *Quan Songci zuozhe cidiao suoyin*, 331–35.
84 See QSC, 523 (He's 9 songs), 1003–4 (Hong's 4 songs). The first of Hong's has a note that reads: "Written on an outing to the garden pond of Wang Deshao, in Raozhou 饒州." Raozhou is located in the area of Poyang Lake, in the northern part of modern Jiangxi province, which is geographically and thematically far from the Tiantai area where the Liu-Ruan romance took place.
85 For a list of variant titles of this tune, see Wu Outing and Wu Xiaoting, *Cidiaoming cidian*, 243–44; Mao Xianshu, *Tianciming jie*, 1.7b (for "Ruyi ling"). For the lyrics to these tunes, see Shen Wei 沈蔚, "Bujian" (2 songs); Zhang Ji 張輯, "Bimei"; anonymous, "Guji" (3 songs), "Ruyi ling." QSC, 707, 2553–54, 3647, 3804.
86 See *Li Qingzhao ji jianzhu*, 14, 40. Her "Springtime in Wuling" ("Wuling chun" 武陵春) also does not deal with anything related to the literal meaning of the tune-title. We will discuss this issue below.

3.4   The Grotto Transcendent in the Northern Song

Writing before this liberation of content from grotto-romance-titled *ci*, Su Shi created an interesting portrayal of the transcendent in his grotto romance lyrics. Since early adaptations such as Zhang Zhuo's *You xianku* (see Chapter 2), Liu and Ruan's romance in the grotto had been used as a figure for the rendezvous of lovers outside of wedlock. This practice was continued in the lyrics to "Ditty-song of the Grotto Transcendent" ("Dongxian ge ling" 洞仙歌令), a tune-title in circulation during the Five Dynasties period and beyond, under which many poets—including Su Shi—created their own lyrics. At that time, only two verses in the beginning of the original song were preserved in Su's memory. He composed lyrics to supplement the snippet according to his understanding of the context and made it a complete song again. He also wrote a preface detailing the textual history of this song:

> When I was seven *sui* I met an old nun of Mount Mei with a family name of Zhu, but forgot her given name. She was over ninety years old. She said: "I once followed my master to enter the palace of Meng Chang (r. 934–965), ruler of the Shu Kingdom. On one very hot day, the Shu king rose at night and went with Lady Huarui (940–976) to Mahā Pond to avoid the heat. He wrote a *ci*-poem." Zhu could recite the words. It had been forty years and Zhu had died; no one knew about this *ci*. I could only remember the first two verses. In my leisure time I reviewed and brooded upon it: is it not [the tune of] "Ditty-song of the Grotto Transcendent"? I therefore completed the lyrics to the tune.
>
> 僕七歲時見眉山老尼姓朱，忘其名，年九十餘，自言：嘗隨其師入蜀主孟昶宮中。一日大熱，蜀主與花蕊夫人夜起避暑摩訶池上，作一詞。朱具能記之。今四十年，朱已死，人無知此詞者。但記其首兩句，暇日尋味，豈〈洞仙歌令〉乎？乃為足之。[87]

This preface has been regarded as historically accurate by those who study *ci*-poetry; we follow this practice and take it at face value in our discussion. Su's poem reads:

---

[87] *QSC*, 297. Mao Xianshu quotes Yang Yuansu 楊元素 (a friend of Su Shi to whom Su wrote a *ci* in company with Yang's when they were both in Mizhou 密州 in modern Shandong province), and argues that this *ci* was not written by Lady Huarui but by Meng Chang. We follow Mao's argument and assume that Meng Chang wrote the first lines remembered by Su Shi. See Mao, *Tianciming jie*, 2.2.9a/b.

1	冰肌玉骨	Your ice-like flesh and jade-like bones,
2	自清涼無汗	Naturally you are fresh, cool, and sweatless.
3	水殿風來暗香滿	At the waterfront basilica come breezes and profound fragrance.
4	繡簾開	As the embroidered drapes are open,
5	一點明月窺人	The dot-shape moon spies on this person.
6	人未寢	This person has not gone to bed,
7	欹枕釵橫鬢亂	Lying on the pillow, with misplaced hairpins and disheveled earlocks.
	***	***
8	起來攜素手	When you get up, I hold your pure-color hand.
9	庭戶無聲	At the courtyard doors there is no sound.
10	時見疏星渡河漢	At times sparse stars are seen crossing the Milky Way.
11	試問夜如何	Let me ask: how is the night?
12	夜已三更	The night has turned to the third watch.
13	金波淡	The lunar gold waves have become light;
14	玉繩低轉	The Jade Rope star has sunk lower.
15	但屈指	We only bend our fingers [to predict]
16	西風幾時來	When the west winds will come.
17	又不道	But again they do not tell;
18	流年暗中偷換[88]	The fleeting years being replaced unnoticed.

Even though Su Shi observed the tune-title and followed the prescribed meter, he was accused by Li Qingzhao of a failure to follow the rules for *ci* writing. What then is the value of Su's completion of the fragments he remembered? As Su Shi's preface calls attention to the historical background of the original lyrics as they relate to the remembered first two lines, the reader must first give due attention to these lines and their relationship to the tune-title. We make three observations here. First, Meng Chang lauds the beauty and supernatural qualities of his beloved consort Lady Huarui who was promoted because of her talent and beauty.[89] Second, Meng took the Lady to the great pond (Mahā means "great" in Sanskrit) and turned her into the grotto transcendent within this beautiful scene. Third, in his first two lines, Meng describes his Lady by

---

[88] *QSC*, 297; translation adapted from Egan, *Word, Image, and Deed*, 345, in which only the second half of the song is translated. Pointing out that Su Shi "could not write in a male voice, his forte," Egan adopts a third-person pronoun in presenting Meng's point of view writing about the female protagonist.

[89] See *Shiguo chunqiu*, 10.748.

borrowing diction from the *Zhuangzi*, in which the famous divine being of Mount Miaoguye 藐姑射 with "ice-like flesh" appears.[90]

Su Shi's subsequent lines may or may not follow Meng's thoughts, but the last line touches on the theme of time passing, a main feature in the Liu-Ruan tale. We hypothesize that Su turned the whole poem into an allegory for his own life in 1082 when he was banished to Huangzhou 黃州 (in modern Huanggang 黃岡, Hubei province) at the age of forty-seven.[91] In this period, Su's lament over the passing of time became a marked theme in his writing. The most representative among Su's works written this year are his lyrics to the tune "The Loveliness of Niannu" ("Niannu jiao" 念奴嬌), in which Su expresses "my hair turned gray too early" 早生華髮. This supports to our reading of his contribution to this poem as autobiography.[92]

Assuming the first two lines did, in fact, belong to a completed work by Meng Chang, we would predict that that *ci*-text would have adhered to the rubric of "tune-title of the original theme." To see how and if Su Shi strayed from that original theme, we must first track down early works under that tune-title. It is a challenging task because of the dearth of reliable information, but, fortunately, our findings about the two Dunhuang songs entitled "Song of the Grotto Transcendent," in *Yunyao ji*, shed some light.[93] A poem to the same tune alleged to be by Meng Chang is found in the Yuan-dynasty anthology *Yangchun baixue* 陽春白雪. Even though this poem has been regarded as a forgery produced in the Southern Song,[94] its content is still revealing for our purposes. It is more loyal to the literal meaning of the tune-title than Su Shi's lyrics just quoted. It reads:

---

90 See *Zhuangzi*, 1/28–29; trans., A. C. Graham, *Chuang-Tzǔ*, 46: "... whose skin and flesh are like ice and snow, who is gentle as a virgin" 肌膚若冰雪，綽約若處子.
91 See *Su Shi ci biannian jiaozhu*, 415; Kong Fanli, *Su Shi nianpu*, 21.557–58.
92 See Egan's translation and discussion of this *ci* in his *Word, Image, and Deed*, 226–28. For Su's works written in 1042, see Kong Fanli, *Su Shi nianpu*, 21.529–62.
93 These two songs have already deviated from the Liu-Ruan thematic convention. They are about the lone wife missing her husband away on a military campaign and, therefore, may still have connection with the motif of the transcendent in love. For the texts, commentary, and discussion of these Dunhuang songs, see Dunhuang manuscript, S.1441; *QTWDC*, "zhengbian," 4.805–6, *DHGC*, 1.150, 1.157; Lin Mei-yi, *Cixue kaoquan*, 103–6, Gao Guofan, *Dunhuang quzici xinshang*, 320–29. This tune-title has variants, such as those made of "Dongxian ge" plus a suffix such as *ling* 令 or *mang* 慢, "Dongxian ci" 詞, "Dongzhong xian" 洞中仙, and "Dongxuan ge" 洞玄歌. These variant titles all have a common musical composition scheme. See Wu Outing and Wu Xiaoting, *Cidiaoming cidian*, 446–48.
94 See Song Fengxiang 宋翔鳳 (1777–1860), *Yuefu yulun* 樂府餘論, quoted in *Su Shi ci biannian jiaozhu*, 421; *QTWDC*, "zhengbian," 3.733.

1	冰肌玉骨	You have ice-like flesh and jade-like bones,
2	自清涼無汗	Naturally you are fresh, cool, and sweatless.
3	貝闕琳宮恨初遠	At the basilica of shells and chamber of carnelian, my regrets begin to fade into the distance.
4	玉闌干倚遍	I have leaned against all the jade balustrades,
5	怯盡朝寒	And feared all the morning chills.
6	回首處	Turning around,
7	何必流連穆滿	It may not be the wandering king, roaming and roving.[95]
	***	***
8	芙蓉開過也	The hibiscus has just bloomed—
9	樓閣香融	Around buildings and lofts, the fragrance pervades.
10	千片紅英泛波面	Thousands of red petals are afloat on ripples.
11	洞房深深鎖	The grotto-chamber is locked away in the fathomless deep.
12	莫放輕舟	Do not let go of the light skiff,
13	瑤臺去	Departing from the Carnelian Terrace.
14	甘與塵寰路斷	I could be cut off from the road to the dusty sphere.
15	更莫遣	Not again would I send
16	流紅到人間	A red leaf to the human realm.
17	怕一似當時	For I worry: just like in the past
18	誤他劉阮[96]	I would lead another Liu and Ruan astray.

This composition does not contain self references, and thus differs from the piece by Su Shi discussed above. We read the protagonist as a grotto transcendent (*dongxian* 洞仙) recalling her love story in the grotto chamber. Assuming this work was written after Su Shi's lyrics, we observe that the fragments of Meng Chang's original composition, as well as Su Shi's preface, most likely served as the inspiration for this and other lyrics descended from the grotto romance tradition. In expressing the protagonist's regret for letting her lover go back to his human realm, the anonymous poet also incorporates the romantic story of the palace lady sending a red leaf out through the moat, a tale that merged with the Liu-Ruan tale in Tang times.[97] With these references established, the poet then writes about Lady Huarui's grievance about the "wandering king"

---

95 An allusion to King Mu of the Zhou 周穆王 (d. 10th c. BC), who indulged himself in roaming and playing.
96 *QTWDC*, "zhengbian," 3.732.
97 See Chan, "A Tale of Two Worlds," 229–30. The two versions of the tale are recorded in *Benshi shi*, 6; *Yunxi youyi*, 3.20a–21a; *TPGJ*, 198.1486.

(l. 7), namely Meng Chang, who has left her alone. The new theme and features may be factors for determining that the poem is a forgery, as additionally supported by Song Xiangfeng's argument that the poem is not about avoiding the heat, and that the images of the basilica, chamber, balustrades, buildings and lofts, grotto-chamber, and Carnelian Terrace are arbitrarily juxtaposed.[98] Regardless of its authenticity, we see that these images and plot design are *not* arbitrarily juxtaposed but are results of the agglomeration and crystallization of components of the grotto romance tradition in this new representation of a lady who has been left alone.

In addition to the earlier versions of "Song of the Grotto Transcendent" mentioned above, a historical review and survey of the other tunes descended from the grotto romance tradition shall help in reconstructing a paradigm, which will further support our reading. These *Yunyao* songs take the perspective of the forlorn wife longing for her campaigning husband (see note 34). Typical examples are the two songs "Bie xianzi" 別仙子 ("Farewell My Transcendent") translated and discussed above. Thematically and aesthetically, these songs fall into the same category of Cao Tang's grotto fantasy poems on the transcendent missing her lover, although the two groups of works differ in the ways they treat the Liu-Ruan tale.[99] Another *Yunyao* song title related to the Liu-Ruan tale is "The Celestial Transcendent" ("Tianxianzi" 天仙子), the two songs of which are also translated and discussed above. In these songs, the lone wife missing her husband is set in the stereotypical "peach blossom grotto" 桃花洞. In the Five Dynasties, *ci*-poets such as Huangfu Song 皇甫松 and Wei Zhuang 韋莊 (836–910) continued this practice. Huangfu begins his "The Celestial Transcendent" with: "On this day, Gentleman Liu bids farewell to the celestial transcendent." Wei outlines a picture of the grieving lady: "I've come to the grotto entrance, gazing at the mist. / Liu and Ruan have not returned, but the vernal sunlight has turned dim."[100] This comparison makes it clear that Su Shi is an exception.

---

98   See Song Fengxiang, *Yuefu yulun*, quoted in *Su Shi ci biannian jiaozhu*, 421.
99   Wang Kunwu argues that the tune-title of these two songs has nothing to do with their content. See Wang, *Sui Tang Wudai yanyue zayan geci yanjiu*, 63.
100 *QTWDC*, "zhengbian," 1.89, 1.165. Mao Xianshu points out that the tune was so named because of Wei Zhuang's verse: "On this day, Gentleman Liu bids farewell to the celestial transcendent." See Mao, *Tianciming jie*, 1.7b. Anna M. Shields points out: "There are twelve references to 'Master Liu' in the *Huajian ji*, five of which are found in 'Nü guanzi' lyrics, two in 'Tian xianzi' lyrics, two in 'Huanxi sha,' and three others in three different tune titles. Four of the twelve references are to Masters Liu and Ruan. Thus, seven of the twelve references appear in tune title sets that are nominally concerned with divinities,

The two songs, "Song of the Grotto Transcendent" and "The Celestial Transcendent," have different music but their lyrics derive from a common source. The examples just discussed show that the Liu-Ruan tale is referenced to different extents. Despite the minor changes and deviations, the lyricists' compliance with the convention sheds light on how one would understand the identity, voice, and sentiments of the female persona in the "Ditty-song on the Grotto Transcendent" by Ouyang Xiu.[101] The lady in these songs is not a copy of the maidens in the Liu-Ruan tale; rather, she comes from the repertoire of images of the grotto transcendent, Daoist priestess, courtesan, and isolated wife. Apart from the persona, the episodic settings also derive from the grotto romance repertoire. They include spring longings, missing her lover, parting, and drinking. These elements assume a new life in juxtaposition with Ouyang's innovative imagery, including overgrown grasses, overnight makeup, a love letter, and infirmity. Despite these new developments, the archetype behind the persona in this poem is still clearly identifiable as the grotto transcendent. In despair and missing her lover in both songs, the grotto transcendent also begins to feature in other lyrics to different tunes with similar amorous content by Ouyang Xiu. In these other poems, we find customary images derived from the grotto romance tradition as well as the familiar lady, but with more tenuous links to the Liu-Ruan tale.

Our quest for the grotto transcendent in Ouyang's lyrics may be informed by the way Liu Yong, who lived some two decades before Ouyang, composed words to the same tune. Accused by Li Qingzhao as being "vulgar" and "low" in style and diction,[102] Liu's songs "broached the subjects of romantic love in its fulfillment (rather than just its sub-version) and sexual desire,"[103] but were mainly composed in adherence to the prescribed themes of their respective tune-titles. The romantic scenes in Liu Yong's lyrics to the tune of "Song of the Grotto Transcendent" are much indebted to the grotto romance tradition. For example, the "grotto chamber" 洞房 and "Peach blossom garden" 桃花園 become the site of romance in the specific context of Liu Yong's own life. When writing about the acquaintance with his lover, Liu Yong bemoans:

| 算國豔仙林 | In this state of beauties and groves of transcendents, |
| 翻恨相逢晚 | I regret that we meet so late. |

---

supporting the argument that poets paid some attention to the meanings of tune titles when composing lyrics." See Shields, *Crafting a Collection*, 321, n. 76.
101 *QSC*, 151–52.
102 Li Qingzhao, "Ci lun," *Li Qingzhao ji jianzhu*, 3.267.
103 Egan, *The Problem of Beauty*, 265. Li Qingzhao considered "Ju hua xin" 菊花新 (*QSC*, 38) to be the most erotic of Liu Yong's lyrics; see Owen, *Just a Song*, 83.

In depictions of sharing a bed with his lover, he writes:

金絲帳暖銀屏亞	In these warm curtains of gold silk, with the screen closed.
......	...
每祇向、洞房深處 痛憐極寵[104]	Always towards the depth of the grotto-chamber, I passionately love and ultimately cosset you.

All these scenes are direct loans from the grotto romance tradition, and they match our image of the poet as a man familiar with the entertainment quarters, and who often associated with singers, about whose performances he often wrote lyrics and for whom he composed "private love songs."[105] In presenting many of these romances in the mode of the Liu-Ruan tale, Liu Yong enhances personal romance with impersonal myth. His two songs under the title of "Pleasure in Day and Night" ("Zhouye le" 晝夜樂) portray a lady's longing for her lover in the spring surrounded by flowers, and thus also fall within the framework of the Liu-Ruan tale. The female protagonist in these songs expresses her longing for a handsome and passionate man with whom she had a bout of drinking and whom she detained for the night in the "grotto-chamber" (*dongfang* 洞房) of her residence on "peach blossom lane" (*taohua jing* 桃花徑).[106] As Stephen Owen observes: "drawing on the lost repertoire of song types in the Entertainment Quarter, Liu Yong often stands at the beginning of these types."[107] And yet, once again, we observe that authors like Liu Yong relied heavily on the diction, images, and sentiments in the grotto romance tradition invoking the Liu-Ruan tale.

Within this line of poetic development, the tune-title "Springtime in the Grotto-heaven" ("Dongtian chun" 洞天春) catches our special attention. The earliest extant lyrics to this tune are by Ouyang Xiu.[108] In this poem, the references to "grotto-heaven" and "spring" are, again, standard references to the grotto romance tradition. The poem reads:

---

104 *QSC*, 42, 36, 50, respectively; the second and third poems, trans. Hightower, "The Songwriter Liu Yung, Part I," 347–48; "The Songwriter Liu Yung, Part II," 51–52.
105 Hightower: "There is ... no need to deny their [Liu's songs; my insertion] author's familiarity with the milieu that is their setting." See idem, "The Songwriter Liu Yung, Part I," 340–41.
106 *QSC*, 15; poem 2, trans. Hightower, "The Songwriter Liu Yung, Part I," 346–47.
107 Owen, *Just a Song*, 94.
108 See Wu Outing and Wu Xiaoting, *Cidiaoming cidian*, 446.

	洞天春	"Springtime in the Grotto-heaven"
1	鶯啼綠樹聲早	Orioles singing among green trees so early,
2	檻外殘紅未掃	Beyond the balustrades are fallen red petals unswept,
3	露點真珠遍芳草	Dewdrops and real pearls all over the fragrant grasses,
4	正簾幃清曉	When my curtains and screens are just showing clear dawn.
	***	***
5	鞦韆宅院悄悄	The swing in my resident courtyard, silent and solitary;
6	又是清明過了	Another Qingming festival has just passed.
7	燕蝶輕狂	Swallows and butterflies are roaming and revelling.
8	柳絲撩亂	Willow catkins stir and disturb
9	春心多少[109]	How many spring hearts?

We observe that the typical scene and theme, as well as the rhetorical devices, appear to have been informed by the grotto romance tradition. The "swallows' chatters and orioles' twitters" 燕語鶯啼 are features of spring, as reflected also in some Dunhuang songs under titles related to the grotto romance. As seen in Part 1 of the present chapter, the spring setting became a customary backdrop for portrayals of forlorn ladies missing their lovers. This setting recurs in Ouyang's poem, which sets the time as the second spring season (l. 6) since the lovers were together. One is reminded of Liu and Ruan's springtime adventure to the grotto, and their six-month detention there (in grotto time). Naturally, images such as swallows, orioles, and spring occur broadly in the repertoire of amorous *ci* in the Northern Song. But here, Ouyang Xiu adds some other less common images to generate a peculiar setting of melancholy: the wilted red blossoms, dewdrops, a swing in the desolate courtyard, and willow catkins enrich the sentiment and aesthetic appeal of the poem. His contribution enlarges this repertoire of romantic images, and enables his *ci* to transcend grotto romance convention. As a result of the sophistication of his technique, the stock images and personae found in his *ci*-poems are not directly traceable to the Liu-Ruan tale. And yet the tale still serves as an important source of Ouyang's poetic vocabulary.

---

109   *QSC*, 145.

3.5   *Writing as Reminiscence of the Peach Spring*

Ouyang Xiu's treatment of the tune-title "Reminiscing about an Acquaintance from the Peach Spring" ("Taoyuan yi guren" 桃源憶故人) more clearly typifies the Liu-Ruan tale prevailed in serving the purpose of writing about amorous topics. The literal meaning of this tune-title pertains to the peach spring adventure, but it is not clear which peach spring is referred to when the tune was first created. As Ouyang Xiu's poems are the earliest extant works under this tune-title, we may rely on them only in our discussion of his sources and creativity. The lyrics show a merging of the two peach springs, namely the one Liu and Ruan entered and the one narrated by Tao Qian in his "Record of the Peach Blossom Spring." This merging of references took place in the Tang and became a common treatment in the *ci* of the Song. In continuing with this style, which was in vogue,[110] Ouyang Xiu practiced new craftsmanship in his versions of love poems within the two frameworks by adding some new imagery and plot elements.

Although the literal meaning of the tune-title "Reminiscing about an Acquaintance from the Peach Spring" seems to be a synopsis of Tao Qian's peach spring tale, there is nothing reminiscent of the fisherman; contextually it makes perfect sense to read it in light of the Liu-Ruan reference. In the poems, it is not clear who the "acquaintance" (*guren* 故人, lit., "one whom one has known for a long time") is, but one can clearly sense the prominent feminine sentiment delivered in the monologue message of "missing my lover" in a feminine voice. It is obviously not the Wuling fisherman's reminiscence. The first poem in the suite reads:

	桃源憶故人	"Reminiscing about an Acquaintance from the Peach Spring"
1	梅梢弄粉香猶嫩	As the plum tree branch's powder-covered tip is fragrant and still fresh,
2	欲寄江南春信	I desire to send a springtime message from South of the River.
3	別後寸腸縈損	After parting, every inch of my insides is entangled and hurt.
4	說與伊爭穩	But how can I dare tell him?
	***	***

---

110   In addition to the *ci* under the tune-title directly related to the grotto romance tradition, one titled "Expressing My Inner Feelings" ("Su Zhongqing" 訴衷情) by Mao Wenxi 毛文錫, an *Among Flowers* poet, also features the same theme. See *QTWDC*, "zhengbian," 3.539.

5	小爐守寒灰燼	Staying by the small oven with its cold ashes,
6	忍淚低頭畫盡	I withhold my tears, my head lowered, drawing all
7	眉上萬種新恨	On my eyebrows a myriad of new grievances.
8	竟日無人問[111]	At the end of the day, no one asks me about it.

Line 2 confirms that this virtual peach spring is in Jiangnan (where the Liu-Ruan tale took place) rather than Wuling (in Hu'nan province). We also recall that Tao Qian's version of the peach spring tale does not have anything to do with love affairs, reinforcing our reading of this as the spring in the Liu-Ruan tale. The theme of a lady troubled by the spring season fits in the grotto romance tradition despite the absence of any grotto. These characteristics are also evident in the other two poems under the same tune-title, which depict the sending off of the lover and remembering him in the spring.[112]

Although Tao Qian's version of the peach spring does not play a role in these lyrics to the tune "Reminiscing about an Acquaintance from the Peach Spring," its popularity occupied a prominent place in literary history, and peach spring references usually recall both his text and the Liu-Ruan tale. This dual reference informs most of the lyrics to the same tune anthologized in *Quan Songci*.[113] In Zhang Xian's lyrics to the variant title of this tune, "Getting Drunk in the Peach Spring" ("Zui Taoyuan" 醉桃源), for example, we read: "On what day will my transcendent gentleman come" 仙郎何日是來期?[114] Throughout the Northern Song, the grotto romance motif was reserved mainly to represent boudoir grievances. The variant title "Getting Drunk in the Peach Spring" seems to prescribe lyrics based on the banquet scene at the grotto heaven where Liu and Ruan met their lovers. The content of an early work under this title by Zhang Xian, however, focuses on the lady missing her lover who has left her after they became drunk in this peach spring.[115] Therefore, these tune-titles on the amorous scenes derived from the grotto romance clearly distinguish themselves from the Tao Qian tale, in which the fisherman is invited to various households in Wuling but pursues no romance. It was the Northern Song lyricists' fondness for writing about amorous matters that sidelined the tale about the Wuling

---

111   *QSC*, 140.

112   *QSC*, 140, 159.

113   After Ouyang Xiu, famous *ci*-poets such as Su Shi, Qin Guan 秦觀 (1049–1100), and Huang Tingjian 黃庭堅 (1045–1105) all wrote lyrics to this tune on a lady missing her lover. See *QSC*, 310, 413, 464.

114   *QSC*, 81.

115   *QSC*, 62, in which the editor Tang Guizhang notes that this poem is also attributed to Ouyang Xiu. The tune-title as a variant of "Gentleman Ruan Returning Home" is in Wu Outing and Wu Xiaoting, *Cidiaoming cidian*, 841.

fisherman. Following this fashion, most *ci* in the tune-title "Springtime in Wuling" ("Wuling chun") were turned into amorous songs. Zhang Xian, again, does position his poem in Qingxi 青溪 (in the vicinity of the peach spring in Wuling), but writes about the flirting between a girl who picks water-chestnuts and her lover.[116] The *ci* "Springtime in Wuling" by Ouyang Xiu illustrates this co-opting of the Wuling peach spring into the grotto romance tradition. It focuses on the lovers bidding farewell soon after their first acquaintance:

Ouyang Xiu, "Springtime in Wuling"

1	寶幄華燈相見夜	Near precious curtains and luxurious lamps—on the night we met.
2	妝臉小桃紅	My made-up face is as red as a small peach.
3	斗帳香檀翡翠籠	The funnel-shape tent, the aromatic sandalwood, and the kingfisher cage—
4	攜手恨忽忽	Hand in hand, I regret that it is too rushed.
	***	***
5	金泥雙結同心帶	Gilded ribbon knotted in the shape of twined hearts,
6	留與記情濃	I leave for you as a token of our deep love.
7	卻望行雲十二峰	Gazing at the wandering clouds around the twelve peaks,
8	腸斷月斜鐘[117]	My insides ache as the moon turns awry towards the bell.

Although the title refers to Tao Qian's Wuling, the amorous scene and feelings presented in the lyrics derive from the *Youming lu* record of Liu and Ruan's meeting with the maidens in the grotto. Like in many other poems with similar references, including those we have seen in this chapter (e.g., by Ouyang Xiu, Mao Wenxi, and Zhang Xian), the persona-speaker here is the forlorn maiden recollecting happy times spent with her lover, and her grievances after parting with him. The allusion to the Goddess of Mount Wu (l. 7) was much loved by *Among Flowers* poets but is not related to Tao Qian's tale.[118] This kind of diversion from the literal meaning of the tune-title and invocation of a wider spectrum of sources here serves to intensify the sorrow of the protagonist by

---

116 *QSC*, 64.
117 *QSC*, 150.
118 See Part 1 of this chapter and Suzanne Cahill's of the tune-title "The Transcendent by the River" for which she identifies the Goddess of Mount Wu as its main source. See Cahill, "Sex and the Supernatural in Medieval China," 199–202.

comparing her with the Goddess of Mount Wu, who had a fleeting romantic experience with her mortal lover, King Xiang of Chu. In short, the Tao Qian reference has been eroticized through its juxtaposition with the grotto romance and the Goddess of Mount Wu references.

The eroticization of the tune "Springtime in Wuling" became a genre feature of these lyrics.[119] In Ouyang's poem, the dual reference to both peach springs served as a standard framework and ensured that the lyrics were not mechanical reproductions of grotto romance tales but instead formed a new poetic discourse.

4 Conclusions

The Dunhuang songs are proto *ci*-poems in Chinese poetic and music history and have been regarded as the most important source materials for tracing the genre's evolution. In this inception stage—when most tune-titles were newly created—vestiges of the referents of the title's literal meaning are still detectable in the lyrics. These songs explore new content while also maintaining traceable connections to the grotto romance tradition. The most remarkable trace is the word and image of *xian*. Here, the transcendent is endowed with the grotto fantasy triple identity, in line with mid-Tang grotto fantasy works in other genres. An understanding of the tune-titles' literal meaning is an important first step in interpreting these works and their relationship with the grotto romance tradition. Grotto fantasy is often indicated by an eponymous title, as in "The Transcendent by the River" and "Gentleman Ruan Returning Home."

Once grotto fantasy is an indicated theme, there is no universally valid interpretation. For example, the tune "Farewell my Transcendent" includes some songs with content unrelated to the literal meaning of the tune-title.[120] A similar example includes the lyrics to the tune "The Transcendent by the River," which begins with a line "Our great king, at your discretion" 大王處分.[121] If we are circumscribed to the myths surrounding the transcendent and the grotto in our reading of this song, we will meet a dead-end because no "transcendent" is found in the song. These exceptional cases are evidence of the early divorce of the song's content from its tune-title's meaning.

---

119 Earlier examples include the lyrics to this tune by Zhang Xian, Yan Jidao, and Lady Wei 魏夫人. See *QSC*, 80, 256, 269.
120 The second song, "Farewell my Transcendent," was written by a monk. See Tang Jun, *Dunhuang quzici diyu wenhua yanjiu*, 117–19.
121 *DHGC*, "buyi," 1757.

In the hands of Northern Song poets, the Liu-Ruan tale evolved to inspire a poetics of boudoir grievance. These male poets demonstrate a range of feminine feelings such that, as Grace Fong observes, "alternatively, these *ci* would present a woman as described by a voyeuristic observer."[122] Living in a time when the form, meter, theme, and music of these tunes were governed by convention mainly developed by *Among Flowers* poets, like most others, Ouyang Xiu conformed to the conventional framework and relied upon stock images inherited from tradition, while at the same time augmenting them with new poetic elements.

However, when encountering these *ci* poems, which appear to be related to or derived from the Liu-Ruan tale, one must guard against reductive readings. Any decent artwork should not be read as a mechanical replication of its source; rather, the new creation has a new life in a new time.[123] As we have seen, most variants of a given tune-title may be understood according to their literal meaning, as indicated by the title, which guides the content of the lyrics, but sometimes the lyrics diverge from this convention. After the inception of a new tune-title, other lyrics may follow tangents, as was the case for "like a dream," thus diverging from the rubric that ties a tune-title to a prescribed theme.[124]

Because they share the Liu-Ruan tale as a source in common, the *ci* and proto-*ci* discussed in this chapter illuminate the three main thematic concerns explored throughout the present book. First, these lyrics directly or indirectly reveal an evolution of the Liu-Ruan tale. Much of that evolution occurred in the role of the female protagonist, leading to our second thematic focus: the triple role of the female protagonist, as the Daoist priestess, the entertainer,

---

122 Fong, "Persona and Mask in the Song Lyric (*Ci*)," 460.
123 For instance, although the tune-title "Butterfly in Love with Blossoms" ("Die lian hua" 蝶戀花) is also named "To the Peach Spring" ("Taoyuan xing" 桃源行), it clearly does not belong to the same textual cycle, because the works with the former tune-title do not reflect grotto romance themes. Ouyang Xiu wrote romantic lyrics under this title by borrowing imagery and diction from the Liu-Ruan tale, but none of these should be qualified as examples of the grotto romance for the same reason. The theme of most lyrics to the tune "Die lian hua" by Ouyang Xiu concerns the forlorn lady's grievances, but they include a variety of topics such as the Yue maidens picking lotus, the courtyard, a spring scene on West Lake, and dreams of the terrace of the Chu State. See *QSC*, 125–28, 149–50. The variant titles of "Die lian hua" are found in Wu Outing and Wu Xiaoting, *Cidiaoming cidian*, 855.
124 Another example includes Ouyang Xiu's poem "Taoyuan yi guren" ("Bisha nongying" 碧紗弄影), which is also attributed to Qin Guan and titled "Yu meiren ying" 虞美人影 ("The Shadow of Yu the Beauty"). It is also on boudoir grievances but has nothing to do with the Liu-Ruan tale. See *QSC*, 159.

and the transcendent. We find this tripartite role present in these works and evolved to include an emphasized sense of anxiety of her extended isolation. After Yuan Zhen and Bai Juyi, her role became prominent in the works of the *Among Flowers* poets, which, in turn, served as one of Ouyang Xiu's models for his own compositions created for singing girls' performances. Third, the theme of time-dilation became a rhetorical device for the expression of grievances of the lady who is left alone. These features are observed in the representation of the themes such as the priestess in love, the campaigner missing his wife and vice versa, and the frustrated career aspirant in the disguise of Liu and Ruan who visited the *xian*. As grotto fantasy provenance of these roles is identified, the entrance of the mysterious grotto is thrown open once again. This rediscovery of the origin of the *xian* image in these contexts allows us to identify and decipher the other figures present in the works, and also aids in establishing the relevant historical background, enabling exploration of nuances in meaning and aesthetic value in these songs.

The findings of this chapter also enable us to reflect on the authenticity of Ouyang Xiu's amorous *ci*. Some of the erotic content of these *ci* poems was inherited from convention but, as mentioned above, the overall content and style was largely fashioned by the poet according to his own circumstances and thoughts. Indeed, there may be no way to substantiate the impeccability of Ouyang's character, but his interactions with entertainers and his composition of songs for their performances should not necessarily tarnish his name. For the more serious charge related to his incestuous relationship with his niece, scholars have made efforts to exculpate him.[125] If, however, we divest from the task of defending his character, we can make use of his biographical details and literary tendencies in the reading of his erotic poetry. One such example is his lyrics to the tune "Xi qun yao" 繫裙腰 ("Fixing My Sashes around My Waist"), which contains a sensual description of a lady who has just woken up.[126] While culturally conservative historians may have condemned him for such writings, Ouyang's outstanding musical skills (especially his proficiency on the zither) may also have served as a pretext for his erotic writing. As Ronald Egan observes, composition of lyrics offered an expedient way to communicate with the entertainers.[127] Tunes for entertainment mainly feature love themes, especially a lady missing her lover; it is thus not surprising that

---

125   The case is called "stealing the niece" (*daosheng* 盜甥). See *Moji*, 3.3b; James T. C. Liu, *Ou-yang Hsiu*, 79–82, and Xie Fei, "Ouyang Xiu yanci feiwen bianyi," 92–97.
126   *QSC*, 152–53; *Ouyang Xiu ci jianzhu*, 166–67.
127   Egan, "The Problem of the Repute of Tz'u," 201.

Ouyang wrote these kinds of works.[128] As time went by, the performers might not even remember "who wrote that [song]," while some of these songs remain under Ouyang's name even after the purge of the allegedly unhealthy works from his oeuvre.[129]

One other *ci*-poem of disputed origins contains lyrics, whether Ouyang Xiu wrote them or not, that are worth some remarks here. This poem in question is "Spring on the Jade Terrace" ("Yulou chun" 玉樓春, no. 4), which begins with the line: "Gold sparrows on the paired ring-shaped coiffures" 金雀雙鬟.[130] This *ci* has long been said to have been forged by Ouyang's enemies who wanted to defile his name but was successfully interpolated into his collected works. No strong argument would support or refute this claim,[131] but we learn in this poem the character of Liu Chen assumes a new role as a seducer of young girls: "Gentleman Liu possesses a great passion for loving blossoms, / But too bad he looks for blossoms slightly too early " 劉郎大有惜花心，只恨尋花來較早.[132] Without concerning ourselves with the authorship of the *ci*, we see clearly that Liu Chen had long become an iconic protagonist of love stories and had been re-created in a large variety of contexts. This example (from "Yulou chun," no. 4) supports this important source of erotic elements in Ouyang's *ci*, in which the Liu-Ruan tale contributes to the making of this specific topos throughout the Northern Song.

---

128   Florence Chia-ying Yeh, "Ambiguity and the Female Voice in Hua-chien Songs," 121; Colin S. C. Hawes, *The Social Circulation of Poetry*, 52.
129   See Stephen Owen's discussion of the issue, especially the part on Ouyang Xiu, in Owen, "Who Wrote That?" 202–20, esp., 212–14.
130   *QSC*, 156.
131   Ronald Egan gives the lyrics "To the tune 'Gazing Toward the Southland'" as an example of "a male persona [who] speaks of his infatuation with a very young girl" in his discussion of how these kinds of writings related to Ouyang's involvement in the alleged incest charges. See Egan, *The Problem of Beauty*, 276–78.
132   *QSC*, 156. See Egan's analysis in his *The Literary Works of Ou-yang Hsiu*, 171.

CHAPTER 5

The Confucian Scholar in Love with the Transcendent in Yuan–Ming Contexts

1   Introduction

Liu Chen and Ruan Zhao's grotto adventure assumed another new life during the Yuan–Ming period, when the story was told in alternative ways to express the frustration of the Chinese literati under Mongol rule. The works under investigation in this chapter are performances and paintings that held great aesthetic appeal for contemporary audiences. Our main interest here is not aesthetics, however. Rather, we focus on a second level of appreciation, namely why and how the Liu-Ruan tale served as a source for purposeful adaptation. This task is achieved by a comprehensive approach to the authors' historical circumstances and political attitudes embedded in these literary and fine art creations. More specifically, we explore how these texts more fully embrace themes of Daoist transcendence as part of the grotto romance repertoire and how these are manipulated to communicate specific, historically relevant political commentary. Literary work and the medium of painting served as peculiar channels for the articulation of political thought under the unprecedented political oppression by the non-Chinese rulers in the period of the thirteenth to fourteenth centuries. Here, we observe how the literati react to the world from which they have been dislocated *en masse*. This disenfranchisement motivates drastic changes to the Liu-Ruan repertoire, in terms of the renewed roles and symbolic meaning of the grotto visitors, their interaction with the transcendents, and the contrast between the transcendent realm and the mortal world.

In our reading of drama scripts and a painting (with inscribed texts), we focus on the unique feature of time dilation in the Liu-Ruan tale, which is adapted as an especially suitable means for the venting of regret over the passing of the previous (native Chinese) dynasty. Our discussion will recover the impulse of art as self-solace, though the play was intended to be performed before an audience. These writers and artists fulfill Liu Chen and Ruan Zhao's previously frustrated wish to return to the grotto, appending a happy ending to a tale that had remained a tragedy for centuries.

We focus on three works in two art forms for discussion, namely 1) a play titled "Celestial Master Zhang's Conviction of Breeze, Flower, Snow, and Moon"

張天師斷風花雪月, attributed to Wu Changling 吳昌齡 (Yuan dyn.), 2) a play titled "Liu Chen and Ruan Zhao's Straying to Mount Tiantai" 劉晨阮肇悞入天台, attributed to Wang Ziyi 王子一 (late Yuan to early Ming dyn.), and 3) "A scroll of paintings of Liu Chen and Ruan Zhao Entering the Tiantai Mountains, by Zhao Cangyun" ("Yuan Zhao Cangyun Liu Chen Ruan Zhao ru Tiantaishan tujuan" 元趙蒼雲劉晨阮肇入天台山圖卷) and the text of the inscription on the painting. Of these three works, only the Liu-Ruan play might have originated in the Yuan Dynasty and been finalized in the Ming; the other two were both produced in the early Ming.[1] Therefore, these works embody the thoughts of Yuan writers and certain ruminations on the Yuan from the perspective of the early Ming.[2] The chapter discusses why and how the Liu-Ruan tale attracted interest from these artists and how it created a new political dimension.

Any discussion of Yuan drama must deal with the problems of textual transmission. In this part of literary history, Li Kaixian and Zang Maoxun 臧懋循 (1550–1620) were two key figures in what was a broad-brush revisionist shaping of Yuan drama to the anthologists' ideals. These and other Ming editors engaged in "appropriation" and "reproductive authorship" when reproducing Yuan works.[3] Modern scholars often refer to works of this kind as "deliverance plays" (*dutuo xi* 度脫戲).[4] While the works analyzed in this chapter reflect this religious theme of deliverance from worldly sorrows, we shall see they also carry more specific meanings when juxtaposed against the language and literary conventions of the Liu-Ruan tradition.

---

1   The name Wang Ziyi is found in Zhu Quan 朱權 (1378–1448), *Taihe zhengyin pu*, 40. Yan Dunyi and Wu Mei read the name literally as "one of the princes," a pseudonym of Zhu Quan who is a member of the Zhu clan, the ruling power of the Ming dynasty. See Yan, *Yuanju zhenyi*, 431; Wu, "Qu'an duqu ji," 418. The play is recorded to have been "written by Wang Ziyi of the beginning of our dynasty" 國初王子一撰. See *Gu mingjia zaju*, vol. 3, 3.1a. A similar attribution, "Wang Ziyi of the Ming" 明王子一, is found in the same play in *Gujin zaju*, 1a. Sun Shulei dates it to the Yuan because Li Kaixian 李開先 (1502–1568) included it in his *Gaiding Yuanxian chuanqi*. See Sun, "*Gaiding Yuanxian chuanqi* kao lun," 10, n. 1. It is generally agreed that Li's anthology was printed between 1558 and 1568. See Tian Yuan Tan, *Songs of Contentment and Transgression*, 224.
2   For Ming period editorial work on Yuan *zaju* plays, see, e.g., Wilt Idema, "Why you never have read a Yuan drama," 765–91; "The Orphan of Zhao," 159–90; "The Many Shapes of Medieval Chinese Plays," 320–34; Stephen West, "A Study in Appropriation," 283–302.
3   See Stephen West, "A Study in Appropriation"; Wilt Idema, "The Many Shapes of Medieval Chinese Plays"; Idema, "Why You Never Have Read a Yuan Drama"; Patricia Sieber, *Theaters of Desire*, 91–119.
4   Stephen West and Wilt Idema define the term *dutuo*: "… in its frequent use in both the Daoist and Buddhist canons [as having] the clear meaning of 'to lead someone beyond [their current existence] and shed [worldly cares].'" See West and Idema, *The Orphan of Zhao and Other Yuan Plays*, 201–2. I am indebted to Stephen West for directing me to this source.

2   Mortality or Immortality: the Values of the Literati

The Song–Yuan-era trend of compiling hagiographies of transcendent beings strengthened the reciprocal relationship between religion and literature. The compilation of such entries for individual transcendents illustrates the deification of certain figures. Specifically, the maidens in the Liu-Ruan tale qualify for the status of *xian* in the *Lishi zhenxian tidao tongjian* 歷世真仙體道通鑑 (*A Comprehensive Reference to the Achievements of the Dao of Perfected Transcendents from All Eras*) and in Luo Ye's 羅燁 (fl. late 13th c.) adapted version of the Liu-Ruan tale in the section on "Fantastic Encounters with the Divinities" (*Shenxian jiahui* 神仙嘉會) of his *Zuiweng tanlu* 醉翁談錄.[5] The deification of the grotto maidens within the Daoist pantheon would have been known to the authors of the works under investigation in this chapter.

While the maidens achieved their immortality, Liu and Ruan have almost always been portrayed as mere mortals. Paradoxically, their mortality contributes to their eternal life in literature, enabling them to serve as literary proxies for literati throughout the ages. In particular, they serve to vicariously satisfy men's pursuit of the transcendent realm, which may stand for the pursuit of love or of a political goal, as we have seen in the previous chapters. To a male member of the literati class, Liu Chen and Ruan Zhao are relatable and malleable characters. In other words, their mortality grants them literary immortality. This paradox is most typically illustrated in a Song-dynasty work, the *Yixian zhuan* 疑仙傳 (*Biographies of Dubious Transcendents*), attributed to Yinfu Yujian 隱夫玉簡, which makes the following remarks on Liu and Ruan:

> I indeed know about people like Liu Chen and Ruan Zhao. They are simply uncultivated individuals who, by accident, strayed to the Peach Spring Grotto. In the end, they had a secular mind and did not attain transcendence. Since then, most of the transcendence pursuers could ascend to heaven under broad sunlight and none ever returned.

---

5   The version of the Liu-Ruan tale included in *Lidai zhenxian tidao tongjian* (HY 296, 7.11b–12a) does not reflect the reality of the Yuan, mainly because the accounts for the "Perfected Transcendents" in this book were mainly taken from previous records. See Jean Lévi, "*Lishi zhenxian tidao tongjian*," 887–92; Ozaki Masaharu, "*Lekisei shinsen taidou tsugan* no tekisuto ni tsuite," 37–54; Zhang Xingfa, *Daojiao shenxian xinyang*, 627, quoting Liu Shipei's *Du Daozang ji*, 17a. One main source of the *Lishi zhenxian tidao tongjian* is the Six-dynasty *Dongxian zhuan* 洞仙傳 (Lévi, op cit., 889). See also Lee Fong-mao, *Liuchao Sui Tang xiandao lei xiaoshuo yanjiu*, 188–89, quoting Yen Yi-ping 嚴一萍. Luo Ye's version is in Luo, *Xinbian zuiweng tanlu*, "Xinji" 辛集, 1.445.

我亦識劉晨阮肇之輩，此皆俗人耳，偶然悮入他桃源洞，終亦有俗心，故不得仙也。爾後好仙者多白日昇天，皆不復回。[6]

As the book title suggests, Liu and Ruan are dubbed "dubious transcendents," but their entry indicates that they are not considered transcendents after all. Their failure to transcend is attributed to their "secular mind" (*suxin* 俗心). From a literary point of view, their secular mindedness may be seen as the power that prompted the writing and rewriting of the Liu-Ruan tale throughout literary history. The two mortal men must transgress borders and boundaries, or, in Yuan Zhen's words, "sneak in and out by stealth" 偷入又偷迴, to complete their romantic adventure.[7] This discourse works especially well in the specific politico-social environment of the Yuan dynasty, as perceived by both the literati under Yuan dominion and those in the Ming period looking back on the Yuan. Political anxiety and oppression invite tales of transgression.

The political frustration experienced by the literati stemmed directly from the civil service (*keju* 科舉) examination being held at irregular intervals and the inequity of official appointments.[8] As a result, the literary works of the time are tinted with despair and discontent.[9] In relevant scholarship, the following testimony by Yu Que 余闕 (1303–1358) from his "Preface to a Special Collection of Yang Xianmin" 楊君顯民特集序, has become the most frequently quoted source explaining the predicament of the literati.

> After annexing the Jin and Song empires, at the beginning of our dynasty, as long as one possessed talent one would be employed with no specific preference, although the majority were Confucius scholars. Since the Zhiyuan reign-period (1335–1340), however, clerks began to

---

[6] *Yixian zhuan* (HY 299), 2.9b. Quoting the editors of the *Siku quanshu*, Ren Jiyu et al. date this source to the Song. See Ren, *Daozang tiyao*, 222. Florian C. Reiter dates it to the Five Dynasties. See Reiter, "*Yixian zhuan*," 432.

[7] Yuan Zhen, "Liu Ruan qi" 劉阮妻, no. 1. *YZJJZ*, "xu buyi," 1.1540; *QTS*, 422.4640.

[8] There were different requirements for different candidates in exam questions, marking criteria, and assignments of official titles for those who passed the examination. Candidates were divided into four groups, in descending order of privilege: 1. Mongols, 2. other categories of peoples ("*semu ren* 色目人" included people of Arab, Alan, and Ouighur decent, among others [Stephen West, private communication, 25 November 2021]), 3. Chinese from the North, and 4. Southern Chinese. See Shen Jianshi, *Zhongguo kaoshi zhidu shi*, 141–43. See also Li Zhian, *Yuandai zhengzhi zhidu yanjiu*, 594–610.

[9] See Shionoya On, *Yuanqu gailun*, 23; Yu Shiao-ling, "Taoist Themes in Yüan Drama," 132–38. Zha Hongde ascribes the prosperity of literary creation in the Yuan to "academic issues not determined by the monarch but through discussion by relevant intellectuals at the imperial court" and "the loosened concepts of rituals and law." See Zha, *Yuandai shixue tonglun*, 20.

be employed even to the extent that they filled the posts of executive ministers. Thereupon, those commoners from the prefectures in central China who could understand only a few characters and process documents could enter the ministry and draft administrative documents. As days and months went by, they could smoothly become renowned. Thus, people with a degree from the Middle Kingdom were used less and less. What is more, the southern regions were so far away that the scholars there were unable to reach the capital by themselves. Those with talents would feel contemptuous about becoming a clerk, so especially few of them would be used. After a while, southern and northern scholars began to criticize each other from their own turf, as a result of the serious situation between the Jin and Qin states [in the Warring States period] and would not share a unified Middle Kingdom. For this reason, the scholars of the south declined. In the Yanyou reign-period (1314–1320), Emperor Renzong (Buyantu Khan, r. 1311–1320) initiated the *keju* examination, but numerous scholars disdained it and preferred to retreat and indulge themselves in mountains and forests. How pitiful indeed. As these scholars were not used in the world, most delved into writing, hoping to achieve an immortal name. However, of these writings some were fortunate and some not. The unfortunate ones found no way to be used as they turned old, and their literary work disappeared without recognition. It was indeed miserable.[10]

Yu Que's analysis provides a Yuan-specific rationale for the literary quest for an alternative "immortality." Yan-shuan Lao's discussion supplements Yu's views on the North-South divide. He argues that "those who were appointed to high offices in the south were invariably northerners" because "before the Mongols conquered the Southern Sung, they had already organized a bureaucracy which absorbed a large number of scholars and ex-bureaucrats from the defunct Jurchen-Chin."[11] As these privileged races and classes occupied most of the official posts, the Han (particularly southern Chinese people) found it hard to get promoted in their official life. As in previous times of political strife in China's history, the literati vented their frustrations in literary and artistic creation, for which there was a ready audience.[12]

---

10   Yu Que, *Qingyang ji*, 2.11b–12a. I acknowledge Stephen West's help in understanding this passage.
11   Lao, "Southern Chinese Scholars," 110.
12   Doubts have been cast as to the credibility of the conventional ten-rank theory of "scholars the ninth and beggars the tenth" 九儒十丐. Instead, the indignation of scholars living in the Yuan had two main causes: 1) The Mongol caste had absolute advantages in pursuing their political career, as *ijaghur* (*genjiao* 根腳, lit., "root and footing," i.e., one's

3   Liu and Ruan's Accidental Straying to Mount Tiantai

One other significant addition to the characterization of Liu Chen and Ruan Zhao in the Yuan is that they were well-educated Confucianists. We find references to the effect that "Confucianism is their family's teaching"; "they were reading the *Documents* and *Odes* from an early age"; and "they emulated the (Confucian) sages."[13] Previous versions of the tale and its adaptations never characterized the pair in this way. The drastic change may be seen as a direct reflection of shared indignation about the perceived decline of Confucian values in Yuan times. In this section, we explore how the pair assume their new Confucian characterization and what significance it has. We focus on the *zaju* play "Accidental Straying to Mount Tiantai" attributed to Wang Ziyi.[14]

The transcendent Venus (Taibai jinxing 太白金星) plays the role of divine guide for Liu and Ruan. He is the first character to take the stage, escorted by some transcendent lads in blue apparel. His opening monologue succinctly summarizes the plot of the play:

> I am Venus from the upper realm. I am solely in charge of good and bad fortune in the mortal realm, I guide the perplexed and astray, and I save people from disaster. Now I have been sent down by an imperial command of the High Thearch to this lower realm to maintain the balance of good and evil in the human realm. At present in Mount Tiantai, there are two transcendent maidens who were jade girls of the Purple Ethereal, but were banished to the dusty world because they were overcome by secular sensuality. Liu Chen and Ruan Zhao of the Tiantai District have long been gifted with Daoist transcendent qualities and are predestined by karma from previous lives to marry these two transcendent maidens. As the Jin royal house deteriorates, and the treacherous and slandering ones have usurped its mandate, these two men live contentedly with their allotment

---

    background) was the most important consideration in the selection criteria; 2) The *keju* examination was suspended from the time the Mongols overthrew the Jurchen-Jin until 1314; during this period, the Chinese literati lost their only path to employment for some eighty years. See Chen Dezhi, "Cong 'jiu ru shi gai' kan Yuandai rushi de diwei" (a revised version is in Chen, *Meng-Yuan shi yanjiu conggao*, 424); Hsiao Ch'i-ch'ing, *Nei beiguo er wai Zhongguo*, 185, 188, 210. Frederick Mote points out additional complexities of Yuan literati life. See Mote, "Chinese Society under Mongol Rule, 1215–1368," 627–48.

13   See Zhao Cangyun's inscription on his painting in appendix; Wang Ziyi, "Liu Chen Ruan Zhao wuru Tiantai," in *Gaiding Yuanxian chuanqi*, 2a, 2b.

14   This play is a relatively complete script compared to others in the same thematic circle. For a list of peach spring dramas of pre-modern times, see Kao Chia-wen, "'Taoyuan xiqu' dui 'Taoyuan zhuti' jieshou zhi yanjiu," 178–80.

in mountains and forests. With talents and skills, they spend their springs and autumns cultivating perfection and refining herbs. Today, they will definitely ascend Mount Tiantai to gather medicinal herbs; I will conjure a stretch of clouds to disorient them on their homeward route. In the disguise of a wood cutter, I will receive them in the mountains. Assuredly, they will ask me for directions, and I will lead them to the transcendent realm for an acquaintance with the transcendent maidens and the consummation of their romantic tryst. Then, I will order my blue-clad lads to herald the transcendent maidens, who should receive the men with transcendent music to enrich their love with harmony and perfection. It is a pity that Liu and Ruan have not severed their karmic link with the dusty world and only a year will pass before they consider returning home. When they are back home, they shall find themselves removed from their own time by generations. Only then will they realize the difference between the transcendent and mortal realms. When they re-enter the mountains, they will lose their way. At that point, it will not be too late to guide them.

吾乃上界太白金星是也。專一掌管人間禍福，指引迷惑，救人急難。今奉上帝勅命，遣臨下界，糾察人間善惡。今有天台山桃源洞二仙子，係是紫霄玉女，凡心一動，降謫塵寰。為天台縣劉晨、阮肇二子，素有仙風道骨，與二仙子有夙世姻緣。此二人因晉室衰頹，奸讒竊柄，甘分山林之下，懷才抱藝，修真練藥，以度春秋。今日必上天台山採藥，吾起白雲一道，迷其歸路。卻化作一樵夫，入山迎之。此人必來問路，吾當引入仙境與二仙子相見，成其良緣。然此必索命青衣童子往洞中報知仙子，使以仙樂相迎，兩情和美。惜乎劉阮二人塵緣未斷，僅及一載，復有思歸之念。比及回家，已經隔世，方惺仙凡有異。再入山中，失其歸路。那時節我再指引他，未爲晚矣。[15]

The adaptation of the familiar Liu-Ruan plot turns the play into a political allegory. Liu Chen's following monologue is delivered upon his and Ruan Zhao's debut in the first act of the play, and represents the frustration of intellectuals under Mongol rule, rather than tropes traditionally attached to the tale:

---

15 Wang Ziyi, "Liu Chen Ruan Zhao wuru Tiantai," in *Gaiding Yuanxian zaju*,1b; *Li Kaixian quanji* (hereafter, LKXQJ), 3: 2159. The *Gu mingjia zaju* version (3.1b–20a) was based on Li Kaixian's text. See Sun Shulei, "*Gaiding Yuanxian chuanqi* kao lun," 24–28. In this chapter, all quotations from this play are based on *Gaiding Yuanxian chuanqi* (quoted as "Wuru Tiantai") and LKXQJ.

[The lead actor performing as Liu Chen—with the support actor as Ruan Zhao, both with props in their hands—ascends to the stage and says:] My surname is Liu and Chen is my given name. The surname of this brother of mine is Ruan and Zhao is his given name. We are both from Tiantai district. In our youth we delved into the *Classic of Poetry* and *Classic of Documents*; we shared the same aspiration when growing up. Now as Emperor Hui of the Jin is on the throne, the codes and laws have decayed and are corrupt. As the road to attaining official chariots and attire has turned muddy, we abscond to forests and straths and have no intent to take part in the competition for deeds and renown. At the foot of Mount Tiantai we've built a thatched cottage and, with my brother, cultivate our conduct and discern the Dao. Have you not heard what the sage said: "When the Dao prevails in the world one shows up [to take office], when it does not, then retreat." Ah, this very much matches the current situation, indeed!

〔正末扮劉晨、外末扮阮肇各帶砌末上云〕某姓劉名晨，這位兄弟姓阮名肇，俱係天台縣人氏，幼攻詩書，長同志趣，方今晉惠帝在位，紀綱頹壞，泥塗軒冕，以此潛形於林壑之間，無志於功名之會。在天台山下，蓋一所茅菴，與兄弟修行辦道。豈不聞聖人之言：天下有道則見，無道則隱。倒大來達時務也呵！16

At the literal level, the play unfolds the usual fantastic story of Liu and Ruan for the enjoyment of its audiences, but it requires correlative reading/viewing to dig out the hidden meaning. This correlation relies on the resonance between the performance and the audience, who were all steeped in the political and literary rationale that a learned man should not pursue personal renown under a morally corrupt regime. This is an artful representation of the plight of the literati under the Yuan dynasty. A political interpretation of the play is reinforced by observing the playwright's alteration of the historical setting of his version of the Liu-Ruan tale from the Yongping era (58–75) of the Han dynasty, as seen in the *Youming lu* original version of the tale, to the reign of Emperor Hui of Jin (r. 291–307), an infamously corrupt period of history. This Jin emperor was considered one of the era's most benighted rulers. His power was eventually usurped by Empress Jia 賈后 (named Jia Nanfeng 南風, 257–300), who was directly responsible for the death of the crown prince and the rebellion of the eight princes, resulting in an invasion by a northern non-Han people who

---

16 *LKXQJ*, 3: 2159–60.

consequently replaced the Jin as the governing power in northern China.[17] This background serves as a historical parallel with the equally chaotic period of the end of the Song dynasty during the reign of Emperor Li (r. 1224–1264), a weak ruler, whose power was usurped by a prime minister—also named Jia (Jia Sidao 賈似道 [1213–1275], who was, coincidentally, a native of Tiantai district, where the Liu-Ruan romance took place)—who became responsible for the Mongol's eventual conquest of the Song.[18] In his monologue, translated above, Venus's damning of "the treacherous and slandering ones" who have usurped the Jin imperial mandate is, therefore, a literary indictment of Jia Sidao.

Wang Ziyi's shifting of the Liu-Ruan tale to the reign of Emperor Hui of Jin reinforces the traditional dating of this drama as a Yuan work. Even if we follow Yan Dunyi 嚴敦易 to understand "Wang Ziyi" as a pseudonym of a member of the Ming royal house named Zhu Quan, the play still reflects social pressure under the Yuan. The surviving fragments from an allegedly similar drama by Ma Zhiyuan 馬致遠 (1250–1321) entitled "Liu and Ruan of the Jin Dynasty Accidentally Strayed to the Peach Spring" 晉劉阮誤入桃源雜劇 also sees the men succeed in returning to the transcendent realm.[19] These plays, adapted from the same thematic source, serve as metaphors for the political desperation of the literati class under the Yuan. Political discontent produced works that were later dubbed "deliverance plays" and a literary preoccupation with lost paradises.[20] As the plot unfolds, the reader is reminded of interpretations of the *Youming lu* Liu-Ruan tale as an expression of the fantastic cravings of the commoners suffering from wars and famine. In this view, the grotto visitors actualize their yearnings for a luxurious house, delicacies, and beautiful girls.[21] In the second act of the drama, Wang Ziyi portrays Liu Chen and Ruan Zhao's encounter with the maidens as a moment akin to all their dreams coming true:

---

17   *Jinshu*, 4.89–108; 31.963–66.
18   *Songshi*, 474.13779–87.
19   See *Quan Yuan xiqu*, vol. 2: 312. Other lost dramas on the Liu-Ruan tale include: Ma Zhiyuan's and Chen Bojiang's 陳伯將 respective *zaju* plays entitled "Jin Liu Ruan wuru Taoyuan" 晉劉阮誤入桃源; Wang Yuanheng 汪元亨, "Liu Chen Ruan Zhao Taoyuandong" 劉晨阮肇桃源洞; anonymous, "Xiangsong chu Tiantai" 相送出天臺. See Zhuang Yifu, *Gudian xiqu cunmu huikao*, 5.338, 6.372, 374, 7.590. Ma Zhiyuan also wrote an aria, "Tiantai lu" 天臺路. See *Quan Yuan sanqu*, 234.
20   On the concept of "deliverance plays," see note 4 above. Lee Fong-mao lays an emphasis on the eschatological backgrounds of the Yuan in his study of the socio-religious backgrounds and art of the *dutuo* plays of the Yuan. See Lee, "Shenhua yu zhefan," 254–63.
21   Lee Fong-mao, *Wuru yu zhejiang*, 133–34.

THE CONFUCIAN SCHOLAR IN LOVE

【叨叨令】	[Daodao ling]
記不的軒轅一枕華胥夢	(I can't remember) Xuanyuan's dream about visiting the State of Huaxu.
學不的淳于一枕南柯夢	(I can't emulate) Chunyu's dream about what he did in Nanke.
盼不的文王一枕非熊夢	(I can't expect) King Wen's dream about his acquaintance with one who was not a bear.
成不的莊周一枕蝴蝶夢	(I can't complete) Zhuang Zhou's dream about turning himself into a butterfly.
到大來福分也麼哥	How great is my bliss—alas!
到大來福分也麼哥	How great is my bliss—alas!
恰做了襄王一枕陽臺夢[22]	(It is just like) having a dream of King Xiang about his romance at Solar Terrace.

Unlike the dreams of Yuan Zhen and the other *ci* poets discussed in Chapters 2 and 4, the first three of these literary dreams and divination of fantastic encounters carry allegorical meanings in a sarcastic tone. They include: 1) the Yellow Emperor dreamed about visiting the State of Huaxu, a utopia-like realm where the citizens enjoyed a carefree life; 2) Chunyu Fen 淳于棼 married a princess and became governor of Nanke in his dream; and 3) in his divination, King Wen of the Zhou Kingdom was told that he would catch some creature that looked like a bear but not really before he met Lü Shang, who later became his minister.[23] These allusions are examples of political successes and, therefore, contrast with Liu and Ruan's failures. The fourth dream is about Zhuang Zhou dreaming of becoming a butterfly and then musing about whether he became a butterfly or the butterfly became him.[24] This reference carries an escapist overtone when read in combination with the Liu-Ruan tale; they may dream of returning to the grotto, but they dream in vain. The fifth dream—concerning King Xiang of Chu who had a love affair with the goddess of Mount Wu—correlates best with the Liu-Ruan tale.[25] This dream represents a *carpe diem* theme as compensation for a failed career. Interestingly, these two

---

22 "Wuru Tiantai," 11b; *LKXQJ*, 2167. The brackets in the beginning (in Chinese and English) mark the tune-title of the aria. The "petty words" (*chenzi* 襯字) are in smaller print in Chinese and in parentheses in the English translation.
23 See, respectively, *Liezi jishi*, 2.41–43; Li Gongzuo 李公佐 (late 8th c.–early 9th c.), "Nanke taishou zhuan" 南柯太守傳, in *Tangren xiaoshuo*, 101–8; *Shiji*, 32.1477–78.
24 *Zhuangzi*, 2/94–96.
25 Song Yu, "Gaotang fu," *WX*, 19.1b–6b.

dreamers are still sober enough to suspect that they will eventually wake up from their dreams. The following aria describes their visit to the peach spring:

【隨煞尾】	[*Sui shawei*]
色籠蔥，光瀲灩	(How flourishing and thriving is the scene. How limpid and lucid is the light.)
山環水繞天台洞	The grotto of Tiantai is encircled by mountains and waters.
勢周旋，形曲折	(How revolving and whirling are the terrains. How winding and meandering are the shapes.)
虎踞龍盤仙子宮	It is the palace of the transcendents, which looks like a crouching tiger and a coiling dragon.
本意閒尋採藥翁	Our original intent was to leisurely look for an herb-gathering elder;
誰想桃源一徑通	Who would expect to find this peach spring accessible through one single path.
謾歎人生似轉蓬	In vain we sigh at human life, that is comparable to tumbling fleabanes.
猶恐相逢是夢中[26]	We still fear that our acquaintance takes place only in a dream.

Upon their return to reality from their dream, they learn the world has changed: their home has been occupied and they are beaten and expelled, and find nowhere to stay. These details are not found in the *Youming lu* version of the tale. Emperor Hui of the Jin is, anachronistically, called by his posthumous title, foreshadowing the brevity of his tenure in the play. The playwright correlates Liu Chen and Ruan Zhao's departure from the grotto with the onset of the Yuan. Upon discovering this unwanted regime change, the men strive to return to the transcendent realm, and, under the guidance of the god Venus, they succeed. This plot "reversal," to borrow Aristotle's term,[27] carries a figurative sense; in reversing their fortunes by returning to the grotto, the parallel implication is that either a return back in time, or forward in time when China is ruled by a Chinese regime, is possible.

In emphasizing the Confucian education of Liu Chen and Ruan Zhao, and facilitating their salvation through a Daoist deity (Venus), the play also illustrates the circular process of how traditional values die and are reborn. It is

---

26 "Wuru Tiantai," 12a; *LKXQJ*, 2167.
27 See Aristotle, *Poetics*, 15 (*Poetics* I, xi.52b9–12).

of interest that this process is brought to completion by means of the omniscient perspective of Venus, rather than by chance. The intervention by an omniscient being dovetails well with the eternal nature of time in the grotto; if both Venus and the grotto represented the triumph of traditional (religious) Chinese values, the reader/audience of the play would feel reassured that foreign oppression must inevitably be short-lived.

4   Beautifying Traumas and Obliteration of Value

A painting entitled "Liu Chen and Ruan Zhao Entering the Tiantai Mountains" attributed to Zhao Cangyun is another artwork that expresses the attitude of the literati under Mongol rule in the Yuan Dynasty.[28] This painting consists of eight parts, each with inscribed texts (see plates below and appendix). The eight inscriptions constitute another Yuan adaptation of the Liu-Ruan tale. In their introduction to this artwork, Maxwell Hearn and Wen C. Fong point out the differences between the role of Liu and Ruan in this work as compared with previous Liu-Ruan lore.[29] The first difference is one of emphasis: in both the painting and inscription text, the description of the banquet is very detailed and occupies a disproportionate amount of space. Here in the peach grove, the clothes and musical instruments of the transcendents serve as a focus. The second difference involves the end of the story: following Liu and Ruan's return to their home village and their ensuing disappointment, the painting and inscription portray them returning to Mount Tiantai. Hearn and Fong emphasize Zhao Cangyun's status as a member of the Song ruling house in their discussion of his uncooperative attitude towards the Mongol rule under the Yuan. They draw a comparison with the story of Bo Yi 伯夷 and Shu Qi 叔齊, who starved to death on Mount Shouyang 首陽山 as a result of refusing to eat any grain that already belonged to the newly founded Zhou dynasty. This may be seen as a parallel to Zhao's loss of his home dynasty to the Yuan.

The details of Zhao's work reveal an obvious political orientation. For example, his introduction to Liu and Ruan's backgrounds reads: "Their family studied Confucianism for generations, paying special attention to medicine. They often displayed a scent of a wish to transcend beyond the auroras." This shares some similarities with Wang Ziyi's play, in which Liu and Ruan are portrayed as

---

28 "Liu Chen and Ruan Zhao Entering the Tiantai Mountains." Permission for the use of these images was granted on November 10, 2014. I acknowledge Timothy M. Davis for calling my attention to this painting.
29 Hearn and Fong, *Along the Riverbank*, 86–88.

Confucian scholars who have no interest in an official career. We are reminded of how Liu Yuxi deals with the same source when he takes on the guise of Qu Boting (see chapter 3). In the context of Yuan–Ming works, the Confucian background of the artists plays a significant role in the construction of political satire.

And yet the emphasis of the painting and inscription is on the appeal of the grotto, rather than on the nature of the grotto's visitors. In the text below the panel depicting the two men lost in the mountains, Zhao seems to flaunt his writing skills with an ornate presentation of the beautiful scene:

> On the ridges the air is fresh and hued. The guise of the mountains looks like a towering snail shell. Gazing at this as though it gave access to the otherworld.
>
> 巒氣翁欝，山色螺聳，望中恍然如接異境。

This kind of ornate elaboration clearly hints at the artist's own fondness for the transcendent realm of the peach spring. This fondness is seen in other similar descriptions of the place throughout the artwork. Here is one such example:

> Consequently, the two girls invited them to their home. On the way, there were craggy and bumpy trails, and peach blossoms were all over the hills. After some three *li* of walking, they arrived at their abode. The living room and chambers were simple and spacious. The clothing was unlike that in the mortal world. The maids on the left and right were clad in blue, all decorous and comely, as glorious as clouds.
>
> 二女因邀歸家，所過山徑崎嶇，滿山桃花燦然。行及三里餘，到其所居，廳館朴廠，服飾非如人間所有，左右侍息青衣，皆端正莊靚，燦然如雲。

In narrating Liu and Ruan's departure from the grotto, the inscription provides a painterly description: "When they turned back they only saw the peach blossoms flourishing and the hues of the mountains as mounds of blue color" 回首惟桃花燦爛，山色堆青而已. These aesthetic depictions emphasize Liu and Ruan's attachment to the scenes and their reluctance to leave. The Liu-Ruan archetype leads us to understand that romance keeps them from leaving, but the descriptions here intensify their passion and attachment. This manner of providing extensive visual cues to Liu Chen's and Ruan Zhao's emotional state represents an innovation in the grotto romance tradition. By

THE CONFUCIAN SCHOLAR IN LOVE   193

FIGURE 1   The two girls inviting Liu and Ruan to their home. Sections 6 and 7 of *Liu Chen and Ruan Zhao Entering the Tiantai Mountains* 元趙蒼雲劉晨阮肇入天台山圖卷
BY ZHAO CANGYUN. THE METROPOLITAN MUSEUM OF ART OF NEW YORK CITY. ACCESSED 25 JULY 2024. HTTPS://WWW.METMUSEUM.ORG/ART/COLLECTION/SEARCH/39545

FIGURE 2   Banquet in the grotto. Section 8 of *Liu Chen and Ruan Zhao Entering the Tiantai Mountains*
BY ZHAO CANGYUN. THE METROPOLITAN MUSEUM OF ART OF NEW YORK CITY. ACCESSED 25 JULY 2024. HTTPS://WWW.METMUSEUM.ORG/ART/COLLECTION/SEARCH/39545

adding these elements, the artist creates a contrast between reality and this transcendent realm. The contrast enhances the attraction of the latter.

This motive is most revealing in the banquet scene in both the painting image and narrative. Here we see a revelry with rich displays of fine wine,

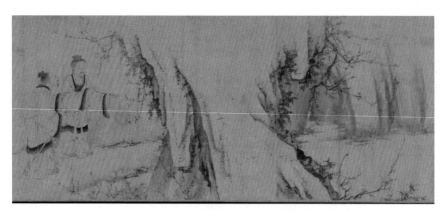

FIGURE 3   Re-visiting the grotto. Section 11 of *Liu Chen and Ruan Zhao Entering the Tiantai Mountains*
BY ZHAO CANGYUN. THE METROPOLITAN MUSEUM OF ART OF NEW YORK CITY. ACCESSED 25 JULY 2024. HTTPS://WWW.METMUSEUM.ORG/ART/COLLECTION/SEARCH/39545

delicacies, music, and transcendent beings presenting peaches. Above all, the two maidens' "complaisance and affability, loveliness like vernal breeze" make "the two men feel they are in heaven paradise."

Although the ending of Zhao's painting and narrative is similar to that of Wang Ziyi's play, their significance differs radically. As discussed, the play ends with Liu and Ruan's success in re-entering the grotto and reuniting with the two maidens. Through the displacement process, Liu and Ruan reach a "new" world with new hopes. In contrast, Zhao Cangyun's artwork does not feature the theme of "brightness after dark." However, the *Youming lu* version of the tale relates: "Suddenly they left again and no one knows where they went." Zhao's painting inscription declares: "The two men entered Mount Tiantai again and no one knows where they went." The panel emphasizes their failure to re-enter the grotto by placing them outside of the closed entrance. Despite their resolution to return to Mount Tiantai, which may be interpreted as their wish to live in reclusion, the painting and the corresponding narrative end in dilemma.

What kind of dilemma? While it was asserted above that Zhao's contradictory characterization of Liu and Ruan as hailing "from a family of Confucianism for generations," while also having "displayed a scent of a wish to transcend beyond the auroras," implied a politicization of the story, we are now in a position to describe this more clearly. Zhao's main concern is the denigration of the status of Confucian scholars under the Yuan. As a member of the Song royal house, Zhao Cangyun descended from generations of Confucianists, and he chose to seclude himself in retreat upon the downfall of the Song.[30] This politically motivated decision may explain the peculiar way in which he recasts the role of Liu and Ruan and their "wish to transcend beyond the auroras." Zhao chooses not to devote details to the romantic encounter,[31] focusing instead on detailed, ornate descriptions of the otherworldly scene.

Hearn and Fong interpret this painting's characterization of Liu and Ruan's frantic wish to return home as one driven by Confucian family values. The fewer amorous elements in Zhao's work form a sharp contrast with Wang Ziyi's play. In addition to some of the different demands of the media, Zhao's painting lacks depictions of romance. As a result, the difference in artistic outcome is clear. The traditional treatment of the romantic encounter as a metaphor is absent from Zhao Cangyun's painting and inscription. Instead, he focuses on themes of transcendence and displacement.

In the disguise of the Confucianized role of Liu and Ruan, Zhao Cangyun expresses his own rationale for reclusion. His sufferings are typical of most scholars' quandary under the rule of the Mongols. Zhao is aware that the Liu-Ruan tale had evolved to combine Daoist thoughts and transcendence-seeking fantasy, and he relies upon this framework. Despite his recasting of Liu and Ruan as Confucian scholars, he also portrays them as "fond of medicine" to account for their herb-gathering trip to the mountains, as well as their having no interest in political careers. Therefore, this unique characterization of Liu and Ruan serves the autobiographical presentation of Zhao, a Confucian scholar who lived in a period of dynastic change and consequently gave up pursuing a career.[32]

The time-dilation theme in the stemmatic line of the Liu-Ruan tale now becomes Zhao Cangyun's artistic device for the expression of his reclusion. Zhao is recorded as "not married and not employed."[33] In his fantasy, he makes use of the Daoist notion of "seven days in the mountains being equal to one thousand years in the human world," representing his strategy to avoid the oppressive Mongol rule. Nathan Sivin's discussion of the "manipulation of

---

30 See Hua Youwu's 華幼武 (1307–1375) "postscript" to "Liu Chen and Ruan Zhao Entering the Tiantai Mountains" appended to the painting inscription.
31 This is particularly evident in the aria "Sui shawei" 隨煞尾, in the end of Act 2 of "Wuru Tiantai," 12a/b; *LKXQJ*, 2168.
32 See Hua Youwu's "postscript" to "Liu Chen and Ruan Zhao Entering the Tiantai Mountains."
33 Ibid.

time" offers a perfect elucidation for Zhao's representation of his escape.[34] Living under foreign rule, he created a different dimension as an artistic means of fleeing. In Zhao's work, Liu and Ruan are arranged to make their way "back" to Mount Tiantai, but Zhao does not concern himself with whether they enter the grotto again; the main goal of escaping from mundane society has been achieved. This ending differs dramatically from the theme of Wang Ziyi's play, and both differ from the ending of the *Youming lu* version. In Zhao Cangyun's case, we may interpret the unique ending as an expression of his strong theme of reclusion.

5   Within and without the Grotto: Enlightenment and Benightedness

Perhaps the motive behind the original Liu-Ruan tale was to "record the uncanny" (*zhiguai* 志怪)—a genre of writing that was not associated with serious literary concerns. And yet the way the tale divides the mortal world and the transcendent realm served as the basis for serious artistic work. This division between parallel worlds is also found in ancient Greek philosophical writings. A brief comparative study may shed light on our reading of the Yuan–Ming texts and the artwork in question.

This in-and-out process as a course of realization may be compared with a similar case in the Western tradition, specifically, Plato's (ca. 427–ca. 347 BC) classic discussion in *The Republic*, in which he contrasts the virtual scene inside a cave and the real scene outside. It is an allegory about enlightenment and ignorance:

> In this chamber are men who have been prisoners there since they were children, their legs and necks being so fastened that they can only look straight ahead of them and cannot turn their heads. Some way off, behind and higher up, a fire is burning, and between the fire and the prisoners and above them runs a road, in front of which a curtain-wall has been built, like the screen at puppet shows between the operators and their audience, above which they show their puppets. ... And so, in every way they would believe that the shadows of the objects we mentioned were the whole truth. ... Suppose one of them were let loose, and suddenly compelled to stand up and turn his head and look and walk towards the

---

34   Sivin, "Chinese Alchemy and the Manipulation of Time," 512–26. Gil Raz uses the term "time manipulation" to refer to the rituals in early Daoist scriptures. See Raz, "Time Manipulation in Early Daoist Ritual," 27–65.

fire; all these actions would be painful and he would be too dazzled to see properly the objects of which he used to see the shadows. ... And if he were made to look directly at the fire's light, it would hurt his eyes and he would turn back and retreat to the things he could see properly, which he would think clearer than the things being shown him. [If] he were forcibly dragged up the steep and rugged ascent and not let go till he had been dragged out into the sunlight, the process would be a painful one ... his eyes would be so dazzled by the flare of it that he wouldn't be able to see a single one of the things he was now told were real. ... And they [i.e., the other prisoners] would say that his visit to the upper world had ruined his sight, and that the ascent was not worth even attempting. And if anyone tried to release them and lead them up, they would kill him if they could lay hands on him.[35]

There are many interpretations of this allegory, but we may note in particular the message that the path of a liberated person is fraught with difficulty. Upon leaving the cave, the escaped prisoner finds that his understanding of reality is instantly broadened, and yet he finds himself persecuted because of his enlightenment. Plato reinforces this message with the following statement: "Those who get so far are unwilling to involve themselves in human affairs." And despite his desire to recuse himself, "While still blinded and unaccustomed to the surrounding darkness, [the liberated prisoner is] forcibly put on trial in the law-courts or elsewhere about the shadows of justice, and made to dispute about the notions of them held by men who have never seen justice itself."[36]

This allegory of the liberated person who suffers persecution may be compared with our Chinese painting and texts. The theme of enlightenment and ignorance in the Platonic classic is also apparent in the Yuan–Ming plays and painting. Only through a process of enlightenment can Liu and Ruan realize the differences between the two realms.

When the two men request to return home after their enjoyment of sexual pleasure and delicacies in a luxurious house, we see in Zhao Cangyun's version:

> The girls respond, "Now you have come here. It was karmic bliss that beckoned you and let you come to our transcendent residence. Compare it with the mundane world. Would you have this kind of enjoyment?"

---

35 Plato, *The Republic*, 256–59, Book VII: 514a–517a.
36 Ibid., 517c, 517e.

女答曰：今來此，皆汝宿福所招，得至予仙館，比之流俗，有此樂否？[37]

This invitation to "compare [the transcendent realm] with the mundane world" is unique to Zhao's work. Naturally, all the previous versions of the Liu-Ruan tale imply comparison between the grotto and the mortal world, but through his explicit encouragement, Zhao places a particular focus on the act of comparison. Clearly, the "mundane world" refers to the new Yuan regime, and the implied comparison is between the Yuan and the Song that preceded it.

In his play, Wang Ziyi highlights the contrast between the mortal (Yuan) and transcendent (Song) realms in a different way. In the second act of his play, we find a hyperbolic depiction of the intense state of bliss experienced by the travelers in the grotto:

【正宮·端正好】	[*Zhenggong* mode: *Duanzhenghao*]
風力緊，羽衣輕，	The wind is strong, our feather clothes are light.
露華濕，烏巾重。	The dewdrops are damp, our black hats turn heavy.
厭紅塵跳出樊籠，	Tired of the red dusty world we now leap out of the cage.
撥開雲霧登丘隴，	Poking away the clouds and fog, we ascend hills and heights.
身世外，無擒縱。	Residing ourselves beyond the mundane, without being caught and released.
……	….
【呆骨朵】	[*Dai guduo*]
你便是	(Even if you are)
鐵石人也	a man of iron and rock,
惹起凡心動。	Your secular heart would be induced and moved.
莫不是	(Are they not)
駕青鸞天上飛瓊。	Feiqiong in the sky riding on blue simurghs?[38]
似這般	(Just like this)
花月神仙，	goddess- or transcendent-like flowers and moon, like goddesses and transcendents.
晃動了	(They have shaken)
文章鉅公	the great scholars of literature.
……	….

---

37 Cf., *Lishi zhenxian tidao tongjiao* (HY 296), 7.12a.
38 Xu Feiqiong 許飛瓊 is an attendant maiden of Queen Mother of the West. See *TPGJ*, 3.15, 70.433, quoting *Hanwu neizhuan* and *Yishi* 逸史, respectively.

沒揣的	(I have no idea how)
撞入風流陣，	we have strayed into this phalanx of romance,
引入花衚衕，	And have been led to the alleys of blossoms.
擺列著	(Arrayed in front are)
金釵十二行。	golden hairpins, twelve rows of them.
莫不是	(Are they not)
巫山十二峰。[39]	the twelve peaks of Mount Wu?

Metaphorically, these two "great scholars of literature" encountering the transcendent maidens in this otherworld may be read as literati having achieved their career goals to pass imperial exams and serve a worthy regime. But here, this achievement takes place in an illusory realm. Upon enjoying their romantic experience, Liu and Ruan are aware that it is only a dream (see above), and they request to return home. The two girls delay them with an exaggerated version of the inducement used in earlier versions of the Liu-Ruan tale; here, they assert that "karmic bliss" brought them together. And yet, six months later, Liu and Ruan are driven by frantic homesickness and petition again to leave this illusory realm and return to the mortal world. Of course, they meet with only cruel reality outside the grotto, which induces their final stage of enlightenment. Like Plato's liberated prisoner, they have become able to distinguish shadow from substance.

They prefer to return to the unreal world of art and enjoy an immortal life. This escapist and reclusive theme is formed through a clear-headed recognition of the benightedness and oppression under the Yuan regime (at least for the Chinese literati). There is also no hero or martyr in these Chinese works, and the overall tone is one of cynicism and despair.

6   Breeze, Flower, Snow, Moon, and Liu and Ruan in Yuan Drama

The Tang-Song practice of poetically encoding love affairs as encounters with a transcendent lady was continued in the Yuan, but with a different emphasis. In addition to the unprecedented developments in drama as a new art form, a new layer of meaning reflecting the Yuan literati's frustration was added to the grotto romance tradition.

In Yuan drama, love themes in works referencing Liu and Ruan's adventure served as a powerful affective factor to move the audience, especially when it converged with political satire. In our continuing exploration of how the

---

39   "Wuru Tiantai," 10a; *LKXQJ*, 2164, 2166.

elements of the Liu-Ruan tale were used to serve the purpose of entertainment imbued with political satire, we turn our focus to a work that may help reconstruct some aspects of the socio-cultural landscape of the time: the *zaju* play "Celestial Master Zhang's Verdict on Breeze, Blossom, Snow, and Moon" 張天師斷風花雪月, which was probably a Ming work falsely attributed to Wu Changling 吳昌齡.[40]

This play script absorbs thematic elements from the Liu-Ruan tale in its arias and dialogues, not only as a metaphor for the love between the main character Chen Shiying 陳世英 and Transcendent Cassia 桂花仙子, but also as a model for the representation of life under the Yuan. The audience may enjoy the elements of romantic comedy without being concerned with political overtones, but this would require an intentional avoidance of "treasure that can be excavated."[41] An attentive reader observes that the main part of the play involves the trial of Cassia, who is accused of seducing Chen, resulting in his illness and failure to attend the civil service examination. The following excerpt from Celestial Master Zhang's prosecution of Cassia and Chen's alleged go-between, a female character ironically called "Transcendent Peach Blossom" 桃花仙, in an obvious nod to the grotto romance tradition:

> [The Celestial Master says:] Peach Blossom, do you admit your crime? [Transcendent Peach Blossom says:] No, I don't. [The Celestial Master says:] You induced Chang'e (i.e., Cassia) to enter the households of the five prominent clans to make trouble for the young man of a fine family. Now I summon you to court. What argument do you have as a defense? [Transcendent Peach Blossom says:] I, as Peach Blossom, [as said in a poem,] in the sea bloom once every millennium, / And once led the transcendent to the Carnelian Terrace. [The Celestial Master says:] Shut up! [As said in a poem,] "Liu and Ruan then succeeded in finding a lover. / Stealthily they followed the currents to Mount Tiantai." If you don't know the details, who does?

---

40 Zhong Sicheng 鍾嗣成 (ca. 1279–ca. 1360) lists only one work titled "Shen gou yue" 鋠勾月, without mentioning "Celestial Master Zhang's verdict on Breeze, Blossom, Snow, and Moon." See Zhong, *Lugui bu* (*wai sizhong*), 1.22. Aoki Masaru 青木正兒 follows Wang Guowei 王國維 in assuming that the two plays are the same. See Aoki, *Yuanren zaju gaishuo*, 73. Yan Dunyi shares Ren Ne's 任訥 view that they seem to be two different plays and concludes that "Celestial Master Zhang" was written by a Ming playwright. See Yan, *Yuanju zhenyi*, 365–66.

41 Wolfgang Iser, *The Act of Reading*, 5: "Meaning is a thing which—as is made explicit in the text—embodies a treasure that can be excavated through interpretation."

〔天師云〕兀那桃花，你知罪麼？〔桃花仙云〕我不知罪。〔天師云〕你引誘嫦娥，輒入五姓之家，纏攪良家子弟，勾至壇前，有何理說？〔桃花仙云〕我這桃花。〔詩云〕海上千年一度開，曾教仙子赴瑤臺。〔天師云〕噤聲。〔詩云〕劉阮當時成配偶，暗隨流水出天台。你不知情誰知情？[42]

Here the playwright personifies the peach blossom—itself a synecdoche for the grotto—into a character with traits accumulated in the textual history of the Liu-Ruan tale. The peach blossom is a crucial image in the original tale and, with its symbolic meaning of love developed in previous literature, now becomes the object of Celestial Master Zhang's criticism for her role as a go-between in the love story of Cassia. Borrowing Yuan Zhen's line, "Once, when the transcendents' grotto opened at its thousand-year interval" 仙洞千年一度聞, the playwright now changes it to the peach blossom blooming every millennium, in telling how Cassia achieved her romance with the help of the other blossom-avatar-transcendents.[43]

One is reminded of the pivotal role of peaches in the Liu-Ruan tale. Peaches save the lives of Liu and Ruan when they almost starve to death, and they are also served at the dinner table. Peach blossoms are in profusion in the grotto. Peaches become a medium for communication between the human world and the transcendent realm, a feature also found in Tao Qian's version of the peach blossom spring, but the love theme is unique to the Liu-Ruan tale. Now, in this *zaju* play, the peach blossom encompasses all these features and is personified.

Another literary tradition is reflected in Celestial Master Zhang's interrogation. The romance of Liu and Ruan with their lovers was consummated, according to one branch of the Liu-Ruan tradition, by means of the petals of peach blossoms drifting outside the grotto on the stream. For this reason, Zhang asks Peach Blossom: "If you don't know the details, who does?" This is in fact a reference to a Tang tradition of "inscribing a poem on a red leaf" 紅葉題詩, derived from respective poems by Lu Wo 盧渥 (*jinshi* mid-9th c.) and Gu Kuang 顧況 (ca. 727–ca. 815).[44] As also mentioned in Chapter 4, these poems concern a palace lady who inscribed a poem on a red leaf and sent it outside by placing it in a moat, thereby inviting a romantic encounter with her lover.[45] This romantic tale shares similarities with the successful romances of Liu

---

42   *Yuanqu xuan*, 186.
43   *QTS*, 422.4640. See Chapter 2 for a full translation and discussion of this poem.
44   See *Benshi shi*, 6, and *Yunxi youyi*, 3.21, respectively.
45   See also my translation of Lu's poem and relevant discussion in Chan, "A Tale of Two Worlds," 229–30.

and Ruan, who also received some utensils and turnip leaves sent afloat on a stream from the grotto. The image of the floating petals of peach blossoms was created as a result of the combination of these two tales. The personified role of the peach blossom in this merged tradition became the reason for Celestial Master Zhang's interrogation.

When Zhang continues his hearing with Breeze, Blossoms, Snow, and Moon, we hear Cassia's aria: "[*Shiliu hua*] On that day when rouge appeared on the flowing stream of Tiantai, who lured Liu Chen and Ruan Zhao to this place?"[46] When other transcendents want to incriminate Cassia for "falling in love with a mortal," she refutes them by testifying *their* "guilt": "these flowers are admirable objects and have long been loved in history. Zhang thereupon orders all of them to be arrested and sent to the Transcendent of Long Eyebrows 長眉仙 of West Pond for formal conviction."[47]

We learn an important message from the Long Eyebrows' verdict, which may be seen as a "sequel" to the adventure of Liu and Ruan, who now re-enter Mount Tiantai. Cassia is convicted as guilty, but considering the illness of Chen Shiying, Long Eyebrows arranges a tryst for the spirit of Chen and his transcendent lover. Here is the scene:

> [Chen Shiying ascends] I, the humble student, am Chen Shiying. Isn't that Cassia Transcendent who has come? [The *zhengdan* sings:] I step down on the carnelian stairs, taking two steps as one. Oh, who is that person who's just turned to me? It is, indeed, Xiucai Chen, my love. How has he himself come so easily to Mount Tiantai? I'm so sure and certain that he misses his old love. Wait, wait, he must be expecting to pick the cassia seeds for harmony. How, oh how, does this not increase my surprise and strange feelings?
>
> 〔陳世英上〕小生陳世英，兀的不是桂花仙子來了也。〔正旦唱〕淹的呵下瑤階，將兩步做一步驀。呀。早轉過甚人來，是是是有情人陳秀才，他他他怎容易到天台。敢敢敢為著我舊情懷，待待待折桂子索和諧。怎怎怎不教我添驚怪。[48]

This scene of the reunion alludes to Liu and Ruan's return to Mount Tiantai as a metaphorical expression of the collective frustration of intellectuals,

---

46　*Yuanqu xuan*, 187.
47　Ibid., 189.
48　Ibid., 191.

and their desire to restore the traditional academic appointment system that existed before the Yuan.

The play does more to ensure that this character Chen Shiying symbolizes and embodies the Yuan literati sentiments. Elsewhere in the play, Chen is referred to as a "cassia branch breaker." This appellation skillfully refers to the well-known expression: "breaking the cassia branch from the palace of toad" 蟾宮折桂, a kenning for passing the *keju* examination.[49] Chen's dream of "breaking the cassia" has taken the form of an affair with Cassia and serves as an ironic and sarcastic layer of significance, which would have been obvious to contemporary audiences. Long Eyebrows's verdict is even more ironic, as he tries to undo all these love-related affairs by asking all these flower-avatar-transcendents to return to their original positions and Chen to continue his studies. Therefore, the play is an obvious satire of the dream of "breaking cassia." The metaphorical meaning of Chen Shiying's sobriquet of the "cassia breaker" is also reflected in a number of extant Yuan tunes. The most prototypical is "Aria of the Palace of Toad" 蟾宮曲, a northern song also known as "Ditty on Breaking the Cassia." The content of most songs under this tune-title aligns with the title. Some refer to the story of Chang'e, some elaborate on the metaphorical meaning of "breaking the cassia in the Palace of Toad." All of these can be read along with the *zaju* play as a symphony of voices reflecting the hopelessness felt by the literati under the Yuan.[50]

7 Conclusion

The well-studied topic of Confucian scholars' career desperation under the Yuan dynasty may be freshly explored through the grotto fantasy of this period. In stage performances of the time, Liu Chen and Ruan Zhao undergo yet another leg of time travel: they are brought back to life in contemporary settings, in which they act out the predicament of the intellectuals of the time. Their final resolution of seeking transcendence reveals a psychological remedy as well as a silent protest. This protest is also implicitly seen in Chen

---

49 Xi Shen 郤詵 (fl. late 3rd c.) is recorded as having compared himself to a branch from a forest of cassia (桂林之一枝). See *Jinshu*, 52.1443.

50 See, e.g., Ma Zhiyuan's expression of having no interest in deeds and renown through writing about history in his "Sighing for the world, to the tune of Palace of Toad" 蟾宮曲・嘆世. Xue Angfu 薛昂夫 (1267–1359) writes about his lament over life in a song with the same title. The most famous songs about renouncing deeds and renown are the three "Zhegui ling" 折桂令 ("Ditty on Breaking the Cassia") by Zhang Yanghao 張養浩 (1270–1329). See *Quan Yuan sanqu*, 243, 712, 424.

Shiying's indulgence in love rather than studying hard to pass the examination, which, in reality, had become a dead end for aspiring intellectuals. In both texts, the playwrights lodge traumatic feelings that would have resonated with audiences who also had lived under (or recalled) the oppressive rule of the Mongols. Given the author's identity and the content of Wang Ziyi's play, however, the intrigue of time-dilated displacement offers the two men a reunion with the maidens in the grotto, where they live happily ever after. This sharp contrast to previous versions of the tale, as well as in Zhao Cangyun's painting and postscript, in which Liu and Ruan never found their way back to the grotto, may be read as the passing of darkness and the coming of brightness, i.e., the advent of a new dynasty.

Zhao Cangyun's presentation of this sentiment is colored with one additional layer. Staying unmarried and out of office is likely a gesture of passive resistance against the Yuan. He provided no service to the Mongol regime and left no descendants. The Mongols had destroyed and replaced the Song, of which he was a royal member. When this indignation is combined with the ethos of the time in his painting and its inscriptions, we see not only a repetition of the old grotto romance themes, but also a highly personal presentation of the beautiful otherworldly realm to which he craves retreat. The Liu and Ruan characters created by Zhao in this context become more eager to return because the grotto represents his bygone dynasty. But their return to the grotto, which stands for Zhao's own return to the Song, is impossible. The metaphorical representation of how Liu and Ruan experience "the good times" in the grotto represents the rupture of dynastic change.

The three works all express a desire for a beautiful life that is found only in a virtual world. The two plays conclude with a "happy ending" to please the audience. This is not only a genre feature of *zaju* plays, but also expresses the playwrights' wishes. Zhao Cangyun's painting with the inscription does not deliver a happy ending but rather an escape from reality: his Liu and Ruan establish their permanence in the world of fantasy. This is also an escape for the author in that his works may be handed down to later generations. In the guise of "Confucian scholars," Liu Chen and Ruan Zhao were predestined to be abandoned by the mortal world because their creators who gave them life in their plays and paintings likewise felt abandoned and mistreated by the Mongol dynasty.

The background of the artworks discussed in this chapter inevitably excludes the female protagonist from assuming the triple role as in Tang–Song literature. Nevertheless, in these works, we observe a new kind of triple role:

lover, grotto-transcendent, and pursuer of fantasy. This new concept marks a shift from the interest in amorous literature to political satire.

Appendix: Text Inscribed on Zhao Cangyun, "Liu Chen and Ruan Zhao Entering the Tiantai Mountains"

　　劉晨阮肇，剡人也，家世儒業，尤留意於醫，嘗飄然有霞表之氣味，漢明帝永安十五年，二人攜鋤筥，往天台山採藥焉。

　　入山既深，尋藥方盈筥，少憩，將返，迷失來路，且糧糗俱盡，二人相顧，方狼狽失措，偶舉目見山頭有桃木穋然，桃實纍然，二人往山上取桃食之，人各食二枚，如覺少健。然食桃尤在手，下山求歸，路轉轉崎嶇，益難辨識。行次不覺至山麓，見澗中水流潺然，清泠可人。二人以手挹水飲之，且各澡其手面。偶見蔓菁，從山腹出，次又有一杯流出，中有胡麻飯屑，二人相顧曰：「去人家不遠矣。」

　　巒氣翁蔚，山色螺聳，望中恍然如接異境。

　　因負藥筥，以鋤探水，水纔四尺許。二人褰裳渡之，行及一里餘，得小徑，又度一山，又見一溪焉。

　　山麓處大溪，隔溪見二女，顏色絕妙，世所未有，便揮手喚劉阮姓名，似有舊交。二人渡溪，二女喜笑而語曰：「郎來何晚也？」意味和懌，香氣襲人。相與相攜，雖合巹之恊，情經數載，未有如此之婉好也。二人始疑為媚，久之，方辨識為人，而亦不之懼焉。

　　二女因邀歸家，所過山徑崎嶇，滿山桃花燦然。行及三里餘，到其所居，廳館朴敞，服飾非如人間所有，左右侍息青衣，皆端正莊靚，燦然如雲。少憩，煮胡麻飯、山羊脯，食之甘美。二人食方畢，不覺饑。欲訊家世，二女但相與談笑亂之，略不之告，二人亦不敢固問，知其為異人。久之，亦不見其家有男子也。

　　既而，又當庭設席，陳酒肴，為二人壽。方飛觴次，有數仙客，持三五仙桃至女家，云：來慶女婿。各至席。二人禮之。各仙客皆仙服，各出樂器，奏之，蕭韶和鳴。暢飲逾二三時，候二女親，各舉巵勸二人酒。歙曲之情，春氣可挹。二子恍然如在天上也。向暮，仙客各還去。

　　二女邀劉阮借止宿，約半月餘，二子求還，女答曰：今來此，皆汝宿福所招，得至予仙館，比之流俗，有此樂否？遂懇留住。及半年，天氣常如三春，山鳥哀鳴。二子求歸甚切。女曰：業根未滅，使令子心如此。於是喚諸仙女共作鼓吹，送劉阮歸。遂告之曰：從此山洞口出去不遠，至大道，至家易矣。

　　二子出洞口，行至大道。回首惟桃花燦爛，山色堆青而已。甫至家鄉，並無相識，鄉里怪異，乃聞得七代子孫，傳上祖入山不出，不知今何在。

　　二子在鄉，既無親屬，棲泊無所；卻同入天台山，尋當年所往，山路已迷，而不知所在。後至晉武帝太康八年，二子復入天台，不知其所之也。

　　蒼雲山人畫書。

EPILOGUE

The Divine Ladies in Love: Romantic Detention in the Liu-Ruan Tradition and *The Odyssey*

1 Introduction

This Epilogue serves as the conclusion of this book. It explores the theme of "the divine ladies in love" from the perspective of comparative literature. We place the Liu-Ruan tale, along with its adapted texts, alongside the Greek classic, *The Odyssey*.

While it may seem an unlikely comparison, our conclusions prove fruitful because these two foundational texts are both structured around the theme of mortal-divine romance. We focus, in particular, on the shared theme of "romantic detention," the struggle against which drives the heroic deeds in the Homeric epic as well as the life-altering choices in the Liu-Ruan tale. We are also able to explore themes of romance in stranded circumstances, surrender to instinctive sexual desire, liberation from romantic detention, and boundary transgression between secular and divine realms.

Certainly, there are far more differences than similarities in the two texts. In addition to their diverse cultural backgrounds, they were composed at different times: *The Odyssey* was supposedly put into writing in ca. 700 BC,[1] while the Liu-Ruan tale was a product of the fifth century AD. The genre of the texts also differs: the former is a heroic epic and the latter, and its adaptations, fall into genres such as *zhiguai* ("recording the uncanny") and *chuanqi* ("transmitting the marvelous") narratives, *shi* and *ci* poetry, drama, and painting. In terms of length, the former comprises twenty books but the original Liu-Ruan tale only a few hundred characters, and its adaptations were also relatively short texts. The protagonists differ enormously; the former tells the story of a hero, Odysseus, on a twenty-year voyage back to his kingdom, Ithaca, where he kills his enemies and restores his throne. Liu and Ruan are common people who enter the transcendent realm of the Peach Spring by accident. Their later avatars, such as those created by Zhang Zhuo, Yuan Zhen, and Liu Yuxi, are commoners who do not qualify as heroes. Yuan Zhen, Bai Juyi, and Liu Yuxi, may well be seen as heroes in the political arena of their time and the Liu and Ruan

---

1 The date the Homeric epics were written is a topic of dispute. See Robert Fowler, "The Homeric Question," 224–32.

in the Yuan–Ming adaptations represent strong, heroic opposition against the Mongol rule, but none of this heroism takes on epic proportions.

In examining the significance of the romantic encounters in these two groups of texts, we are able to comment on the relative value placed on home, as well as on the meaning of eternity in each text. The constructs of home and polis in *The Odyssey* are grounded in the mortal realm rather than the otherworld, and are essential in molding the image of a hero. The concept of home in the Liu-Ruan tale and its adaptations, on the other hand, becomes a foil to comment on the fragility of human nature, the impermanence of human life, and the transient nature of love. Both groups of texts also highlight their respective concepts of home through a contrast between the transcendent and human realms.[2] The texts resolve in diametrically opposite ways: one in a "happy return" and the other in "tragedy."[3]

These kinds of differences have not impeded other comparative studies involving the Homeric epic. Comparative mythology is a field that deals with "myths and mythic themes drawn from a wide variety of cultures."[4] Homeric epics have been compared with, for instance, the great Indian epics—the *Ramayana* and the *Mahabharata*, the Iranian *Book of Kings*, and the Scandinavian *Ynglinga saga*.[5] Odysseus's ordeals are juxtaposed against those of Arjuna[6] and other heroic figures in the Christian Bible and the *Epic of Gilgamesh*.[7] The comparison here between the great hero in *The Odyssey* and two Chinese commoners, Liu Chen and Ruan Zhao along with their variations, contributes to this growing body of scholarship.

2   Recurring Romance and the Realm of Remembrance

The theme of "the divine ladies in love" sees its recurrences in the Western classic and the circle of our Chinese texts. Although the notion of "the divine ladies in

---

2 In *The Odyssey*, we note that there is a notion of *nymphaea*—caves with many literary features equivalent to those of Chinese grotto-heavens (Verellen, "The Beyond within," 266). The difference in the treatment of *nymhaea* is that they do not serve the Greek poets as a way to provide literary tension in contrast to their protagonists' earthly home, as they do in the Chinese texts studied here. This cave is not where Odysseus's romantic episodes take place; Kalypso's cavern is a place of this kind but it has nothing to do with otherworldly adventure. See discussion below.
3 These are terms borrowed from Joseph Campbell, *The Hero with a Thousand Faces*, 178.
4 Covington Scott Littleton, *The New Comparative Mythology*, 32.
5 Julian Baldick, *Homer and the Indo-Europeans*.
6 N. J. Allen, *Arjuna–Odysseus*.
7 Bruce Louden, *Homer's Odyssey and the Near East*.

love" is derived from Chinese literature, it applies well to the romantic episodes in *The Odyssey*. The idea is first found in Song Yu's 宋玉 (fl. ca. mid-3rd c. BC) two rhapsodies, "*Fu* on the Gaotang Temple" ("Gaotang fu" 高唐賦) and "*Fu* on the Divine Lady" ("Shennü fu" 神女賦),[8] which mark early developments of amorous interactions between mortals and divinities in Chinese literary history. This tradition of a mortal pursuing the love of a divine being is believed to have originated in the "Lisao," which relates the mortal protagonist's failed courting of Consort Fu 宓妃, Jiandi 簡狄, and the two daughters of the You Yu 有虞 state. These episodes have long been given allegorical readings.[9] The Liu-Ruan tale differs, however, as its earliest versions do not necessarily invite allegorical meaning. Predating the Liu-Ruan tale by a thousand years, the Homeric epic similarly carries no apparent allegorical meaning, serving instead as a "prototype of the human soul on its journey through this world of darkness and danger."[10] In our comparison of the two groups of texts, therefore, we focus on the text as a commentary on the human journey, independent of politics. One common theme in both stories sees the protagonists imperiled and saved by beautiful ladies, with whom they fell in love. As the romance recurs in *The Odyssey*, and in the Liu-Ruan literary circle, a cycle of remembrance is formed.

Odysseus experienced three such romantic encounters. After the fall of Troy when all generals under the Greek alliance each led their warships back to their respective home kingdoms, Odysseus and his crew met thirteen ordeals on their homeward-bound voyage to Ithaca. His first romantic interlude was with Circe, the daughter of Helios, the god of the sun. She was proficient at music, knitting, and mantic skills. On her island Aiaia, where Odysseus and his crew landed, Circe transformed his crewmen into swine. Hermes disclosed to Odysseus the method for breaking Circe's tricks and obtained some magical grass called moly as protection. Hermes also told him not to refuse Circe's invitation to sexual pleasure. It all worked out as instructed and expected: Circe's powers were overcome and his crewmen were changed back to human form. In the year that followed, Odysseus and his crew enjoyed delicacies at Circe's home; he himself found great sexual pleasure every day. This enjoyable life ended with his crewmen's reminder of their ultimate goal of returning home.[11]

The encounter with Circe is regarded as having been copied from the one about Kalypso's detainment of Odysseus, which takes place later in the book.[12]

---

8   Wei Fengjuan, "Xianfan qingyuan gui hechu," 43.
9   *CCBZ*, 1.31–34, commentaries. See also Pauline Yu, *The Reading of Imagery*, 85, 88.
10 See Howard W. Clarke, *The Art of The Odyssey*, 48–49.
11 Lattimore, trans. *The Odyssey of Homer*, 10.133–486 (pp. 155–64).
12 William G. Thalmann assumes that Circe is more civilized than Kalypso. See Thalmann, *The Odyssey*, 76–78. Other different views include: that the part on Circe was written by a different hand; that the images and plots of these two goddesses were copied from

This divine lady saved Odysseus from the sea when all his crewmen had died as a result of failing to comply with the advice of Circe and eating the herds of Helios, god of the sun, who punished them.[13] When all his hopes for return had become impossible, Kalypso saved him. Thereafter, they lived together on her island, Ogygia, for seven years. The hero felt distressed that he could not go home, but, fortunately, he had this beautiful nymph who saved him and took him to be her lover and who wanted to keep him as her husband forever.[14] The island was so isolated from the human realm that it may be seen as an otherworldly realm.

The third romantic encounter of Odysseus was not with a divine lady but with Nausikaa, princess of Scheria, where the Phaeacians lived. At the command of Zeus, Kalypso agreed to let Odysseus go. With the help of the nymph, Odysseus made a raft and started his voyage towards home. But on the way, Poseidon, the god of sea, took revenge on him because Polyphemos, son of Poseidon, was tricked by Odysseus who blinded his eye.[15] His raft was destroyed but he managed to reach Scheria, where he was saved by the princess, "looking like a goddess."[16] She led him to see her father, King Alkinoös, who immediately offered his beautiful young daughter's hand in marriage to him, desiring to keep him in his kingdom.[17] In the end, Odysseus was moved to tears by the lyrics of the songs performed by Domodokos, which narrated the scenes of the Trojan war and revealed his real identity. The startled king then gave him gifts and assigned a flotilla to escort him to his kingdom Ithaca.[18] This episode brings the hero another step closer back to the "mortal realm."

The three proposed marriages pose challenges to the hero, each more difficult than the other. His refusals were driven by his determination to return home. He struggled to regain his heroic courage and strengthen his determination through a gradual awakening, from submission to temptation to refusal. Following in parallel is the diminishment of the supernatural hold over him, which leads to his escape.

---

each other; and that the two goddesses were put together and regarded as interchangeable multiforms of the same basic character. See Karl Reinhardt, "The Adventures in *The Odyssey*," 90–99; Gregory Crane, *Calypso*, 31. Bruce Louden points out that "their relationships with Odysseus thus run in opposite directions." See Louden, *The Odyssey*, 104–5, 158, n. 5, 107–22. See also Suzanne Saïd, *Homer & The Odyssey*, 171–74.

13 See Lattimore, *The Odyssey of Homer*, 12.260–419 (pp. 192–96).
14 Ibid., 1.13–15 (p. 27), 5.151–58 (p. 92).
15 Ibid., 9.368–565 (pp. 146–67).
16 Ibid., 7.291 (p. 118).
17 Ibid., 7.312–314 (p. 119).
18 Ibid., 8.531–585 (p. 135); 13.1–46 (p. 198).

One major ordeal on Odysseus's long homeward journey is that he was repeatedly forced to forget his native land. Additionally, marriage is a bond that would have dashed the hero's hopes to return home. A physical manifestation of this theme involves the realm of the Lotus-Eaters. Upon landing there, Odysseus's crewmen are given the fruit of the lotus. But any who eat the honey-sweet fruit grow unwilling to take any messages away, or to depart the island themselves, preferring instead to stay with the lotus-eating people, feeding on lotus.[19] Ralph J. Hexter points out that the episode on Kalypso is a repetition of Odysseus's detainment by the Lotus-Eaters and that Homer's keyword is "forget" (*lathoiato*).[20] The temptation to forget also colors Odysseus's two romantic encounters, and each time the hero must choose to overcome this temptation. The notion of returning (rather than remembering) serves as the opposite of forgetting and is another keyword of great significance. It not only implies his return to his own kingdom, but its meaning also extends to Odysseus re-seizing his lost sovereignty as well as his restoration of disordered family ethics.[21]

These two opposite forces, forgetting and remembering, are in constant competition. The retelling of the protagonist's ordeal itself constitutes a new layer of narrative within that contest. In this regard, Domodokos's singing of Odysseus's adventures finds a counterpart in Bai Juyi's mention of Liu Yuxi's (see chapter 2). Bai concludes in his poem: "The east wind has returned for twenty-four spring seasons."[22] Hearing this, Liu Yuxi is agonized by his past, which frequently alludes to the fantasies of the two peach springs. Most of the writings that recall the Liu-Ruan tale include a thematic element of forgetting, which, in turn, intensifies the protagonist's remembrance. We have seen numerous examples of the male lover forgetting his wife or his transcendent lover. These episodes of forgetting contribute to a "grotto of remembrance," which means different things to different roles. For the jilted lady, this displacement is a source of lasting grievance.

---

19   Ibid., 9.93–97 (p. 139).
20   Hexter, *A Guide to* The Odyssey, 143, note on ll. 260–61.
21   Thalmann, *The Odyssey*, 9–11.
22   *BJYJJ*, 1756.

3   Expedient Means and the Intended Morals

Recalling the inducement of a "karmic blessing" (*sufu* 宿福), a pretext of the grotto maidens for detaining Liu and Ruan, we may, by extension, employ some other Buddhist concepts to explore the nature of Liu Chen and Ruan Zhao's detainment. Being on the verge of death, in a religious sense, serves as an "expedient means" (a Mahāyāna Buddhist term *fangbian li* 方便力 [Sanskrit, *upāya-kauśalya*]) of obtaining access to Buddhahood.[23] For an aspirant not on one's deathbed, this "expedience" may be replicated through a combination of Buddhist "metaphor" (*piyu* 譬喻) and "discourse" (*yanci* 言辭). These paired teaching methods enable an aspirant to achieve Buddhahood, usually through the conjuring of an illusion of temporary enjoyment, before destroying it. Through this process, the aspirant becomes aware of the transient nature of sensual pleasure. This theory fits well with the poetry of the Tang-Song, in which the grotto transcendents make use of this predestined bliss as a pretext for detaining their mortal lovers, and, when their mortal lovers resolve to leave, the ladies feel helpless, despite the divine "bond."

We have explored the device of time dilation (see Chapter 1), such that seven human generations have passed when Liu and Ruan exit the grotto. We also explored the dangers of transiting between the grotto and mortal realms, ameliorated by the consumption of certain magic substances and foods. Cao Tang even portrays the grotto transcendent hurriedly feeding her mortal lover some magic food to help him survive.[24] Similarly, in *The Odyssey*, we read about a "deal" proposed by Kalypso, who wanted to grant her mortal lover "immortality" as a reward for his remaining with her.[25] Although the epic does not detail how the nymph could accomplish this, the text does not question her capacity to do so. Her promise of immortality is not unlike the grotto transcendents' offer to Liu and Ruan. The time dilation in the grotto is comparable, in a literary sense, to the immortality of the Greek gods.

---

[23]   The term is usually translated as "power of great skillful means," referring to "extraordinary powers" or "adaptability." See William Edward Soothill and Lewis Hodous, *A Dictionary of Chinese Buddhist Terms*, 106a, 424b. For the translation of *upāya* as "expedient means," see Donald S. Lopez Jr., *Critical Terms for the Study of Buddhism*, 238, 302–3. Examples of *fangbian li* are passim in early Buddhist sutras, e.g., *Abhiniṣkramaṇa-sūtra* (*Fo benxing ji jing*), T 190, 3.725c09–10; *Saddharma-puṇḍarīka-sūtra* (*Miaofa Lianhua jing*), T 262, 9.7b20–21, 26–27; 9.13.c17–15a29; 9.25c26–26a19.

[24]   QTS, 641.7347.

[25]   Lattimore, *The Odyssey of Homer*, 5.136, 5.209, 7.256–57, 23.335–36 (pp. 91, 209, 117, 343–44).

4   Otherworld and This-World

The two groups of texts are both set at the boundary between two realms: this-world and an otherworld. In this liminal space, the ideas of isolation and separation are expressed in similar ways.

Structured around boundary transgression, the adventures in *The Odyssey* set the hero entering the otherworld (sometimes in a figurative sense) from the mortal world. In ancient Greek cosmology, the world is divided into three parts: Zeus rules Heaven; Hades the underworld; and Poseidon the sea.[26] This tripartite structure has a counterpart in early medieval China, where the world was believed to be divided into heaven, earth, and the underworld.[27] At one point, Odysseus is depicted as traveling to the underworld through sacrificial rituals, which do not always involve physical travel.[28] The locales of some of the adventures in the epic are also fictional.[29] All these geographic locales function metaphorically as another world and become a counterpart of this-world, a realm where Odysseus originally belonged in a political and family sense. This antithetical structure not only demarcates a geographic separation and enforces isolation, but, most significantly, generates two points of tension: 1) the interaction between mortals and divinity and 2) the desire to return from the otherworld to this-world.

The first and second romantic encounters of Odysseus each took place on an Island occupied by a nymph. In ancient Greece, we imagine, this kind of island must have been considered distant, uninhabited, and out of the reach of mortals. As our hero makes his first footstep onto this island dominated

---

26   See Lattimore, *The Iliad of Homer*, 15.187–93 (p. 315).
27   See, e.g., Hsiao Teng-fu, *Han Wei Liuchao Fo Dao liangjiao*, 3–333; Needham et al., *Science and Civilisation in China, Vol. 5: Part III*: 114. Michael Loewe distinguishes four ideas of paradise or life after death in Han times, namely the notion that the whole structure of these isles underlies the universe, the magical realm of the west, and the Yellow Springs. See Loewe, *Chinese Ideas of Life and Death*, 27–34. For how the notion of the underworld evolved since early times and how hell was introduced via Buddhist sutras to China in Han times, see Sun Changwu, "Zhongguo wenxue li de diyu xunyou," 146–57. See also Zhang Zhenjun, *Buddhism and Tales*, 106–37, in which the relevant *Youming lu* tales are discussed in this light.
28   Lattimore, *The Odyssey of Homer*, 11.23–635 (pp. 168–84). The "visit" to the underworld is in fact "the rite by which ghosts were summoned and questioned." This rite is called Nekuia (ἠνέκυια). See Mark P. O. Morford and Robert J. Lenardon, *Classical Mythology*, 490–91.
29   Lattimore identifies some place names in the epic which correlate to historical places, but there are also many that do not. See Lattimore, "Introduction," *The Odyssey of Homer*, 12–16.

by the nymph and is later possessed by her beauty and his sexual desire, this realm may well be seen as an otherworld. In a metaphorical sense, the locale, along with the related romance, may be seen as a product of the "expedient means" of the poet. The episode, on the one hand, describes this locale as a "sea-washed island, the navel of all the water" and a "far-lying island";[30] on the other hand, the island is teeming with growth:

> There was a growth of grove around the cavern, flourishing,
> alder was there, and the black poplar, and fragrant cypress,
> and there were birds with spreading wings who made their nests in it,
> little owls, and hawks, and birds of the sea with long beaks
> who are like ravens, but all their work is on the sea water;
> and right about the hollow cavern extended a flourishing
> growth of vine that ripened with grape clusters. Next to it
> there were four fountains, and each of them ran shining water,
> each next to each, but turned to run in sundry directions;
> and round about there were meadows growing soft with parsley
> and violets, and even a god who came into that place
> would have admired what he saw, the heart delighted within him.[31]

This otherworldly scene attracts even Hermes, god of boundaries and guide of souls, to the underworld. This piece of land is the home of the nymph and became a secluded realm; even the divinities (other than Hermes) remained largely unaware of it. In this realm, with such a beautiful lady as a companion, why would the sojourning hero still yearn for his own home? Therefore, his initial choice to just pass by became a decision to stay, for obvious reasons.

This otherworld, represented by the grotto heaven in the Chinese tradition, is often depicted as a spring surrounded by peach blossom trees, but the natural surroundings are secondary to the man-made. The realm first appears as a paradise where Liu and Ruan strayed, but later changed to a site of revelry and romance. Even in the Liu-Ruan tale, the chamber's promise of a luxurious life becomes the focus and provides a rationale for the protagonists' initial desire to remain. The most typical realm embodying secular values on the Chinese side is the grotto (re)created by Zhang Zhuo in his *You xianku*. This encounter shares some features with the Greek counterpart. Firstly, both realms are set within the human world, rather than in the sky or underground. For the hero/intruder, the realm is a place of revelry and is free of social censure, but

---

30   Ibid., 1.50, 5.55 (pp. 28, 89).
31   Ibid., *The Odyssey of Homer*, 5.63–74 (p. 90).

the pleasure is only temporary as the protagonist must return to normal life. Finally, the parting leaves the ladies (the nymphs in one and the *xian*-like ladies in the other text) holding lasting grievances.

In both groups of texts, the initial allure is replaced by reluctance. As Irene de Jong reminds us: "The narrator stresses that Odysseus now sleeps with the nymph 'unwillingly' and 'only by constraint' (ἀνάγκῃ) just as she keeps him with her 'by constraint' ... Odysseus simply does not have the means to leave her."[32] This strained situation reminds us of the one faced by Liu Chen and Ruan Zhao, who could not leave the realm, although at first, they enjoyed the pleasure offered by the ladies. Likewise, for Zhang Zhuo, Yuan Zhen, and other male protagonists in later adaptations, this kind of accidental romance means an initial happy time followed by renunciation of transient pleasure and return to the human world. This romantic encounter, however, becomes a force luring the men to return. Only after the protagonists witness the crudity of the outside world do they realize how good it is in the grotto. Ironically, their reluctance to remain in the grotto changes into a reluctance to stay in the mortal world, especially for political reasons. Liu Yuxi, Wang Ziyi, and Zhao Cangyun are examples of this take on the theme.

The nature of Odysseus's third romantic encounter differs from the previous ones. It did not take place in an otherworld, was not an interaction between mortal and immortal, and did not involve any sexual relations, but has a narrative function similar to the other two occasions. Here, we include this romantic encounter in the same category as the first two because Scheria was presented as a kingdom cut off from the world. It was not only remote but also served as a gateway to lands even more remote. Put another way, Scheria "stands at the crossroads between two worlds [and] functions as a transition between the mythical universe of Odysseus's adventures and the real world of Ithaca."[33] Structurally and thematically, Scheria forms "the last obstacle to Odysseus's return" despite the hospitality he enjoys, because "he is tempted to marry her [Nausicaa] and remain in Scheria." The hospitality of the Phaeacians may deprive the hero of his ability to return home.[34] This isolation served a definite narrative purpose. As M. I. Finley comments: "The first thing we are told about the Phaeacians—immediately establishing the Utopianism of the tale—is that they existed in almost complete isolation; in fact, Alchinous's

---

32   De Jong, *A Narratological Commentary on the Odyssey*, 133. Odysseus's being detained by Kalypso against his will is evident *passim* in Lattimore, *The Odyssey of Homer*, 1.55–56, 1.197, 4.498, 4.552, 23.334 (pp. 28, 32, 78, 79, 343).
33   See Saïd, *Homer & The Odyssey*, 179, n. 90, citing various views.
34   Steve Reece, *The Stranger's Welcome*, 120, 203–4.

father, Nausithous, had transplanted the community from Hypereia to Scheria (both mythical places) to that very end."[35]

In his formulaic poetics, Homer, to a certain degree, repeats the previous two romantic encounters and modifies them to make this third one.[36] Scheria is only a quasi-mythical world, which was "so very dear to the immortals,"[37] but was closer to the mortal world on the hero's homecoming journey. This transition marks a change from the hero under the manipulation of the nymphs to his acquaintance with Nausicaa, a demi-god princess.

The transcendent realm entered by Liu and Ruan serves a similar function in the tale's plot, but with a different outcome. Unlike other *zhiguai* tales of the time, the Liu-Ruan tale does not record an "anomalous" visit to the underworld, a boat voyage to the moon, or a journey into a flagon. Rather, as discussed in Chapter 1, this fifth-century Chinese tale presents a moderately realistic, humanized vision of an encounter with otherworldly beings. Rather than celestial flight, the text shows physical travel to a land located within the human realm, in which normal human appetites (for food and sex) are satisfied. This kind of "enclosed paradise" (see Introduction) is only accessible to those who have "karmic blessings." Although we read this as an inducement for the men to stay, rather than a narrative fact, "karma" reflects a common belief in a supernatural force, of which there is a parallel in the Homeric classic. The key difference, however, is in the outcome. While the focus of *The Odyssey* is on the heroism of the protagonist in overcoming obstacles, the focus in the Liu-Ruan tale is on the survival of time dilation and the consequences of indulgence.

The adventure to the otherworld in both groups of texts involves a process of entering and exiting. The transgression across borders facilitates the protagonists' romantic ordeals and their determination to renounce them. Through the "expedient means," the protagonists are brought from indulgence to awakening, as we see in Bai Juyi's remonstration of his friend Yuan Zhen. The discourse of transgression enhances the ideology of the work, testing the determination of the characters, and expanding the ups and downs of the plots. These factors contribute to a picture of the vulnerability of human nature.

---

35   Finley, *The World of Odysseus*, 105. Lattimore, *The Odyssey of Homer*, 6.4 (p. 102).
36   Milman Perry and Albert B. Lord rely largely on oral tradition in their theory of "formulaic" poetry. They employ the Greek terms "cyclic" and "Epic Cycle" in their discussion of the repetitive nature of the songs. See Lord, *The Singer of Tales*, 9, 121, 152–53, et passim.
37   Lattimore, *The Odyssey of Homer*, 6.203 (p. 107).

5 Human Needs and Values

Desire and passion are two main aspects of human nature that serve as prominent focuses in the Chinese and Greek texts in question. These emotions are reflected in the representation of eating, drinking, and sensuality. The pursuit of pleasure creates the tension that reveals the marked qualities of our protagonists, which emerge through their assertion of higher values in the choices in front of them. In *The Odyssey*, the hero is finally driven by his sense of obligation to family and society. The main themes of the epic may thus be summarized as: 1) the recovery of losses and 2) liberation from displacement. This process in which values are perverted and later recovered is not as clearly featured in the Liu-Ruan tale, owing to the vastly different conventions of the *zhiguai* genre. And yet the pair's decision to return home is also borne of a sense of duty and responsibility.

Satisfaction of basic human needs is a common feature in both groups of texts. When Liu and Ruan got lost and were out of food and drink, they were taken care of by the two girls who satisfied their hunger and thirst as well as sexual pleasure. This change from a crisis to fortune looks radical and incredible. Similarly, of Odysseus's three romantic encounters two are given a similar portrayal—a "reversal" occurs in a dire situation, after which the hero's hunger and sexual desire were fulfilled.[38]

In the religious and moral traditions of both cultures, the suffering of the protagonist would naturally have been regarded as a divinely influenced ordeal. The romantic encounters of Odysseus, one after another, inspire the hero's and the reader's contemplation of the process of awakening from confusion. These episodes have long been adopted as teaching materials, guiding people to be positive and good.[39] The Liu-Ruan tale in its original version may not deliver a didactic moral of similar force, but the men's ordeal becomes a rationale for the conversion of the protagonists in the Yuan–Ming contexts. When they are on the verge of starving to death, Venus ascends to save them. When they try to return to the grotto after witnessing the temporal changes in the mortal world, they fail to find the entrance, resulting in suicidal impulses. This makes a second "reversal" of the dramatic text and serves as a religious means by which the protagonists are converted. This line of thought leads to a political resolution: all the pleasures and ensuing disappointments are but a

---

38 Aristotle points out: "… *The Odyssey* is complex (for it is recognition right through) and full of character." "A recognition is finest when it happens at the same time as a reversal." Aristotle, *Poetics*, 24.59b11, 11.52a33–34; trans., Janko, *Poetics*, 34, 14.

39 Lionel Pearson, *Popular Ethics in Ancient Greece*, 36–38.

mirage, which stands as a metaphor for the fallen Song dynasty. The climax of these artworks forces the protagonists toward transcendence (in the drama) and absence (in the painting). Tang–Song adaptations in the grotto romance tradition ascribed more complex motives to the pair. Liu and Ruan's homesickness is allegorized by some poets as an awakening from a dream, a euphemism for the ending of an illicit love affair. In the original tale, when the two men exit from the mountains and return to their village only to discover that seven human generations have passed, it is too late for regret. The tale evolved into a tryst with the transcendent, the identity of whom assumes a triple role of the *xian*, a Daoist priestess, and a geisha in the Tang and opened up new poetry on love. Yuan Zhen and Bai Juyi learned the lesson on awakening, while most other Tang and Song poets and lyrists focused on the erotic dimensions of grotto fantasy.

Human needs are manifested in family values in both bodies of texts. In dealing with the theme of alienation and its effects on the relationships between the individual, society, and family, the Greek epic does not rely upon the intrigue of time dilation, but moves its readers with familiar romantic encounters and the ensuing isolation. One of Odysseus's heroic traits is his will that unflaggingly sustains his wish to return home. Before Odysseus's fleet set sail, Circe gave the hero instructions on how to enter the underworld through sacrificial rituals to seek prophetic guidance from the ghost of the prophet Teiresias. During his visit to this realm, Odysseus learned from the ghost of Agamemnon that Penelope, wife of Odysseus, had remained chaste and loyal, but had been making the utmost efforts to refuse unreasonable requests from suitors.[40] These suitors had something else on their minds rather than love—they each conspired to usurp power and take over the throne of the long-absent Odysseus to become the new king of Ithaca. The prophecy provided by the ghosts of Teiresias and Agamemnon was crucial in strengthening Odysseus's courage and will to return home, kill his enemies, and restore his power after so many years of wandering. To Odysseus, this series of actions meant much more than just ensuring his homecoming; their larger significance was in the restoration of his sovereignty, which had been on the verge of being usurped. To those around him (and to Homeric audiences) his restoration also signified the return of the inherent social order and moral norms in the kingdom and, therefore, the victory of justice and righteousness.

Liu and Ruan do not assume heroic qualities, but the implications of their loss of family, relatives, and social network may be of similar magnitude in

---

40 Lattimore, *The Odyssey of Homer*, 11.445–46 (p. 179).

medieval China. One important function of their romantic encounter is the undermining of family norms and social bonds. Once the transgression begins, a centrifugal force is formed and becomes more and more formidable as the plot unfolds. The greater the temporal separation and the more deeply the protagonists indulge in the temptation, the greater this force. Eventually, the protagonists are completely estranged from the world to which they originally belonged and are placed in a strange, unfamiliar state akin to a moral vacuum. It is a state of spiritual displacement, as much as it is one of time and place.[41] As this time-dilated dimension is not where/when they belong, the centrifugal force continuously pushes them away. Back home, their families and social relations have likewise been distanced from them and all bonds permanently severed. The unique device of temporal displacement in the Chinese narrative executes power over the alienation process by heightening the protagonist's plight to an irreparable extent. As such, the discourse may be seen as a perfect realization of an old Chinese proverb, "a single misstep leads to a thousand years of regret." The moral is crystal clear: seeking extramarital sensual pleasure causes irreparable damage to one's family. This rupture works in similar ways in the political satires discussed in the book, but in the romantic encounters in Zhang Zhuo's and Yuan Zhen's works, they make efforts to flee or remedy the consequences of their transgressive acts. In Tang–Song lyrics, this rupture becomes the source of the female protagonist's agony. To Zhao Cangyun, the family value may carry a much more significant meaning because he was descended from the royal Zhao family. Therefore, the loss of family means the loss of *his* Song dynasty. This reading construes Liu and Ruan's failure to rediscover the grotto after leaving.

Although Odysseus's romantic encounters do not occur in dilated time, time and space still form major challenges in his longing to return to his home and kingdom. In his case, the damage is repairable, as it is the will of the gods and he is under the constant protection of Athena. Odysseus's challenge mainly depends on his personal agency, which is clearly reflected in his ambivalence during his seven years of romantic life on the island of Ogygia. Sexual desire seems to be the only reason for his tarrying, yet is also a driver behind resuming his destiny and returning home.[42] The hero's hesitation about leaving his

---

41 Joseph Campbell discusses spiritual displacement in an analysis of the adventures of the Future Buddha, Gautama Śākyamuni, and gives the respective adventures of Theseus and Odysseus as parallel cases. See Campbell, *The Hero with a Thousand Faces*, 46–48.

42 George E. Dimock, for example, questions: "We may be tempted to ask why this Kalypso is not at least as good as home." See Dimock, *The Unity of The Odyssey*, p. 12; Howard W. Clarke: "It is true that he is going home, but he does not want to miss a thing—or a gift—on the way." See Clarke, *The Art of The Odyssey*, 51.

romantic life reflects human nature and, indeed, makes an excellent component of moral education. As time elapses, the hero's will to return home is on the decline and on the verge of vanishing; on the other hand, his lust and excitement for the lovely nymph is also in decline, as he has enjoyed this illegitimate pleasure for long enough.[43] After the seven years, the hero's sense of responsibility and great mission finally supersedes his transgressive pursuit of sexual pleasure. The name of the nymph in this romance, Kalypso (καλύπτω, kalyptō), which means "hide" or "conceal," is most revealing. She not only hides her lover Odysseus on this island, which no mortal can reach, but, more importantly, conceals and cuts off the hero's identity, deeds, family, and social relations.[44] In addition to these two common connotations, Bruce Louden also adds: "Kalypso, living up to her name, not only hides the hero but threatens to conceal the plot as well." By this, he means that, if she had not released the hero, Odysseus would not have met the two bards, Demodokos and Phemios, who "both meet the hero face to face, and consequently will be able to pass on authoritative accounts about him to the subsequent tradition."[45] Louden's hypothesis touches on how the epic poet structures his narrative and generates the moral of the epic. In addition, as Fajardo-Acosta puts it, Kalypso may be read as the "goddess of death," and Ogygia "the very land of spiritual death."[46] This oxymoronic notion of "death" refers to the dead-end of Odysseus's road to heroism, which would have won him immortality in a different sense. The stumbling block for Odysseus's heroism, represented by the nymph, is thus tied to the passage of time: stumble and fall into immortality, or overcome and continue walking in mortal time. Imperatively, one may say, the hero is predestined to break the concealment as the plot unfolds.

Focusing on the passage of time, John H. Finley, Jr. discusses Odysseus's seven-year romantic encounter and sums up the subjective nature of how time elapses in this "realm of immortality." He argues: "The quiet of his seven years with her [Kalypso] conveys his half-entrance into timelessness; his recovery at Scheria of his old heroic power is slow, a kind of rebirth."[47] This "timeless" stage is thus like a gestation for Odysseus's inevitable recovery. And yet this gestation is not always slow and quiescent, especially when he saw "the very smoke

---

43 Lattimore, *The Odyssey of Homer*, 5.151–54 (p. 92).
44 Kalypso's name carries the connotation of "hiding," as reflected in her being called "the hidden one" and "hiding" Odysseus. She tries "... not only to hide Odysseus from his world but to hide his world from him." See Seth L. Schein, "Introduction," in his *Reading The Odyssey*, 14–15.
45 Louden, *The Odyssey*, 106.
46 Fajardo-Acosta, *The Hero's Failure*, 203.
47 John H. Finley, Jr., *Homer's Odyssey*, 77.

uprising from his own country."[48] This urgency reveals the predestined nature of the reassertion of Odysseus's heroic desire to return.

This kind of moral lesson has a parallel in Liu and Ruan's adventures. The common moral elements include the inevitable lure of the fulfilment of appetite and lust and the enjoyment of a luxurious life in the grotto, and the resulting moral dilemma when enjoyment turns to ennui. At the beginning of the Chinese tale, we read: "The sweetness of the voices and words of these girls swept away the two men's worries." Their "worries" refer not only to their mixed feelings of cheer and fear when they first arrived at the scene, but also to their general sense of family and social responsibility in the human world. Their worries may, furthermore, extend to the political and social turmoil that was in abundance when the tale was written. How could anyone resist a luxurious escape during a chaotic time? Nevertheless, "ten days later, the two men requested to return home." This request marks the inevitable resilience of the inherent value of society, family, and ethics, which had temporarily been repressed and displaced by extramarital excitement and rapture but then regained sufficient strength to reach the muddled minds of the two men. From a religious perspective, one observes the suffering endured by Liu and Ruan, including bouts of hunger, fear, temptation, anxiety, and homesickness, the experience of which foments and catalyzes a strong wish to renounce suffering and pleasure alike, and to return to mortal society, marking a process of redemption and recovery. But the process is not smooth. In response to the ladies' persuasions, Liu and Ruan agree to stay for another half year. Perhaps they are not satisfied and want to indulge more before returning, or perhaps they do not want to give up their "karmic blessing" so easily. If we see this as a religious test for the men, they fail and are consequently punished.

The conflict between opposing emotional impulses is common in the Western classic and the Liu-Ruan literary tradition. Liu and Ruan are faced with the choice between the enjoyment of sexual pleasure and a return home to their families to live a mortal life. In these contexts, the role of the maidens is mechanical, and serves only to generate the moral momentum that enables the Chinese men's departure from the grotto, which is predestined by the storyteller/poet, or the "expedient means." It is the moral dilemma faced by the men that drives the narrative tension and the catastrophic consequences.

---

48   Lattimore, *The Odyssey of Homer*, 1.57–59 (p. 28).

6   Real and Unreal

The Liu-Ruan tale and *The Odyssey* are both shaped by a dichotomy in which the human realm is legitimate while the otherworld represents deviance and anomaly. The latter serves to challenge the protagonists' moral fiber, and thereby strengthen the narrative tension and the story's eventual edifying impact. The authors of the two groups of texts make ingenious use of the lure of immortality as a plot intrigue. The original Liu-Ruan tale might have intended to deliver a moral by discouraging the unbridled pursuit of transient pleasure, sensual enjoyment, and carnal longevity. This possible moral gave rise to variations of motifs and representations in later adaptations. The dichotomy of real vs. unreal is a crucial literary device in the two groups of texts. These generically disparate texts share the narrative progression from survival, confusion, enjoyment, and hesitation, to determination. Odysseus resolves to abandon the offer of immortality, which would have destroyed his heroic nature over time, and instead determines to return to the human world, where time (in his lifespan) resumes its normal passage. This marks a return from unreality to reality. This does not mean that the passage of time moves at a different speed on the outlying islands, but that the longer he lingers there, the longer his heroic destiny is postponed. Liu Chen and Ruan Zhao also renounce the otherworldly realm, where they could have lived much longer, wishing to return to their native land, but upon returning they only found themselves displaced in time and no longer have homes or practical purposes to their lives. The open ending in the original tale as well as in Zhao Cangyun's version, which has Liu and Ruan wandering to an unknown fate, completes the progression from reality to unreality, back to reality, but finally ending up in unreality again. The moral in these early versions of the grotto romance tale produces a lesson on transgression between reality and unreality. This transgression in the *Youming lu* version might have been accidental but is clearly purposeful in Liu Yuxi's and Zhao Cangyun's hands in their political satires. In Tang–Song poetic grotto fantasy, this kind of yoyoing between the real and unreal becomes the source of the forlorn lady's anxiety.

The two stories present the eternal in different ways. Kalypso promises Odysseus eternal life as an incentive for his stay. Athena, the patron goddess of Odysseus, has been with him throughout his plight and assists him in achieving his exploits upon returning home. However, had Odysseus remained obsessed with the nymph's beauty and chosen eternal life in lieu of returning home, the significance of the eternal in the epic would have been limited. Had he opted for eternal life instead of eternal fame, his great accomplishments in the Trojan

War would have perished altogether; his kingdom would also have fallen into the hands of the vicious suitors; and the narrative impact of the epic would have been drastically reduced. The significance of Liu and Ruan's eternity was much more limited. As soon as the men depart the grotto, the wheel of time has turned and cannot be reset. The two groups of texts compared in this chapter represent two different views of eternity, but the moral they share is itself timeless: it is human nature to covet carnal pleasures, but when indulgence goes too far, serious consequences ensue.

The resilience of the Greek classic and the Chinese tale is astonishing. Both endured for millennia after they were first introduced into circulation. In the case of the Liu-Ruan tale, what remains unchanged is the capacity of the narrative to enable writers to explore values via exploration of and interplay with an otherworld. This quest is enlivened when the texts are reread and contemplated with reference to our own, always changing, lives. The grotto fantasy textual and contextual circles, with their capacity to generate new thematic twists and turns, comprise a tradition that is defined by a fascinating degree of flexibility. It is this instability that guaranteed the relevance of grotto fantasy over centuries of turbulent socio-political history.

Works Cited

A list of abbreviations of frequently cited works is on pp. XV–XVI of this book.

Daoist Scriptures (by HY Number)

Edition: *Zhengtong Daozang* 正統道藏. Rpt. Taipei: Xinwenfeng chuban gongsi, 1985–88.

The HY sequence number is according to Wen Dujian 翁獨健, comp., *Daozang zimu yinde* 道藏子目引得, Harvard-Yenching Institute Sinological Index Series, no. 25.

HY 6	*Shangqing dadong zhenjing* 上清大洞真經.
HY 166	Ge Hong 葛洪 (284–364). *Yuanshi shangzhen zhongxian ji* 元始上真眾仙記.
HY 167	Tao Hongjing 陶弘景 (456–536). *Dongxuan Lingbao zhenling weiye tu* 洞玄靈寶真靈位業圖.
HY 294	*Liexian zhuan* 列仙傳. Attributed to Liu Xiang 劉向 (77–6 BC).
HY 296	Zhao Daoyi 趙道一 (Yuan). *Lishi zhenxian tidao tongjian* 歷世真仙體道通鑑.
HY 299	*Yixian zhuan* 疑仙傳. Attributed to Yinfu yujian 隱夫玉簡 (ca. 10th–13th c.).
HY 388	*Taishang Lingbao Wufu xu* 太上靈寶五符序.
HY 595	Wu Shu 吳淑 (10th c.). *Jiang-Huai yiren lu* 江淮異人錄.
HY 596	Wang Songnian 王松年 (Tang). *Xianyuan bianzhu* 仙苑編珠.
HY 836	Ge Hong. *Zhenzhong ji* 枕中記.
HY 998	Zhu Xi 朱熹 (1130–1200), ed. *Zhouyi cantongqi* 周易參同契.
HY 1010	Tao Hongjing, comp. *Zhen'gao* 真誥.
HY 1026	Zhang Junfang 張君房 (fl. early 11th c.), comp. *Yunji qiqian* 雲笈七籤.
HY 1130	*Wushang biyao* 無上祕要.
HY 1252	Ma Zhong 馬總 (Tang), ed. *Yilin* 意林.

Buddhist Sutras (by *T* Number)

Sequence number of Buddhist sutras according to *Taishō shinshū Daizōkyō* 大正新脩大藏経. Comps. Takakusu Junjirō 高楠順次郎 (1866–1945) and Watanabe Kaikyoku 渡邊海旭 (1872–1932). Tokyo: Iaishō Issaikyō kankōkai, 1924–32.

T 99	*Saṃyuktâgama-sūtra (Za Ahan jing)* 雜阿含經. Trans. Guṇabhadra 求那跋陀羅 (394–468).

T 186   *Lalitavistara (Fo shuo Puyao jing)* 佛說普曜經. Trans. Dharmarakṣa 竺法護 (233–310).

T 190   *Abhiniṣkramaṇa-sūtra (Fo benxing ji jing)* 佛本行集經. Trans. Jñānagupta 闍那崛多 (523–600).

T 210   *Dharmapada (Faju jing)* 法句經. Trans. Vighna 維祇難 (3rd c.), et al.

T 262   *Saddharma-puṇḍarīka-sūtra (Miaofa Lianhua jing)* 妙法蓮華經. Trans. Kumārajīva 鳩摩羅什 (334–413).

T 263   *Saddharma-puṇḍarīka-sūtra (Zheng Fahua jing)* 正法華經. Trans. Dharmarakṣa 竺法護 (W. Jin).

T 278   *Avataṃsaka-sūtra (Dafang guang fo Huayan jing)* 大方廣佛華嚴經. Trans. Buddhabhadra 佛馱跋陀羅 (fl. early 5th c.).

T 475   *Vimalakīrti-sūtra (Weimojie suoshuo jing)* 維摩詰所說經 (in 3 *juan*). Trans. Kumārajīva.

T 670   *Laṅkâvatāra-sūtra (Lengqieabaduoluo baojing)* 楞伽阿跋多羅寶經. Trans. Guṇabhadra.

T 1585 *Vijñaptimātratāsiddhi-śāstra (Cheng weishi lun)* 成唯識論. Trans. Xuanzang 玄奘 (602–664).

T 2008 *Liuzu dashi fabao Tanjing* 六祖大師法寶壇經. Comp. Fahai 法海 (Tang).

T 2035 *Fozu tongji* 佛祖統紀. By Zhipan 志磐 (fl. mid-13th c.).

T 2122 *Fayuan zhulin* 法苑珠林. Comp. Shi Daoshi 釋道世 (fl. early to mid-7th c.).

T 2901 *Dharmapada (Fo shuo Faju jing)* 佛說法句經.

In addition to *Taishō shinshū Daizōkyō*:

Fo wei Xinwang pusa shuo Toutuo jing 佛為心王菩薩說頭陀經. In *Zangwai Fojiao wenxian* 藏外佛教文獻, vol. 1, ed. Fang Guangchang 方廣錩. Beijing: Zongjiao wenhua chubanshe, 1995.

Other Primary Sources (by Title)

Baopuzi neipian jiaoshi 抱朴子內篇校釋. Ed. & comm. Wang Ming 王明. Beijing: Zhonghua shuju, 1985.

Bencao gangmu 本草綱目. By Li Shizhen 李時珍 (1518–1593). Rpt. Taipei: Wenguang tushu youxian gongsi, 1983.

Benshi shi 本事詩. By Meng Qi 孟棨 (*jinshi* 870s). In *Lidai shihua xubian* 歷代詩話續編, ed. Ding Fubao 丁福保 (1874–1952). Beijing: Zhonghua shuju, 1983, pp. 4–22.

Bowu zhi jiaozheng 博物志校證. By Zhang Hua 張華 (513–581). Ed. Fan Ning 范寧. Beijing: Zhonghua shuju, 1980.

Caidiao ji buzhu 才調集補注. Comm. Song Bangsui 宋邦綏 (d. 1779). *XXSK*, vol. 1611.

WORKS CITED 225

"Changsheng le" 長生樂 ("Joy of Eternal Life"). Attributed to Yuan Yuling 袁于令 (1599–1674) or Zhang Yun 張勻 (fl. late 17th c.). In *Guben xiqu congkan sanji* 古本戲曲叢刊三集. Shanghai: Shangwu yinshuguan, 1955.

Chaoye qianzai 朝野僉載. By Zhang Zhuo 張鷟 (ca. 660–ca. 740). Issued in one volume with *Sui Tang jiahua* 隋唐嘉話. Beijing: Zhonghua shuju, 1997.

Chaxiangshi congchao 茶香室叢鈔. By Yu Yue 俞樾 (1821–1906). Ed. Zhen Fan 貞凡, Gu Xin 顧馨 and Xu Minxia 徐敏霞. Beijing: Zhonghua shuju, 1995.

Gujin cihua 古今詞話. By Yang Shi 楊湜 (S. Song). In Tang Guizhang 唐圭璋, comp., *Cihua congbian* 詞話叢編. Beijing: Zhonghua shuju, 1986, pp. 13–54.

Ciyuan congtan 詞苑叢談. By Xu Qiu 徐釚 (1636–1708). *SKQS*, vol. 1494.

Dongming ji 洞冥記. By Guo Xian 郭憲 (E. Han). In *Han Wei liuchao biji xiaoshuo daguan* 漢魏六朝筆記小說大觀, ed. Shanghai guji chubanshe 上海古籍出版社. Shanghai: Shanghai guji chubanshe, 1999.

Dunhuang manuscripts:

    P.2506. In *Fa cang Dunhuang Xiyu wenxian* 法藏敦煌西域文獻, vol. 14, ed. Shanghai guji chubanshe and Bibliothèque nationale de France. Shanghai: Shanghai guji chubanshe, 2001, p. 377 (plate 6–1).

    S.1441. In *Ying cang dunhuang wenxian: Hanwen Fojing yiwai bufen* 英藏敦煌文獻：漢文佛經以外部份, vol. 3. Chengdu: Sichuan renmin chubanshe, 1990, pp. 48–49.

    S.2607. In *Ying cang dunhuang wenxian: Hanwen Fojing yiwai bufen*, vol. 4: pp. 113–16.

    S.7111. In *Ying cang dunhuang wenxian: Hanwen Fojing yiwai bufen*, vol. 12. Chengdu: Sichuan renmin chubanshe, 1995, p. 52.

Dunhuang quzici ji 敦煌曲子詞集. Comp. Wang Zhongmin 王重民. Shanghai: Shangwu yinshuguan, 1950.

Dunhuang quzici ji (xiuding ben) 敦煌曲子詞集（修訂本）. Comp. Wang Zhongmin 王重民. Shanghai: Shangwu yinshuguan, 1956.

Dunhuang Yunyao ji xin jiaoding 敦煌雲謠集新校訂. Ed. Shen Yingming 沈英名 and Meng Yu 孟玉. Taipei: Zhengzhong shuju, 1979.

Gaiding Yuanxian chuanqi 改定元賢傳奇. Comp. Li Kaixian 李開先 (1502–1568). *XXSK*, vol. 1760.

Gu mingjia zaju 古名家雜劇. Comp. Chen Yujiao 陳與郊 (1544–1611). In *Guben xiqu congkan siji* 古本戲曲叢刊四集. Shanghai: Shangwu yinshuguan, 1958.

Guanyinzi 關尹子. *SKQS*, vol. 1055.

Gujin zaju 古今雜劇. In *Maiwang guan chaojiaoben gujin zaju* 脈望館抄校本古今雜劇, vol. 33, *Guben xiqu congkan siji* 古本戲曲叢刊四集. Shanghai: Shangwu yinshuguan, 1958.

Guxiaoshuo gouchen 古小說鉤沈. Comp. Lu Xun 魯迅. Beijing: Renmin wenxue chubanshe, 1953.

Han Tang dili shuchao 漢唐地理書鈔. Comp. Wang Mo 王謨 (ca. 1731–1817). Beijing: Zhonghua shuju, 1961.

Hanshu 漢書. By Ban Gu 班固 (32–92). Beijing: Zhonghua shuju, 1987.

Han Yu quanji jiaozhu 韓愈全集校注. By Han Yu 韓愈. Ed. & comm. Qu Shouyuan 屈守元 and Chang Sichun 常思春. Chengdu: Sichuan daxue chubanshe, 1996.

Hejiao Shuijing zhu 合校水經注. Ed. Wang Xianqian 王先謙 (1842–1917). *SBBY*.

Houqing lu 侯鯖錄. By Zhao Lingzhi 趙令畤 (1061–1134). *CSJC*, vol. 2859.

Huajian ji jiaozhu 花間集校注. Ed. & comm. Yang Jinglong 楊景龍. Beijing: Zhonghua shuju, 2014.

Hua'an cixuan 花庵詞選. By Huang Sheng 黃昇 (S. Song). *SKQS*, vol. 1489.

Jiading Chicheng zhi 嘉定赤城志. Comp. Chen Qiqing 陳耆卿 (1180–1236). In *Song Yuan fangzhi congkan* 宋元方志叢刊. Beijing: Zhonghua shuju, 1990.

Jiaofang ji 教坊記. By Cui Lingqin 崔令欽 (early 8th c). In *Zhongguo gudian xiqu lunzhu jicheng* 中國古典戲曲論著集成, vol. 1, ed. Zhongguo xiqu yanjiuyuan 中國戲曲研究院. Beijing: Zhongguo xiju chubanshe, 1982.

Jiaofang ji jianding 教坊記箋訂. By Cui Lingqin 崔令欽 (early 8th c). Ed. & comm. Ren Bantang 任半塘. Beijing: Zhonghua shuju, 1982.

Jinshu 晉書. By Fang Xuanling 房玄齡 (579–648), et al. Beijing: Zhonghua shuju, 1987.

Jiping jiaozhu Xixiang ji 集評校注西廂記. Ed. & comm. Wang Jisi 王季思 and Zhang Renhe 張人和. Shanghai: Shanghai guji chubanshe, 1987.

Koji dan 古事談. By Minamotono Akikane 源顯兼 (1160–1215). N.d.: N.p. Copy preserved in Kokuritsu Kokkai toshokan 国立国会図書館. Call number: ほ-45.

Li Qingzhao ji jianzhu 李清照集箋注. Comm. Xu Peijun 徐培均. Shanghai: Shanghai guji chubanshe, 2002.

Liji zhengyi 禮記正義. Comm. Zheng Xuan 鄭玄 (127–200) and Kong Yingda 孔穎達 (574–648). *SSJ*.

Lishi 隸釋. Comp. Hong Gua 洪适 (1117–84). *SBCK*.

Liu Chen and Ruan Zhao Entering the Tiantai Mountains 元趙蒼雲劉晨阮肇入天台山圖卷. By Zhao Cangyun 趙蒼雲 (active late 13th–early 14th century). Yuan dynasty (1271–1368). Handscroll; ink on paper. 8 7/8 in. × 18 ft. 5 in. (22.5 cm × 564 cm). Sections 6, 7, 8, 9, and 11. The Metropolitan Museum of Art of New York City. Accessed 25 July 2024. https://www.metmuseum.org/art/collection/search/39545.

Liu Mengde wenji 劉夢得文集. *SBCK*.

Liu Yuxi quanji biannian jiaozhu 劉禹錫全集編年校注. Ed. & comm. Tao Min 陶敏 and Tao Hongyu 陶紅雨. Changsha: Yuelu shushe, 2003.

Liu Zhangqing shi biannian jianzhu 劉長卿詩編年箋注. Ed. & comm. Chu Zhongjun 儲仲君. Beijing: Zhonghua shuju, 1996.

Lugui bu (wai sizhong) 錄鬼簿（外四種）. By Zhong Sicheng 鍾嗣成 (ca. 1279–ca. 1360). Shanghai: Gudian wenxue chubanshe, 1957.

Lunheng jiaoshi 論衡校釋. Comm. Huang Hui 黃暉 and Liu Pansui 劉盼遂. Beijing: Zhonghua shuju, 1990.

Lunyu 論語 (*The Analects*). Section and line numbers are based on *Lunyu yinde* 引得. Harvard-Yenching Institute Sinological Index Series, Supplement no. 16.

Lunyu zhushu 論語注疏. Comm. Kong Anguo 孔安國 (ca. 156–ca. 74 BC). *SSJ*.

Mengzi 孟子 (*Mencius*). Section and line numbers are based on *Mengzi yinde* 引得. Harvard-Yenching Institute Sinological Index Series, Supplement no. 17.

Moji 默記. By Wang Zhi 王銍 (12th c.). *SKQS*, vol. 1038.

Ouyang Xiu ci jianzhu 歐陽修詞箋注. Comm. Huang She 黃畬. Beijing: Zhonghua shuju, 1986.

Qingyang ji 青陽集. By Yu Que 余闕 (1303–1358). *SKQS*, vol. 1214.

Quan Jin Yuan ci 全金元詞. Comp. Tang Guizhang 唐圭璋. Beijing: Zhonghua shuju, 1979.

Quan Liang wen 全梁文. *QSGSD*.

Quan Tangwen 全唐文. Comp. Dong Gao 董誥 (1740–1818), et al. Beijing: Zhonghua shuju, 1983.

Quan Yuan sanqu 全元散曲. Comp. Sui Shusen 隋樹森. Beijing: Zhonghua shuju, 1986.

Quan Yuan xiqu 全元戲曲. Ed. Wang Jisi 王季思. Beijing: Renmin wenxue chubanshe, 1999.

Riben fangshu zhi 日本訪書志. By Yang Shoujing 楊守敬 (1839–1915). *XXSK*, vol. 930.

Ruan Bubing Yonghuai shi zhu 阮步兵詠懷詩註. Comm. Huang Jie 黃節. Beijing: Renmin wenxue chubanshe, 1984.

Ruan Ji ji jiaozhu 阮籍集校注. Ed. & comm. Chen Bojun 陳伯君. Beijing: Zhonghua shuju, 1987.

Sanguo zhi 三國志. By Chen Shou 陳壽 (233–297). Beijing: Zhonghua shuju, 1982.

Shanhai jing jiaozhu 山海經校注. Comp. & comm. Yuan Ke 袁珂. Shanghai: Shanghai guji chubanshe, 1980.

Shengxian gaoshi zhuan 聖賢高士傳. By Ji Kang 嵇康 (223–262). In *Quan Sanguo wen* 全三國文, *QSGSD*.

Shennong bencao jing 神農本草經. Ed. Sun Xingyan 孫星衍 (1753–1818) and Sun Fengyi 孫馮翼 (fl. early 19th c.). *Congshu jicheng xinbian* 叢書集成新編, vol. 46. Taipei: Xinwenfeng chuban gongsi, 1986.

Shiguo chunqiu 十國春秋. By Wu Renchen 吳任臣 (ca. 1628–ca. 1689). Beijing: Zhonghua shuju, 1983.

Shiji 史記. By Sima Qian 司馬遷 (ca. 145–ca. 86 B.C.). Beijing: Zhonghua shuju, 1982.

Shijing 詩經. Poem and section numbers are based on *Maoshi yinde* 毛詩引得. Harvard-Yenching Institute Sinological Index Series, Supplement no. 9.

Shishuo xinyu jianshu 世說新語箋疏. Comm. Yu Jiaxi 余嘉錫. Shanghai: Shanghai guji chubanshe, 1993.

Shiyi ji 拾遺記. Comp. Wang Jia 王嘉 (E. Jin). Beijing: Zhonghua shuju, 1988.

Shuowen jiezi gulin 說文解字詁林. Comp. Ding Fubao 丁福保. Beijing: Zhonghua shuju, 1988.

Shuyi ji 述異記. By Ren Fang 任昉 (460–508). *Longwei bishu* 龍威祕書 edn.

Songshi 宋史. By Tuotuo 脫脫 (1313–55), et al. Beijing: Zhonghua shuju, 1985.

Soushen hou ji 搜神後記. Attributed to Tao Qian 陶潛 (365–427). Comp. & comm. Wang Shaoying 汪紹楹. Beijing: Zhonghua shuju, 1981.

Soushen ji 搜神記. By Gan Bao 干寶 (fl. early 2nd c.). Ed. & comm. Wang Shaoying. Beijing: Zhonghua shuju, 1985.

Su Shi ci biannian jiaozhu 蘇軾詞編年校注. Ed. & comm. Zou Tongqing 鄒同慶 and Wang Zongtang 王宗堂. Beijing: Zhonghua shuju, 2002.

Su Shi wenji 蘇軾文集. Comp. Kong Fanli 孔凡禮. Beijing: Zhonghua shuju, 1986.

Suishu 隋書. By Wei Zheng 魏徵 (580–643). Beijing: Zhonghua shuju, 1982.

Taihe zhengyin pu 太和正音譜. By Zhu Quan 朱權 (1378–1448). In *Zhongguo gudian xiqu lunzhu jicheng* 中國古典戲曲論著集成, vol. 3, ed. Zhongguo xiqu yanjiuyuan 中國戲曲研究院. Beijing: Zhongguo xiju chubanshe, 1982.

Taiping jing hejiao 太平經合校. Ed. Wang Ming 王明. Beijing: Zhonghua shuju, 1960.

Tangqian zhiguai xiaoshuo jishi 唐前志怪小說輯釋. Comp. & comm. Li Jianguo 李劍國. Shanghai: Shanghai guji chubanshe, 1986.

Tangren xiaoshuo 唐人小說. Comp. Wang Pijiang 汪辟疆. Hong Kong: Chung Hwa Book Company (Hong Kong) Limited, 1987.

Tangren xuan Tangshi xinbian 唐人選唐詩新編. Ed. Fu Xuancong 傅璇琮. Xi'an: Shaanxi renmin jiaoyu chubanshe, 1996.

Tao Jingjie xiansheng shi zhu 陶靖節先生詩註. Comp. & comm. Tang Han 湯漢 (ca. 1265). Rpt., Beijing: Zhonghua shuju, 1987.

Tao Yuanming ji 陶淵明集. Comp. & comm. Lu Qinli 逯欽立. Beijing: Zhonghua shuju, 1979.

Tao Yuanming ji jianzhu 陶淵明集箋注. Comp. & comm. Yuan Xingpei 袁行霈. Beijing: Zhonghua shuju, 2003.

The Analects. See *Lunyu*.

Tianciming jie 填詞名解. By Mao Xianshu 毛先舒 (1620–88). In *Siku quanshu cunmu congshu* 四庫全書存目叢書, vol. 425, ed. Siku quanshu cunmu congshu bianzuan weiyuanhui 四庫全書存目叢書編纂委員會. Tainan: Zhuangyan wenhua shiye youxian gongsi, 1997.

Tiangong kaiwu 天工開物. xxsk, vol. 1115.

Tiaoxi yuyin conghua houji 苕溪漁隱叢話後集. By Hu Zi 胡仔 (1095–1170). Beijing: Renmin wenxue chubanshe, 1962.

Wang Wei ji jiaozhu 王維集校注. Ed. & comm. Chen Tiemin 陳鐵民. Beijing: Zhonghua shuju, 1997.

Wang Wugong wenji (wujuanben huijiao) 王無功文集（五卷本會校）. Ed. Han Lizhou 韓理洲. Shanghai: Shanghai guji chubanshe, 1987.

Wenyuan yinghua 文苑英華. Comps. Li Fang 李昉 (925–996), et al. Beijing: Zhonghua shuju, 1966.

Xiaojing yuanshen qi 孝經援神契. In *Isho shūsei (Weishu jicheng)* 緯書集成, ed. Yasui Kōzan 安居香山 and Nakamura Shōhachi 中村璋八. Tokyo: Kangi Bunka Kenkyūkai, 1959–64. Rpt. Shijiazhuang: Hebei renmin chubanshe, 1994.

Xijing zaji 西京雜記. *SBCK*.

Xin Tangshu 新唐書. By Ouyang Xiu 歐陽修, et al. Beijing: Zhonghua shuju, 1987.

Xinbian zuiweng tanlu 新編醉翁談錄. By Luo Ye 羅燁 (fl. late 13th c.). *XXSK*, vol. 1266.

Xinji Soushen ji, Xinji Soushen hou ji 新輯搜神記，新輯搜神後記. Ed. Li Jianguo 李劍國 Beijing: Zhonghua, 2007.

Xunzi jijie 荀子集解. Comp. Wang Xian Qian 王先謙 (1842–1918). In *Zhuzi jicheng* 諸子集成, ed. Guoxue zhengli she 國學整理社. Rpt. Beijing: Zhonghua shuju, 1986.

Yiyuan 異苑. Comp. Liu Jingshu 劉敬叔 (mid-5th c.). In *Shuoku* 說庫, comp. Wang Wenru 王文濡. Hangzhou: Zhejiang guji chubanshe, 1986. Reprint of Wenming shuju edn.

Yu Zishan ji zhu 庾子山集注. Comp. Ni Fan 倪璠 (late 17th c.). Beijing: Zhonghua shuju, 1985.

Yuefu shiji 樂府詩集. Ed. Guo Maoqian 郭茂倩 (ca. 1084). Beijing: Zhonghua shuju, 1979.

Yunxi youyi 雲谿友議. By Fan Shu 范攄 (fl. 877). *SKQS*, vol. 1035.

Yuan Zhen ji biannian jianzhu 元稹集編年箋注. Ed. & comm. Yang Jun 楊軍. Xi'an: San Qin chubanshe, 2002.

Yuanqu xuan 元曲選. Comp. Zang Jinshu 臧晉叔 (1550–1620). Beijing: Zhonghua shuju, 1989.

Yuanqu xuan jiaozhu 元曲選校注. Ed. & comm. Wang Xueqi 王學奇, et al. Shijiazhuang: Hebei jiaoyu chubanshe, 1994.

Yuding Peiwenzhai guang Qunfang pu 御定佩文齋廣群芳譜. *SKQS*, vols. 845–47.

Yuefu zalu 樂府雜錄. By Duan Anjie 段安節 (late 9th c.). In *Zhongguo gudian xiqu lunzhu jicheng* 中國古典戲曲論著集成, vol. 1, ed. Zhongguo xiqu yanjiuyuan 中國戲曲研究院. Beijing: Zhongguo xiju chubanshe, 1982.

Yuxuan lidai shiyu 御選歷代詩餘. Comp. Shen Chenyuan 沈辰垣 (*jinshi* 1685). *SKQS*, vols. 1491–93.

Yūsenkutsu shō 遊仙窟鈔. Dated 1671. Rpt., Osaka: Gunhōdō 群鳳堂. N.d.

Zhenglei bencao 證類本草. Comp. Tang Shenwei 唐慎微 (N. Song), et al. *SKQS*, vol. 740.

Zhilin 志林. By Yu Xi 虞喜 (ca. 270–ca. 345). In *Shuofu yibai ershi juan* 説郛一百二十弓, comp. Tao Zongyi 陶宗儀 (1329–1410). In *Shuofu sanzhong* 説郛三種. Shanghai: Shanghai guji chubanshe, 1988.

Zhuangzi 莊子. Section and line numbers are based on *Zhuangzi yinde* 引得. Harvard-Yenching Institute Sinological Index Series, Supplement no. 20.

Zhuangzi jishi 莊子集釋. Ed. & comm. Guo Qingfan 郭慶藩 (1844–ca. 1896). Beijing: Zhonghua shuju, 1985.

Zizhi tongjian 資治通鑑. Comp. Sima Guang 司馬光 (1019–1086), et al. Beijing: Zhonghua shuju, 1986.

Zuozhuan 左傳. Year and section numbers are based on *Chunqiu jingzhuan* 春秋經傳引得. Harvard-Yenching Institute Sinological Index Series, Supplement no. 11.

Secondary Works in Chinese and Japanese (by Author)

Aoki Masaru 青木正兒. *Yuanren zaju gaishuo* 元人雜劇概說. Trans. Sui Shusen 隋樹森. Hong Kong: Zhonghua shuju, 1977.

Bai Zhaojie 白照傑. "Qu Boting" 瞿柏庭. In *Lidai gaodao zhuan* 歷代高道傳. Unpublished manuscript.

Bian Xiaoxuan 卞孝萱. *Liu Yuxi nianpu* 劉禹錫年譜. Beijing: Zhonghua shuju, 1963.

Bian Xiaoxuan 卞孝萱. *Yuan Zhen nianpu* 元稹年譜. Ji'nan: Qi Lu shushe, 1980.

Chai Jianhong 柴劍虹 and Xu Jun 徐俊. "Dunhuang ci jijiao sitan" 敦煌詞輯校四談. *Dunhuangxue jikan* 敦煌學輯刊 1988.1 & 2: 53–59.

Chan, Timothy Wai Keung 陳偉強. "Cong wuru dao daoru: 'Liu Ruan Tiantai' zaju zhuti de xinbian" 從誤入到導入：《劉阮天台》雜劇主題的新變. *Daojia wenhua yanjiu* 道家文化研究 24. Beijing: Shenghuo, dushu, xinzhi Sanlian shudian, 2009, pp. 438–61.

Chan, Timothy Wai Keung 陳偉強. "Dao buruo shen: Ruan Ji de yuzhou shengmie xunhuan lun" 道不若神——阮籍的宇宙生滅循環論. In *Han Wei Liuchao wenxue yu zongjiao* 漢魏六朝文學與宗教, ed. Ge Xiaoyin 葛曉音. Shanghai: Shanghai guji chubanshe, 2005, pp. 215–44.

Chan, Timothy Wai Keung 陳偉強. "Lu Ji 'Lingxiao fu' de youxixing yu jingdianxing" 陸機《陵霄賦》的遊戲性與經典性. *Zhongguo gudianxue* 中國古典學 1. Beijing: Zhonghua shuju, 2020, pp. 308–22.

Chan, Timothy Wai Keung 陳偉強. "Yixiang feixiang: Shangqing Dadong zhenjing suoshu zhi cunsi xiulian" 意象飛翔：《上清大洞真經》所述之存思修煉. *Journal of Chinese Studies* 中國文化研究所學報 53 (July 2011): 217–48.

Chan, Timothy Wai Keung 陳偉強. "Yujingshan Chaohui: cong Liuchao buxuyi dao Chu Tang youxianshi" 玉京山朝會：從六朝步虛儀到初唐遊仙詩. *Journal of Chinese Studies* 72 (January 2021): 1–26.

Chan, Timothy Wai Keung 陳偉強. "Zhongshen huxing, buxu Yujing: Li Bai de Zhexian shixue" 眾神護形，步虛玉京——李白的謫仙詩學. *Tsing Hua Journal of Chinese Studies* 清華學報 52.4 (2022), 675–715.

Chang Yi-jen 張以仁. "Cong Lu Qianyi de 'Linjiang xian' tandao tade yishou 'Nüguanzi'" 從鹿虔扆的〈臨江仙〉談到他的一首〈女冠子〉. In idem., *Huajianci lunji* 花間詞論集. Taipei: Zhongyang yanjiuyuan Zhongguo wenzhe yanjiusuo, 1996, pp. 263–74.

Chang Yi-jen 張以仁. "Wen Tingyun liangshou 'Nüguanzi' de xunjie yu tizhi de wenti" 溫庭筠兩首〈女冠子〉的訓解與題旨的問題. In idem., *Huajianci lunji*, 169–82.

Chen Bohai 陳伯海, comp. *Tangshi huiping* 唐詩彙評. Hangzhou: Zhejiang jiaoyu chubanshe, 1995.

Chen Dezhi 陳得芝. "Cong 'jiu ru shi gai' kan Yuandai rushi de diwei" 從「九儒十丐」看元代儒士的地位. *Guangming ribao* 光明日報, June 18, 1986. Also in idem., *Meng-Yuan shi yanjiu conggao* 蒙元史研究叢稿. Beijing: Renmin chubanshe, 2005, pp. 424–29.

Chen Yinke 陳寅恪. "'Taohuayuan ji' pangzheng" 桃花源記旁證. In idem., *Jinmingguan conggao chubian* 金明館叢稿初編. Rpt. Beijing: Shenghuo, dushu, xinzhi sanlian shudian, 2001, pp. 188–200.

Chen Yinke 陳寅恪. *Yuan Bai shi jianzheng gao* 元白詩箋證稿. Shanghai: Shanghai guji chubanshe, 1978.

Chen Zhiyuan 陳致遠. "Cong Wuling gu fangzhi kan 'Taohuayuan ji' yuanxing" 從武陵古方志看《桃花源記》原型. *Wuling xuekan* 武陵學刊 2011.4: 45–49.

Cheng Qianfan 程千帆. "Guo Jingchun, Cao Yaobin 'Youxian' shi bianyi" 郭景純、曹堯賓〈遊仙〉詩辨異. In idem., *Gushi kaosuo* 古詩考索. Shanghai: Shanghai guji chubanshe, 1984, pp. 296–307.

Dong Kang 董康. *Quhai zongmu tiyao* 曲海總目提要. Taipei: Xinxing shuju, 1985.

Dong Shangde 董上德. "Luelun Zhongguo gudai yanyuxing 'youxian' gushi de chengchuan yu bianyi: yi *You xianku* 'yinan shuangmei' gushi kuangjia wei zhongxin" 略論中國古代豔遇型"遊仙"故事的承傳與變異——以《遊仙窟》"一男雙美"故事框架為中心. *Kyūshū Chūgoku gakukai hō* 九州中國學會報 41 (2003): 38–51.

Gao Guofan 高國藩. *Dunhuang quzici xinshang* 敦煌曲子詞欣賞. Nanjing: Nanjing daxue chubanshe, 1989.

Gao Feng 高鋒. *Huajian ci yanjiu* 花間詞研究. Nanjing: Jiangsu guji chubanshe, 2001.

Gao Mingqian 高明乾, ed. *Zhiwu gu Hanming tu kao* 植物古漢名圖考. Zhengzhou: Daxiang chubanshe, 2006.

Gao Xitian 高喜田 and Kou Qi 寇琪, comps. *Quan Songci zuozhe cidiao suoyin* 全宋詞作者詞調索引. Beijing: Zhonghua shuju, 1992.

Ge Zhaoguang 葛兆光. *Zhongguo Chan sixiang shi: cong 6 shiji dao 9 shiji* 中國禪思想史：從6世紀到9世紀. Beijing: Beijing daxue chubanshe, 1995.

Goldin, Paul R. (Jin Pengcheng 金鵬程). "Qi de hanyi jiqi jiji yiyi" 氣的含義及其積極意義. *Sino-humanitas* 人文中國學報 25 (2017): 305–39. Chinese translation of Goldin, 2000, cited below in Secondary Works in Western Languages, q.v.

Hanabusa Hideki 花房英樹 and Maegawa Yukio 前川幸雄. *Gen Shin kenkyū* 元稹研究. Kyoto: Ibundō Shoten, 1977.

Hatano Tarō 波多野太郎. "Yūsenkutsu shin kō" 遊仙窟新攷. *Tōhō shūkyō* 東方宗教 8 & 9 (1955): 1–28.

Hatano Tarō 波多野太郎. "Yūsenkutsu shin kō (shita)" 遊仙窟新攷（下）. *Tōhō shūkyō* 東方宗教 10 (1956): 21–58.

Hiraoka Takeo 平岡武夫 and Imai Kiyoshi 今井清. *Tōdai no Chōan to Rakuyō: Chizu* 唐代の長安と洛陽：地図. Kyoto: Kyōto Daigaku Jinbun Kagaku Kenkyūjo, 1956.

Hisamatsu Sen'ichi 久松潜一. *Man'yōshū no kenkyū (ichi)* 万葉集の研究（一）. Tokyo: Shibundō, 1976.

Hsiao Ch'i-ch'ing 蕭啟慶. *Nei beiguo er wai Zhongguo: Meng-Yuan shi yanjiu* 內北國而外中國：蒙元史研究. Beijing: Zhonghua shuju, 2007.

Hsiao Teng-fu 蕭登福. *Han Wei Liuchao Fo Dao liangjiao zhi tiantang diyu shuo* 漢魏六朝佛道兩教之天堂地獄說. Taipei: Taiwan xuesheng shuju, 1989.

Hu Zhengwu 胡正武. "Liu Ruan yuxian gushi yu Yuezhong chuantong zaozhi fawei" 劉阮遇仙故事與越中傳統造紙發微. *Zhejiang shifan daxue xuebao (shehui kexue ban)* 浙江師範大學學報（社會科學版） 119 (2002): 14–19.

Jao Tsung-i 饒宗頤. "'Tang ci' bian zheng"「唐詞」辨正. In idem., *Jao Tsung-i ershi shiji xueshu wenji* 饒宗頤二十世紀學術文集. Taipei: Xinwenfeng chuban gongsi, 2003, vol. 8: pp. 1098–1117.

Jin Pengcheng 金鵬程. See Goldin, Paul R.

Kao Chia-wen 高嘉文. "'Taoyuan xiqu' dui 'Taoyuan zhuti' jieshou zhi yanjiu"「桃源戲曲」對「桃源主題」接受之研究. *Oriental Humanities* 東方人文學誌 4 (2007): 171–86.

Kim Hyun Choo 金賢珠 and Lee Eun Ju 李恩周. "Guanyu Dunhuang quzici de mingcheng yu fanchou de shangque (xia)" 關於敦煌曲子詞的名稱與範圍的商榷（下）. *Zhongguo yuwen* 中國語文 2010.3: 86–92.

Kadowaki Hirofumi 門脇廣文. *Dōkutsu no naka no den'en: Soshite hutatsu no "Tōka genki"* 洞窟の中の田園：そして二つの「桃花源記」. Tokyo: Kenbun shuppan, 2017.

Kominami Ichirō 小南一郎. *Chūgoku no shinwa to monogatari: koshōsetsushi no tenkai* 中国の神話と物語り：古小説史の展開. Tokyo: Iwanami Shoten, 1984.

Kominami Ichirō 小南一郎. "Momo no densetsu" 桃の傳說. *Tōhō gakuhō* 東方學報 72 (2000): 49–77.

Kominami Ichirō 小南一郎. "Seiōbo to tanabata denshō" 西王母と七夕傳承. *Tōhō gakuhō* 46 (1974): 33–81.

Kominami Ichirō 小南一郎. *Tōdai denki shōsetsuron: kanashimi to akogare* 唐代伝奇小說論：悲しみと憧れ. Tokyo: Iwanami Shoten, 2014.

Kong Fanli 孔凡禮. *Su Shi nianpu* 蘇軾年譜. Beijing: Zhonghua shuju, 1998.

Lee Fong-mao 李豐楙. *Liuchao Sui Tang xiandao lei xiaoshuo yanjiu* 六朝隋唐仙道類小說研究. Taipei: Taiwan xuesheng shuju, 1986.

Lee Fong-mao 李豐楙. "Xian, ji yu dongku: cong Tang dao Bei Song chu de changji wenxue yu Daojiao" 仙、妓與洞窟——從唐到北宋初的娼妓文學與道教. In *Songdai wenxue yu sixiang* 宋代文學與思想, ed. Guoli Taiwan daxue Zhongguo wenxue yanjiusuo 國立臺灣大學中國文學研究所. Taipei: Taiwan xuesheng shuju, 1989, pp. 473–515.

Lee Fong-mao 李豐楙. *Wuru yu zhejiang: Liuchao Sui Tang Daojiao wenxue lunji* 誤入與謫降：六朝隋唐道教文學論集. Taipei: Taiwan xuesheng shuju, 1996.

Lee Fong-mao 李豐楙. *You yu you: Liuchao Sui Tang youxianshi lunji* 憂與遊：六朝隋唐遊仙詩論集. Taipei: Taiwan xuesheng shuju, 1996.

Lee Fong-mao 李豐楙. "Shenhua yu zhefan: Yuandai dutuo ju de zhuti jiqi shidai yiyi" 神化與謫凡：元代度脫劇的主題及其時代意義. In *Wenxue, wenhua yu shibian* 文學、文化與世變, ed. Lee Fong-mao. Taipei: Institute of Chinese Literature and Philosophy, Academia Sinica, 2002, pp. 237–72.

Lee Fong-mao 李豐楙. "*Shizhou ji* yanjiu"《十洲記》研究. In Lee, *Xianjing yu youli* 仙境與遊歷. Beijing: Zhonghua shuju, 2010, pp. 264–317.

Lee Fong-mao 李豐楙. "Dongtian yu neijing: Xiyuan er zhi wushiji Jiangnan Daojiao de neixiang youguan" 洞天與內景：西元二至五世紀江南道教的內向遊觀. In Liu Yuan-ju 劉苑如, ed., *Tixian ziran: Yixiang yu wenhua Shijian* 體現自然：意象與文化實踐. Taipei: Academia Sinica, 2012, pp. 37–80.

Lee, Lily Hsiao Hung 蕭虹. "Shishuo xinyu zuozhe wenti shangque" 世說新語作者問題商榷. *Guoli zhongyang tushuguan guan kan* 國立中央圖書館館刊 n.s. 14.1 (1981): 8–24.

Li Fan 李璠. *Zhongguo zaipei zhiwu fazhanshi* 中國栽培植物發展史. Beijing: Kexue chubanshe, 1984.

Li Jianguo 李劍國. *Tang qian zhiguai xiaoshuo shi* 唐前志怪小說史. Tianjin: Nankai daxue chubanshe, 1984.

Li Sheng 李晟. *Xianjing Xinyang yanjiu* 仙境信仰研究. Chengdu: Ba Shu shushe, 2010.

Li Zongwei 李宗為. *Tangren chuanqi* 唐人傳奇. Beijing: Zhonghua shuju, 1985.

Liao Mei-yun 廖美雲. *Tangji yanjiu* 唐伎研究. Taipei: Taiwan xuesheng shuju, 1995.

Lin Mei-yi 林玫儀. *Cixue kaoquan* 詞學考詮. Taipei: Lianjing chuban shiye gongsi, 1987.

Liu Kairong 劉開榮. *Tangdai xiaoshuo yanjiu* 唐代小說研究. Shanghai: Shangwu yinshuguan, 1956.

Liu Shipei 劉師培. *Du Daozang ji* 讀道藏記. In idem., *Liu Shenshu yishu* 劉申叔遺書, vol. 2. Nanjing: Jiangsu guji chubanshe, 1997.

Liu Zhongyu 劉仲宇. "Liu Chen Ruan Zhao ru taoyuan gushi de wenhua toushi" 劉晨阮肇入桃源故事的文化透視. *Zhongguo daojiao* 中國道教 2002.6: 15–20.

Long Yusheng 龍榆生. "Tianci yu xuandiao" 填詞與選調. In *Long Yusheng cixue lunwenji* 龍榆生詞學論文集. Shanghai: Shanghai guji chubanshe, 1997, pp. 176–88.

Lu Qian 魯茜. "Lun 'hongye tishi' de wenben liuchuan" 論「紅葉題詩」的文本流傳. *Yibin xueyuan xuebao* 宜賓學院學報 8 (2007): 11–13.

Maegawa Yukio 前川幸雄. "Chiteki yūgi no bungaku: Gen Haku shōwashi no shujusō" 知的遊戲の文学——元. 白唱和詩の種々相. In *Chūgoku bungaku no sekai* 中国文学

の世界, vol. 5, ed. Chūgoku Koten Bungaku Kenkyūkai 中国古典文学研究会. Tokyo: Kasama Shoin, 1981, pp. 115–58.

Miura Kunio 三浦國雄. "Dōten Fukuchi shōron" 洞天福地小論. *Tōhō shūkyō* 東方宗教 61 (1983): 1–23.

Miyagawa Hisayuki 宮川尚志. "Takusen kō" 謫仙考. *Tōhō shūkyō* 東方宗教 34 & 35 (1969): 1–15.

Nakamura Hajime 中村元, ed., *Bukkyōgo daijiten* 佛教語大辭典. Tokyo: Tōkyō Shoseki, 1975.

Nomura Takeo 野村岳陽. "Shinjin ron" 真人論. *Kangaku kenkyū*, Fukkan 漢學研究, 復刊 3 (1965): 1–12.

Ogawa Tamaki 小川環樹. *Chūgoku Shōsetsushi no kenkyū* 中國小説史の研究. Tokyo: Iwanami shoten, 1968.

Ozaki Masaharu 尾崎正治. "*Lekisei shinsen taidou tsugan* no tekisuto ni tsuite"『歷世真仙体道通鑑』のテキストについて. *Tōhō shūkyū* 東方宗教 88 (1996): 37–54.

Pan Chung-kwei 潘重規. *Dunhuang ci hua* 敦煌詞話. Taipei: Shimen tushu gongsi, 1981.

Qian Zhongshu 錢鍾書. *Guanzhibian* 管錐編. Beijing: Zhonghua shuju, 1979.

Ren Erbei 任二北. *Dunhuang qu chutan* 敦煌曲初探. Shanghai: Shanghai wenyi lianhe chubanshe, 1954. Note: Ren Erbei is a variant name of Ren Bantang (q.v.).

Ren Bantang 任半塘. *Tang shengshi* 唐聲詩. Rpt., Shanghai: Shanghai guji chubanshe, 2006. See also Ren Erbei (q.v.).

Ren Jiyu 任繼愈, ed. *Daozang tiyao (xiuding ben)* 道藏提要（修訂本）. Beijing: Zhongguo shehui kexue chubanshe, 1995.

Seo Tatsuhiko 妹尾達彦. "'Caizi' yu 'jiaren': jiushiji Zhongguo xinde nannü renshi de xingcheng" "才子"與"佳人"——九世紀中國新的男女認識的形成. In *Tangdai nüxing yu shehui* 唐宋女性與社會, ed. Deng Xiaonan 鄧小南. Shanghai: Shanghai cishu chubanshe, 2003, vol. 2: pp. 695–722.

Seo Tatsuhiko 妹尾達彦. "Koi o suru otoko: kyūseiki no Chōan niokeru atarashii danjo ninshiki no keisei" 恋をする男：九世紀の長安における新しい男女認識の形成. *Chūō daigaku Ajia shi kenkyū* 中央大学アジア史研究 26 (2002): 43–66.

Shang Yongliang 尚永亮. *Tang Wudai zhuchen yu bianzhe wenxue yanjiu* 唐五代逐臣與貶謫文學研究. Wuhan: Wuhan daxue chubanshe, 2007.

Shi Zhecun 施蟄存. *Tangshi baihua* 唐詩百話. Shanghai: Shanghai guji, 1987.

Shimode Sekiyo 下出積與. *Shinsen Shisō* 神仙思想. Tokyo: Yoshikawa Kōbunkan, 1995.

Shionoya On 鹽谷溫. *Yuanqu gaishuo* 元曲概說. Trans. Sui Shusen 隋樹森. Shanghai: Shangwu yinshuguan, 1947.

Sun Changwu 孫昌武. *Han Yu shiwen xuanping* 韓愈詩文選評. Shanghai: Shanghai guji chubanshe, 2003.

Sun Changwu 孫昌武. "Tangdai wenren de Weimo xinyang" 唐代文人的維摩信仰. *Tang yanjiu* 唐研究 1 (1995): 87–117.

Sun Changwu 孫昌武. "Zhongguo wenxue li de diyu xunyou" 中國文學裏的地獄巡遊. In *Religious Writings on the Other Worlds: China and Beyond* 中外宗教與文學裏的他界書寫 (*Zhongwai zongjiao yu wenxue li de tajie shuxie*), ed. Sher-shiueh Li 李奭學 and John Tsz Pang Lai 黎子鵬. Taipei: Institute of Chinese Literature and Philosophy, Academia Sinica, 2015, pp. 146–75.

Sun Qifang 孫其芳. "Ci (fu Foqu)" 詞（附佛曲）. In *Dunhuang wenxue* 敦煌文學, ed. Yan Tingliang 顏廷亮. Lanzhou: Gansu renmin chubanshe, 1989, pp. 196–216.

Sun Qifang 孫其芳. "*Yunyao ji zaquzi* jiaozhu"《雲謠集雜曲子》校注. In *Yunyao ji yanjiu huilu* 雲謠集研究彙錄, ed. Chen Renzhi 陳人之 and Yan Tingliang 顏廷亮. Shanghai: Shanghai guji chubanshe, 1998, pp. 268–300.

Sun Shulei 孫書磊. "*Gaiding Yuanxian chuanqi* kao lun"《改定元賢傳奇》考論. In idem., *Nanjing tushuguan cang guben xiqu congkao* 南京圖書館藏孤本戲曲叢考. Beijing: Zhonghua shuju, 2011, pp. 9–99.

Sun Wang 孫望. "'Yingying zhuan' shiji kao"《鶯鶯傳》事跡考. In idem., *Wosou zagao* 蝸叟雜稿. Shanghai: Shanghai guji chubanshe, 1982, pp. 56–99.

Sunayama Minoru 砂山稔. "Ku Dō tōsen kō: chūban Tō no shitaifu to Bōzanha Dōkyō" 瞿童登仙考——中晚唐の士大夫と茅山派道教. *Tōhō shūkyō* 東方宗教 69 (1987): 1–23.

Tang Jun 湯湮. *Dunhuang quzici diyu wenhua yanjiu* 敦煌曲子詞地域文化研究. Shanghai: Shanghai guji chubanshe, 2004.

Tay Lian Soo 鄭良樹. *Xu Weishu tongkao* 續偽書通考. Taipei: Taiwan xuesheng shuju, 1984.

Tsuzuki Akiko 都築晶子. "Nanjin kanmon, kanjin no shūkyō sōzōryoku" 南人寒門·寒人の宗教想像力. *Tōyōshi kenkyū* 東洋史研究 47.2 (1988), pp. 252–283.

Wang Kunwu 王昆吾. *Sui Tang Wudai yanyue zayan geci yanjiu* 隋唐五代燕樂雜言歌辭研究. Beijing: Zhonghua shuju, 1996.

Wang Kuo-liang 王國良. *Wei Jin Nanbeichao zhiguai xiaoshuo yanjiu* 魏晉南北朝志怪小說研究. Taipei: Wenshizhe chubanshe, 1984.

Wang Shengduo 汪聖鐸. *Zhongguo qianbi shi hua* 中國錢幣史話. Beijing: Zhonghua shuju, 1998.

Wang Shiyi 王拾遺. *Yuan Zhen lun gao* 元稹論稿. Xi'an: Shaanxi renmin chubanshe, 1994.

Wang Shunu 王書奴. *Zhongguo changji shi* 中國娼妓史. Shanghai: Shenghuo shudian, 1935.

Wei Bin 魏斌. "*Shanzhong*" de Liuchao shi "山中"的六朝史 (*History of the Six Dynasties "in Mountains"*). Beijing: Shenghuo, dushu, xinzhi, Sanlian shudian, 2019.

Wei Fengjuan 韋鳳娟. "Xianfan qingyuan gui hechu: guanyu Liuchao zhiguai zhong 'tianxian pei' de wenhua chanshi" 仙凡情緣歸何處——關於六朝志怪中 "天仙配" 的文化闡釋. *Zhongguo gudai xiaoshuo yanjiu* 中國古代小說研究 3. Beijing: Renmin wenxue chubanshe, 2008, pp. 42–56.

Wei Guangxia 魏光霞. "Xiwangmu yu daojiao xinyang" 西王母與道教信仰. In *Xiwangmu wenhua yanjiu jicheng, lunwen juan* 西王母文化研究集成・論文卷, vol. 2, ed. Lu Zhihong 陸志紅. Guilin: Guangxi shifan daxue chubanshe, 2008, pp. 930–93.

Wong Young-tsu 汪榮祖. *Shijia Chen Yinke zhuan* 史家陳寅恪傳. Taipei: Lianjing chuban shiye gongsi, 1984.

Wu Fuxiu 吳福秀. *Fayuan zhulin fenlei sixiang yanjiu*《法苑珠林》分類思想研究. Beijing: Zhongguo shehui kexue chubanshe, 2014.

Wu Mei 吳梅. "Qu'an duqu ji" 瞿安讀曲記. In *Wu Mei xiqu lunwenji* 吳梅戲曲論文集. Beijing: Xiju chubanshe, 1983.

Wu Outing 吳藕汀 and Wu Xiaoting 吳小汀. *Cidiaoming cidian* 詞調名辭典. Shanghai: Shanghai shudian chubanshe, 2005.

Xiang Chu 項楚. *Dunhuang geci zongbian kuangbu* 敦煌歌辭總編匡補. Taipei: Xinwenfeng chuban gongsi, 1995.

Xie Qian 謝謙. "Ouyang Xiu yanci feiwen bianyi" 歐陽修艷詞緋聞辨疑. *Sichuan daxue xuebao (zhexue shehui kexue ban)* 四川大學學報（哲學社會科學版） 2006.4: 92–97.

Xie Siwei 謝思煒. *Bai Juyi ji zonglun* 白居易集綜論. Beijing: Zhongguo shehui kexue chubanshe, 1997.

Xie Siwei 謝思煒. "Yuan Zhen 'Dai Qujiang laoren baiyun' shi zuonian zhiyi" 元稹《代曲江老人百韻》詩作年質疑. *Qinghua daxue xuebao (zhexue shehui kexue ban)* 清華大學學報（哲學社會科學版） 19.2 (2004): 42–44.

Xu Jun 徐俊. "Bo 2506 quzici chao: 'Dunhuang quzici ji xinjiao' zhiyi" 伯二五〇六曲子詞鈔——《敦煌曲子詞集新校》之一. *Huaxue* 華學 9/10 (2008): 934–43.

Xu Wei 許蔚. "Liu Ruan gushi de wenben cengci, yujing bianqian yu yiyi zhuanyi" 劉阮故事的文本層次、語境變遷與意義轉移. *Bulletin of the Department of Chinese Literature National Chengchi University* 政大中文學報 31 (2019): 59–76.

Yamamoto Kazuyoshi 山本和義. "Gen Shin no Enshi oyobi Tōbōshi ni tsuite" 元稹の豔詩及び悼亡詩について *Chūgoku bungaku hō* 中國文學報 9 (1958): 54–84.

Yan Dunyi 嚴敦易. *Yuanju zhenyi* 元劇斟疑. Beijing: Zhonghua shuju, 1960.

Yang Yi 楊義. *Zhongguo xushixue (zengding ben)* 中國敘事學（增訂本）. Beijing: Shangwu yinshuguan, 2019.

Ye Shuxian 葉舒憲. "Shiyu xinyang yu xibu shenhua de jian'gou" 食玉信仰與西部神話的建構. *Root Exploration* 尋根 2008.4: 4–12.

Yen Chin-hsiung 顏進雄. *Liuchao fushi fengqi yu wenxue* 六朝服食風氣與文學. Taipei: Wenjin chubanshe, 1993.

Yin Zhanhua 尹占華. *Yuan Zhen pingzhuan* 元稹評傳. In Jian Changchun 蹇長春 and Yin Zhanhua, *Bai Juyi pingzhuan fu Yuan Zhen pingzhuan* 白居易評傳附元稹評傳. Nanjing: Nanjing daxue chubanshe, 2002.

Yu Jiaxi 余嘉錫. *Siku tiyao bianzheng* 四庫提要辨證. Beijing: Zhonghua shuju, 1985.

Zha Hongde 查洪德. *Yuandai shixue tonglun* 元代詩學通論. Beijing: Beijing daxue chubanshe, 2014.

Zhang Jian 張劍. *Dunhuang quzici baishou yizhu* 敦煌曲子詞百首譯注. Lanzhou: Dunhuang wenyi chubanshe, 1991.

Zhang Jianwei 張建偉. "Lun Tangshi zhong Taoyuan diangu yu Liu Ruan ru Tiantai gushi zhi heliu" 論唐詩中桃源典故與劉、阮入天台故事之合流. *Jiangxi shifan daxue xuebao (zhexue shehui kexue ban)* 江西師範大學學報（哲學社會科學版） 43.4 (2010): 72–76.

Zhang Xincheng 張心澂. *Weishu tongkao* 偽書通考. Shanghai: Shangwu yinshuguan, 1954.

Zhang Xingfa 張興發. *Daojiao shenxian xinyang* 道教神仙信仰. Beijing: Zhongguo shehui kexue chubanshe, 2001.

Zhao Guoping 趙國平, Dai Shen 戴慎, and Chen Renshou 陳仁壽, comps. *Zhongyao dacidian* 中藥大辭典. Shanghai: Shanghai kexue jishu chubanshe, 2006.

Zhou Yao 周瑤. "Cong Tang Wudai wenxian shitan 'quzi,' 'quzici' zhiming de youlai: yi Dunhuang xieben wei zhongxin" 從唐五代文獻試探「曲子」、「曲子詞」之名的由來——以敦煌寫本為中心. *Qiusuo* 求索 2009.1: 158–60.

Zhuang Yifu 莊一拂. *Gudian xiqu cunmu huikao* 古典戲曲存目彙考. Shanghai: Shanghai guji chubanshe, 1982.

Secondary Works in Western Languages (by Author)

Allen, N. J. *Arjuna–Odysseus: Shared Heritage in Indian and Greek Epic*. New York: Routledge, 2019.

Allen, Sarah. *Shifting Stories: History, Gossip, and Lore in Narratives from Tang Dynasty China*. Cambridge, MA: Harvard University Asia Center, 2014.

Arthur, Shawn. *Early Daoist Dietary Practices: Examining Ways to Health and Longevity*. Lanham, MD: Lexington Books, 2013.

Aristotle. *Poetics*. Trans. Richard Janko. Indianapolis and Cambridge: Hackett Publishing Company, 1987.

Augustine. *On Christian Doctrine*. Trans. D. W. Robertson, Jr. New York: Macmillan Publishing Company, 1958.

Baldick, Julian. *Homer and the Indo-Europeans: Comparing Mythologies*. London: I. B. Tauris, 1994.

Bodde, Derk. *Festivals in Classical China: New Year and Other Annual Observances During the Han Dynasty, 206 B.C.–A.D. 220*. Princeton: Princeton University Press, 1975.

Bokenkamp, Stephen R. *Early Daoist Scriptures*. Berkeley and Los Angeles: University of California Press, 1997.

Bokenkamp, Stephen R. "The Peach Flower Font and the Grotto Passage." *JAOS* 106.1 (1986): 65–77.

Burke, Kenneth. *Permanence and Change: An Anatomy of Purpose*. Berkeley: University of California Press, 1954.

Cahill, Suzanne E. "Sex and the Supernatural in Medieval China: Cantos on the Transcendent Who Presides over the River." *JAOS* 105.2 (1985): 197–220.

Cahill, Suzanne E. *Transcendence and Divine Passion: The Queen Mother of the West in Medieval China*. Stanford: Stanford University Press, 1993.

Campany, Robert Ford. *A Garden of Marvels: Tales of Wonder from Early Medieval China*. Honolulu: University of Hawai'i Press, 2015.

Campany, Robert Ford. *Making Transcendents: Ascetics and Social Memory in Early Medieval China*. Honolulu: University of Hawai'i Press, 2009.

Campany, Robert Ford. *Strange Writing: Anomaly Accounts in Early Medieval China*. Albany: SUNY Press, 1996.

Campany, Robert Ford. "Tales of Strange Events." In *Early Medieval China: A Sourcebook*, ed. by Wendy Swartz, Robert Ford Campany, Yang Lu, and Jessey J. C. Choo. New York: Columbia University Press, 2014, pp. 576–91.

Campany, Robert Ford. "The Meanings of Cuisines of Transcendence in Late Classical and Early Medieval China." *T'oung Pao* 91 (2005): 1–57.

Campany, Robert Ford. *To Live As Long As Heaven and Earth: A Translation and Study of Ge Hong's Traditions of Divine Transcendents*. Berkeley: University of California Press, 2002.

Campbell, Joseph. *The Hero with a Thousand Faces*. Novato, CA: New World Library, 2008.

Chan, Timothy Wai Keung. "A Re-evaluation of Chen Ziang's 'Manifesto of a Poetic Reform.'" *Journal of the Oriental Society of Australia* 36–37 (2004–05): 56–85.

Chan, Timothy Wai Keung. "A Tale of Two Worlds: The Late Tang Poetic Presentation of the Romance of the Peach Blossom Font." *T'oung Pao* 94 (2008): 209–45.

Chan, Timothy Wai Keung. *Considering the End: Mortality in Early Medieval Chinese Poetic Representation*. Leiden and Boston: Brill, 2012.

Chan, Timothy Wai Keung. "Engulfing and Embracing the Vast Earth: Li Bai's Cosmology in His 'Ballad on the Sun Rising and Setting.'" *Tang Studies* 37 (2019): 30–58.

Chan, Timothy Wai Keung. "Ruan Ji's and Xi Kang's Visits to Two 'Immortals.'" *Monumenta Serica* 44 (1996): 141–65.

Chan, Timothy Wai Keung. "The *Jing/zhuan* Structure of the *Chuci* Anthology: A New Approach to the Authorship of Some *Chuci* Poems." *T'oung Pao* 84 (1998): 293–327.

Chan, Timothy Wai Keung. "The Transcendent of Poetry's Quest for Transcendence: Li Bai on Mount Tiantai." In *Buddhism and Daoism on the Holy Mountains of China*, ed. Thomas Jülch. Leiden: Peeters, 2021, pp. 203–43.

Chan, Timothy Wai Keung. "Amorous Adventure in the Capital: Lu Zhaolin and Luo Binwang Writing in the 'Style of the Time.'" *Tang Studies* 40 (2022), 1–45.

Chan, Wing-tsit. *A Source Book in Chinese Philosophy*. Princeton: Princeton University Press, 1963.

Chang, Kang-i Sun. *The Evolution of Chinese Tz'u Poetry: From Late T'ang to Northern Sung*. Princeton: Princeton University Press, 1980.

Chen Shih-hsiang. "The Genesis of Poetic Time: The Greatness of Ch'ü Yuan, Studied with a New Critical Approach." *Tsing Hua Journal of Chinese Studies* n.s. 10.1 (1973): 1–44.

Ch'en, Kenneth K. S. *Buddhism in China: A Historical Survey*. Princeton: Princeton University Press, 1973.

Clarke, Howard W. *The Art of The Odyssey*. Englewood Cliffs, NJ: Prentice-Hall, Inc., 1967.

Cleick, James. *Time Travel: A History*. London: 4th Estate, 2016.

Crane, Gregory. *Calypso: Backgrounds and Conventions of the* Odyssey. Frankfurt am Main: Athenäum, 1988.

Dange, Sindhu S. *The Bhāgavata Purāṇa: Mytho-Social Study*. Delhi: Ajanta Publications, 1984.

Dalby, Michael T. "Court Politics in Late T'ang Times." In *The Cambridge History of China, Volume 3: Sui and T'ang China, 589–906, Part 1*, ed. Denis Twitchett. Cambridge: Cambridge University Press, 1979, pp. 561–681.

Davies, Paul. *About Time: Einstein's Unfinished Revolution*. New York: Simon & Schuster, 1995.

DeWoskin, Kenneth and J. I. Crump, Jr. *In Search of the Supernatural: The Written Record*. Stanford: Stanford University Press, 1996.

De Jong, Irene J. F. *A Narratological Commentary on the Odyssey*. Cambridge: Cambridge University Press, 2001.

De Voragine, Jacobus (ca. 1229–1298). *The Golden Legend: Readings on the Saints*. Trans. William Granger Ryan. Princeton, NJ: Princeton University Press, 1993.

DeBlasi, Anthony. *Reform in the Balance: The Defense of Literary Culture in Mid-Tang China*. Albany, NY: State University of New York Press, 2002.

Dimock, George E. *The Unity of the Odyssey*. Amherst: University of Massachusetts Press, 1989.

Dong, Lorraine. "The Many Faces of Cui Yingying." In *Women in China: Current Directions in Historical Scholarship*, ed. Richard W. Guisso and Stanley Johannesen. Youngstown, NY: Philo Press, 1981, pp. 75–98.

Doniger, Wendy. *Hindu Myths: A Sourcebook Translated from The Sanskrit*. London: Penguin Books, 1975.

Dudbridge, Glen. *The Tale of Li Wa: Study and Critical Edition of a Chinese Story from the Ninth Century*. London: Ithaca Press, 1983.

Egan, Ronald C. "On the Commentary of the *Yu hsien k'u* Commentary." *HJAS* 36 (1976): 135–46.

Egan, Ronald C. *The Burden of Female Talent: The Poet Li Qingzhao and Her History in China*. Cambridge, MA: Harvard University Asia Center, 2013.

Egan, Ronald C. *The Literary Works of Ou-yang Hsiu (1007–72)*. Cambridge, MA: Cambridge University Press, 1984.

Egan, Ronald C. *The Problem of Beauty: Aesthetic Thought and Pursuits in Northern Song Dynasty China*. Cambridge, MA: Harvard University Asia Center, 2006.

Egan, Ronald C. "The Problem of the Repute of *Tz'u* during the Northern Sung." In *Voices of the Song Lyric in China*, ed. Pauline Yu. Berkeley: University of California Press, 1994, pp. 191–225.

Egan, Ronald C. *Word, Image, and Deed in the Life of Su Shi*. Cambridge, MA: Council on East Asian Studies, Harvard University, and Harvard-Yenching Institute, 1994.

Einstein, Albert. "Zur Elektrodynamik bewegter Körper." *Annalen der Physik* 17 (1905): 891–921.

Eliade, Mircea. *Shamanism: Archaic Techniques of Ecstasy*. Trans. Willard R. Trask. Princeton: Princeton University Press, 1964.

Eskildsen, Stephen. *Asceticism in Early Taoist Religion*. Albany: State University of New York Press, 1998.

Fidel, Fajardo-Acosta. *The Hero's Failure in the Tragedy of Odysseus: A Revisionist Analysis*. Lempeter, Dyfed, Wales: The Edwin Mellen Press, 1990.

Finley, John H., Jr. *Homer's Odyssey*. Cambridge, MA: Harvard University Press, 1978.

Finley, M. I. *The World of Odysseus*. New York: Viking Press, 1965.

Fong, Grace S. "Persona and Mask in the Song Lyric (*Ci*)." *HJAS* 50.2 (1990): 459–84.

Fowler, Robert. "The Homeric Question." In idem., *The Cambridge Companion to Homer*. Cambridge: Cambridge University Press, 2004, pp. 220–32.

Frankel, Hans H. "The Contemplation of the Past in T'ang Poetry." In *Perspectives on the T'ang*, ed. Arthur F. Wright and Denis Twitchett. New Haven: Yale University Press, 1973, pp. 345–65.

Freud, Sigmund. *The Interpretation of Dreams*. Trans. James Strachey. New York: Avon Books, 1965.

Frye, Northrop. *Anatomy of Criticism: Four Essays*. Princeton: Princeton University Press, 1973.

Ganguli, Kisari Mohan, trans. *Mahabharata of Krishna-Dwaipayana Vyasa*, vol. 3, *Santi Parva*. New Delhi: Munshiram Manoharlal Publishers, 2000.

Goldin, Paul R. "What is *Qi* 氣 and Why Was It a Good Idea?" In Goldin, *The Art of Chinese Philosophy: Eight Classical Texts and How to Read Them*. Princeton: Princeton University Press, 2000, pp. 229–44. A Chinese translation is in Goldin, 2017 under Chinese sources, q.v.

Greenblatt, Stephen. *Shakespearean Negotiations: The Circulation of Social Energy in Renaissance England.* Berkeley and Los Angeles: University of California Press, 1988.

Gregory, Peter N. *Inquiry into the Origin of Humanity: An Annotated Translation of Tsung-mi's* Yüan jen lun *with a Modern Commentary.* Honolulu: University of Hawai'i Press, 1995.

Graham, A. C., trans. *Chuang-tzŭ: The Inner Chapters.* London: Unwin, 1989.

Gott III, J. Richard. *Time Travel in Einstein's Universe: The Physical Possibilities of Travel Through Time.* Boston and New York: Houghton Mifflin Company, 2001.

Gupta, S. V. *Units of Measurement Past, Present and Future: International System of Units.* Heidelberg: Springer, 2010.

Hansen, William. *The Book of Greek and Roman Folktales, Legends and Myths.* Princeton: Princeton University Press, 2017.

Hartman, Charles. *Han Yü and the T'ang Search for Unity.* Princeton: Princeton University Press, 1986.

Hawes, Colin S. C. *The Social Circulation of Poetry in the Mid-Northern Song: Emotional Energy and Literati Self-Cultivation.* Albany: State University of New York Press, 2005.

Hawkes, David. "The Quest of the Goddess." In *Studies in Chinese Literary Genres*, ed. Cyril Birch. Berkeley: University of California Press, 1974, pp. 42–68.

Hawkes, David. *The Songs of the South: An Ancient Chinese Anthology of Poems by Qu Yuan and Other Poets.* Harmondsworth, Middlesex: Penguin Books, 1985.

Hearn, Maxwell K. and Wen C. Fong. *Along the Riverbank: Chinese Paintings from the C. C. Wang Family Collection.* New York: The Metropolitan Museum of Art, 1999.

Hendrischke, Barbara. *The Scripture on Great Peace: the* Taiping jing *and the Beginnings of Daoism.* Berkeley: University of California Press, 2006.

Hexter, Ralph J. *A Guide to The Odyssey: A Commentary on the English Translation of Robert Fitzgerald.* New York: Vintage Books, 1993.

Hightower, James Robert. *The Poetry of T'ao Ch'ien.* Oxford: Oxford University Press, 1970.

Hightower, James Robert. "The Songwriter Liu Yung: Part I." *HJAS* 41.2 (Dec. 1981): 323–76.

Hightower, James Robert. "The Songwriter Liu Yung: Part II." *HJAS* 42.1 (Jun. 1982): 5–66.

Hightower, James Robert. "Yüan Chen and the Story of Ying-ying." *HJAS* 33 (1973): 90–123.

Hilton, James. *Lost Horizon.* First Published in 1933. Rpt. Chichester: Summersdale, 2003.

Holzman, Donald. *Poetry and Politics: The Life and Works of Juan Chi* A.D. *210–263.* Cambridge: Cambridge University Press, 1976.

Honig, Edwin. *Dark Conceit: The Making of Allegory.* Hanover and London: University Press of New England, 1982.

Hutcheon, Linda. *A Theory of Adaptation*. New York: Routledge, 2006.

Idema, Wilt L. "The Many Shapes of Medieval Chinese Plays: How Texts Are Transformed to Meet the Needs of Actors, Spectators, Censors, and Readers." *Oral Tradition* 20/2 (2005): 320–34.

Idema, Wilt L. "The Orphan of Zhao: Self-Sacrifice, Tragic Choice and Revenge and the Confucianization of Mongol Drama at the Ming Court." *Cina* 21 (1988): 159–90.

Idema, Wilt L. "Why You Never Have Read a Yuan Drama: The Transformation of Zaju at the Ming Court." In *Studi in onore di Lanciello Lanciotti*, ed. S. M. Carletti, M. Sacchetti, and P. Santangelo. Napoli: Istituto Universiatorio Orientale, Dipartimento di Studi Asiatici, 1996, pp. 765–91.

Iser, Wolfgang. *The Act of Reading: A Theory of Aesthetic Response*. Baltimore: John Hopkins University Press, 1978.

Jia Jinhua. *Gender, Power, and Talent: The Journey of Daoist Priestesses in Tang China*. New York: Columbia University Press, 2018.

Jia Jinhua. "New Poetry from the Turquoise Pond: Women Poets in Eighth and Ninth Century China." *Tang Studies* 37 (2019): 59–80.

Kirkova, Zornica. *Roaming into the Beyond: Representations of* Xian *Immortality in Early Medieval Chinese Verse*. Leiden: Brill, 2016.

Kohn, Livia, ed. *Dao and Time: Classical Philosophy*. St Petersburg: Three Pines Press, 2021.

Kohn, Livia. *Time in Daoist Practice: Cultivation and Calculation*. St Petersburg: Three Pines Press, 2021.

Knechtges, David R. "Tuchkahoe and Sesame, Wolfberries and Chrysanthemums, Sweet-Peel Orange and Fine Wines, Pork and Pasta: The *Fu* as a Source for Chinese Culinary History." *Journal of Oriental Studies* 45.1 & 2 (December 2012): 1–26.

Knechtges, David R. *Wen xuan or Selections of Refined Literature, Volume One: Rhapsodies on Metropolises and Capitals*. Princeton: Princeton University Press, 1982.

Knechtges, David R. *Wen xuan or Selections of Refined Literature, Volume Three: Rhapsodies on Natural Phenomena, Birds and Animals, Aspirations and Feelings, Sorrowful Laments, Literature, Music, and Passions*. Princeton: Princeton University Press, 1996.

Knechtges, David R. and Taiping Chang, eds. *Ancient and Early Medieval Chinese Literature: A Reference Guide*. Leiden and Boston: Brill, 2010.

Kroll, Paul W. *A Student's Dictionary of Classical and Medieval Chinese*. Leiden and Boston: Brill, 2015.

Kroll, Paul W. "In the Halls of the Azure Lad." *JAOS* 105.1 (1985): 75–94.

Kroll, Paul W. "Li Po's Transcendent Diction." *JAOS* 106.1 (1986): 99–117.

Kroll, Paul W. "On Far Roaming." *JAOS* 116.4 (1996): 653–69.

Lai, C. M. "The Art of Lamentation in the Works of Pan Yue: 'Mourning the Eternally Departed.'" *JAOS* 114.3 (1994): 409–25.

Lao, Yan-shuan. "Southern Chinese Scholars and Educational Institutions in Early Yüan: Some Preliminary Remarks." In *China under Mongol Rule*, ed. John D. Langlois, Jr. Princeton: Princeton University Press, 1981, pp. 107–33.

Lattimore, Richmond, trans. *The Iliad of Homer*. Chicago: University of Chicago Press, 1962.

Lattimore, Richmond, trans. *The Odyssey of Homer*. Rpt. New York: Harper & Row, 2009.

Lau, D. C., trans. *Lao Tzu: Tao Te Ching*. Harmondsworth, Middlesex: Penguin Books, 1963.

Lau, D. C., trans. *Mencius*. Harmondsworth, Middlesex: Penguin Books Ltd., 1970.

Laufer, Berthold. *Sino-Iranica: Chinese Contributions to the History of Civilization in Ancient Iran: With Special Reference to the History of Cultivated Plants and Products*. Chicago: Field Museum of Natural History, 1919. Rpt. Taipei: Ch'eng Wen Publishing Company, 1978.

Lee, Lily Hsiao Hung. "Hypothesis Regarding the Gender of the Creator of the Song Lyrics in the *Yunyao ji*, a Collection Discovered in the Mogao Caves at Dunhuang." *Huaxue* 9/10 (2008): 890–933.

Lévi, Jean (Revised by Franciscus Verellen). "*Lishi zhenxian tidao tongjian* 歷世真仙體道通鑑." In Schipper and Verellen, *The Taoist Canon*, vol. 2: pp. 887–92.

Levy, Howard S., trans. *The Dwelling of Playful Goddesses: China's First Novelette*. Tokyo: Dai Nippon Insatsu, 1965.

Levy, Howard S. "The Original Incidents of Poems." *Sinologica* 10 (1969): 1–54.

Lewis, C. S. *The Discarded Image: An Introduction to Medieval and Renaissance Literature*. Cambridge: Cambridge University Press, 1964.

Lewis, Mark Edward. *The Construction of Space in Early China*. Albany: State University of New York Press, 2006.

Littleton, Covington Scott. *The New Comparative Mythology: An Anthropological Assessment of the Theories of Georges Dumézil*. Berkeley and Los Angeles: University of California Press, 1966.

Liu, James T. C. *Ou-yang Hsiu: An Eleventh Century Neo-Confucianist*. Stanford: Stanford University Press, 1967.

Loewe, Michael. *Chinese Ideas of Life and Death: Faith, Myth and Reason in the Han Period (202 BC–AD 202)*. London and Boston: Allen & Unwin, 1982.

Loewe, Michael. *Ways to Paradise: The Chinese Quest for Immortality*. London and Boston: Allen & Unwin, 1979.

Lopez, Donald S., Jr. *Critical Terms for the Study of Buddhism*. Chicago: University of Chicago Press, 2004.

Lord, Albert B. *The Singer of Tales*. Cambridge, MA: Harvard University Press, 1960.

Louden, Bruce. *Homer's Odyssey and the Near East*. Cambridge and New York: Cambridge University Press, 2011.

Louden, Bruce. *The Odyssey: Structure, Narration, and Meaning*. Baltimore and London: The John Hopkins University Press, 1999.

Luo, Manling. *Literati Storytelling in Late Medieval China*. Seattle: University of Washington Press, 2015.

Ma, Y. W. and Joseph S. M. Lau, eds. *Traditional Chinese Stories: Themes and Variations*. Boston: Cheng & Tsui Company, 1996.

MacGregor, Rob. *Indiana Jones and the Last Crusade*. New York: Ballantine Books, 2008.

Mair, Victor H., trans. *Wandering on the Way: Early Taoist Tales and Parables of Chuang Tzu*. New York: Bantam Books, 1994.

Maspero, Henri. *Le taoïsme et les religions chinoises*. Paris: Gallimard, 1971.

Mather, Richard B., trans. *Shih-shuo Hsin-yü: A New Account of Tales of the World*. Minneapolis: University of Minnesota Press, 1976.

Menon, Ramesh, trans. *Bhagavata Purana*. New Delhi: Rupa & Co., 2007.

Meulenbeld, Mark. "The Peach Blossom Spring's Long History as a Sacred Site in Northern Hunan." *T'oung Pao* 107 (2021): 1–39.

Morford, Mark P. O. and Robert J. Lenardon. *Classical Mythology* (7th edition). New York: Longman, 1985.

Mote, Frederick W. "Chinese Society under Mongol Rule, 1215–1368." In *The Cambridge History of China, Volume 6: Alien Regimes and Border States, 907–1368*, ed. Herbert Franke and Denis Twitchett. Cambridge: Cambridge University Press, 2006, pp. 616–64.

Nahin, Paul J. *Time Machines: Time Travel in Physics, Metaphysics, and Science Fiction*. New York: American Institute of Physics, 1993.

Needham, Joseph, Ho Ping-yü, and Lu Gwei-djen. *Science and Civilisation in China, Volume 5: Chemistry and Chemical Technology, Part III, Spagyrical Discovery and Invention: Historical Survey, from Cinnabar Elixirs to Synthetic Insulin*. Cambridge: Cambridge University Press, 1974.

Needham, Joseph and H. T. Huang. *Science and Civilisation in China, Volume 6: Biology and Biological Technology, Part V: Fermentations and Food Science*. Cambridge: Cambridge University Press, 2000.

Newman, John. "Eschatology in the Wheel of Time Tantra." In *Buddhism in Practice*, ed. Donald S. Lopez, Jr. Princeton: Princeton University Press, 1995, pp. 284–89.

Nienhauser, William H., Jr. "Floating Clouds and Dreams in Liu Tsung-yüan's Yung-chou Exile Writings." *JAOS* 106.1 (1986): 169–81.

Owen, Stephen. *Just a Song: Chinese Lyrics from the Eleventh and Early Twelfth Centuries*. Cambridge, MA: Harvard University Asia Center, 2019.

Owen, Stephen. *Remembrances: The Experience of the Past in Classical Chinese Literature*. Cambridge, MA: Harvard University Press, 1986.

Owen, Stephen. *The End of the Chinese 'Middle Ages': Essays in Mid-Tang Literary Culture*. Stanford: Stanford University Press, 1996.

Owen, Stephen. *The Late Tang: Chinese Poetry of the Mid-ninth Century (827–860)*. Cambridge, MA: Harvard University Asia Center, 2006.

Owen, Stephen. *The Making of Early Chinese Classical Poetry*. Cambridge, MA: Harvard University Asia Center, 2006.

Owen, Stephen. "Who Wrote That? Attribution in Northern Song *Ci*." In *Reading Medieval Chinese Poetry: Text, Context, and Culture*, ed. Paul W. Kroll. Leiden: Brill, 2015, pp. 202–20.

Pearson, Lionel Ignacius Cusack. *Popular Ethics in Ancient Greece*. Stanford: Stanford University Press, 1962.

Plato. *The Republic*. Trans. H. D. P. Lee. London: Penguin Books, 1987.

Prasad, Sheo Shanker. *The Bhāgavata Purāṇa: A Literary Study*. Delhi: Capital Publishing House, 1984.

Price, A. F. and Wong Mou-Lam, trans. *The Sutra of Hui Neng*. Issued in a volume with *The Diamond Sutra*. Boston: Shambhala, 1969.

Proust, Marcel (1871–1922). *Remembrance of Things Past, Volume 1: Swann's Way and Within A Budding Grove*. Trans. C. K. Scott Moncrieff and Terence Kilmartin. New York: Vintage Books, 1982.

Puett, Michael J. *To Become a God: Cosmology, Sacrifice, and Self-divinization in Early China*. Cambridge, MA: Harvard University Asia Center, 2002.

Pulleyblank, Edwin G. *Lexicon of Reconstructed Pronunciation in Early Middle Chinese, Late Middle Chinese, and Early Mandarin*. Vancouver: UBC Press, 1991.

Pulleyblank, Edwin G. "The An Lu-shan Rebellion and the Origins of Chronic Militarism in Late T'ang China." In *Essays on T'ang Society: The Interplay of Social, Political, and Economic Forces*, ed. John Curtis Perry and Bardwell L. Smith. Leiden: Brill, 1978, pp. 33–60.

Raz, Gil. "Time Manipulation in Early Daoist Ritual: The East Well Chart and the Eight Archivists." *Asia Major* 3rd series 18.2 (2005): 27–65.

Read, Bernard E. *Chinese Medicinal Plants from the Pen Ts'ao Kang Mu* 本草綱目 A.D. *1596 of a Botanical, Chemical and Pharmacological Reference List*. Rpt. Taipei: SMC, 1982.

Reece, Steve. *The Stranger's Welcome: Oral Theory and the Aesthetics of the Homeric Hospitality Scene*. Ann Arbor: University of Michigan Press, 1993.

Richards, I. A. *The Philosophy of Rhetoric*. Oxford: Oxford University Press, 1965.

Reinhardt, Karl. "The Adventures in *The Odyssey*" (trans. Harriet I. Flower). In *Reading The Odyssey: Selected Interpretive Essays*, ed. Seth L. Schein. Princeton: Princeton University Press, 1996, pp. 63–132.

Reiter, Florian C. "Yixian zhuan 疑仙傳." In Schipper and Verellen, *The Taoist Canon*, vol. 1: p. 432.

Robinet, Isabelle. *Taoist Meditation: the Mao-shan Tradition of Great Purity*. Albany: State University of New York Press, 1993.

Rouzer, Paul. *Articulated Ladies: Gender and the Male Community in Early Chinese Texts*. Cambridge, MA: Harvard University Asia Center, 2001.

Saïd, Suzanne. *Homer & The Odyssey*. Oxford and New York: Oxford University Press, 2011.

Sanders, Graham. *Words Well Put: Visions of Poetic Competence in the Chinese Tradition*. Cambridge, MA: Harvard University Asia Center, 2006.

Sanders, Julie. *Adaptation and Appropriation*. Second edition. London and New York: Routledge, 2016.

Schafer, Edward H. "Empyreal Powers and Chthonian Edens: Two Notes on T'ang Taoist Literature." *JAOS* 106.4 (1986): 667–77.

Schafer, Edward H. *Mirages on the Sea of Time: The Taoist Poetry of Ts'ao T'ang*. Berkeley and Los Angeles: University of California Press, 1985.

Schafer, Edward H. "Notes on T'ang Geisha." *Schafer Sinological Papers*, no. 2. Privately printed. February 6, 1984.

Schafer, Edward H. *Pacing the Void: T'ang Approaches to the Stars*. Berkeley: University of California Press, 1977.

Schafer, Edward H. "The Capeline Cantos: Verses on the Divine Loves of Taoist Priestesses." *Asiatische Studien* 32 (1978): 5–65.

Schafer, Edward H. *The Divine Woman: Dragon Ladies and Rain Maidens in T'ang Literature*. Berkeley and Los Angeles, University of California Press, 1973.

Schafer, Edward H. "The Jade Woman of Greatest Mystery." *History of Religions* 17, no. 3/4 (February–May 1978): 387–98.

Schafer, Edward H. *The Vermilion Bird: T'ang Images of the South*. Berkeley: University of California Press, 1985.

Schafer, Edward H. "The World Between: Ts'ao T'ang's Grotto Poems." *Schafer Sinological Papers*, no. 32. Privately printed. October 15, 1985.

Schafer, Edward H. "Thoughts About A Students' Dictionary of Classical Chinese." *Monumenta Serica* 25 (1966): 197–206.

Schein, Seth L. Ed. "Introduction." In idem., ed., *Reading The Odyssey: Selected Interpretive Essays*. Princeton: Princeton University Press, 1996, pp. 3–31.

Schipper, Kristofer Marinus. *L'empereur wou des Han dans la légende Taoïste: Han Wou-ti nei-tchouan*. Paris: École française d'Extrême-Orient, 1965.

Schipper, Kristofer Marinus and Franciscus Verellen, eds. *The Taoist Canon: A Historical Companion to the* Daozang. Chicago: University of Chicago Press, 2004.

Schlegel, Gustave. *Uranographie chinoise*. Leyde: E. J. Brill, 1875.

Sieber, Patricia. *Theaters of Desire: Authors, Readers, and the Reproduction of Early Chinese Song-drama, 1300–2000*. New York: Palgrave Macmillan, 2003.

Shang, Biwu. *Unnatural Narrative across Borders: Transnational and Comparative Perspectives*. Abingdon, Oxon; New York, NY: Routledge, 2019.

Shields, Anna M. *Crafting a Collection: The Cultural Contexts and Poetic Practice of the Huajian ji* 花間集 (*Collection from Among the Flowers*). Cambridge, MA: Harvard University Asia Center, 2006.

Shields, Anna M. "Defining Experience: The 'Poems of Seductive Allure' (*Yanshi*) of the Mid-Tang Poet Yuan Zhen (779–831)." *JAOS* 122.1 (2002): 61–78.

Shields, Anna M. *One Who Knows Me: Friendship and Literary Culture in Mid-Tang China*. Cambridge, MA: Harvard University Asia Center, 2015.

Simmons, Richard VanNess. *The Sōushén hòujì: Latter Notes on Collected Spirit Phenomena Attributed to Táo Yuānmíng (365–427)*. New Haven: American Oriental Society, 2022.

Sivin, Nathan. "Chinese Alchemy and the Manipulation of Time." *Isis* 67.4 (1976): 512–26.

Soothill, William Edward and Lewis Hodous, comps. *A Dictionary of Chinese Buddhist Terms: With Sanskrit and English Equivalents and a Sanskrit-Pali Index*. First published 1937. Rpt. Abingdon, Oxon: Routledge, 2014.

Spring, Madeline K. "T'ang Landscapes of Exile." *JAOS* 117.2 (1997): 312–23.

Stanford, William Bedell. *The Odyssey of Homer* (2nd edition). New York: St Martin's Press, 1959.

Stein, Rolf A. *The World in Miniature: Container Gardens and Dwellings in Far Eastern Religious Thought*. Trans. Phyllis Brooks. Stanford, Stanford University Press, 1990.

Strickmann, Michel. "The Mao Shan Revelations: Taoism and the Aristocracy." *T'oung Pao* 63.1 (1977): 1–64.

Stuart, G. A. *Chinese Materia Medica: Vegetable Kingdom*. Shanghai: American Presbyterian Mission Press, 1911. Rpt., Taipei: Southern Materials Center, Inc., 1987.

Tan, Tian Yuan. *Songs of Contentment and Transgression: Discharged Officials and Literati Communities in Sixteenth-century North China*. Cambridge, MA: Harvard University Asia Center, 2010.

Thalmann, William G. *The Odyssey: An Epic of Return*. New York: Twayne Publishers, 1992.

Tuan, Yi-fu. *Space and Place: The Perspective of Experience*. Minneapolis: University of Minnesota Press, 1977.

Verellen, Franciscus. "The Beyond Within: Grotto-Heavens (*Dongtian* 洞天) in Taoist Ritual and Cosmology." *Cahiers d'Extrême-Asie* 8 (1995): 265–90.

Wang, Ao. *Spatial Imaginaries in Mid-Tang China: Geography, Cartography, and Literature*. Amherst, NY: Cambria Press, 2018.

Washington, Irving (1783–1859). *Rip Van Winkle and Other Stories*. London: Puffin Books, 1905; rpt. 1994.

Watson, Burton. *Zhuangzi: Basic Writings*. New York: Columbia University Press, 2003.

West, Stephen H. "A Study in Appropriation: Zang Maoxun's Injustice to Dou E." *JAOS* 111.2 (1991): 283–302.

West, Stephen H. and Wilt L. Idema. *The Orphan of Zhao and Other Yuan Plays: the Earliest Known Versions.* New York: Columbia University Press, 2015.

Williams, Nicholas Morrow. *Chinese Poetry as Soul Summoning: Shamanistic Religious Influences on Chinese Literary Tradition.* New York: Cambria Press, 2022.

Williams, Nicholas Morrow. *Elegies of Chu: An Anthology of Early Chinese Poetry.* Oxford: Oxford University Press, 2022.

Wu, Lu-Chiang and Tenney L. Davis. "An Ancient Chinese Treatise on Alchemy Entitled Ts'an T'ung Ch'i." *Isis* 18, no. 2 (October 1932): 210–89.

Wu Fusheng. *The Poetics of Decadence: Chinese Poetry of the Southern Dynasties and Late Tang Periods.* Albany, NY: State University of New York Press, 1998.

Xiong, Victor Cunrui. *Sui-Tang Chang'an: A Study in the Urban History of Medieval China.* Ann Arbor: Center for Chinese Studies, The University of Michigan, 2000.

Yamada Toshiaki. "Longevity Techniques and the Compilation of the *Lingbao Wufu xu*." In *Taoist Meditation and Longevity Techniques*, ed. Livia Kohn. Ann Arbor: Center For Chinese Studies, The University of Michigan, 1989, pp. 99–124.

Yeh, Florence Chia-ying. "Ambiguity and the Female Voice in Hua-chien Songs." In *Studies in Chinese Poetry*, ed. James R. Hightower and Florence Chia-ying Yeh. Cambridge, MA: Harvard University Asia Center, 1998, pp. 115–49.

Yu, Pauline. *The Reading of Imagery in the Chinese Poetic Tradition.* Princeton: Princeton University Press, 1987.

Yu Shiao-ling. "Taoist Themes in Yüan Drama (with Emphasis on the Plays of Ma Chih-yüan)." *Journal of Chinese Philosophy* 15.2 (1988): 123–49.

Yü Ying-shih. "Life and Immortality in the Mind of Han China." *HJAS* 25 (1964–65): 80–122.

Zhang Zhenjun. *Buddhism and Tales of the Supernatural in Early Medieval China: A Study of Liu Yiqing's (403–444) Youming Lu.* Leiden and Boston: Brill, 2014.

Zhang Zhenjun, trans. *Hidden and Visible Realms: Early Medieval Chinese Tales of the Supernatural and the Fantastic.* New York: Columbia University Press, 2018.

Index

adaptation   53*n*1, 150–51, 200
Albert Einstein   47–48
alienation   101, 125, 217–18
Alkinoös (king of Scheria)   14, 209
appropriation   53, 151, 181
Aristotle   190
Athena   218, 221

Bachao qiongguai lu 八朝窮怪錄   54*n*7, 55
Bai Juyi 白居易   11, 53, 54, 62, 70, 76–77, 81, 83, 85, 88–90, 95, 123, 125, 178, 206, 210, 215, 217
   "He 'Meng youchun shi' yibai yun bingxu" 和夢遊春詩一百韻并序 (Harmonizing Yuan Zhen's "Dream of Spring Roaming," with a preface)   12, 79–82, 84–88, 90, 91–94, 139, 141
   "Xingyuan huaxia zeng Liu Langzhong" 杏園花下贈劉郎中 ("Beneath the Flowers in Apricot Garden, Presented to Gentleman Liu")   123
Banished transcendent
   chudi 黜帝   90*n*130
   zhexian 謫仙   10
beef   17, 18, 41, 49–50, 51*n*132
Bhāgavata Purana   24
Bo Yi 伯夷 and Shu Qi 叔齊   132*n*107, 191
Brahma the creator   24
Buddhist parables
   conjured city   80*n*95, 85
   house on fire   84–85
   moth rushing to lamps and candles   87*n*113
   thirsty deer running to the mirage of water   87*n*114

Cai Nan 蔡枏   159
   "Tanpo Su zhongqing" 攤破訴衷情 ("Enhanced Version of Telling of My Sincere Feelings")   159
Cao Pi 曹丕
   Lieyi zhuan 列異傳   30, 31
Cao Tang 曹唐   48, 56, 169, 211
   "Da youxian shi" 大遊仙詩 ("Greater Poems on Roaming in Transcendence")   147
   "Xiao youxian shi" 小遊仙詩 ("Lesser Poems on Roaming in Transcendence"), no. 23   48, 147, 211
Cao Zhi 曹植
   "Luoshen fu" 洛神賦 ("*Fu* on the Goddess of River Luo")   55
Chan 禪 Buddhism   101
Chang'an 長安   7, 12–13, 62, 103–4, 108, 119–22
Chen Shiying 陳世英   200, 202–3
   See also Wu Changling: "Celestial Master Zhang's Conviction of Breeze, Flower, Snow, and Moon"
Chen Ziang 陳子昂   69
Chonghua 重華 (variant name of Shun 舜)   22
Chuanqi 傳奇 ("transmitting the marvelous")   66, 69, 206
Chuci 楚辭 (*Songs of the South*)   20–23, 24, 29, 49, 153
   "Lisao" 離騷   20–21, 23, 118, 208
   "Shejing" 涉江 ("Crossing the River")   22
   Wang Yi's 王逸 commentary   21–22
   "Yuanyou" 遠遊 ("Far-off Roaming")   21
   "Yufu" 漁父 ("The Fisherman")   115–17
Chunyu Fen 淳于棼   189
Ci-poetry   5
   developments   134–37, 146, 157, 159–60, 166, 173, 176–78
   grotto romance themes   142, 146, 162, 165, 169, 172–73
   See also tune-titles
Circe   208*n*12, 208–9, 217
civil service examination (*keju* 科舉)   56*n*14, 183–84, 185*n*12, 200, 203
Consort Fu (Fu fei 宓妃). *See* Goddess of the Luo River
Cui Shiniang 崔十娘   55, 57–59, 59*n*29, 63, 65, 67
   See also Zhang Zhuo: *You xianku*
Cui Yingying 崔鶯鶯   62, 64–69, 71, 86*n*110, 90, 137, 147
   See also Yuan Zhen: "Story of Yingying"
cunsi 存思 (aka *cun*, meditation method)   31

Daode jing 道德經 23
Demodokos 123, 209–10, 219
Deliverance plays (*Dutuo xi* 度脫戲) 181, 188*n*20
diaoming benyi 調名本意 ("tune-title of the original theme") 13, 135–36, 146, 148, 167
Ding Lingwei 丁令威 48*n*117, 62
displacement 5, 13, 68, 73, 98, 103–4, 115–18, 119, 121, 124, 125, 151, 194–95, 204, 210, 216, 218
Dongfang Shuo 東方朔 26–27, 29, 32, 33, 39–40
Dongming ji 洞冥記. *See* Guo Xian: *Bieguo dongming ji*
Duyixiang 都夷香 35–36

E Lühua 萼綠華 2, 10
Emperor Gaozu of Han 漢高祖. *See* Liu Bang
Emperor Hui of Jin 晉惠帝 187
Emperor Li of Song 宋理宗 188
Emperor Shun of Tang 唐順宗 108
Emperor Wu of Han 漢武帝 39
Emperor Xian of Tang 唐憲宗 108
Emperor Zhuang of Later Tang 後唐莊宗. *See* Li Cunxu
Empress Jia 賈后 (Jia Nanfeng 賈南風) 187
Empress Wu 武后 (Wu Zhao 武曌) 56, 58
Esoteric Biography of Ziyang the Perfected (*Ziyang zhenren neizhuan* 紫陽真人內傳) 44
expedient means (*fangbian li* 方便力; Sanskrit, *upāya-kauśalya*) 211, 211*n*23, 213, 215, 220

fairy 9–10
Fan Ye 范曄 31
Fei Changfang 費長房 30–31, 33–34, 47
Feng Yansi 馮延巳 152, 159*n*63, 163
Fisherman 173–74
  "fishermanism" 115
  Huang Daozhen 黃道真 2
  in Tao Qian's Peach Blossom Spring 41, 96–97, 109–10, 142, 173–74
  Liu Yuxi's self-identification 12, 98–101, 106–9, 114–19, 121, 125, 126
  Lü Shang 呂尚 (aka Jiang Ziya) 115
Fudi 福地 (Blissful land) 6

Fu fei 宓妃. *See* Consort Fu and Goddess of the Luo River
Fu Zai 符載 111–12

Gan Bao 干寶
  Soushen ji 搜神記 16*n*4, 53*n*2
Gaotang 高唐 goddess (aka Goddess of Mount Wu) 2, 18, 65, 73, 82*n*102, 152–53, 175–76, 189
Ge Hong 葛洪
  Baopuzi neipian 抱朴子內篇 22*n*23, 45*n*107
  Shenxian zhuan 神仙傳 31, 33, 42
geisha 7, 61*n*35, 64, 137, 142, 147, 158, 217
Gentleman Liu. *See* Liulang
Goddess of Mount Wu. *See* Gaotang goddess
Goddess of the Luo River 洛神 (aka Consort Fu, Fu fei 宓妃) 152–53, 208
goat jerky 17, 18, 41, 49–51
Gourd Elder (Hugong 壺公) 2, 10, 34, 126*n*82
Grand Lord of the East 東皇太一 102
Grotto-heaven (*dongtian* 洞天) 6, 7, 36, 38, 111, 171, 207*n*2
Guanyinzi 關尹子 43
Gu Kuang 顧況 201
Guo Pu 郭璞
  commentary on *Shanhai jing* 山海經 39
Guo Xian 郭憲
  Bieguo dongming ji 別國洞冥記 (aka *Dongming ji*) 26, 33, 35
Guo Xiang 郭象
  commentary on *Zhuangzi* 20

Hades 212
Han Xin 韓信 20*n*13
Han Yu 韓愈 104
  poetic exchange with Liu Yuxi 105–15, 125
  "Taoyuan tu" 桃源圖 ("Painting of the Peach Spring") 104–10, 115
Hanwudi neizhuan 漢武帝內傳 33, 40*n*89
Hanwu gushi 漢武故事 40
Hermes 208, 213
Homer 210, 215
  Homeric epic 206–8
Hongniang 紅娘 (Cui Yingying's maid) 64, 67
  See also Yuan Zhen: "Story of Yingying"
Hou Han shu 後漢書 33

INDEX

Hou Wencan 侯文燦 161
huaigu 懷古 ("reminiscence of the past") 117
Huajian ji 花間集 (*Poems Gathered from among Flowers*, also abbreviated as *Among Flowers*) 46, 136, 152–53, 155–62, 169*n*100, 175, 177–78
Huang Daozhen 黃道真. *See* Fisherman
Huang Dongyuan 黃洞元 112
Huangfu Song 皇甫松 143, 169
Huang Sheng 黃昇
    Hua'an cixuan 花庵詞選 134–35
Huayang 華陽 36–37
Hugong 壺公. *See* Gourd Elder
Huineng 慧能 89*n*126, 101

immortality 9, 27, 30, 36, 39, 52, 76, 182, 184
    in Daoism 8, 27
    in *The Odessey* 211, 219, 221
    peach and 39–41
    people of 39
    sesame and 42–45
    "state of immortality" 常世国 49*n*121
"instantaneous enlightenment" (*dunwu* 頓悟) and "gradual enlightenment" (*jianwu* 漸悟) 85–89
intrusion/straying/going astray (to an otherworld by accident; *wuru* 誤入) 6–7, 12, 25, 74, 76, 97, 99, 168, 182, 185, 199, 213
Isaac Newton 48

Jiang Ziya 姜子牙. *See* Lü Shang
Jiaofang ji 教坊記 74
Jia Sidao 賈似道 188
jujube seeds 33, 35–36
jusheng 巨勝 ("giant victory"), variant name of sesame, q.v.

Kalypso 68, 207*n*2, 208, 209, 219, 221
karmic bliss (*sufu* 宿福) 197–99, 211
keju 科舉 (civil service examination, q.v.)
King Kakudmi 24
King Wen of Zhou Kingdom 周文王 116, 189
King Xiang of Chu 楚襄王 46, 65*n*51, 73, 82*n*102, 135*n*4, 152, 176, 189

Lady Huarui 花蕊夫人 165–66, 168
Li Cunxu 李存勖 (Emperor Zhuang of Later Tang) 162
    "Yi xianzi" 憶仙姿 ("Remembering the Beauty of the Transcendent") 162–63
Li Kaixian 李開先
    Gaiding Yuanxian chuanqi 改定元賢傳奇 181, 181*n*1
Lingfen 靈氛 (diviner in "Lisao") 20
Li Qingzhao 李清照 162, 166, 170
    "Ci lun" 詞論 162*n*78, 170
    "Rumeng ling" 如夢令 ("Dreamlike Ditty") 164
    "Wuling chun" 武陵春 ("Springtime in Wuling") 164*n*86
Liu Bang 劉邦 (Emperor Gaozu of Han) 106*n*28, 108, 112
Liu Bei 劉備 120
Liulang 劉郎 (aka Gentleman Liu, Master Liu)
    sobriquet of Liu Chen, the putative lover 143, 156, 159–62, 169, 169*n*100, 179
    sobriquet of Liu Yuxi 13, 62, 98, 119, 121–25
Liu Xiang 劉向
    Lienü zhuan 列女傳 153*n*48
    Liexian zhuan 列仙傳 42
Liu Yiqing 劉義慶 1, 16
    See also Youming lu 幽明錄
Liu Yong 柳永 160
    "Dongxian ge" 洞仙歌 ("Song of the Grotto Transcendent") 170–71
    "Zhouye le" 晝夜樂 ("Pleasure in Day and Night") 171
Liu Yuxi 劉禹錫 12, 62, 95–102, 104–5, 108, 110–16, 120, 123–24, 125, 192, 206, 210, 214, 221
    "At Year's End, I Ascended the Walls of Wuling, …, Felt the Onset of Melancholy, and Composed This" 116–17
    "In the Jiawu Year of the Yuanhe Reign-period (815), … . On My Way to the Capital from Wuling, … . Thinking of the Other Gentlemen who Would Continuously Arrive" 119

Liu Yuxi (*cont.*)
   "In the twenty-first year of the Zhenyuan reign-period (805), ..., I wrote another 28-word poem for my new visit. ... the third month of the second year of the Dahe reign-period (828)" 122
   on exile 98
   on Qu Boting 瞿柏庭 (*see also* Qu Boting, q.v.) 110–14
   poetic "exchange" with Han Yu 韓愈 109
   political alienation 101
   "Taoyuan xing" 桃源行 ("Ballad of the Peach Blossom Spring") 99–100
   "To the Gentlemen who Viewed the Flowers, Written in ... the Eleventh Year of the Yuanhe Reign-period (816) when I was Summoned... back to the Capital from Langzhou" 121
   "Wuling shuhuai wushi yun" 武陵書懷五十韻 ("Writing My Inner Feelings in Wuling in Fifty Rhymes") 102–3
   "You Taoyuan yibai yun" 遊桃源一百韻 ("An Excursion to the Peach Blossom Spring, in One Hundred Rhymes") 12, 104, 109–11, 113–14, 125–33
   See also Liulang
Liu Ziji 劉子驥 (aka Liu Linzhi 劉驎之) 97, 101, 104, 104*n*21, 126
Li Ye 李冶 (aka Li Jilan 李季蘭) 11, 73
   "Song Yan Ershiliu fu Shanxian" 送閻二十六赴剡縣 ("Sending Yan the Twenty-sixth to Shan District") 74
Li Ying 李郢 142
Li Yu 李煜 (last emperor of Southern Tang dynasty) 159*n*63
Longaevi 9
Lord Azure Lad 青童君 37
Lotus-Eaters 210
Lu Nüsheng 魯女生 46–48
Lü Gong 呂恭 33
Luo Ye 羅燁
   Zuiwen tanlu 醉翁談錄 182
Lü Shang 呂尚 (aka Jiang Ziya 姜子牙) 115–16, 189
Lu Wo 盧渥 201

magical eating
   and time-dilated travel 24, 18–19, 32–33
   in *Chuci* 21–23
   in the Liu-Ruan tale 18, 41
Magu 麻姑 73
Maiden Xie 謝女 152–53
Maoshan 茅山 5, 37
Mao Wenxi 毛文錫 152, 175
   "Su Zhongqing" 訴衷情 ("Expressing My inner Feelings") 173*n*110
Ma Zhiyuan 馬致遠
   "Jin Liu Ruan wuru Taoyuan zaju" 晉劉阮誤入桃源雜劇 ("Liu and Ruan of the Jin Dynasty Accidentally Strayed to the Peach Spring") 188
   "Changong qu, tanshi" 蟾宮曲・嘆世 ("Sighing for the world, to the tune of Palace of Toad") 203*n*50
Meng Chang 孟昶 (ruler of Later Shu Kingdom) 165–69
   "Dongxian ge ling" 洞仙歌令 ("Ditty-song of the Grotto Transcendent") 168
Mongol(s) 180, 183n8, 185–86, 188, 191, 195, 204, 206
Most High Lord of the Dao 太上道君 44
Mount Buzhou 不周山 20
Mount Jishi 積石山 53
Mount Juqu 句曲山. *See* Maoshan
Mount Kunlun 崑崙山 20, 86
Mount Leiping 雷平山 37
Mount Liangchang 良常山 37
Mount Mao 茅山. *See* Maoshan
Mount Miaoguye 藐姑射之山 167
Mount Shouyang 首陽山 132*n*107, 191
Mount Tiantai 天台山 13, 38, 181, 185–87, 191, 194, 196, 200, 202
Mount Tongbo 桐柏山 38
Mysterious Capital Abbey (Xuandu guan 玄都觀) 120–23

Nausikaa 5, 68, 209
Nongyu 弄玉 152–53

Odysseus xii, 5, 14, 68, 123, 206–21
otherworld 2, 3, 7, 18, 33, 34, 51, 53, 56, 101, 138, 150, 156, 192, 199, 207, 212–15, 221–22
otherworldly

INDEX

otherworldly (cont.)
    adventure/travel 14, 21, 23, 25, 55, 56, 63, 207n2
    beings 215
    paradise/realm/scene/setting 5, 12, 20, 25, 32, 33, 38, 41, 55, 76, 105, 106, 150, 195, 204, 209, 213, 221
Ouyang Xiu 歐陽修 13, 136–37, 157–63, 177n123, 177–79
    "Dongtian chun" 洞天春 ("Springtime in the Grotto-heaven") 172
    "Dongxian ge ling" 洞仙歌令 ("Ditty-song on the Grotto Transcendent") 170
    "Ruanlang gui" 阮郎歸 ("Gentlemen Ruan Returning Home") 157, 160–61, 163
    "Taoyuan yi guren" 桃源憶故人 ("Reminiscing about and Acquaintance from the Peach Spring") 173–74, 177n124
    "Wuling chun" 武陵春 ("Springtime in Wuling") 175
    "Xi qun yao" 繫裙腰 ("Fixing My Sashes around My Waist") 178
    "Yulou chun" 玉樓春 ("Spring on the Jade Terrace") 179

Pan Yue 潘岳 86
peach 33, 39–42, 48, 52, 175
    peach blossom/flower 4, 46, 57, 58, 59, 72, 75, 77, 116, 122, 124, 144, 160, 161, 192, 201–2
    peach blossom garden 170
    peach brook 59
    peach forest/grove 41, 73, 191
    peach stone/seed 39, 128
    peach tree 2, 16, 41, 75, 77, 106, 121, 122, 213
    peach wood 41
    Queen Mother of the West's 39–40
Peach Blossom Spring 38
    Han Yu's criticism 106–7
    Liu Yuxi's 99–101, 121
    Tao Qian's compared with the Liu-Ruan tale's 1, 2, 5, 12, 201
    See also Peach Spring; Tao Qian: "Record of the Peach Blossom Spring"

Peach Spring 2, 12, 48, 95, 98, 125, 142, 153, 173, 174, 175, 190, 192, 206
    drama 185n14
    grotto 2, 140–41, 162, 163, 182
    tale 12, 174
    See also Peach Blossom Spring
Penelope 14, 68, 217
Plato 199
    The Republic 196–97
Playing girl of Han'gao 漢皋遊女 152, 153, 168–69
Polyphemos 68n61, 209
Poseidon 209, 212

qiamagu 恰瑪古. See wujing
Qin Guan 秦觀
    "Yu meiren ying" 虞美人影 ("The Shadow of Yu the Beauty") 117n124
Qu Boting 瞿柏庭 (aka Qu Tong 瞿童) 12, 98, 110–15, 125, 192
Qu Yuan 屈原 102–3, 114, 118
    and Liu Yuxi 103, 117
    See also Chuci
Queen Mother of the West 西王母 39–40

Rip Van Winkle xii
Romantic detention 5, 14, 172, 206

Saint Augustine 83, 88
sesame 16, 33, 41–45
Shangqing School 上清派 31, 44–45
Shanhai jing 山海經 39
Shennong bencao jing 神農本草經 43
Shenxiu 神秀 101
Shi Daoshi 釋道世
    Fayuan zhulin 法苑珠林 53, 88
Sima Chengzhen 司馬承禎
    "Shenxian fu huma fa" 神仙服胡麻法 ("Transcendents' Methods of Huma Consumption") 46
Song Yingxing 宋應星 42
Song Yu 宋玉 71
    "Dengtuzi haose fu" 登徒子好色賦 ("Fu on Master Dengtu the Lecher") 71
    "Gaotang fu" 高唐賦 ("Fu on the Gaotang Temple") 152, 208

"Shennü fu" 神女賦 ("*Fu* on the Divine Lady") 208
Soushen houji 搜神後記 3*n*3, 16*n*4, 83
Student Zhang 張生 (lover of Cui Yingying, q.v.). *See* Zhang Junrui
See also Yuan Zhen: "Story of Yingying"
Sun Chuo 孫綽
 "You Tiantaishan fu" 遊天台山賦 38*n*82
Sun Simiao 孫思邈
 Zhenzhong ji 枕中記 48
Su Shi 蘇軾 13, 162, 163, 167–69
 criticized by Li Qingzhao 164
 "Dongxian ge ling" 洞仙歌令 ("Ditty-song of the Grotto Transcendent") with a preface 165–66
 "Fu huma fu" 服胡麻賦 ("*Fu* on Consuming Sesame") 43*n*103
 "Niannu jiao" 念奴嬌 ("The Loveliness of Niannu") 167

Taibai jinxing 太白金星 185–86, 191
Taishang Lingbao wufu xu (aka *Wufu xu*) 太上靈寶五符序 28, 42, 50
Tao Hongjing 陶弘景 36
 Zhen'gao 真誥 36–37, 45
Tao Qian 陶潛 (aka Tao Yuanming 淵明) 2, 16, 38, 41, 98, 115, 118
 author of the Liu-Ruan tale 16
 Fisherman. *See* fisherman
 "Taohuayuan ji" 桃花源記 ("Record of the Peach Blossom Spring") 2–3, 4, 32, 38, 41, 51, 59*n*27, 60, 95–99, 101–2, 104, 108, 112, 116, 120, 125, 142, 173–76, 201
Tao Yuanming 陶淵明. *See* Tao Qian.
The Odyssey 5, 14, 68, 206–11, 214–22
time-dilated displacement/realm/travel 12, 15, 18, 22, 23, 24, 27, 32, 34, 36, 46, 51, 52, 204, 218
 See also time dilation
time dilation 1, 4, 5, 12, 18, 24, 28, 32, 33, 34, 42, 47, 48, 51, 90, 154, 178, 180, 195, 211, 215, 217, 218
 in Zhao Cangyun's work 195
 King Kakudmi in *Bhāgavata Purāna* 24
 See also magical eating, time-dilated displacement/realm/travel

Transcendent Cassia 桂花仙子 (aka Cassia) 200–2
 See also Wu Changling: "Celestial Master Zhang's Conviction of Breeze, Flower, Snow, and Moon"
Transcendent of Long Eyebrows 長眉仙 202–3
 See also Wu Changling: "Celestial Master Zhang's Conviction of Breeze, Flower, Snow, and Moon"
Transcendent Peach Blossom 桃花仙 200–201
 See also Wu Changling: "Celestial Master Zhang's Conviction of Breeze, Flower, Snow, and Moon"
transcendent (*xian* 仙)/transcendent being 1–13, 23–25, 27, 32, 37, 40–41, 44, 45, 48, 52, 58, 59, 65, 68, 73, 74, 78–79, 81, 90, 105, 108, 109, 110, 127, 128, 132, 134, 136–78, 182, 185–86, 188, 194, 198, 199–202, 204, 207, 210–11, 217
 elixir 56
 grotto 75
 palace 49*n*121
 peach tree 122
 realm/otherworld/mountain 7, 8, 18, 27*n*42, 38*n*83, 38*n*85, 48, 51, 68, 81, 101, 104, 109, 114, 120, 125, 141, 156, 180, 182, 186, 188, 190, 192, 193, 196, 197, 198, 201, 206, 215
 triple role/identity (transcendent maiden, entertainer, Daoist priestess) 1, 7, 52, 74, 78, 90, 142, 144, 154, 156, 176, 177, 204, 217
triple identification of the protagonist, narrator, and poet 64, 81
triple role of the transcendent maiden, entertainer, Daoist priestess. *See* Transcendent: triple role/identity (transcendent maiden, entertainer, Daoist priestess)
tune-titles (of lyrics and arias)
 "Bie xianzi" 別仙子 ("Farewell My Transcendent") 13, 138, 144–48, 168–69, 176
 "Bimei" 比梅 ("Comparing with the Plum Blossoms") 164
 "Bitao chun" 碧桃春 ("Spring Season of the Emerald Peaches") 158

INDEX

tune-titles (of lyrics and arias) (*cont.*)
   "Biyun chun" 碧雲春 ("Spring Season of the Emerald Clouds") 158
   "Bujian" 不見 ("Not Seeing") 164
   "Changong qu" 蟾宮曲 ("Aria of the Palace of Toad") 203
   Dai guduo 呆骨朵 198–99
   "Dao cheng gui" 道成歸 ("Going Home upon Attainment of the *Dao*") 158
   Daodao ling 叨叨令 189
   "Die lian hua" 蝶戀花 ("Butterfly in Love with Blossoms") 177*n*123
   "Dongxian ge" 洞仙歌 ("Song of the Grotto Transcendent") 13, 138, 167, 169–70
   Duanzhenghao 端正好 198–99
   "Guji" 古記 ("Ancient Record") 164
   "Hao xishan" 好溪山 ("Fine Brooks and Mountains") 158
   "He chongtian" 鶴沖天 ("The Crane Soaring to the Sky") 159*n*66
   "Linjiang xian" 臨江仙 ("The Transcendent by the River") 13, 134, 148–49, 151–56, 159, 176
      by Zhang Bi 張泌 155–56
   "Nüguanzi" 女冠子 ("The Capelined Priestess") 134, 138, 159, 160
      by Liu Yong (3 poems) 160*n*71
      by Wen Tingyun 溫庭筠 155
      by Xue Zhaoyun 薛昭蘊 159
      by Zhang Bi 155–57
   "Ruanlang gui" 阮郎歸 ("Gentleman Ruan Returning Home") 13, 134, 157–59, 161–62, 163, 176
      by Ouyang Xiu 13, 157–58, 160–62, 163
      by Sima Guang 司馬光 159*n*65
      by Yan Jidao (5 poems) 159*n*65
   "Ruanlang mi" 阮郎迷 ("Gentleman Ruan Going astray") 74
   "Rumeng ling" 如夢令 ("A Dreamlike Ditty") 163–64
      by Li Qingzhao 164
   "Ruyi ling" 如意令 ("A Ditty on Fulfilling My Intent") 164
   Sui shawei 隨煞尾 190
   "Taoyuan yi guren" 桃源憶故人 ("Reminiscing about an Acquaintance from the Peach Spring") 13, 173–74

   "Tiantai xianzi" 天台仙子 ("The Celestial Transcendent of Tiantai") 144
   "Tianxianzi" 天仙子 ("The Celestial Transcendent") 13, 138–43, 139*n*15, 148–50, 169–70
      by He Ning 和凝 143–44
      by Huangfu Song 143
      by Wei Zhuang 韋莊 143, 169
   "Yan Taoyuan" 宴桃源 ("Banqueting at the Peach Spring") 158, 164
   "Yan Taoyuan" 宴桃園 ("Banqueting at the Peach Garden") 158, 164
   "Yulou chun" 玉樓春 ("Spring on the Jade Terrace"), no. 4, attributed to Ouyang Xiu 179
   "Zhegui ling" 折桂曲 ("Ditty on Breaking the Cassia") 203
      by Zhang Yanghao 張養浩 203*n*50
   "Zhuoying qu" 濯纓曲 ("Washing My Hat Tassel") 159*n*66
   "Zui Taoyuan" 醉桃源 ("Getting Drunk at the Peach Spring") 158

Urashimako 浦島子 (aka Urashima Tarō 浦島太郎) 6*n*8, 49*n*121

Vimalakirti 80*n*96
Vimalakirti sutra 80, 83

Wang Can 王粲
   "Qiai shi" 七哀詩 ("Seven Sorrows") 103
Wang Chong 王充 10, 24–26, 28*n*46, 30
Wang Ji 王績 95
Wang Jia 王嘉
   Shiyi ji 拾遺記 25*n*36, 33, 43
Wang Pi 王伾 108
Wang Pou 王裒 (sobriquet: Qingxu zhenren 清虛真人) 10
Wang Shuwen 王叔文 97, 108, 109*n*33
Wang Songnian 王松年
   Xianyuan bianzhu 仙苑編珠 2
Wang Wei 王維 3*n*4, 89, 120
   "Taoyuan xing" 桃源行 ("Ballad of the Peach Spring") 3*n*4, 100*n*9
Wang Yi 王逸 21, 22
Wang Zhi 王質 33, 35

Wang Ziyi 王子一
　"Liu Chen Ruan Zhao wuru tiantai" 劉晨阮肇悞入天台 ("Liu Chen and Ruan Zhao's Straying to Mount Tiantai")　13, 181, 185–90, 194, 198–99
"weft texts" 緯書 (apocryphal writing)　6
Wei Boyang 魏伯陽　30
Wei Cong 韋叢 (wife of Yuan Zhen)　73n75, 86
Wei furen 魏夫人. See Wei Huacun
Wei Huacun 魏華存　10, 45n109
Wei Zhuang 韋莊
　"Tianxianzi 天仙子 ("The Celestial Transcendent")　143–44, 169
Wen Tingyun 溫庭筠　155
wheel of time　28, 222
Wu Changling 吳昌齡
　"Zhang tianshi duan feng hua xue yue" 張天師斷風花雪月 ("Celestial Master Zhang's Conviction of Breeze, Flower, Snow, and Moon")　13, 181, 200–3, 204
wujing 蕪菁 (aka manjing 蔓菁; rape-turnip; qiamagu, Brassica rapa-depressa)　50–51
Wuling 五陵　139
Wuling 武陵　2, 99, 102, 107–9, 115, 116, 119, 120, 174, 175
　Fisherman of　96, 109, 121, 173
　painting of　125
　peach spring of　12, 98, 175
　taishou 太守 (Governor/Grand Protector)　104, 105
Wusao 五嫂 (fifth sister-in-law)　55, 67
　See also Zhang Zhuo: You xianku

xian 仙. See transcendent (xian)/transcendent being
Xiang Consort (Xiang furen) 湘夫人　152–53
Xiang Ji 項藉　102
Xiang Mandu 項曼都 (aka Mandu)　10, 24–25, 27, 29, 32, 41
Xiaojing yuanshen qi 孝經援神契　43
Xuandu guan 玄都觀 (Mysterious Capital Abbey)　120–21
Xue Zhaoyun 薛昭蘊　159
Xu Lingfu 徐靈府
　"Tiantaishan ji" 天台山記　38n82
Xu Qiu 徐釚　162

Yangchun baixue 陽春白雪　167
Yang Shoujing 楊守敬　54, 63
Yang Xi 楊羲　10
Yang Xiong 揚雄　130n96
　"Fan 'Lisao'" 反離騷 ("Counter-Lisao")　23
Yan Jidao 晏幾道
　"Ruanlang gui" 阮郎歸 ("Gentleman Ruan Returning Home")　159n65
Yan Shu 晏殊　13, 159n63
　"Changsheng le" 長生樂 ("Joy of living long")　160
Yaochi xin yong ji 瑤池新詠集 (Anthology of New Poetry from the Turquoise Pond)　136n9
Yinfu yujian 隱夫玉簡
Yixian zhuan 疑仙傳 (Biographies of Dubious Transcendents)　182
Yiyuan 異苑 (Garden of Anomalies)　32
Youming lu 幽明錄 (Record of the Hidden and Manifested)　1, 14–16, 33, 48, 53, 67, 73, 96, 98, 121–22, 141, 150–51, 175, 187–88, 190, 194, 196, 221, 265
youwu 尤物 (lit., "fault-causing creature")　64–66
Yuan Xiang 袁相 and Gen Shuo 根碩
　Tale of　56
Yuan Zhen 元稹　11, 12, 54, 55, 61–65, 68–69, 76–77, 81, 83–90, 141
　"Chou Bai Letian xinghua yuan" 酬白樂天杏花園 ("In Response to Bai Letian's Poem, The Garden of Apricot Blossoms")　124
　"Dai Qujiang laoren baiyun" 代曲江老人百韻 ("One Hundred Rhymes Written on behalf of Elder of Qujiang")　62
　"Gu yanshi er shou" 古豔詩二首 ("Two Amorous Poems in Ancient Style")　70
　"Huizhen ji" 會真記 ("A Tryst with the Perfected"; variant title of "Story of Yingying," q.v.)　72n71, 76n87
　"Huizhen shi sanshi yun" 會真詩三十韻 ("A Tryst with the Perfected, in Thirty Rhymes")　64, 71
　"Lisi" 離思 ("Parting Thoughts"), nos. 1, 2, and 4　72–73

INDEX

Yuan Zhen (*cont.*)
   "Liu Ruan qi er shou" 劉阮妻二首 ("Wives of Liu and Ruan," Two poems)   75, 201
   "Meng youchun qishi yun" 夢遊春七十韻 ("Dream of Spring Roaming in Seventy Rhymes")   54*n*5, 77–78, 91–93
   "Story of Yingying" 鶯鶯傳   11, 12, 60–67, 69–72, 78–81, 147
   Yanshi juan 豔詩卷 (*A Fascicle of Amorous Poems*)   70*n*67
   "Zayi" 雜憶 ("Miscellaneous Remembrances")   72–75
Yuefu 樂府 (Music Bureau poetry)   138, 157
   "Taoyuan xing" 桃源行 ("Ballad of the Peach Spring")   3*n*4, 177*n*123
Yunyao ji 雲謠集 (*Anthology of Tunes from the Clouds*)   136, 138, 167
Yu Que 余闕
   "Yangjun Xianmin teji xu" 楊君顯民特集序 ("Preface to a Special Collection of Yang Xianmin")   183–84
Yu Xuanji 魚玄機   11, 142

Zang Maoxun 臧懋循   181
Zhang Chengfeng 張承奉   146
Zhang Heng 張衡   23
   "Nandu fu" 南都賦   153*n*50
   "Sixuan fu" 思玄賦 ("*Fu* on Contemplation on the Mysterious")   23
Zhang Hua 張華
   Bowu zhi 博物志   39–40
Zhang Junrui 張君瑞 (aka Student Zhang 張生, lover of Cui Yingying, q.v.)   56*n*14, 63–69, 71
Zhang Wenchang 張文成, variant name of Zhang Zhuo (q.v.)

Zhang Xian 張先
   "Ruanlang gui" 阮郎歸 ("Gentleman Ruan Returning Home")   160–61
   "Taoyuan yi guren" 桃源憶故人 ("Reminiscing about an Acquaintance from the Peach Spring")   174
   "Wuling chun" 武陵春 ("Springtime in Wuling")   175, 176
   "Zui Taoyuan" 醉桃源 ("Getting Drunk at the Peach Spring")   159n165, 174
Zhang Zhuo 張鷟   56, 58, 62, 206
   You xianku 遊仙窟 (*Roaming to the Grotto of the Transcendents*)   6*n*8, 11, 12, 53*n*3, 53–60, 63, 77, 90, 165, 213, 214, 218
Zhan the Superior Lord 展上公   37
Zhao Cangyun 趙蒼雲   191–92, 194, 196, 204, 214, 218, 221
   "Yuan Zhao Cangyun Liu Chen Ruan Zhao ru Tiantaishan tujuan" 元趙蒼雲劉晨阮肇入天台山圖卷 ("A scroll of paintings of Liu Chen and Ruan Zhao Entering the Tiantai Mountains, by Zhao Cangyun")   181, 192–95, 197–98, 205, 221
Zhao Daoyi 趙道一   7
Zhao Lingzhi 趙令畤   63
Zhen Fu 甄宓   55
zhenren 真人 (The Perfected One)   10, 10*n*30
zhexian 謫仙. *See* Banished transcendent
zhiguai 志怪 ("recording the uncanny")   1, 5, 10, 12, 16, 196, 206, 215, 216
Zhong Yi 鍾儀   103, 132
Zhouyi cantong qi 周易參同契 (aka *Cantong qi*)   28–29
Zhou Yishan 周義山 (sobriquet: Ziyang zhenren 紫陽真人)   44
Zhuangzi 莊子   20, 48, 115, 167
Zhuge Liang 諸葛亮   120

Printed in the United States
by Baker & Taylor Publisher Services